THE NIGHTLESS CITY OF THE GEISHA

The Japanese geisha is the ultimate erotic icon - the courtesan par excellence - and this is her definitive book. The life of the geisha is the most secret and traditional in Japan, and today remains largely unchanged and unknown behind the tea house doors. This remarkable work was the first to reveal the hidden world of the geisha of the famous Yoshiwara quarter of Tokyo, the 'nightless city', and it has never been surpassed. Written over a hundred years ago, it is a meticulous description of every aspect of geisha life there, including the history of the geisha, life stories of famous geisha, the decoration of the tea houses, the different grades of courtesans, their costumes and hairstyles, the instruction of young girls brought to the tea houses, the art of selecting a geisha for the evening, proper conduct on the morning after, erotic practices and charms used by geisha to attract lovers. The vibrant life of the Yoshiwara quarter is evoked with finesse, portraying the procurers and madames, the festivals and geisha processions, even the menus of the tea houses, along with such matters as forms of contracts between brothels and courtesans. Profusely illustrated with photographs, prints and drawings, this is an essential volume for all who are fascinated by the sophisticated sensuality of the willow, the cherry blossom and the silken kimono.

J.E. DE BECKER was a lawyer and long time resident of Japan.

THE NIGHTLESS CITY OF THE GEISHA

The Japanese geisha is the ultimate erotic icon - the courtesan par excellence - and this is her definitive book. The life of the geisha is the most secret and traditional in Japan, and today remains largely unchanged and unknown behind the tea house doors. This remarkable work was the first to reveal the hidden world of the geisha of the famous Yoshiwara quarter of Tokyo, the 'nightless city', and it has never been surpassed. Written over a hundred years ago, it is a meticulous description of every aspect of geisha life there, including the history of the geisha, life stories of famous geisha, the decoration of the tea houses, the different grades of courtesans, their costumes and hairstyles, the instruction of young girls brought to the tea houses, the art of selecting a geisha for the evening, proper conduct on the morning after, erotic practices and charms used by geisha to attract lovers. The vibrant life of the Yoshiwara quarter is evoked with finesse, portraying the procurers and madames, the festivals and geisha processions, even the menus of the tea houses, along with such matters as forms of contracts between brothels and courtesans. Profusely illustrated with photographs, prints and drawings, this is an essential volume for all who are fascinated by the sophisticated sensuality of the willow, the cherry blossom and the silken kimono.

J.E. DE BECKER was a lawyer and long time resident of Japan.

THE NIGHTLESS CITY OF THE GEISHA

THE HISTORY OF THE YOSHIWARA

By J. E. DE BECKER

Routledge
Taylor & Francis Group
LONDON AND NEW YORK

First published in 2002 by
Kegan Paul International

This edition first published in 2010 by
Routledge
2 Park Square, Milton Park, Abingdon, Oxfordshire OX14 4RN
711 Third Avenue, New York, NY 10017

First issued in paperback 2016

Routledge is an imprint of the Taylor & Francis Group, an informa business

British Library Cataloguing in Publication Data
A catalogue record for this book is available from the British Library

ISBN 13: 978-1-138-99448-5 (pbk)
ISBN 13: 978-0-7103-0717-0 (hbk)

Contents

List of Illustrations.

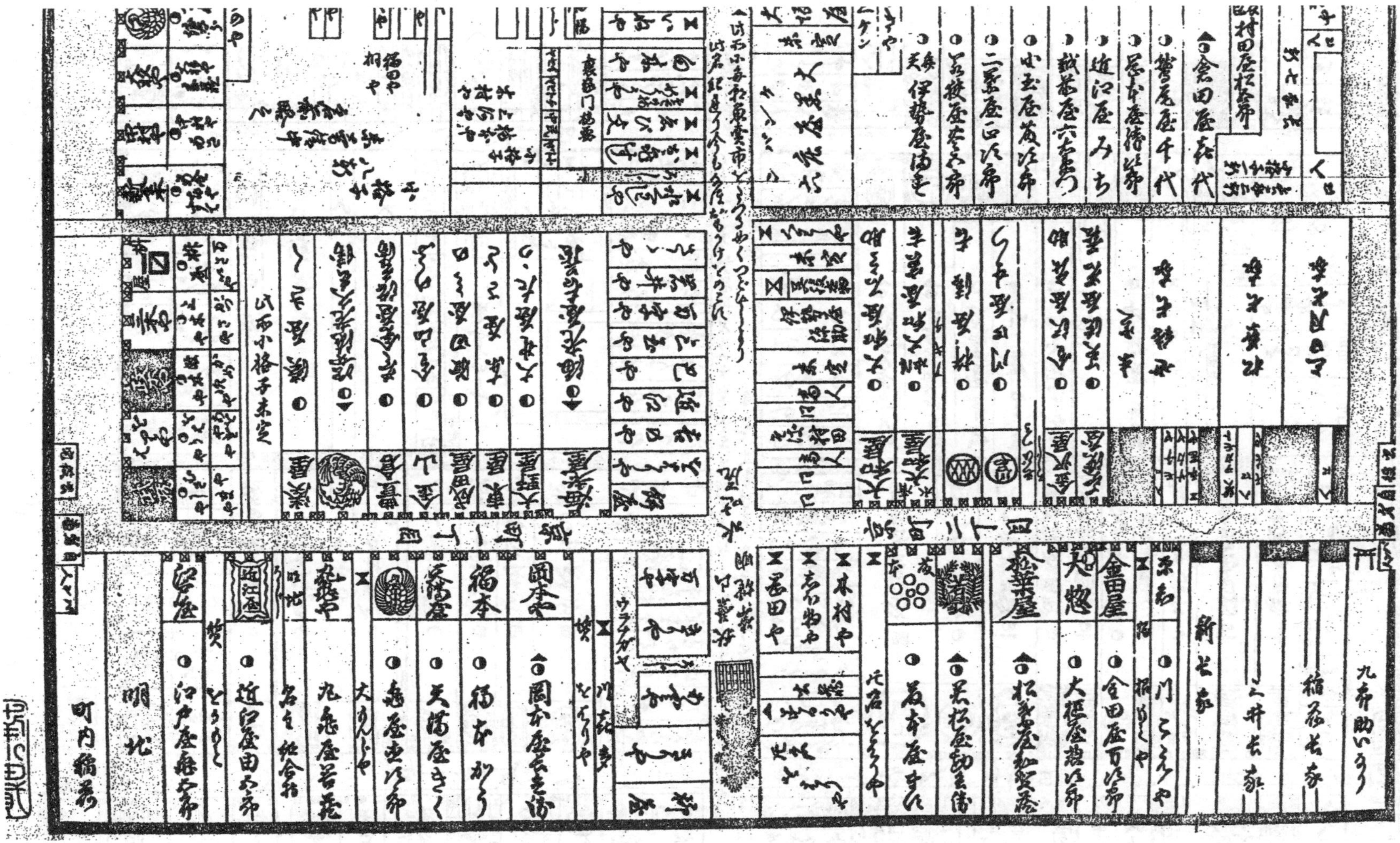

京町一丁目
京町二丁目
町内稲荷
明地
岡本屋
福本
金田屋
大惣
松葉屋
新長家

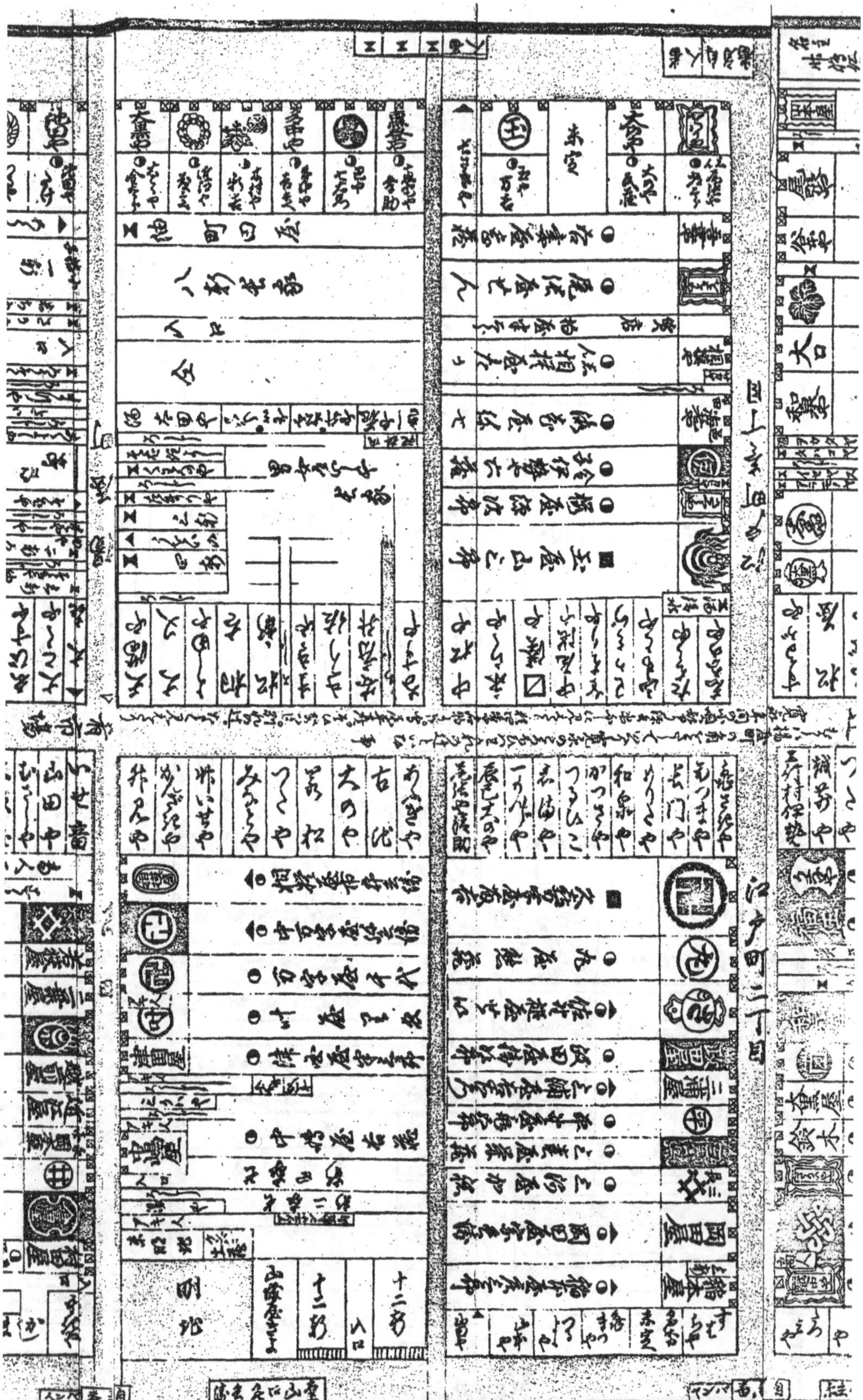
江戸町二丁目

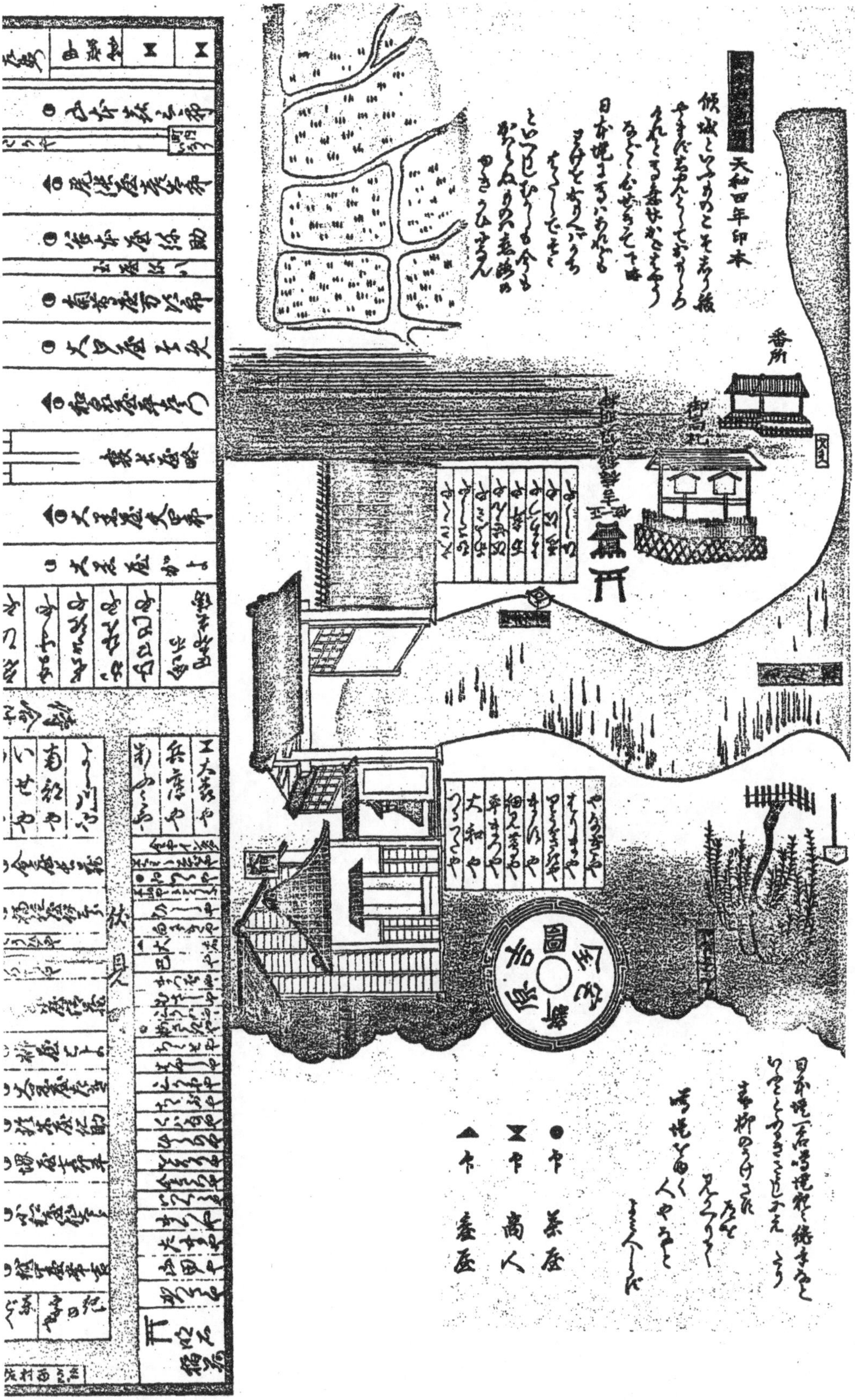

天和四年印本
番所
御高札
新吉原圖
● や 茶屋
⧗ や 商人
▲ や 揚屋

PREFACE TO THE FIRST EDITION.

SO long as the human race shall last, so long as human appetites demand illegitimate gratification, so long as human blood shall course hot in the veins, so long as men have passions, so long as women are frail, so long as illicit pleasure has attraction for bewildered wallowing humanity, and so long as lust—"the headstrong beast"—stalks through the earth, venery and dissipation will undoubtedly continue to claim thousands of unhappy victims.

"Vice, like disease, floats in the atmosphere," and notwithstanding the strenuous efforts which have been made in all countries and ages to eradicate prostitution, it still exists rampant and invincible.

History demonstrates the sad truth that all human efforts have been—and probably will ever be—unequal to the task of stamping out the social evil from our midst, and we are therefore forced to recognize that the most we can hope to achieve in the direction of ameliorating its consequences is to regulate and control its worst features.

Many and earnest have been the vain attempts of European reformers to grapple with the evil, but their efforts have invariably ended in disappointment. The Church has thundered and anathematized, the secular authorities have enacted severe and even cruel laws, but the courtesan still survives and will doubtless survive and flourish until the waters of Time have engulfed the World.

Japan has not stood still among the nations in her endeavour to solve the problem of prostitution, and the present system of legal control is to all intents and purposes a development of that inaugurated *well-nigh three centuries ago.*

While admitting the existence of objectionable features in the Yoshiwara, it is evident that a system which has stood the test of three hundred years must possess *some* good points to account for its long lease of life, and it is also manifest that in the course of three centuries a great many curious customs—some good, some bad—must have crystallized around the institution.

Being no partizan or special pleader, I have simply confined myself to what I believe to be assured facts, and hope that the contents of the volume will be of interest and service to persons who are anxious to impartially investigate the customs of one of the most remarkable institutions in this country. I have compiled this book with the object of providing foreign students of sociology, medical men, and philanthropists, with some reliable *data* regarding the practical working of the system in the leading prostitute quarter of the Japanese Metropolis, and I leave my readers to form their own opinions as to the pros and cons of the success or otherwise achieved by the plan of strict segregation adopted in this country.

To Japanese who may think that the Yoshiwara is a disgrace to Japan I would remark that this Empire has by no means a *monopoly* of vice; and to foreigners who declaim against the "immorality of Japanese" I would say frankly—"Read the '*History of Prostitution*' by Dr. W. W. Sanger of New York, also the '*Maiden Tribute of Modern Babylon*' which appeared in the Pall Mall Gazette fourteen years ago. You cannot afford to criticize this country too closely, for you certainly dare not lay the flattering unction to your souls that you, as a race, have any *monopoly* of virtue."

THE AUTHOR.

Tōkyō, 1899.

PREFACE TO THE THIRD EDITION.

SUBSEQUENT to the anonymous publication of the first edition of "*The Nightless City*" in 1899, the author was severely remonstrated with by certain unctuous persons for writing a work which lays bare a phase of Japanese social phenomena before which all writers (with the notable exception of Mr. Henry Norman) have studiously drawn a veil. To this class of persons he neither owes, nor offers an apology; but, in order to obviate any misunderstanding of his motives, it may be well to explain the *raison d'être* of the book.

The voluminous *data* on which is based the science of Medical Jurisprudence, the records of all Courts, and the experience and common knowledge of mankind, prove the universal existence of the "social evil" to be a present and undeniable *fact.*

History shows that from the earliest ages society was never free from the devastating influences of a vice which arises from an apparently inextinguishable natural impulse inherent alike in human beings and in the lower creation. Wrap ourselves up as we may in a mantle of prudery, refuse as we may to recognize the evil, it is still there, and like the poor, it will probably "be with us always."

We can no more hope to eradicate or suppress it than to control an earthquake or harness the winds and waves! Its existence being thus palpable, is it not far wiser to frankly recognize and investigate the phenomenon with a view to control, by judicious regulations, the current of the vice and direct it into channels where it may be, at least to a certain extent, grappled with and arrested, than to foolishly close our eyes and refuse to discuss the subject on the cowardly plea that we may possibly disturb the "conventionalities" by publicly and fully investigating the evils of prostitution?

The author utterly denies the proposition that there can be any impropriety in enquiring into the facts of a matter which virtually affects, either directly or indirectly, the whole community; on the other hand he affirms that much good may be done by collecting facts and statistics which may prove of value to the legislator, the philanthropist, and the clergy. Without adequate *data*, how can we ever hope to devise measures of a preventative or ameliorative nature, and how can such *data* be obtained if we are all to be deterred from necessary investigations by the mawkish sensibility of Mrs. Grundy?

Legislators of all nations, at different times, have apparently endeavoured to crush out or control prostitution, and by various high-handed methods sought to single out and distinguish, for the alleged protection of the public, women known to be guilty of leading a professedly abandoned life. Moses, the great Jewish law-giver, hurled cruel and oppressive edicts against improper unions among the children of Israel. Greece made the *Disteriads* wear a distinguishing costume, and, branding these women with infamy, made regulations by which they were subjected to the control of the municipal police, and were forbidden to offend the public by open indecency. Rome required the registration of its prostitutes, who, under the directions of the *Ædile* were forced to wear special garments and to dye their hair a certain colour. Mediæval Europe tried (among other gentle (!) measures) sumptuary laws, banishment, scourging, branding, the stake, the gibbet, the block, outlawry; while the spiritual powers launched against prostitution all the terrors of religious anathema, threatening physical torment and strict excommunication in this world, and in the world to come everlasting damnation!

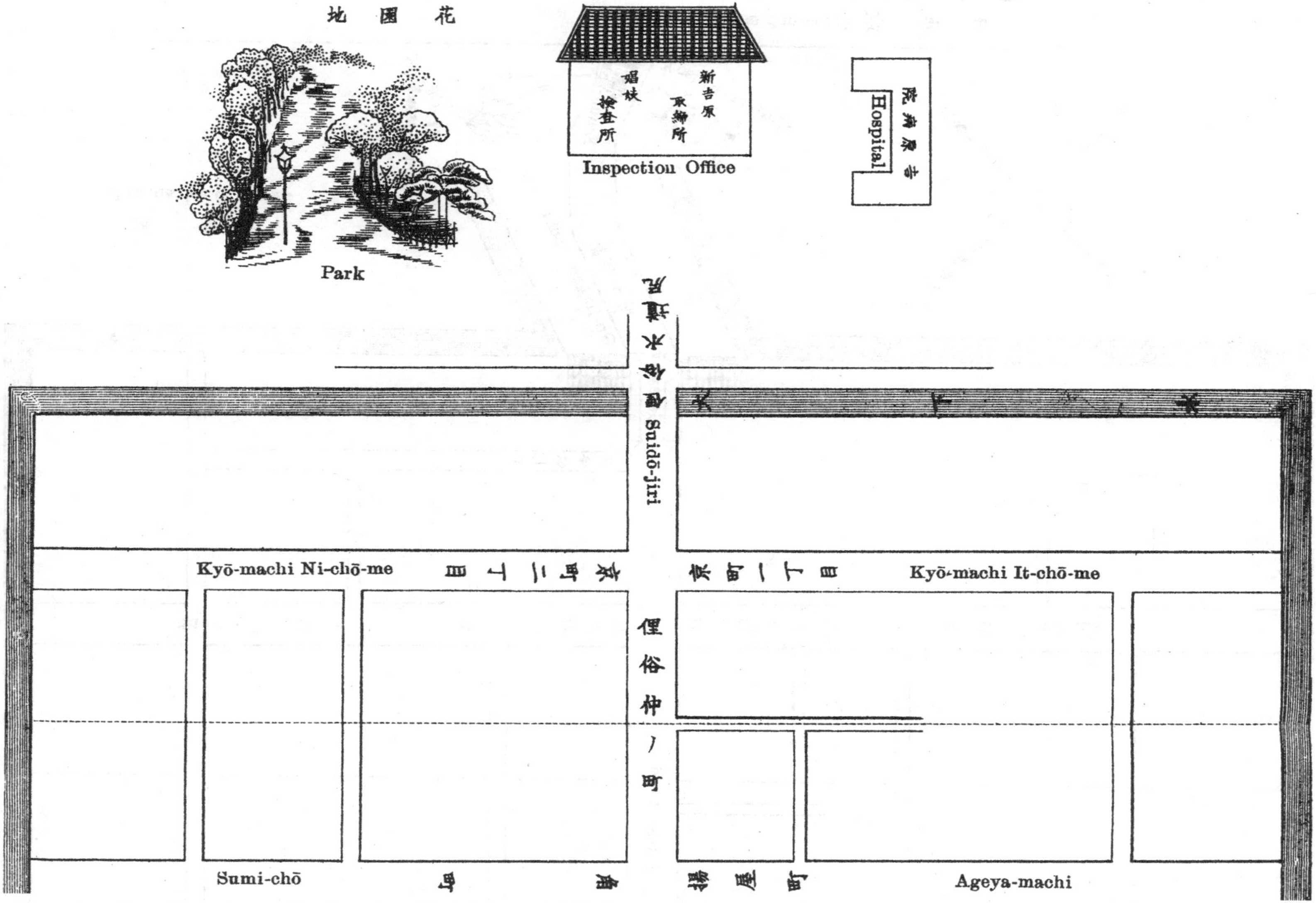
Park
Inspection Office
Hospital
Suidō-jiri
Kyō-machi Ni-chō-me
Kyō-machi It-chō-me
Sumi-chō
Ageya-machi

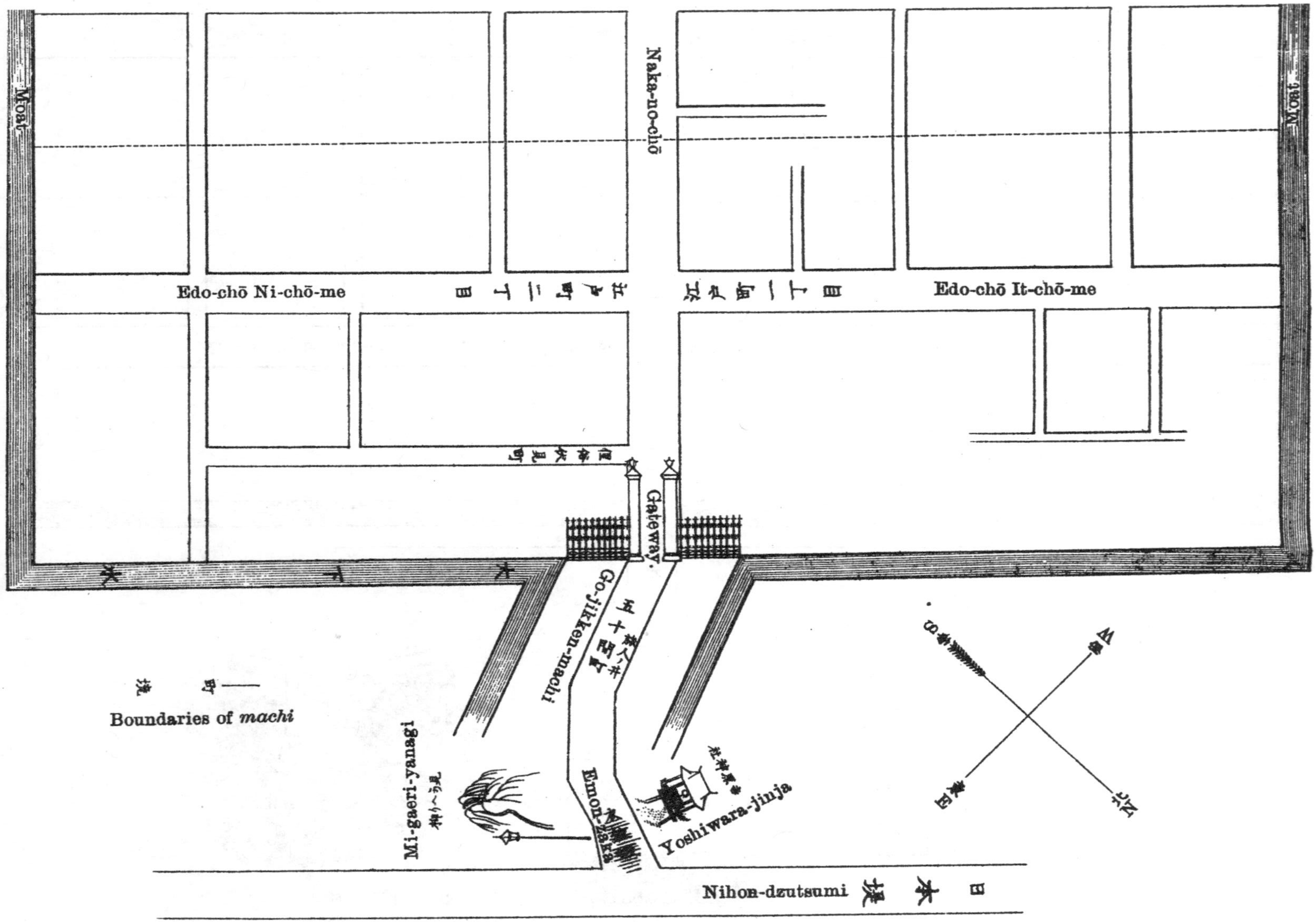

Present Plan of the Yoshiwara.

Modern Europe, while outwardly wearing a spotless garment of professed self-righteousness, and turning up its goggling eyeballs in sanctimonious horror at the bare suggestion of anything being amiss with *its* morality, knows well enough that its various Governments are secretly struggling with the problem through their police, and that the latter have found no satisfactory solution of the matter notwithstanding many serious essays.

Thousands of miles away from Europe, and practically cut off from all intercourse with the rest of the world at large, the Japanese found themselves confronted with the same problem and, after various attempts at control, they endeavoured to solve the question in a manner far more practical than that of the Europeans. They were astute enough to see that human passions could not be changed by human legislation, and instead of attempting impossibilities they started in to limit and control what they knew they had not the power to prevent; so, with the object of rendering the evil as inoffensive as possible, the authorities decided upon setting aside certain areas within which prostitutes were allowed to pursue their calling subject to various stringent laws. These quarters were fenced in and moated, their great gateways carefully guarded, and so successful did the system prove in many respects that it has been maintained (with certain modifications) up to the present day.

Human nature is fixed and immutable, is, always was, and ever will be the same; and while race environment and education may affect its outward form, the *animal* man is essentially the same throughout the entire globe. This being so, it is evident that the experience of one nation or country may often be of considerable value to other peoples if accepted and applied *mutatis mutandis* to the circumstances and needs of the latter; thus it is always well to investigate the results of institutions foreign to our own in a candid and receptive frame of mind before concluding that we possess a monopoly of wisdom in our own home lands. Moreover, human nature is so constituted that when a separate community is established in such a manner as to be practically unaffected by pressure from the outside, its units are sure to co-operate, however unconsciously, in moulding new customs and habits and even superstitions, which gradually crystallize into time-honoured precedents by immemorial usage. The Yoshiwara, during its three centuries of existence, proved no exception to the rule, and in the course of years its inhabitants became slaves to numberless precedents, with the result that some extraordinary customs were developed and even yet linger on in a modified form. A serious consideration of these facts induced the author to believe that it would be of value to students of sociology throughout Europe and America to be provided with all available *data* as to the ins and outs and the working of this unique and purely native Japanese system of control—a system of which the Westerners have had no experience whatsoever. The result of his labours was "*The Nightless City*," this new edition of which he now publishes together with an appendix which brings the work up to date so far as is possible.

The author's best thanks are due to Prof. Dr. Tōichirō Nakahama, Director of the "*Kai-Sei-Byō-in*" and Member of the Central Board of Health, who kindly furnished certain medical statistics and *data*. He also desires to express a deep debt of gratitude to Mr. E. Beart for lightening his task by assisting in seeing the book through the press, and has pleasure in acknowledging the strenuous endeavours of the Box of Curios Printing & Publishing Company in producing in Japan, notwithstanding certain drawbacks and disadvantages, a handsome volume worthy of the great printing houses of London or New York.

THE AUTHOR.

Kamakura, December, 1905.

Procession of Courtesans.

History of the Yoshiwara Yukwaku.*

IT was not until after the City of Yedo had become the seat of the Tokugawa government that regular houses of ill-fame were established, and up to the period of Keichō (1596-1614) there were no fixed places set apart for brothels and assignation houses. Under these circumstances, the brothels of Yedo were to be found scattered all over the city in groups of twos or threes, but among the many localities in which such stews were situated were three spots where the houses were to be found in larger numbers plying their shameful trade side by side.

(1.)—In Kōjimachi, hat-chō-me, there were fourteen or fifteen houses: these had been removed from Roku-jō in Kyōto.

(2.)—In Kamakura-gashi (Kanda district) the numbers of houses was the same as in Kōjimachi: these had been removed from Miroku-machi of Fuchū (now Shidzu-oka ?) in Suruga province.

(3.)—In Uchi-Yanagi-machi, near Ōhashi (Ōhashi is now the Tokiwa-bashi gate, and Yanagi-machi is now Dōsangashi-dōri) there were twenty houses. This group was inhabited by Yedo women exclusively. It is stated by some writers that the name of this street "Yanagi-machi" (Willow Street) was derived from the fact that at the entrance of the street stood two gigantic weeping-

* *Yūkwaku* is a segregated town provided with brothels and assignation houses.

willows. Prior to this date, in the period of Tenshō (1573-1591), a person named Hara Saburōzaemon had established a brothel quarter at Made-no-Koji, Yanagi-no-baba, in Kyōto, but although it is true that the name of Yanagi-machi was given to this place, the Yanagi-machi of Yedo did not derive its title from the one in the Western city.

In the 10th year of Keichō (1605) Yanagi-machi was selected by the Government in connection with the construction of the castle of Yedo, and consequently all the brothels were removed to a place in front of the Moto-Sei-gwanji (temple).

As Yedo prospered and her population increased, various enterprising individuals gradually arrived from Shumoku-machi in Fushimi, Kitsuji-machi in Nara, and other places near Kyōto, and established themselves in the brothel-keeping business.

But as Yedo still grew more and more prosperous and thriving, and her marts busier, various municipal improvements were projected, numerous new roads were opened, and bridges constructed, and, as gradually the work of organizing the urban districts progressed, many houses had to be pulled down; consequently large numbers of persons were forced to remove their residences. Under these circumstances, the brothel-keepers considered the moment to be an opportune one for the presentation to the powers that were of a petition requesting the Government to allow of the collection, into one special locality, of the Yedo *demi-monde.* They therefore petitioned the authorities to establish a regular *Keisei-machi,**

* *Keisei-machi*:—A courtesan quarter. *Keisei* means a castle falling into ruins, the idea being that such women lead to the destruction and ruin of the State.

but their petition was unsuccessful and matters remained *in statu quo.*

In the 17th year of Keichō (1612) a certain *Shōji Jinyemon* (a native of Odawara in Sagami province) conceived the idea of collecting all the brothels and assignation houses of Yedo into one special quarter of the city, and after many consultations with his *confrères* (for this gentle "reformer" was in the "profession" himself) he made a representation to the Government to the effect that:—

> "In *Kyōto* and in *Suruga*, and also in all other thickly "populated and busy places (to the number of more than "twenty) there have been established, in accordance with "ancient custom and precedent, regular licensed *Keisei-machi*, "whereas in *Yedo*, which is growing busier and more populous "day by day, there is no fixed *Yūjo-machi.** In consequence of "this state of affairs houses of ill-fame abound in every part of "the city, being scattered hither and thither in all directions. "This, for numerous reasons, is detrimental to public morality "and welfare, *etc., etc.*"

The petitioner further enumerated the advantages which would be gained by the system he advocated, and he submitted a memorandum of reasons and arguments divided into three headings, the substance of the same being:—

> "(1.) As matters stand at present, when a person visits a "brothel he may hire, and disport himself with, *Yūjo* (*filles de* "*joie*) to his heart's content, give himself up to pleasure and "licentiousness to the extent of being unable to discriminate as "to his position and means and the neglect of his occupation or "business. He may frequent a brothel for days on end, giving "himself up to lust and revel, but so long as his money holds "out the keeper of the house will continue to entertain him as "a guest. As a natural consequence, this leads to the neglect "of duty towards masters, defalcations, theft, etc., and even "then the keepers of the brothels will allow the guilty guests "to remain in their houses as long as their money lasts. If

* *Yūjo-machi*:—A courtesan quarter.

"brothels were all collected into one place a check would be put "to these evils, as, by means of investigation and enquiry, a "longer stay than twenty-four hours could be prohibited and "such prohibition enforced.

"(2.) Although it is forbidden by law to kidnap children, "yet, even in this city, the practice of kidnapping female "children and enticing girls away from their homes under false "pretences is being resorted to by certain vicious and unprinci-"pled rascals. It is a positive fact that some evil-minded "persons make it a regular profession to take in the daughters "of poor people under the pretext of adopting them as their "own children, but when the girls grow-up they are sent out "to service as concubiness or prostitutes, and in this manner "the individuals who have adopted them reap a golden harvest. "Perhaps it is this class of abandoned rascals that even dare to "kidnap other people's children? It is said to be a fact that "there are brothel-keepers who engage women knowing per-"fectly well that they are the adopted children of the parties "who wish to sell the girls into prostitution. If the prostitute "houses be all collected into one place, strict enquiries will be "made as to the matter of kidnapping and as to the engage-"ment of adopted children, and should any cases occur in "which such reprehensible acts are attempted, information "will be immediately given to the authorities.

"(3.) Although the condition of the country is peaceful, "yet it is not long since the subjugation of *Mino** province was "accomplished, and consequently it may be that there are "many *ronin*† prowling about seeking for an opportunity to "work mischief. These ruffians have, of course, no fixed place "of abode and simply drift hither and thither, so it is impos-"sible to ascertain their whereabouts in the absence of properly "instituted enquiries even although they may be staying in "houses of ill-fame for a considerable number of days. If the "authorities grant this petition, and permit the concentration "of the existing brothels in one regular place, the brothel-"keepers will pay special attention to this matter and will cause "searching enquiries to be made about persons who may be "found loafing in the prostitute quarters: should they discover "any suspicious characters they will not fail to report the same "to the authorities forthwith.

---

* The decisive battle between Ieyasu and Hideyori, son of the great Hideyoshi ("Taikō Sama") was fought at Seki-ga-hara, Mino Province, in the year 1600.

† Masterless swashbucklers.

"It will be deemed a great favour if the august authorities "will grant this petition in the fulness of their magnanimous "mercy."

In the following spring (1613) Shōji Jinyemon was summoned to the Magistrate's Court and examined on various points by Honda Lord of Sado, after which he was informed that the result of the petition would be made known at a later date. He was then dismissed.

In the spring of the 3rd year of Genna (1617) Jinyemon was again summoned to the Court and, in the presence of several other judicial officials, Honda Lord of Sado notified him that the petition was granted. He was also informed that two square *chō* of land would be devoted to the purpose of founding a prostitute quarter, and that the site had been selected at Fukiya-machi. In return for this privilege, Jinyemon promised that no prostitutes should be allowed in the city of Yedo and neighbourhood except in the licensed quarter, and further covenanted that in case of any of the women being found elsewhere the matter should be communicated to the authorities, as in duty bound, either by himself or by the other brothelkeepers. At the same time, Shōji Jinyemon was appointed *Keisei-machi Nanushi* (director of the prostitute quarter) and was instructed by the *Bugyō* (Governor possessed of administrative, military, and judicial functions) to observe the following regulations:—

"(1.) The profession of brothel-keeping shall not be carried "on in any place other than the regular prostitute quarter, "and in future no request for the attendance of a courtesan at "a place outside the limits of the enclosure shall be complied "with.

"(2.) No guest shall remain in a brothel for more than "twenty-four hours.

"(3.) Prostitutes are forbidden to wear clothes with gold "and silver embroidery on them; they are to wear ordinary "dyed stuffs.

"(4.) Brothels are not to be built of imposing appearance, "and the inhabitants of prostitute quarters shall discharge the "same duties (as firemen, etc.,) as ordinary residents in other "parts of *Yedo* city.

"(5.) Proper enquiries shall be instituted into the person "of any visitor to a brothel, no matter whether he be gentle-"man or commoner, and in case any suspicious individual "appears information shall be given to the *Bugyō-sho* (office of "the city Governor).

"The above instructions are to be strictly observed.

"(Date............) The *Bugyō*."

On the low land of Fukiya-chō, which was thus granted by the authorities, now stand Idzumi-chō, Takasago-chō, Sumi-yoshi-chō, and Naniwa-chō, and the *ko-hori* (or small ditch) at Hettsui-gashi which was once the outer moat of the prostitute quarters. The present Ō-mon-dōri (Great Gate Street) was formerly the street leading to the Ō-mon (Great Gate). At the time about which I am writing the place was one vast swamp overrun with weeds and rushes, so Shōji Jinyemon set about clearing the Fukiya-machi, reclaiming and filling in the ground, and building an enclosure thereon. Owing to the number of rushes which had grown thereabout the place was re-named Yoshiwara (葭原=Rush-moor) but this was after-wards changed to Yoshi-wara (吉原=Moor of Good luck) in order to give the locality an auspicious name.

The work of filling in and levelling the ground, and the construction of houses, was commenced in the 3rd year of Genna (1617) and by November of the following year "business" commenced. The work of laying out the streets and completing the quarters was not however finished until the 9th day of the 10th month of the 3rd year of Kwan-ei (28th November 1626).

The following were the names of the wards of the Yoshiwara:—

Yedo-chō, It-chō-me: This was the pioneer prostitute quarter established in the city after the Tokugawa government had made Yedo the seat of their administration; and in the hope and expectation of sharing in the prosperity of the city itself the felicitious name of Yedo-chō (Yedo ward) was chosen as appropriate for the new ward. All the houses at Yanagi-chō removed to this Yedo-chō, and among them was the "Nishida-ya" (House of the Western Ricefield) which was kept by Shōji Jinyemon himself.

Yedo-chō, Ni-chō-me: To this ward (Second ward of Yedo-chō) were transferred all the houses formerly kept at Moto-Kamakura-gashi.

Kyōmachi, It-chō-me: To this ward were transferred the houses at Kōjimachi. The majority of these establishments having had their origin in Roku-jō, Kyōto, the ward was named Kyō-machi, thus using the first character 京 (Kyō) of Kyōto and preserving the old association with the capital.

Kyōmachi, Ni-chō-me: The brothelkeepers of Hisago-machi in Ōsaka, Kitsuji in Nara, and other localities, having heard of the opening of the Yoshiwara, many of them immigrated to this place. The buildings in this ward were completed two years later than those in the other streets, and accordingly this ward was commonly called Shim-machi (新町 New Street).

Sumi-chō: The brothels at Sumi-chō, Kyōbashi, having been removed to this ward, the name of the original place was copied when "christening" the new street.

After many vicissitudes, the brothelkeepers believed that they had now found an abiding place, and that no further changes would be made, but they were doomed to disappointment. On the 19th day of the 10th month of the 2nd year of Meireki (4th December 1656) Ishigaya Shōgen, the Bugyō, summoned the elders (*toshi-yoridomo*) of the Yoshiwara and informed them that the existing site of the prostitute quarter being required by the authorities for building purposes, the houses must be removed elsewhere. Ishigaya added that, in lieu of the Yoshiwara, the authorities were prepared to grant either a plot of land in the vicinity of the Nihon-dsutsumi (Dike of Japan) behind the Asakusa temple, or one in the neighbourhood of Honjō.

The representatives of the Yoshiwara people were filled with consternation at the action of the government, and they submitted a petition of grievances to the effect that the brothels had been in existence for 44 years and that the keepers would be put to great inconvenience and caused serious loss if they were suddenly forced to remove to a remote district. After reciting the above facts, and pointing out the injury which would be done to "vested interests," the petition wound up with a prayer that the authorities would be pleased to permit the brothels to continue to ply their profession in the same place as hitherto. This petition, however, was rejected, and after mature deliberation the elders now applied for a grant of land at the Nihon-dsutsumi: they also petitioned that a sum of money might be given them from the public funds to assist their removal.

In response to the last petition, the authorities provided a suitable site near Nihon-dsutsumi, and in consideration of the removal of the houses to such a distant and out-of-the-way locality, Ishigaya Shōgen, and Kamio, Lord of Bizen, agreed to the following conditions in connection with the new Yoshiwara :—

"(1.) Hitherto the ground to be occupied has been limited "to 2 square *chō:* in the new place these limits will be increased "by 50 per cent., and extended to 3 *chō* by 2 *chō* (3×2).

"(2.) Whereas hitherto the profession has been allowed to "be carried on in the day-time only, in consideration of the "quarter being moved to such a distant place, it is in future "permitted both day and night alike.

"(3.) More than 200 *Furo-ya* (風呂屋=Bath-houses)* now "existing in the city shall be abolished.

"(4.) In consideration of the *Yoshiwara* being removed to "a distant place, its people shall hereafter be exempted from "the duties of acting as guards against fire on the occasion of "the festivals at *Sannō* and at *Kanda*, or as firemen in time of "conflagrations, etc.

"(5.) The sum of 10,500 *ryō* will be granted to assist the "expenses of removal, at the rate of 14 *ryō* per small room."†

It is very curious to note that Japan was not the only country where shady "bath-houses" were to be found. In a German book by Wilhelm Rudeck, entitled "*Geschichte der Oeffentlichen Sittlichkeit In Deutschland,*" it is stated that "bath-houses" were plentiful. Early in the morning a horn announced that everything was ready, and men, women and

* These "*bath-houses*" were in reality houses of assignation and unlicensed brothels. Carrying on their business under this innocent title they engaged women called "*Kami-arai-onna,*" or (for want of a better word) "shampooers," but these females were really "*jigoku*" ("Hell women") and were selected for their beauty in order to attract persons to "*take baths.*" The "*bath-house*" women were not only as beautiful and accomplished as the regular courtesans, but they were cheaper and would accommodate guests either day or night, whereas, the regular girls were only permitted to exercise their calling in the day time. These unlicensed prostitutes were so numerous that they seriously interfered with the business of the real *Yoshiwara*, and it was to the interest of regular brothel-keepers that they should be suppressed.

† It is interesting to note that even in those times the Government recognized the principle of granting compensation when the right of eminent domain was exercised.

maids undressed at home and went nearly naked to the bath-houses, where the attendants were mostly girls who had a very liberal idea of their duties. The tubs in many cases were large enough for two, and a board was laid across, upon which food and drink was served to the bathers, who were not compelled to produce a marriage certificate. In the castles of the knights, the ladies often attended on the male guests in the bath and *vice versa*, and in bathing resorts, such at Wiesbaden, for instance, Frau Venus seems to have reigned supreme. A very free illustration, reproduced from an old volume, shows a row of tubs with a long board laid across them, upon which food and drink is served, and there are other illustrations, reproduced from old cuts, of some more than merely suggestive scenes, which we must presume were nothing out of the common in bath-houses.

On the 27th day of the 11th month of the same year (January 11th, 1657) the elders and monthly managers (月行司 =*tsuki-gyō*-ji) of the Yoshiwara repaired to the Treasury office at Asakusa and received the sum granted by the authorities to defray the expenses of removal: at the same time they applied to the officials to be allowed to remain in the Yoshiwara during the next three or four months, promising to complete the removal by the following April.

The request being a reasonable one, it was granted, and the removal was postponed until the fourth month, but on the 2nd March 1657 (Meireki 3 nen, Shōgwatsu, 18 nichi) Hi-no-to-tori (cycle of the Water Fowl) that disastrous fire known as the "*Furisode kwaji*" (fire of the long-sleeved garment) broke out in the Hom-myōji (temple) at Maru-yama in Hongō and raged through the city of Yedo during three days and three nights burning everything before it.* The fire swept away a large portion of the city and gutted the Yoshiwara completely, so there was no further excuse left for not moving forthwith. The head-man of the Yoshiwara was again summoned to the Bugyō's office and ordered to take advantage of the fire to carry out the removal without further delay.

In May 1657 Ishigaya Shōgen, Kamio Lord of Bizen, and Sone Genzaemon proceeded to Nihon-dsutsumi to inspect the site of the new quarter, and while the houses were being built and prepared temporary shanties called "Koya-gake" (小屋掛 =a temporarily built shed or house) were erected in the neighbourhood of Sanya and Imado, and in these (and also in private houses which were hired for the purpose) the loathesome trade was carried on as usual.

In September 1657, the new brothels were completed and the "profession" crowded into the "Shin-Yoshiwara."

The "Shin-Yoshiwara" (new Yoshiwara) was so named in contra-distinction to "Moto-Yoshiwara" (former Yoshiwara). It is situated at a place formerly known as Senzoku-mura and is only a few *chō* distant from the Asakusa-ji (temple).

There is a hill (or rather slope) leading down from the Nihon-dsutsumi on the way to the Shin-Yoshiwara which is called "Emon-zaka" or "Dress(ing) Hill," because it is supposed that visitors to the gay quarter began to adjust their garments and smarten themselves up in passing along this road. Another account states that the name was taken from the Emon-zaka of Kyōto.

* *Vide* chapter entitled "The *Furisode Kwaji.*"

The road leading from Emon-zaka to the Yoshiwara is known as Gojikken-machi. Tradition says that there was a servant named Koheiji in the employ of Shōji Jinyemon (the founder of the quarter) and that he advised his master to construct the road in three curved lines as this was considered more tasteful than one constructed in a plain line. Another tradition says that the road was constructed in that way in accordance with the commands of Kamio Lord of Bizen, but, at any rate, it is certain that the plan of the road was conceived by some person gifted with a (from a Japanese point of view) poetical imagination. On either side of the curved section of roadway twenty-five tea-houses (cha-ya) were built, making a total of fifty houses (go-jik-ken), hence the popular name "Go-jik-ken machi" (fifty house street) or "Go-jik-ken-machi" (fifty house town). At the end of the road stood a gateway which formed the entrance of the Yoshiwara, and the vicinity of this gateway was known as the Ōmon-guchi (entrance to the great gate). The gate itself was called the Ō-mon (great gateway). Having passed through the Ō-mon, the visitor would find himself within the precincts of the "Shin-Yoshiwara."

The Shin-Yoshiwara was about half as large again as the old place (Moto-Yoshiwara), measuring about 3 chō (1074 feet) from North to South, and 2 chō (716 feet) from East to West, and therefore embracing nearly 18 acres of land. The enclosure was surrounded by a kind of moat, and the streets within were laid out something in the shape of the Chinese character 田 (ta=a ricefield). As will be seen from the plan of the Shin-Yoshiwara annexed, Nakano-chō goes through the centre while Yedo-chō (It-chō-me and Ni-chō-me), Sumi-chō, and Kyō-machi (It-chō-me and Ni-chō-me) branch out to right and left on either side. As was the case with the Moto-Yoshiwara, another street was added for the convenience of "*Age-ya*" and called "Ageya-machi."* This street was situated opposite Sumi-chō, to the right of the Naka-no-chō when facing Suidō-jiri.

In the 8th year of Kwambun (1668) a raid was made on the "jigoku" (unlicensed prostitutes) and the captives were transported to the Yoshiwara, but as they numbered 512 souls it was difficult to find accommodation for them and apparently there was not enough room in the quarter to erect new brothels. Under these circumstances, a little plot of ground was requisitioned at the back of each brothel in Yedo-chō Ni-chōme, and some seventy-five small houses were built there for the reception of the new immigrants to this earthly paradise. As the majority of the these fresh arrivals were natives of Fushimi and Sakai, the streets where their houses stood were called Fushimi-chō and Sakai-machi. Sakai-machi was destroyed by fire during the era of Meiwa (1764-1771) and has ceased to exist, but Fushimi-chō is to be seen to this day.

At first the five streets of the Shin-Yoshiwara consisted wholly of brothels, Ageya-machi of "*age-ya*" and Naka-no-chō of tradesmen's stores, but as time rolled away the "*age-ya*" ceased to exist and in their place sprang up "*cha-ya*" (tea-houses). Gradually, also, the shopkeepers in Naka-no-chō removed elsewhere and their stores were turned into tea-houses. Subsequently tea-houses began to increase in number at Ageya-machi, and nowadays there are even many brothels to be seen in this street.

---

* *Ageya* (揚屋) were houses of assignation were, in accordance with the customs of the time, a visitor could stay and to which he could invite any prostitute with whom he had, or wished to have, a *liaison*. The *age-ya* made all arrangements for procuring the attendance of courtesans when required.

The following extract from the "Tsuikō Yoshiwara Taizen" (追考吉原大全 an old descriptive book on these matters) may be of interest to my readers:—

"The corner between *Maka-no-chō* and *Yedo-chō It-chō-me* and "*Ni-chō-me* is called "*Machi-ai no tsuji*, or "Waiting lane" be- "cause the women used to sit down here before their houses "waiting for guests * * * * The corner of *Yedo-chō Ni-chō-me* "was called the *Ao-mono Ichiba* (Vegetable Market) and that of "Sumi-chō the "*Sakana Ichiba*" (Fish Market) because during "the day-time green-grocers and fishmongers were in the habit "of assembling in those places. In the summer evenings "dealers in fire-flies (*hotaru-uri*) would also be found hanging "around these streets. As to the origin of the *Suido-jiri* ("End "of the Aqueduct") it is said that formerly there were no wells "in the *Yoshiwara* and that all the water used there had to be "carried from the wells at *Jariba* and *Tambo*, but in the eras of "*Genroku* (1688-1703) and *Hōyei* (1704-1710) the famous *Yedo* "merchant prince—*Kinokuni-ya Bunzayemon*—caused a well to "be sunk in the compound of *Owari-ya Seijūrō* in *Ageya-machi* for "the first time, with the result that a plentiful supply of water "was provided * * * * * As the pipes in which this water was "conducted to the various portions of the *Yoshiwara* terminated "at the end of *Naka-no-chō*, the name "*Suidō-jiri*" (see above) "was given to that spot." The "*Jisekigōkō*" 事蹟合考 (another "book) says:—"The name of *Suidō-jiri* did not originate in the "*Moto-Yoshiwara*, but in the *Shin-Yoshiwara*. In the plans of the "old *Yoshiwara*, however, it would seem that a place with a "similar name *did actually* exist, and so it is mentioned here for "the sake of reference. The street along the creek at *Kyō-machi* "*It-chō-me* is called *Jōnen-gashi* which name is said to have been "derived from the name of a son of the Headman, *Shōji Jin-* "*yemon*, who formerly had his residence there."

"The "*Kiyū Shōran*" 嬉遊笑覽 (another book) says:—During "the era of *Kwanbun* (1661-1672) the *san-cha*" (a class of low and "cheap prostitutes about whom an explanation is given else- "where) came into existence, and at the same period, on the "application of *Genyemon*, headman of *Kyō-machi*, new houses "were built at *Sakai-machi*, *Fushimi-chō*, and *Minami-chō*. The "first street was so named because it was situated on the "border (*sakai*) of *Sumi-chō Ni-chō-me*, the second on account of "the forefathers of the elders of the street* (*Yamada-ya Yama-*

*"Named after their native place in order to perpetuate the memory of their ancestors."

Artist Painting Mural Decorations in a Brothel.

" *zaburō, Yamaguchi-ya Shichiroemon, Adzuma-ya Jihei*, and *Okada-* " *ya Kichizaemon*) having come over to the *Yoshiwara* from " *Kotobuki-chō, Bungo-bashi*, etc., in *Fushimi*, at the time of the " founding of the *Yoshiwara*. The street along the creek at " *Kyō-machi It-chō-me* is called the *Nishi-gashi* in remembrance of " a younger brother of *Shōji Jinyemon*, (founder of the *Yoshiwara*) " named *Tachibana-ya Sainen*, having lived there.* The street " along the creek at *Kyō-machi Ni-chō-me*, known as *Rashōmon-* " *gashi*—or more commonly as " *Waru-gashi*" (the wicked creek- " side)—was so-called owing to the fact that there was a small " brothel there—named *Ibaraki-ya* "—the inmates of which used " to accost passers-by and clutch tenaciously at their sleeves, " somewhat after the fashion of the warrior *Watanabe no Tsuna* " who seized the arm of an ogre and cut in off in the course of " his well-known adventures at the *Rashō-mon*, near *Kyōto*.† The " *Tenjin-gashi* was situated at *Suidō-jiri*, and here there were some " 25 low brothels established. This creek-side was called "*Tenjin-* " *gashi*" after *Sugawara-no-Michizane*, a great scholar who had " been deified and whose festival fell on the 25th of each " month."‡

Nihon-dsutsumi.

(The Dyke of Japan.)

It is mentioned in the " Dōbō Goyen " 洞房語園 that there was an hereditary farmer at Minowa named Shibazaki Yohei, and according to his story he had heard from his grandfather that the Nihon-dsutsumi was constructed about a hundred years ago in the year of the " large monkey." Now countrymen often call the year of Kōshin the " year of the large monkey," so the year referred to by Yohei's grandfather may be the 7th year of Genna (1621). It is also mentioned, in a

* The Japanese pronunciation of the character 西 (*sai*) in the name " *Sainen* " is " *Nishi* " (West); hence the name of *Nishi* (West) + *gashi* (river bank). It is a very common custom in Japan to compose names in this manner.

† The story of *Watanabe no Tsuna's* adventures has been published in the *Kōbunsha* " " Fairy Tale Series " under the head of " *The Ogre's Arm.*"

‡ *Tenjin* is the name under which *Sugawara-no-Michizane* is apotheosized. He was a great minister and scholar, but falling a victim to calumny was banished and finally died in exile. He is worshipped as the God of Calligraphy.

supplement to the book, that the characters formerly used in writing the name were 二本 (ni hon=2 lines) and not 日本 (Nihon=Japan), because there were two roads one of which led from Shōden-chō to Sanya-bashi. As, however, Yedo increased in prosperity, hills were levelled and canals dug, after a while the road to Sanya-bashi disappeared as part of the changes made in the city; and accordingly the characters 二本 were altered to 日本 in describing the remaining road. At the time of the construction of the Nihon-dsutsumi, a large number of lacquer-trees (*urushi-no-ki*) were planted on both sides of the road, forming a veritable avenue,* and it was a common joke to warn an *habitué* of the Yoshiwara by saying significantly—"When you pass along the Sanya road, mind you don't get poisoned by lacquer!" The bank commenced at Shōden-chō in the West and Yoshino-machi (Asakusa) in the East, and extended to Harajuku (Shitaya), the total length being 834 Ken (5004 feet), the width of the road 10 Ken (60 feet) and the horse-path 5 Ken on the average (30 feet).

Mi-kaeri Yanagi.

(Gazing back Willow-tree.)

This well-known willow-tree stands at the entrance of Go-jik-ken-machi, on the left, below the Nihon-dsutsumi. It has been so called because many a visitor to the Yoshiwara has looked regretfully back as he passed the willow tree, feeling reluctant to leave the pleasures of the quarter and to be separated from his fair, even though frail, inamorata.

* Trees planted in this manner by the authorities were called "*goyō-boku,*" or "government trees." Lacquer trees are poisonous, and the sap produces a severe rash on the skin if handled.

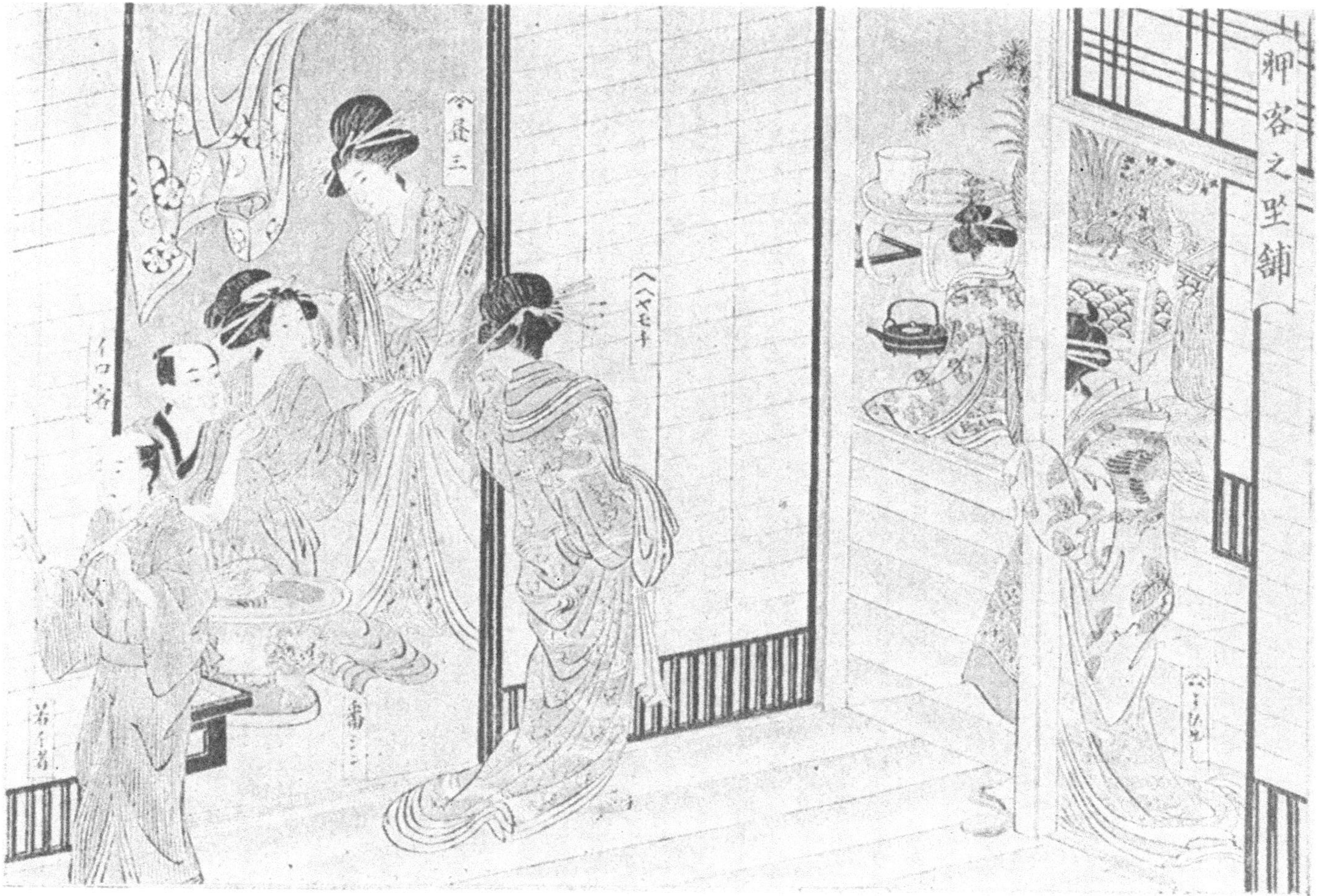

A Familiar Guest. Period of Kiōwa (1801 to 1803).
(After the Picture by Kitagawa Utamaro.)

Yoshiwara Jinja.

(Yoshiwara Shrine).

This is situated on the right hand side of the Go-jik-ken-michi. Formerly there was on this site a shrine called Yoshitoku Inari, but of late years the Enomoto Inari (at the corner of Yedo-chō Ni-chō-me) the Kai-un Inari (at the corner of Kyō-machi, It-chō-me) the Kurosuke Inari (at the corner of Kyō-machi Ni-chō-me) and the Akashi Inari at the corner of Yedo-chō Ni-chō-me—Fushimi-chō) were all amalgamated into one. The name of "Yoshiwara Jinja" was given to the new shrine and it has been made the guardian shrine of the "enclosure." Every twelve days, on the day of the horse, the festival of this shrine is celebrated, crowds of people visit the neighbourhood including sundry itinerant dealers known as "*ennichi akindo*" (festival dealers) and the fête has become one of the popular features of the Yoshiwara. According to the "*Shimpen Yedo-shi*," (新編江戸志) the Kurosuke Inari was in the old Yoshiwara, having been founded in the 4th year of Wadō? (711?). Later on, a person named Chiba Kurosuke removed it to a space on the border of a paddy-field, and since the establishment of the Yoshiwara, in the era of Keichō (1596-1614), this Inari became the guardian deity of the prostitude quarter. Again, according to the "*Kwagai Manroku*" (花街漫錄) the shrine of the Kurosuke Inari was situated beneath Kyō-machi Ni-chō-me since its removal from the old to the new Yoshiwara, and about the era of Tenna (1681-1683) it began to be called "Kurosuke" Inari because a man called Kurosuke lived in front of the building.

As to the origin of the "*Byakko-seki*" (white fox stone) of the Akashi-Inari—which was the presiding deity of Yedo-chō Ni-chō-me—its shrine formerly stood on the estates of a certain Mr. Nishimura, but at the request of the local inhabitants to consecrate it shrine of the guardian deity it was removed to the present site. While the shrine was in course of construction a curiously shaped object was unearthed, and on closer examination it was found to be a beautiful blackish coloured stone resembling the figure of a *byakko* (white fox) gambolling in the fields. The people, thinking this a good omen, consecrated the image under the name of Akashi Inari (明石=*aka-ishi* "the bright stone," or even, by forced rendering, "the bright and revealed stone") and prayed to it as a god which would bring prosperity and good-luck to the town and protect the quarter from disastrous fires.

The "Aisome-zakura."

(Cherry-tree of first meeting.)

AND

The "Koma-tsunagi-matsu."

(Colt teathering pine-tree.)

The above trees stand close to the Yoshiwara shrine.

The "Ryo-jin no Ido."

(Traveller's Well.)

This well is situated about the centre of the Go-jik-ken-michi, on the right hand side.

Government Edict-board and Regulations at the Ōmon.

Up to the time of the Restoration—some 30 odd years ago —the following official regulations were posted up before the O-mon (great gateway) of the Yoshiwara:—

The "*Ō-mon*" or Entrance Gateway of the Yoshiwara.

"Persons other than doctors are forbidden to enter riding "in *Kago* (palanquin) or *norimono* (sedan chair).

"Long weapons are forbidden."* [This meant spears or "long swords, and also other warlike weapons which formed "part of the ordinary paraphernalia of a *Daimyō's* (noble's) "train.]

The Present Ōmon.

On the present Ō-mon (great gateway) are inscribed the following characters from the pen of Mr. Fukuchi Genichirō (a well-known playwright) better known under his *nom de plume* of "Ōchi Koji":—

春夢正濃滿街櫻雲。秋信先通兩行燈影

"*Shum-mu masa ni komayaka nari, mangai no ō-un. Shū-shin saki ni tsūzu ryōkō no tō-yei,*" or freely translated into English :—

"*A dream of Spring-tide when the streets are full of the cherry blossoms. Tidings of the autumn when the streets are lined on either side with lighted lanterns.*"

This poem is a eulogy composed of four sentences each containing four Chinese characters, the style being an imitation of that of the blank verses which were in vogue in the *Tsin* dynasty. The depth of meaning conveyed by these sixteen ideographs is almost incredible to the uninitiated, and to explain the full sense of the composition in English is well-nigh impossible. The words which are rendered "*A dream of Springtide when the streets are full of the cherry blossoms*" refer to the custom of planting cherry-trees right down the centre of the *Naka-no-chō* from the main gateway (*Ō-mon*) to *Suidō-jiri*. The cherry trees are in full bloom about the first week in the third month (according to the old calendar—now April) and when one then glances down

* It should not be forgotten that no *samurai* (feudal warrior class) was allowed to enter the brothels wearing his swords. The swords were taken charge of by attendants at the doors before the *samurai* guest went into the house. Mr. A. B. Mitford says in his "Tales of old Japan"—"When a Japanese enters a house of ill-fame he is forced to leave his sword and dirk at the door for two reasons—first, to prevent brawling; secondly because it is known that some of the women inside so loathe their existence that they would put an end to it, could they get hold of a weapon."

the avenue at night, after the place is lighted up with thousands of brilliantly coloured lanterns and flashing electric lamps, the whole quarter appears as if smothered in flowers. The commingling blossoms, seemingly transmuted into dense masses of soft and fleecy cloud, braid the trees in a wealth of vernal beauty, and the gay dresses both of the unfortunate women, and those of the passers-by, ever kaleidoscopic in effect and vividly oriental in colour, all go to make up a scene at once strange, fascinating, and well-nigh dream-like in character. The women in the Yoshiwara are likened in a certain poem to "*cherries of the night which blossom luxuriantly,*" and their power of fascination is expressed by another poem which says "*Cherry blossoms of the night at length become those of the morning and again those of the night*": and yet another poem runs—"*Naka-no-chō, where the night-cherries* (courtesans) *blossom luxuriantly.*" There is a *double entendre* in the sentence, for the words not only refer to the intermingling cherry blossoms in the *Naka-no-chō* but imply that joy and pleasure is to be found in "*A dream of spring, in a town inhabited by beautiful and voluptuous women to whom their lovers cleave as the commingling blossoms of the cherries blend together.*" The poem also implies an indirect allusion to an episode in the life of one of the Chinese Emperors, who was distinguished for his Solomon-like proclivities in his admiration for the fair sex, and the harem of ravishingly beautiful damsels he kept at Fuzan.* The words "*Tidings of the autumn when the streets are lined on either side with lighted lanterns*" refer to the custom of hanging out *tōrō* (lanterns) in front of every tea-house in the Naka-no-chō during one month from the 1st day to the last day of the 7th month (old calendar.) These *tōrō* were first hung out as an offering to the soul of one Tamagiku, a popular courtesan in olden days. When one enters the great gate at the time of this festival it is a very pretty sight to see the rows of lanterns after they are lighted up. Some of these lanterns bear pictures by celebrated painters and are therefore quite works of art, and the effect of the display is heightened at times by artifical flowers being placed between them. It is said that the approach of Autumn is heralded by the cry of the wild geese, but that it is also foretold by the display of lanterns in the Naka-no-chō during the festival of the dead. The sight of these lanterns moreover remind the sightseers of the words of an old poem which runs—"*Alas! it is the night when the dead Tamagiku comes to visit the tōrō.*"

* Chi Hwan-ti (始皇帝), builder of "Great Wall."

Of the Reason Why Going to the Yoshiwara was Called "Chō ye yuku."

In the "Yoshiwara Ō-kagami," (吉原大鑑 "Great Mirror of the Yoshiwara") it is mentioned that the origin of the common expression in former days of "Chō ye yuku" (going to Chō)—meaning "going to the Yoshiwara"—was as follows: Formerly the streets of the Yoshiwara were laid out in the shape of a cross, but afterwards one of the entrances was closed, changing the cross into a shape like that of the Chinese character "Chō" (丁), hence the saying. In later times this expression was changed, and nowadays people speak of going to the Yoshiwara as "*naka ye yuku*" (to go inside").

Classes of Brothels.

In ancient times the houses were classified according to the position and standing of their inmates. As we mention elsewhere, the courtesans were formerly classed as Tayū, Kōshi-joro, Tsubone, Sancha-joro, Umecha-joro (also read "Baicha-joro") and Kirimise-joro, and in a similar manner brothels were also divided as Tayū-mise, Kōshi-mise, Tsubone-mise, Sancha-mise, Umecha-mise (or "Baicha-mise") Kirimise, etc. Afterwards, the name of the Tayū-mise and Kōshi-mise was changed to "Yobidashi," and the "Umecha-mise" having disappeared the so-called "Zashiki-mochi" and "Heya-mochi" came into existence. After the era of Kwansei (1789-1800) the following classes of brothels sprang into existence:— 1st class:—Ōmagaki; 2nd class:—Hammagaki; 3rd class:—Dai-chō ko-mise; 4th class:—Kogōshi; 5th class:—Kirimise, etc. Courtesans classed as Yobidashi, Hirusan, and Tsuke-mawashi belonged to the Ōmagaki, while the Zashiki-mochi and Heya-mochi were attached to the Dai-chō ko-mise.

The style of architecture employed in the erection of the "Tsubone-mise" is elaborately described in the "*Dōbō Go-yen,*" (洞房語園) and the fact that the general features of the "Sancha-mise" were similar to those of the Furo-ya in the city is also mentioned in the same book. After the era of Kwansei (1789-1800) the classes of brothels, it appears, were determined according to the height of the bars of the cages. The highest *magaki* (籬) are said to have reached to the ceiling while the lowest were about 2 feet high. The wood used in the lattice window of an *Ō-magaki* (a first-class house with bars running up to the ceiling) was about 8 inches in width and was painted red. The houses themselves were generally as large as 13 *ken* by 22 *ken* (78 × 132 ft). The lattice bars of the lower class houses, on the contrary, were 3 inches in width and therefore these houses were called Ko-gōshi (small lattices). The lowest class houses had bars which ran horizontally instead of vertically. These distinctions were maintained up to the time of the general liberation of prostitutes in the 5th year of Meiji (1872) but since that time the brothels have been classified as either *Ō-mise, Chū-mise,* or *Ko-mise* (Large, medium, and small "shops.)"

At present there is no uniform style of architecture, but as the better class of houses are naturally visited by a superior class of guests, the leading establishments are fine buildings, and are noted as much for the luxurious character of their furniture and appointments as for the beauty of the women who inhabit them. The best houses do not exhibit the women in cages.

Street Scene in the "Naka-no-chō," Yoshiwara.

The following are the names of the 126 existing brothels of the Yoshiwara (1899).

Ō-mise
(*First-class houses.*)

Kado-ebi-rō	in Kyō-machi It-chō-me
Inamoto-rō	" Sumi-chō.
Daimonji-rō	" Yedo-chō It-cho-me.
Shinagawa-rō	" Ageya-machi.
Nomura-rō	" Kyō-machi Nichō-me.

Naka-mise
(*Second-class houses.*)

Man-kwa-rō	in Yedo-chō Nichō-me.
Hōrai-rō	" Ageya-machi.
Ai-idzumi-rō.	" Sumi-chō.
Naka-gome-rō.	" Kyō-machi Ni-chō-me.

Ko-mise
(*Third-class houses.*)

Shin Hanai-rō	in Yedo-chō	It-chō-me.	
Shō-yei-rō.	"	"	"
Shin Ichino-rō	"	"	"
Nari-hisa-rō	"	"	"
Sugimoto-rō	"	"	"
Kikuya-rō	"	"	"
Ichino-rō	"	"	"
Shin Kinkwa-rō	"	"	"
Kajita-rō	"	"	"
Nishihashi-rō	"	"	"
Yoshi-Inaben-rō	"	"	"
Fuku-Suzuki-rō	"	"	"

Fukurai-rō	in Yedo-chō It-chō-me.
Katsu Nakagome-rō	" " "
Shō-yū-rō	" " "
Izutsu-rō	" " "
Seikwa-rō	" " "
Hanaoka-rō	" " "
Moto Fujiyoshi-rō.	" " "
Fukuyosu-rō	" " "
Kawa-tachibana-rō	" " "
Kyōchū-rō	" " "
Kyō-shin-rō.	" " "
Kiku-matsu-kane-rō	" " "
Matsu-mi-rō.	in Yedo-chō Ni-chō-me.
Katsu-moto-rō	" " "
Tama Mikawa-rō	" " "
Tama Hanai-rō.	" " "
Tsune-Matsu-kane-rō.	" " "
Hikota-rō	" " "
Ōsaka-rō.	" " "
Kiyo Fujimoto-rō	in Yedo-chō It-chō-me.
Oto Hanai-rō	" " "
Musashi-rō	" " Ni-chō-me.
Hisa Hanai-rō	" " "
Yawata-rō	" " "
Ryūgasaki-rō	" " "
Toku Hanai-rō	" " "
Kikkō-rō.	" " "
Matsu Yebi-rō	" " "
Sugito-rō	" " "
Sumi-Yawata-rō	" " "

Suke-Komatsu-rō	in Yedo-chō-Ni-cnō-me.
Iwa Hanai-rō	" " "
Moto Komatsu-rō	" " "
Hanai-rō	" " "
Asahi-rō	" " "
Matsu-Nakagome-rō	" " "
Tsuru-yoshi-rō	" " "
Chisei-rō	" " "
Fuji-yoshi-rō	" " "
Naka-Hanai-rō	" " "
Nakamura-rō	" " "
Yū-sen-rō	" " "
Kane Koshikawa-rō	" " "
Manji-rō	" " "
Kinkwa-rō	" " "
Hira Hanai-rō	" " "
Moto Kawachi-rō	" " "
Shin Yoshiwara-rō	in Yedo-chō Ni-cho-me.
Yasu Nakagome-rō	" " "
Masui-rō	" " "
Shin Ryū-ga-saki-rō.	" " "
Kyōsei-rō	in Ageya-machi.
Ogawa-rō	" "
Nishi-naka-rō.	" "
Sei-kwa-rō	" "
Takahashi-rō	" "
Naka Inaben-rō	" "
Kikumoto-rō	" "
Shin-Fujimoto-rō	" "
Hei-Daikoku-rō	" "

Seihō-rō	in Ageya-machi.
Nari-Yamata-rō	" "
Masu-Kawachi-rō	" "
Nishioka-rō	" "
Hōrai-rō	" "
Kin-Nakagome-rō	" "
Ise-rō	" "
Sawa-Inaben-rō	" "
Owari-rō	" "
Tama Hōrai-rō	" "
Kiku Inaben-rō	" "
Yamada-rō	" "
Sawa Nakagome-rō	" "
Sada Kawachi-rō	" "
Shin-Matsu-Daikoku-rō	" "
Ume-man-rō	" "
Shimotake-rō	" "
Tanaka-rō	" "
Takeman-rō	" "
Tama-Kawachi-rō	" "
Aichū-rō	" "
Tatsu-Inaben-rō	" "
Shin-Inaben-rō	" "
Shin-Matsu-kin-ro	" "
Kame-Inaben-rō	" "
Toku-Inaben-rō	" "
Ni-masu-rō	" "
Shō-Nakagome-rō	" "
Tsuta-Inaben-rō	" "
Fuku-Yamato-rō	" "

Hiroshima-rō	in Ageya-machi.		
Niikawa-rō	"	"	
Naga-Idzumi-rō	"	"	
Takara-rō	"	"	
Matsuoka-rō	"	"	
Koshikawa-rō	"	"	
Daikoku-rō	"	"	
Tama-Kawachi-rō	"	"	
Shin-Ai-idzumi-rō	"	"	
Inaben-rō	in Kyō-machi	It-chō-me.	
Shin-man-rō	"	"	"
Ai-man-rō	"	"	"
Shin-Fukuoka-rō	"	"	"
Is-shin-rō	"	"	"
Hyō-Daikoku-rō	"	"	"
Toyo-Matsu-Kin-rō	"	"	"
Matsumoto-rō	"	"	"
Shin-Hōrai-rō	"	"	"
Inage-rō	"	"	"
Fujimoto-rō	"	"	"
Man-nen-rō	"	"	"
Yedo-rō	"	"	"
Shin-Okamoto-rō	"	"	"
Hoku-yetsu-rō	"	"	"
Mikawa-rō	"	"	"
Matsu-Owari-rō	"	"	"
Sen-Inaben-rō	"	"	"
Kimman-rō	"	"	Ni-chō-me.
Matsuyama-rō	"	"	"
Matsu-Kin-rō	"	"	"

Sen-Nakagome-rō	in Kyo-machi Ni-chō-me.
Matsu-Daikoku-rō	" " "
Yoshida-rō	" " "
Kawachi-rō	" " "
Moto-Higashi-rō	" " "
Koiman-rō	" " "
Bitchū-rō.	" " "
Kane-Nakagome-rō	" " "
Shin-Nakagome-rō	" " "
Gyokusai-rō	" " "
Waka-take-rō	" " "
Kin-Hōrai-rō	" " "
Shin-Adzuma-rō.	" " "
Tatsu-Komatsu-rō	" " "
Kado-Owari-rō	" " "

Hikite-jaya.*

("Introducing Tea-houses.")

The business of *hikite-jaya* is to act as a guide to the various brothels, and to negotiate introductions between guests and courtesans. There are seven of these introducing houses within the enclosure (*kuruwa*), fifty in Naka-naga-ya, Suidō-jiri, and outside of the Ō-mon (great gate).

Besides these there are many houses in Yedo-chō, Sumi-chō, Kyō-machi (It-chō-me and Ni-chō-me) Ageya-machi, etc. The first-mentioned seven houses are first-class, those in Naga-naga-ya second-class, while those at Suidō-jiri and Gō-jik-ken are very inferior indeed. The reception of guests, and arranging affairs for them, is attended to by servant maids, three or four of whom are generally employed in each *hikite-jaya*. As,

* "Leading-by-the-hand tea-houses."

1. Entertainment given by a *Yūjo* who has been Redeemed from a Brothel.
2. Guests in a Tea-house Diverting themselves with Dancing Girls.
3. A Guest being conducted to a Brothel by the Servants of a *Hikite-jaya*.

of course, the reputation of the house depends on these servant maids, their employers generally treat them very considerately, well knowing that if the girls attend to their duties satisfactorily the number of guests will continue to increase.

When a visitor arrives before the entrance of a *hikite-jaya*, the mistress of the house and her maid-servants run to welcome him with cries of "*irrasshai*" (you are very welcome!), and on entering the room to which he is conducted (in case of his being a stranger) the attendant will ask him the name of the brothel to which he desires to go, as well as that of the particular lady he wishes to meet. If he has no "friend" with whom he is acquainted, photographs are produced for inspection and the guest chooses his *oiran* from them. Then the attendant will guide him to the brothel selected, act as a go-between in negotiating for the courtesan's favours, and after all preliminaries have been settled will wait assiduously upon the guest throughout the banquet which inevitably follows, taking care to keep the *saké* bottles moving and the cups replenished. By and by, when the time comes for retiring, the attendant conducts the guest to his sleeping apartment, waits until the arrival of the "lady friend" and then discreetly slips away and leaves the brothel. When one of these servant maids takes charge of a visitor she becomes, for the time being, the actual personal servant of such guest and attends to everything he requires. To perform the services rendered by her is professionally spoken of as "*mawasu*" (廻 to turn round, to move round) because she goes bustling round in order to arrange a hundred and one matters for the guest upon whom she is in attendance. If the guest calls *geisha* (dancing and singing girls) the maid carries (supposing it to be night-time) the *geisha's samisen* (guitar) and the guest's night-dress in the left hand, and a "*Kamban chōchin*"* and a white porcelain *saké* bottle (*haku-chō*)† in the right—a performance which requires considerable experience to achieve successfully.

With the exception of the guests, no persons are allowed to wear *zōri* (sandals) inside the brothels.

Of late it has become a rule that the office which manages all affairs in the Yoshiwara shall distribute to the various tea-houses registration books, of a uniform style, in which are to be minutely recorded the personal appearance of visitors, status and place of registration, profession, general figure and build, aspect, style of clothes, personal effects (i. e. rings, chains, watches, etc., etc.) The books are carefully ruled off in columed blanks headed :—"Nose, Ears, Mouth, Status, Place of registration," etc., etc.; and the descriptions have to be written in under the respective headings. In short, these books (for which, by the way, a charge of 20 to 30 sen is made) are something like the usual Japanese hotel registers but more complex and detailed, and when the blanks are faithfully filled up an exceedingly good description of guests is secured. In all brothels similar books are kept, and the duty of comparing the entries in these with the entries in those of the *hikite-jaya* devolves on the staff of the Yoshiwara office. In

* Literally a "sign-board lantern" so called because the lantern bears the name of the *hikite-jaya*. It is the custom for the maid to carry a lighted lantern (even inside the brothel) as far as the door of the room of the courtesan to whom the visitor is introduced. This lantern serves as a token to identify the *hikite-jaya* to which the maid belongs. On arriving before the door of the room the lantern is extinguished by shaking it, and not by blowing out the light in the usual way. A supersition exists against blowing out the light with one's lips :—it is supposed to be unlucky.

† The *haku-chō* or white porcelain *saké* bottles used on these occasions hold about 1 *shō*, or say about 3 pints.

addition to these duties there are a good many harassing and vexatious police regulations to be observed by the introducing houses. Should any *hikite-jaka* keeper or employé secretly introduce a guest who is in possession of explosives, a sword, or poison, he is severely punished and caused no end of trouble. The payment of the guest's bill is made through the *hikite-jaya* on his return to the introducing house in the morning. The guest pays his total bill to the *hikite-jaya* and the latter squares up accounts with the brothel. The strict rule is for the *hikite-jaya* to settle up these accounts daily with the brothels, but it has become a custom with the majority to balance accounts only twice a month—viz:—on the 14th and 30th day of each month. In case of a frequent visitor being without money, and unable to pay his bill, the *hikite-jaya* will not, as a rule, refuse him credit in consideration of the patronage he has extended to the house and in anticipation of future visits. Sometimes, however, it happens that a regular customer becomes heavily indebted to a certain house, and turning his back on this establishment he seeks for new pastures and fresh credit; but here the extraordinary secret intelligence system upsets his calculations. Among these tea-houses exists a kind of "honor among thieves" *esprit de corps*, and besides, self-protection has forced the houses to give secret information to each other where their mutual interests are threatened; so when a party is in debt to one of the *hikite-jaya* he will be boycotted by the others. A smart hand may successfully pretend to be a new arrival in the Yoshiwara once or twice, but his trick is sure to be discovered ere long. Faithful service of employés is ensured in the Yoshiwara in a similar manner. In case of a servant-maid employed in one house being desirous to enter the service of another establishment, she must first obtain the consent of her employer, and the master of the house to which she wishes to go will certainly confer with the master of the establishment she wishes to leave. In ordering food from a *dai-ya* (a cook-house where food is cooked and sent out to order), or in making purchases from storekeepers in the Yoshiwara, a maid-servant belonging to any of the *hikite-jaya* requires no money with her because the dealers all place confidence in the house from which she has come, and this they know at once by the inscription on the lantern she carries. Immediately an order is given by a maid-servant the goods are handed over without the slightest hesitation, so under these circumstances an evil-minded woman might resort to fraud without any difficulty; but should she once be detected she would never again be able to get employment in the Yoshiwara.

The fifty tea-houses outside the *Ō-mon* (great gate) were in former times called "*Kitte-jaya*" (ticket tea-houses) or "*Kitte-mise*" (ticket shops); they were also colloquially termed in *Yedo* slang—"*Yoshiwara no go-jū-mai kitte*" (the fifty "tickets" of the Yoshiwara) because they had the monopoly of issuing tickets or passes for the Yoshiwara. In a book called the "*Hyōkwa Manroku*" (苹華漫錄) it is recorded that in the 3rd year of *Keian* (1650) one of the tea-houses named "*Kikuya*" (sign of the Chrysanthemum Flowers) issued tickets—or rather passes—for the passage of women through the great gate. On one of these old passes was written:—

> I certify that these six ladies belong to the household of a gentleman who patronizes my establishment.
>
> January 26th—.
>
> Ticket-shop,
>
> To (signed) Kikuya Hambei.
>
> The keeper af the great gate.

It appears from this that every lady who wished to enter the precincts for the purpose of sightseeing, or for any other reason, had to obtain a pass from the tea-houses abovementioned. Afterwards, the "*Midzu-chaya*" (rest-houses) began to be built on the *Nihon-dsutsumi* (Dyke of Japan) and as they gradually increased and prospered they at length encroached upon the *Naka-no-chō* where the tradesmen of the quarter were living. This continued until the street came to be monopolized by *Midzu-chaya*, and from the latter the present *hikite-jaya* were finally evolved. It is recorded that since the era of *Genroku* (1688-1703) the keepeers of *funa-yado* (a sort of tea-house where pleasure boats are kept and let out on hire for excursions and picnics) used to arrange for guests to go and come in their river-boats, "and among the sights of Yedo were the long lines of boats floating up and down the river with gaily-dressed courtesans and the *jeunesse dorée* of the city in them." During the 8th years of Kwambun (1668) all the unlicensed prostitutes in Yedo city were pounced upon by the authorities and placed in the Yoshiwara, and about this time the inconvenient custom of being obliged to visit brothels through an *ageya* was abolished. The tea-houses which had their origin on the banks of the *Nihon-dsutsumi*, now acted as guides (*tebiki*) to intending visitors to brothels, the old custom of the place was broken, and the name of *hikite-jaya* come into existence. [The tea-houses belonging to the *Ageya* which were removed from the old Yoshiwara, and the "*Amigasa-jaya*" (see this heading further on) which sprang into existence while the brothels were temporarily situated at Sanya, after the *Furisode-kwaji* (fire) of the era of Meireki, are separate establishments.] In this way the newly evolved tea-houses prospered greatly, and their influence grew apace until the older houses in Ageya-machi began to lose their trade. No doubt but the decadence of the older institutions is attributable to the superior facilities afforded to guests by the new houses. In the old days the tea-houses in Ageya-machi were allowed to construct balconies on the second stories of their establishments for the convenience of those guests who desired to witness the processions of courtesans (*Yūjo no dō-chū*) that formed one of the most interesting features in the life of the Yoshiwara. Prior to the fire of the Meiwa era (1764-1771) the second stories of all the tea-houses in *Naka-no-chō* were fitted with open lattice-work in front, but subsequent to that memorable conflagration this restriction was removed and the houses were built so as to render them convenient for sight-seeing from the upper floor. This freedom did not prove of much advantage to many of the houses, however, as it was decided that the processions should thenceforward be confined to the *Naka-no-chō*. In the 10th year of Hōreki (1760) the "*Ageya*" completely disappeared, and the receiving of and arranging matters for guests became the monopoly of the tea-houses. Taking advantage of the position attained, the tea-houses abused their prosperity and influence and allowed their establishments to be used by courtesans, *geisha, taiko-mochi*, and various guests, for the purpose of carrying on illicit intrigues and advancing amours between men and women of loose morals. Not only this, but the houses allowed their accounts with the brothels to fall into arrears, or made payment in an unpunctual and perfunctory manner, and for these reasons many were suspended from exercising their business. In the era of Tempō (1830-1843) all food served to the guests in *hikite-jaya* was prepared on the premises by professional cooks in the service of the houses.

At present, a first customer to a tea-house is called "*shōkwai*" (first meeting): the second time he comes "*ura*" (behind the scenes) and the third time "*najimi*" (on intimate terms). According to prevalent custom, guests have to pay a certain sum of money as "footing" on their second and third visits, and persons who are anxious to pass as "in the swim" are often willing to pay both these fees (*ura-najimi-kin* and *najimi-kin*) down at once. Ordinarily the *najimi-kin* is fixed at from 2½ *yen* or 3 *yen*, according to the brothels to which a visitor wishes to go, and the tea-houses do not guide visitors who do not patronize either a first (*ōmise*) or second (*naka-mise*) class establishment. In addition to other small fees the visitor is expected to give a tip of 20 or 30 *sen* to the maid who acts as his guide, but if he does not hand it over voluntarily it is carefully included in his bill under the heading of "*o-tomo*" (your attendant). *Jinrikisha* fares advanced will also appear in the bill (*tsuké*=contraction of "*kakitsuke*"= an account, writing, or memo) under the title of "*o-tomo*" (your attendant). Experience of *hikite-jaya* will convince visitors that these establishments never fail to charge up every possible or impossible item in their accounts: when a man is returning home in the morning with a "swollen head" after a night's debauch his ideas of checking a bill are generally somewhat mixed up.

The expenses of planting flowers in the streets in Spring, setting up street lanterns (*tōrō*) in Autumn, and maintaining street dancing (*niwaka*) are defrayed by the tea-houses.

The profits of *hikite-jaya* are chiefly derived from return commissions on the fees paid to courtesans and dancing girls, and percentages levied on the food and *sakê* consumed by guests. (A large profit is made upon *sakê*, as this is kept in stock by tea-houses themselves). Besides, they draw a handsome revenue from visitors in the shape of "*chadai*" (tea money) which rich prodigals bestow upon them in return for fulsome flattery and cringing servility. The guests will also often give a *sōbana* (present to all the inmates of the house) when they are well treated, and at special seasons of the year, festivals, and occasions of rejoicing, the liberality of visitors brings quite a shower of dollars, all nett profit, into the coffers of the *chaya* proprietor.

It is one of the many curious customs of the Yoshiwara that the expression "*fukidasu*" (to blow out) is disliked, as also is the blowing out of the ground cherry (*hozuki*).*

* As these places depend upon the custom of persons entering them, it is considered as unlucky to speak about blowing anything out. The *hozuki* is bitter or acid, and as a pregnant woman is supposed to like sour or acid things courtesans think that to blow the winter cherry is most ominous as it may presage pregnancy and injure their profession. The ordinary *geisha* (dancing girl) in Japan delights to sit making a squeaking noise by means of blowing and squeezing between her lower lip and teeth the dried and salted berry of the winter-cherry, from which the pulp has been deftly extracted at the stem. This practice seems as pleasant to the *geisha* as that of chewing gum does to some foreigners.

Outside of a Third-class Brothel at night.

I must not omit to state that there is a low class of tea-houses which resort to extortion and barefaced robbery in dealing with strangers to the Yoshiwara. These houses are known by the general term of "*bori-jaya*" and their *modus operandi* is to detail their rascally employés to prowl about outside the quarter and inveigle uninitiated visitors to the *kuruwa*. Under various pretexts, inexperienced persons are guided to *bori-jaya* by these touters, welcomed effusively, and pestered with the most fulsome flattery and attention. *Saké* and food is served to them, including a number of dishes never even ordered by the guest, and by and by *geisha* are called in to sing and dance, although the visitors have not requisitioned their services. Later on, when the guests are primed with liquor, they are urged to visit a brothel on the condition that the expenditure shall be kept as low as possible, but, once within the low stews to which they are taken, they are persuaded to squander money on *geisha* and other things. If meanwhile the visitor, fearing heavy expenses, should desire to settle his bill, the keeper of the house will put off the matter and invent various plausible excuses for delaying the making up of the account. Time flies and morning succeeds the night, but no bill is rendered, and every artifice and trick is employed to detain the guest, until the latter, overcome with *saké* and fatigue, rolls over on the floor in a drunken sleep. Meanwhile the pockets of the unfortunate victim are surveyed in order to discover the extent of his means, and as soon as it is evident that there is no more money left to be sucked he is allowed to depart. Sometimes, however, the visitors prove too smart to be successfully swindled, but in these cases the houses afford them a very cold reception indeed. Sometimes it happens that the *bori-jaya* proprietors overestimate the pecuniary resources of guests who have fallen a prey to their wiles, and find that their purses are not lined sufficiently well to meet the bills run up against them. In such a case the proprietors will allow the guest to depart under the escort of one of the employés of the house. This man exercises strict surveillance over the guest, and follows him like grim death wherever he goes until the bill is settled. He is known as a *tsuki-uma* (an attendant—or "following"—horse) and if payment is not made he will inflict the disgrace of his presence upon the luckless wight he follows, tracking the latter home to his very doorstep and there making a noisy demand for the money owing. It is only fair to add, however, that such low tea-houses are not to be found in the *Naka-no-chō.*

Name of the Present "Hikite-jaya (1899.)

In Go-jikken-machi.

Yamato-ya	kept by	Kuwagata Saku	(w)*
Hama-Yamato	"	Sakamoto Komajirō.	
Ōmi-ya	"	Tanaka Fumi	(w)
Wakamatsu-ya	"	Wakamatsu Tomi	(w)
Suzuki-ya	"	Suzuki Naka	(w)
Ōsaka-ya	"	Ōta Tama	(w)
Tsurutsuta-ya	"	Ieda Hanzaburō	
Shin-Wakamatsu	"	Ogiwara Riye	(w)
Naniwa-ya	"	Sada Koto	(w)
Yawata-ya	"	Kobayashi Kiku	(w)
Taka-Yamato	"	Takamatsu Kame	(w)

In Yedo-chō It-chō-me.

Gin-Yamato	kept by	Onozuka Ginjirō
Takeji	"	Takenouchi Jihei
Nagasaki-ya	"	Koboso Kihei
Yamaguchi Tomoye	"	Shimura Tsunejirō

* Those marked "w" are kept by women.

Fukudama-ya	kept by	Sugenuma Fuku	(w)
Komi-Nomura	"	Kuga Mitsu	(w)
Takasago-ya	"	Hagii Tetsu	(w)
Rō-Nakamura	"	Otsuka Tatsu	(w)
Owari-ya	"	Oda Tarōbei	
Wakamizu	"	Ōkubo Aikichi	
Masu-dawara	"	Okamura Iku	(w)
Chikahan	"	Shimizu Hanshir	
Hayashi-ya	"	Ishii Mine	(w)
Kane-Ōsaka	"	Takata Kane	(w)
Nishinomiya	"	Saruhashi Shōzō	
Ise-matsu-ya	"	Sugiyama Chisa	(w)
Fuku-no-ya	"	Miyazaki Fuku	(w)
Saiken-Tsuta-ya	"	Matsumae Saku	(w)
Masu-minato	"	Ishiguro Nobutarō	
Den-Daikoku	"	Itō Shin	(w)
Yonekawa	"	Ishikawa Eizaburō	
Uwajima	"	Uwajima Kichizō	
Kameda-ya	"	Tanaka Harutarō	
Kiri-ya	"	Kimura Kin	(w)
Ume-no-ya	"	Kagawa Ichizō	
Kanō-ya	"	Kuriyama Tsuru	(w)
Matsu-zumi-ya	"	Sakigawa Rin	(w)
Yoshi-mura-ya	"	Yoshimura Tameshichi	
Awa-manji	"	Ōta Masa	(w)
Morita-ya	"	Mori Nao	(w)
Adzuma-ya	"	Ogiya Fuku	(w)
Tsuruhiko Ise-ya	"	Ōmori Hikojirō	
Ine-ya	"	Katsuya Heisuke	
Tani-Iseya	"	Katō Chika	(w)

In Yedo-chō Ni-chō-me.

Ueki-ya	kept by	Kakubari Chō	(w)
Kanzaki-ya	"	Hirano Fuku	(w)
Hisa Ono	"	Ishizaka Hisa	(w)
Idzutsu-ya	"	Yamagoshi Kane	(w)
Iwa-Yamato	"	Kobayashi Hide	(w)
Tatsumi-Ōno	"	Ōno Saki	(w)
Mon-Matsumura	"	Nemoto Mon	(w)
Myōga-ya	"	Koidzumi Fuku	(w)
Yamazaki	"	Yamazaki Mitsu	(w)
Kanedama-ya	"	Nozaki Yura	(w)
Mon-Kadzusa	"	Tomizawa Hanshichi	

Shin-Owari	kept by	Kuroda Genjirō	
Matsu-Iseya	"	Sugiyama Kayo	(w)
Hisa-Yamato	"	Ozawa Masu	(w)
Kirisa	"	Hiroto Sahei	
Nobuzen	"	Nakajima Kin	(w)
Minomura	"	Shinowara Natsu	(w)
Kotobuki-ya	"	Hozaka Kamekichi	
Shin-Nagashima	"	Takashima Iku	(w)
Tokushima	"	Sugimoto Nisaburō	

In Ageya-machi.

Hanagawa-ya	kept by	Katagiri Ito	(w)
Matsumura	"	Ikeda Kayo	(w)
Umemura	"	Momooka Matsunosuke	
Idzutora	"	Tsuji Toku	(w)
Horikawa-ya	"	Uchida Tokuji	
Dai-yoshi	"	Minagawa Fuku	(w)
Tamasei	"	Satō Kin	(w)
Ichimonji-ya	"	Saitō Katsu	(w)
Ōshima-ya	"	Saotome Kiku	(w)
Daichū	"	Wakizaka Kenjirō	

In Sumi-chō.

Shin-Kirihan	kept by	Shimidzu Matsuzō	
Suzuki Kadzusa	"	Suzuki Shige	(w)
Shinakin	"	Miyazawa Kin	(w)
Tamasano-ya	"	Shimidzu Tamasaburō	
Nobuki	"	Yamamoto Kisaburō	
Matsumoto	"	Itō Kihei	
Hatsune-ya	"	Nakamura Shintarō	
Ishigaki-ya	"	Minoura Jingorō	
Masumiya	"	Yamazaki Tetsu	(w)
Aoyagi	"	Ishii Rihei	
Ōzaki-ya	"	Miyazaki Tano	(w)
Mansen	"	Kōno Teru	(w)

In Kyo-machi It-chō-me.

Akashi-ya	kept by	Akashi Shika	(w)
Kawagoe-ya	"	Matsumoto Jūbei	
Tamayoshi	"	Suzuki Rika	(w)

In Kyo-machi Ni-chō-me.

Naka-Ōmi	kept by	Hagiwara Yoshi	(w)
Masuda-ya	"	Amano Kin	(w)
Hyōgo-ya	"	Yoshida Rui	(w)
Komatsu-ya	"	Akao Yoshizō	

The Ju-hachi-ken-jaya.

(*Eight Tea-houses.*)

The "*Yoshiwara Zatsuwa*" 吉原雜話 states that there were in Ageya-machi, besides the "*Ageya*" themselves, eighteen tea-houses to which persons repaired for the purpose of watching the *tayū* entering the various "*ageya.*" According to the regulations of the Yoshiwara in ancient times, the construction of *tsuki-age-do* (shutters which slide up into a groove above the window, like shop-shutters) in the windows of the second stories of these houses was permitted, whereas it was prohibited in any other part of the *kuruwa.* In the tea-houses in Naka-no-chō, lattice work doors were used in their upper floors. It is stated that originally only the central portion of the Yoshiwara leading from Ageya-machi was called Naka-no-chō, the other portions being named Yedo-chō division, Kyō-machi division, etc. According to an old resident of Ageya-machi, Naka-no-chō was formerly amalgamated with Ageya-machi owing to the number of officials being small in the former street, and about that time there was a fireman's ensign (*matoi*) in existence in Ageya-machi bearing the character 中 ("*Naka*"), clearly showing the connection between the wards. [Nowadays the whole central street is called *Naka-no-chō*—middle street—because it passes right through the centre of the enclosure.]

The "Amigasa-jaya."

(*Braided hat tea-houses.*)

It is mentioned in the "*Yoshiwara Taizen*" (吉原大全) that there were tea-houses, standing on each side of the Go-jik-ken-michi outside the great gate, which were known as "*Amigasa-jaya*" because they lent to samurai, nobles, and people who wished to conceal their identity, "*amigasa*" which covered the entire head, face and all.* These hats were usually made of rush, and being very deep looked something like inverted baskets. The twenty tea-houses are still to be seen in Go-jikken-machi, but the rush hats formerly supplied are conspicuous by their absence. In passing, it may be noted that it was a custom for these houses to be built without second-stories facing the street.

AMIGASA.

The "*Yoshiwara Kagami*" 吉原鑑 says:—In ancient times "there were *amigasa-jaya* outside the great gate and visitors "used to enter the Yoshiwara wearing the deep rush hats sup-"plied by those houses. Each hat cost 100 *mon* (10 *sen*), but if "the purchaser returned it on the way home the keeper of the "*amigasa-jaya* would exchange it for 54 *mon* (about 6½ *sen*).

"These hats are no longer used, but the old name still "clings to the tea-houses."

The "Kujaku Nagaya."

In the "*Yedo Sunago*" (江戸砂子) we find this passage:—

"The *Kujaku-nagaya* (a *nagaya* is a long building in which "are several separate residences. The old *nagaya* were used as "a species of barracks for the retainers of the feudal lords.

---

* In ancient Rome, until the lowest age of Roman degradation, no man of any character entered a houses of ill-fame without hiding his face with the skirt of his dress.

"*Kujaku*=peacock) are situated at the rear of the street at the "end of the paddy-fields, and are so called because from this "place the brilliant spectacle of the lighted Yoshiwara can be "seen to great advantage. The spot has therefore been com- "pared to the body of a peacock, and the dazzling splendour of "the Yoshiwara to the magnificent tail of that vain bird."

"In the "*Bokusui Shōkaroku*" (墨水消夏錄) it is written:—"A "row of houses on the eminence along that part of the Nihon- "dzutsumi which leads to Tamachi, is called the "Peacock "*nagaya.*" The origin of this picturesque name is that about "the era of *Kwanbun* (1661-1672) there lived in the extremity of "the *nagaya* a lovely girl whose wonderous beauty was noised "about the neighbourhood, and, owing to the dingy block of "houses having such an enchanting damsel residing in the end "building, some admirers of the fair nymph, by a quaint con- "ceit, compared the block of houses to the body and the dainty "maiden to the gorgeous tail of a peacock."

The "Kembansho."

(Office which manages the affairs of geisha and other professionals.)

"The "*Yedo-Kwagai Enkaku-shi*" (江戸花街沿革誌) says:—"In "the 7th year of Anyei (1778) there were about 100 professional "artists in the Yoshiwara including 20 *otoko-geisha* (male *geisha*) "50 female *geisha*, and 16 young dancing girls (*geiko*)."

These people had to obtain licenses from the headmen of their respective districts, but as no fixed taxes were imposed upon them, all their earnings, including tips (*shūgi*) and fees (*gyokudai*), went into their pockets intact. Under these circumstances, many persons began to consider the advisability of taxing the *geinin* (*artists* and *artistes*) and appropriating such taxes towards defraying the common public expenses of the Yoshiwara. At this time the morals of the *geinin* were at a very low ebb, and their conduct so lax that great trouble was experienced in the quarter. Female *geisha* began to compete with the regular courtesans and openly offered themselves as prostitutes, while the male professionals contracted intimacies with the women in the brothels and carried on liaisons with the latter. All these abuses clearly showed the absolute necessity of putting the *geinin* under proper control and of framing regulations for putting a check to their unrestrained intrigues, amours, and general gross misconduct. In the 8th year of Anyei (1779) a certain person named Shōroku (who was the keeper of a brothel known as "*Daikoku-ya*") agitated the question, and after consultation with his confrères established a *Kemban-sho* (registry office for *geisha* of both sexes). Abandoning his profession of brothel-keeping, Shōroku became the director (*tori-shimari-yaku*) of this institution, and under his supervision a system was inaugurated by which all *geinin*, including men, women, and children, *jōruri*-singers, *samisen*-players, etc., were brought under authoritative control. The business of the *Kemban-sho* was transacted by two *bantō* (head-clerks) and some ten assistant clerks (*te-dai*), the latter acting in the capacity of a modern *hako-ya* (attendant who carries a *geisha's* musical instruments) and attending to female *geisha* when the latter went out to fill an engagement.

The male *geisha*, it appears, were all bound to do duty at the *Kemban-sho* in turn.

Classes of Prostitutes.

The custom of dividing courtesans into higher and lower classes had already sprung into existence while the Yoshiwara was situated at Yanagi-machi (close by the present Tokiwa-bashi). They were then classified as *Tayū* and *Hashi-jōro.** During the period of the Yoshiwara three classes were added,

* The best women in a brothel were always placed in the middle of the *misé* (shop) and those of inferior beauty or attainments were placed at the sides. Whence the name *hashi-jōro* ("end" courtesan.)

Types of Modern Courtesans.

viz:—*Kōshi-jōro*, *Tsubone-jōro*, and *Kirimise-jōro*. After the opening of the new (*Shin*) Yoshiwara, *Hashi-jōro* and *Tsubone-jōro* ceased to exist, while at the same period (*Genroku*=1688-1703) *Sancha-jōro* and *Umecha-jōro* came into existence. After the era of Kwansei (1789-1800) the classes in existence were:—*Yobi-dashi*, *Chūsan*, *Tsuke-mawashi*, *Zashiki-mochi*, *Heya-mochi*, and *Kirimise-jōro*. Particulars of these changes are mentioned in various old books and can also be gathered from the lists of courtesans published in those times. As to the origin of the names *Tayū*, *Kōshi*, *Tsubone*, etc., these terms appear to have been derived from a similar classification in vogue in Kyōto, and if my readers are curious to trace these derivations they will do well to refer to a book called the *Dōbō-Goyen* (洞房語園) for further information.

The *Tayū* was a courtesan of the highest class, excelling her unfortunate sisters both in respect to her beauty and accomplishments, and, as previously mentioned, this appellation had come into existence while the *kuruwa* was yet in Yanagi-chō. In the 20th year of Kwan-ei (1642) there were 18 *tayū*, in the era of Manji (1658-1660) 19, and in the 2nd year of Kyōhō (1718) 14, but between the 21st year of Kyōhō (1736) and the 1st year of En-kyō (1744) the number of *tayū* decreased to 5. In the 4th year of Kwan-en (1751) we only find one *tayū* in the whole Yoshiwara, and by the end of the Hōreki era (1751-1763) the class had entirely disappeared. The *age-dai-kin* (fee) of a *tayū* was at first fixed at 37 *momme* (about Yen 6.14), but by the era of Teikyō (1684-1687) it had been doubled. In the era of Kwampō it appears to have been 97 *momme* of silver (about Yen 16.00). At that period the class of courtesans styled *Hashi-jōro* was a very low one, and no reliable record is extant from which we can obtain particulars of their fees.

The *Kōshi-jōro* were similar to those known as *Tenjin* in Kyōto. These women had their rooms within the *ō-gōshi* (great lattice doors or bars) and the *Dōbō-Goyen* (洞房語園) states that these women had the prefix of *Kōshi* placed before the word *jōro* (courtesan) to distinguish them from *Tsubone-jōro*. *Kōshi-jōro* were next in position to the *Tayū*, and their fee was at first 25 *momme* (Yen 4.15), but in the era of Kwampō (1741-1743) it rose to 60 *momme* of silver (about Yen 10.00). It is mentioned in the Naniwa Seirōshi (浪花青樓誌) published in the 10th year of Hōreki (1760) that the term *Tenjin* was in use not only in Kyōto but in Shim-machi, Ōsaka city. Next to the *Kōshi-jōro* came the *Tsubone-jōro*,* and their fee was originally 20 *momme* silver (about Yen 3.32), but, after the appearance of the *Sancha-jōro*, competition reduced it to 15 *momme* (about Yen 2.49).

In the front of the houses where *Tsubone-jōro* resided, wooden lattice work screens, cut in a "figure of eight" all over pattern, of six feet in height were erected, presenting a most curious spectacle. This class of courtesans were in their turn ousted from popularity by the *Umecha-jōro* about the era of Genroku (1688-1703). It is true that after the era of Temmei (1781-1788) a class of prostitutes bearing a similar

---

* *Tsubone-jōro* were generally quartered in the second story. *Tsubone*,—the "women's apartments" in the courts of princes and daimyō—was added to *jōro* to find an appellation for a daughter of Ichinomiya, a noble. She set out on a journey, so the story runs, to Hatake in Tosa, but was driven by stress of weather to Hiroshima, where poverty presently forced her to become a prostitute.

The country folk of that district possessed no word in their vocabulary, applicable to a *jōro* of such high social status, so they coined one and handed down to future generations in the Yoshiwara the name *tsubone-jōro*.

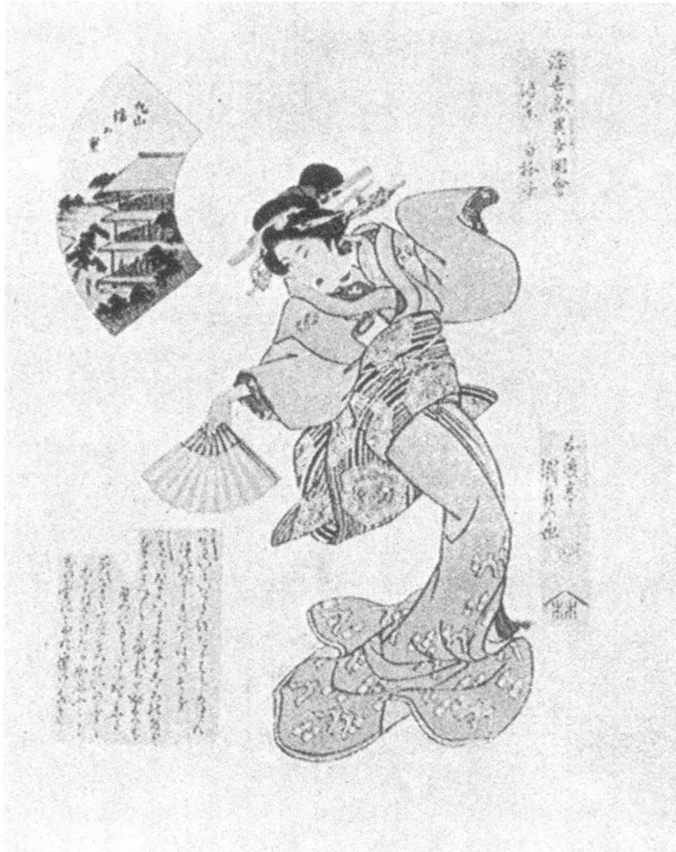

An Ancient "*Shirabyōshi.*"   A "*Yobidashi*" of the Yoshiwara.

name came into existence, but these latter-day *Tsubone-jōro* were the lowest of low women and are not to be confounded with their predecessors.

Kirimise-jōro were the predecessors of the present *Ko-mise-jōro* (" small-shop-courtesans ") to be found by the creek. These women lived in *naga-ya* (barrack-like tenement houses) and offered their services for the modest sum of 100 *mon* (10 *sen*): in consequence of this latter fact they were described as *hyaku-zō* (or freely rendered—" 100 *mon* women ").

At the beginning of Kwambun (1661-1672) a still lower class of harlot, called *Kendon*, arose, and later on another lower grade of strumpets came into existence under the euphonious name of *Teppō* (a gun). The *Teppō* charged 2 *shu* (about Yen 1.25 for a day and night, but after 10 o'clock at night even this sum was reduced, on strictly business principles, to 400 *mon* (40 *sen*).

Sancha-jōro was the name of a class of women which sprang up when a raid was made on the *jigoku* (" *Hell women* ") of Yedo and the *furo-ya* (bath-house) women were brought into the Yoshiwara in the 5th year of Kwambun (1665). The derivation of the word *Sancha* is very curious, and its explanation lies in a phonetically evolved pun. *Sancha* was the old time word for powdered tea, nowadays known as *matcha* or *hikicha*. In ancient times ordinary leaf tea was infused by placing it in a bag, and shaking this bag about in boiling water until the liquor was extracted. In the Japanese the verb "to shake" is *furū*, but this word is also used (especially by courtesans) to mean—" to repel " or " manifest dislike to " a guest. Ground tea (*Sancha*)—on the contrary—was not placed in a bag, but put right into the water, and therefore it required no shaking. The negative form of the word *furū* is *furazu*, and *furazu* has the sense not only of "not to shake" but "not to repel." In the *Dōbō-Goyen* it is stated that many of the better class courtesans were proud as peacocks, and in the zenith of their prosperity they would at times display marked antipathy to some of their guests, going so far as to repel (*furū*) the visitor altogether. The newly arrived courtesans who had been brought into the Yoshiwara from all parts of Yedo City were quite tractable and docile and did not attempt to rebuff (*furazu*) would-be guests and hence the name *Sancha-jōro* ("Ground-tea harlots"). The fee of the *Sancha-jōro* was at first 1 *Bu* (gold) about Yen 2.50). This class of women became very popular in course of time, and by the era ōf An-yei (1772-1780) and Temmei (1781-1788) this popularity had become so marked that the number and value of *Tayū* and *Kōshi* began to decrease. By the end of Hōreki (1763) the last-named classes disappeared, and as soon as they ceased to exist the *Sancha-jōro* succeeded in monopolizing the whole field. About that time, however, there arose a superior class called the *Yobi-dashi*, and these again were divided into two grades, distinguished in the *Yoshiwara Saiken* (list of prostitutes) of the period by the marks  and  respectively. Those marked  corresponded in all respects to the *tayū*. Their *age-dai* for 24 hours was 1 *ryō* 1 *bu* (about Yen 12.50) while those bearing the sign  were similar to the *Kōshi-jōro*, their *age-dai* for a day and a night being 1 *ryō* (about 10.00 Yen).

The *Sancha* were divided into *Chūsan* (or *Hirusan*) and *Tsuke-mawashi*, their charges being 3 *bu* (about Yen 7.50) and 2 *bu* (silver) (about Yen 5.00) respectively. Both the *Yobi-*

Type of Modern Courtesan in "State" Costume.

dashi and *Chūsan* walked about the *Naka-no-chō* on *hachimonji geta* (clogs) whereas the other women, with the exception of the *Tsuke-mawashi*, appeared in the *hari-mise* (or cage-like enclosure where the courtesans sat on exhibition). About the era of Genroku (1688-1703) a class of women named *Baicha-jōro* came into existence and entered into competition with the *San-cha*, but failed to maintain their footing. The fee of these *Bai-cha* was originally 10 *momme* (silver) (about Yen 1.66) but it was raised to 15 *momme* (about Yen 2.50) afterwards. By the era of Kwampō (1741-1743) the *Baicha* had well-nigh disappeared. The *Zashiki-mochi* and *Heya-mochi* who existed up to the time of the Restoration are said to have been the remnants of the *Baicha-jōro*.

Since the Restoration (*I-shin*) the different classes of prostitutes have not been distinguished by any special names, but their *age-dai* varies according to the position of the brothels to which they belong. At present (1899) the fees charged run from 20 *sen* to 1 *Yen* 20 *sen*, and the women are divided into nine classes. The fees of the women in *ō-mise* (large brothels) and *naka-mise* (medium brothels) are *Yen* 1.20 and 90 *sen* respectively. These large and medium-sized establishments must be visited through the agency of *hikite-jaya*, and the latter receive a commission of 10 per cent. on the business introduced by them.

In passing, it may be of interest to readers to peruse the following extracts from the "Kōshoku-Shūgyō-Shokoku-Monogatari," (好色修行諸國物語), written by the well-known novelist Kyōden (京傳) under the *nom de plume* of Shōzan (笑山). In this work elaborate descriptions of *Yobi-dashi*, *Zashiki-mochi*, and *Heya-mochi* are given, and they portray a vivid picture of the lives and customs of those women between the era of Temmei (1781-1788) and Bunsei (1818-1829).

△ *Yobidashi.* (Fee from 1 *Ryō* 1 *Bu* to 1 *Ryō* 3 *Bu*: about Yen 12.50 to Yen 17.50). The gorgeousness of her wearing apparel almost defies description. Her dress consists of a long robe of richly embroidered silk brocade. Her head is ornamented by a dazzling glory of hair-pins (made of the finest tortoise-shell) which glitter around her head like the lambent aureole of a saint, while her ravishing beauty is such that the mere sight of her face will steal away one's very soul * * * * * From this description, the neatness of her apartments, the tasteful arrangement of her furniture, and the dainty elegance of her personal effects may well be imagined. Every *oiran* of the *Yobidashi* class goes out walking in the *Naka-no-chō* as soon as it is dusk. She is attended by two *kamuro* (young female pages), two grown up female attendants (*shinzō*), a man bearing a box-lantern (*hakojōchin*), a footman holding an open long-handled umbrella, and an old woman (*yarite*) who acts as her chaperone.

△ *Zashiki-mochi.* (Fee 1 *Bu* about Yen 2.50). These women belong to the *ham-magaki* brothels. Their "business hours" in the day-time are from 12 o'clock at noon to 4 o'clock in the afternoon; and in the evening from sunset until 12 o'clock (midnight) * * * * * Their garments are made chiefly of velvet, crêpe, satin, figured satin, or *habutaye*, and their girdles (*obi*) of gold brocade, velvet, damask, etc. A couple of rooms of eight mats each are generally placed at the disposal of each courtesan.

Their *futon* (a kind of soft mattress) are of velvet or damask (heavily wadded to a thickness of about nine inches) covered on the surface with a specially woven crêpe, and each woman possesses two such *futon*. The coverlets used at night are of black velvet lined with red crêpe.

△ *Heyamochi.* (Fee 2 *shu*: about Yen 1.25).

Although these belong to the smaller establishments, there are many fine looking women among them * * * * * Velvets, crêpes, and other silken fabrics are employed in making their garments and bedding.

△ *Tsubone-jōro.* (Fee 100 *mon*—about 10 sen—or 200 *mon*—about 20 *sen* for a day and night).

These are an exceedingly low class of women and their houses are frequented by the riff-raff and scum of the neighbourhood exclusively.

Type of Dress worn by a Courtesan.

In this neighbourhood there is some strange slang employed. A *samurai*—for example—is called "*Yama San;*" a priest "*Gen San;*" a merchant "*Chōnin San;*" a young man "*Musuko San;*" and other queer nicknames are given to the various classes of people who visit the locality. These women used to lie in wait for passers-by, and pulling in any likely patron they could find would slam to the door. A few minutes afterwards the door would reopen and the guest depart, and this process would be repeated *ad infinitum.*

In a humorous work by Ikku called the "Sato Kanoko Shina Sadame" (里鹿子品定) the *tayū*, *kōshi*, *sancha*, *zashiki-mochi* and *heya-mochi* are wittily compared to flowers, as follows:—*Tayū* being scarce nowadays may be compared to the cherry-blossom, for as no other flowers can equal the cherry in point of colour and fragrance, in like manner the beauty and loveliness of the *tayū* surpasses that of all courtesans. *Kōshi-jōro*, being mild and gentle, are like the single-petaled cherry-flower booming luxuriantly, for they impose no sense of restraint on anyone. The prosperity of the *Sancha* and *Zashiki-mochi* may be likened to the red plum blossom (*kōbai*) because its colour is so deep (by means of a *double entendre* this means that the amours of these women are very numerous).

The *heya-mochi* are like the white plum-blossom, pale in colour but very odoriferous. (!!!).

The following is a chronological table of the various changes of class and nomenclature of the *joro*:—

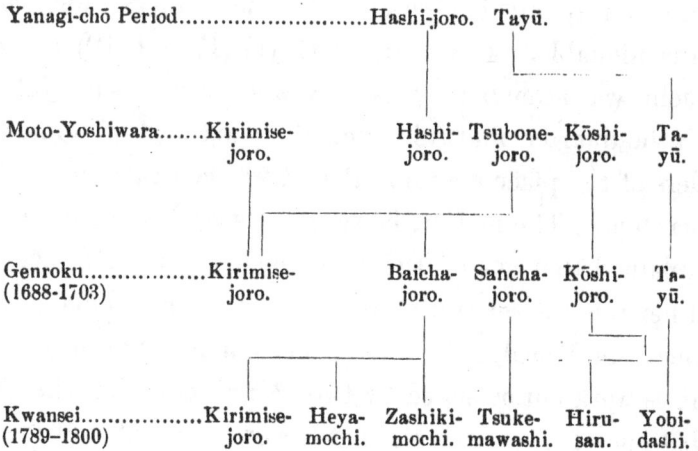

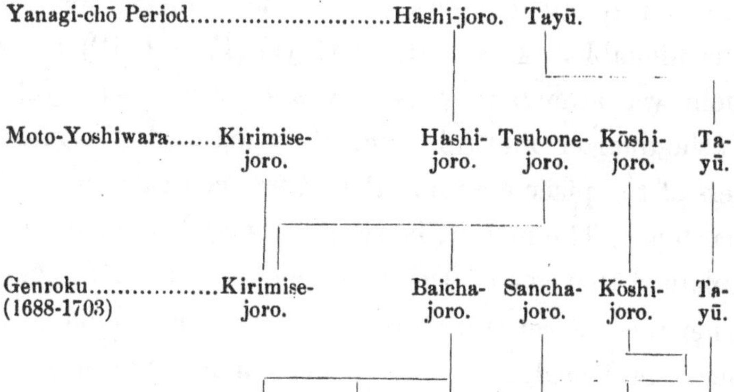

Kamuro

(*Young Female Pages.*)

It is mentioned in the "*Yoshiwara Daizen*" (吉原大全) that *Kaburo* (or *Kamuro*) was the name of young females in the Imperial Court who had the greater part of their head shaven and only a long kind of scalp-lock left hanging. The little girls who attended to the courtesans in ancient times were dressed in imitation of the child attendants formerly attached to the Court, and were styled *Kiri-Kamuro.* Their portraits are often seen in pictures of the Tosa and Hishikawa *ukiyō-e* (realistic pictures) schools. The clothes of the *Kamuro* were *cha-jōro* named *Miyakoji,* belonging to the Naka-Ōmiya in chiefly made of white bleached linen, on which was dyed a pinetree pattern) *waka-matsu no some-moyō*), or of dyed calico.

The *Tayū* and *Kōshijōro* were entitled to two and three *Kamuro* attending upon them respectively while the *Sancha-jōro* had only one; this system of limiting the number of the *Kamuro* of a courtesan was instituted to distinguish the class to which she belonged. The wearing of a kind of clothes, made of material called *ōgiya-zome,* by the *Kamuro* was considered fashionable. In the era of Hōyei (1704-1710) a *San-*Sim-machi, was attended by two *Kamuro* when she walked through the quarter, and this excited a good deal of comment, the elders of the place claiming that it was contrary to established custom. The matter, however, was settled when Miyakoji explained that one of the little maids who had accompanied her was the servant of a sister courtesan. This precedent once established, it became a custom for *Sancha-jōro* to sometimes walk out attended by two *Kamuro* under the pretext that one of these girls was not her own servant. It is said

Modern Courtesan and Her Attendants.

that this Miyakoji was a very popular woman, and that in the house of Naka Ōmiya, to which she belonged, her memory was preserved for several generations by means of calling her successors by a similar name. Since then *Wakashu-Kamuro* and *Bōzu-Kamuro* came into fashion, and of later years it became the custom for *Kamuro* to wear the same kind of beautiful clothes as the courtesan on whom she was in attendance. Even at the present day it is the custom for the *Kamuro* to wear cotton clothes, dyed with a pine-tree pattern, during the first week in January, a period which is known by the Japanese as *matsu no uchi*.

The "*Yedo Kwagai-Enkwaku-Shi*" (江戸花街沿革誌) says:—When a young girl was brought to a brothel as a *Kamuro*, it was usual for the keeper of the house to see and name her. In the selection of these names high-flown cognomens such as were bestowed on courtesans were carefully avoided, and pretty innocent names were chosen. These names rarely exceeded three syllables, and never four in any case. In the event of two *Kamuro* being attached to one courtesan, names were given them to match: e.g. one being called "*Namiji*" (waves) the other would be named "*Chidori*" (plover), or if one was called *Kureha* (呉織 was one of the weavers who came from *Go*—a kingdom of China—in ancient times) the other would receive the name of *Ayaha* (a weaver from another kingdom in China.) The courtesan to whom the *Kamuro* belonged was called her "*ane-jōro*," and this *ane-jōro* found the *Kamuro* in clothes and paid all other expenses in connection with the child. The keeper of the brothel watched the behaviour and disposition of all the *Kamuro* in his houses, and if any promised to become famous courtesans he had them instructed in every branch of deportment, and taught the banjo (*samisen*), harp (*koto*), floral arrangement (*ikebana*), incense-burning (*senkō* 燃香), tea ceremonial (*cha-no-yu*), and other accomplishments which were considered necessary in aspirants for the "profession." The behaviour of *Kamuro* towards their *ane-jōro* was generally gentle and submissive, and they waited on her most assiduously. They attended to all her wants, waited on her at meals, lit her pipe when she desired to smoke, accompanied her when she promenaded in the Naka-no-chō, and ran all her errands in the neighbourhood. The *Kamuro* would also perform trifling services for the guests of her *ane-jōro* such as bringing water for washing their hands, etc. It was the custom originally that no *Kamuro* should assist at a wine party, as she was expected to remain sitting by the side of her mistress in the same manner as the page of a feudal lord sat behind his master, but later no this custom was changed and now the *Kamuro* wait on guests and pour out the *saké.* When there was no available *ane-jōro* the *Kamuro* used to wait on the master of the house, and if the latter found her smart, beautiful, and likely to become a popular courtesan, he took her himself as a sort of adopted daughter, and had her educated at his own expense so as to fit her for the calling. On the other hand, girls who gave no promise of turning out well in the business were left without any education whatever, became household drudges pure and simple, and ended their days in dismal ignorance: under the most favourable circumstances, this latter class of *Kamuro* would not be able to attain to reading characters other than *hiragana* (an easy form of native script) and to a slight smattering of *samisen* playing. When a *Kamuro* attached to a courtesan was sick, her place was taken by one of the girls

Modern Courtesan, Attendant, and *Kamuro*.

attending on the master, and it was also a custom for one brothel to make a loan of *Kamuro* to a neighbouring house whose keeper was short of these children. There were no particular rooms assigned to the *Kamuro* but they generally slept in a room next to that of their *ane-jōro.* They took their meals in the kitchen together with *Shinzo* (see chapter headed thus) and *Wakaimono* (see that heading) and in the day-time were allowed to romp about the galleries of the brothels and play together.

The term *Kamuro* has only been employed in the Yoshiwara, and in the *Okabasho* (which includes the prostitute quarters at Shinagawa, Shinjuku, Senju, etc.) young servant maids were either called *mame-don* or *ko-shoku.* Even in the Yoshiwara there was a rule limiting the number of *kamuro* to attend to a courtesan of a particular grade.

Shinzo.

In the "*Yoshiwara Daizen*" (吉原大全) it is mentioned that the name of *Shinzō* (newly constructed) has been borrowed owing to the fact that a newly launched ship is so called. When *kamuro* (these girls generally entered service between the ages of five to seven years) had grown up to thirteen or fourteen they were made *Shinzō*, according to the discretion of the *ane-jōro.* About ten days prior to this event the girls obtained some *ohaguro** (collected from seven different friends of their *ane-jōro*) and blackened their teeth for the first time. On the actual day of the ceremony *soba* (buckwheat macaroni)

* *Ohaguro* is a dye made by immersing heated iron scrapes in water and then adding to it a small quantity of *saké.* It is used (mixed with powdered gall-nuts) by married women, and formerly by court nobles, to blacken their teeth. The custom is dying out fast.

was made and partaken of by all the inmates of the house, and presents of the same food were sent to every *jōro-ya*, *tea-house*, *hikite-jaya*, and *funa-yado* with which the brothel was acquainted and on friendly terms. Sometimes *sekihan* (rice boiled with red beans) was distributed instead of buckwheat macaroni. It was also the custom on these occasions to put out a large number of *seirō* (vessels for steaming food) ranged in a row in front of the brothel, and to place them on a long table of unpainted board measuring from 9 to 18 feet in length. On a table (also of unpainted wood) inside the brothel, in the room of the *ane-jōro*, were exhibited rolls of dress materials, tobacco-pouches, fans, towels, etc., which were to be given as congratulatory presents to friends of the house as souvenirs of the ceremony. In front of the tea-house or *funa-yado*, where the guest who was supposed to finance the ceremony was wont to come, a number of *seirō* were piled up, and to all the tea-houses and *funa-yado* presents of *mushi-gwashi* (steamed cakes) were distributed. On this day the interior decorations of the brothel were so magnificent and splendid that according to ancient writers the spectacle defies the power of language to adequately portray them. The *shinzō*, or *imōto-jōro* did not at once appear in the " *mise.*" For a week or more from the day of her initiation she promenaded the *Naka-no-chō* (clad each day in different garments) under the guidance of her *ane-jōro*, and in case of the latter having any *imōto-jōro* she would bring her along. When the week of introduction was past, the fellow-courtesans of the girl would " *shimai-tsukawasu* " her to their ranks by engaging her and paying her *agedai* every day in turn, and she would receive congratulatory presents from her friends. Sometimes two or more *shinzo*

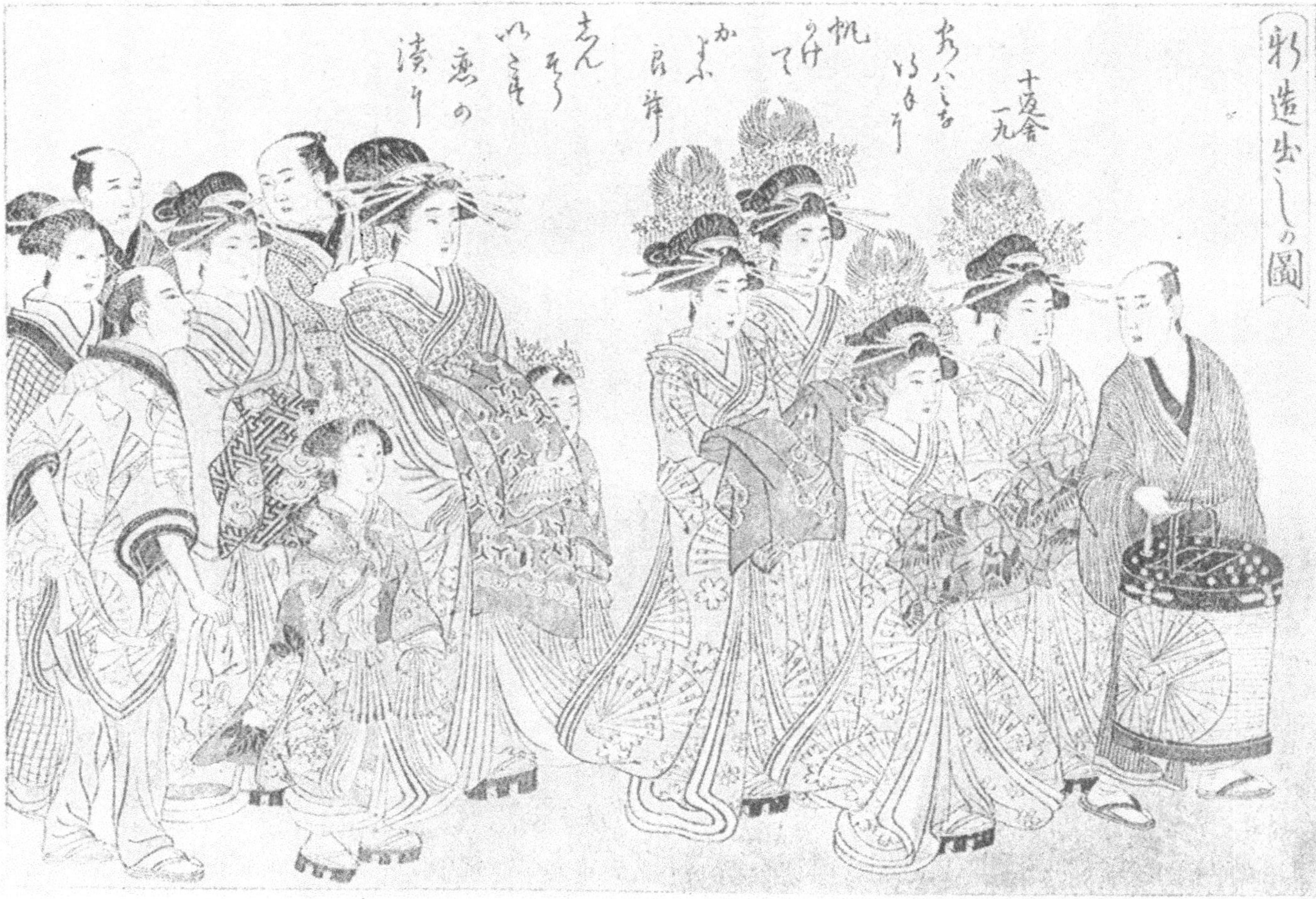

First début of a "*shinzō*" in the Kiōwa period (1801 to 1803).
(After the Picture by Kitagawa Utamaro.)

were initiated in one house at the same time. When a girl who had not been brought up in the Yoshiwara was made a *shinzō* she was technically termed a "*tsuki-dashi*" (one who is pushed out to the front) and as, in this case, there would be no *ane-jōro* to look after her interests, the *kutsuwa* (explained further on) provided her with the necessary bedding, wearing apparel, and furniture suited to a *heya-mochi*, *chūsan* (*hiru-san ?*), or *tsuke-mawashi* as the circumstances required. The amount of money spent greatly depended on the personal attractions and beauty of the girl. As in the case of a regularly trained *fille de joie*, she promenaded the *Naka-no-chō*, accompanied by another *shinzō*, for the space of a week from the day when she made her *dêbut*, and, as a necessary accessory to this ceremony, a present of *sakazuki* (small *sakê* cups), each bearing the name and crest of the debutante, was made to all the various tea-houses and *funa-yado*.

There was another class of prostitutes in the Yoshiwara called *yakko* which originally, it seems, was generally recruited from the ranks of *samurai* women. Every now and again a female of gentle birth would be guilty of a lapse from virtue, and, in order that the stern code of *samurai* honour might be vindicated, she would be sent to the public stews for a term of three, or even five, years as an exemplary punishment for her immoral behaviour. In later times all public women who were sold into the Yoshiwara from other quarters were similary termed *yakko*.

In the "*Yedo-Kwagai Enkakushi*" (江戸花街沿革誌) it is stated that the *shinzō* were divided into two classes, viz—the *furi-sode-shinzō* and *tome-sode-shinzō*. For the sake of brevity, the former was sometimes called "*Furi-sode*" or "*Furi-*

shin," and the girls themselves were either recruited from among the *kamuro* who had attained the age of 13 or 14 years, or by outsiders specially engaged for the purpose. When the *furi-shin* had reached an age when *furi-sode* (long sleeves) were no longer suitable to them, they were attired in the same manner as their seniors. With the change of their garments came the change of the general name by which they were known, and they were now called "*tome-shinzō*" (short-sleeves *shinzō*) or more simply "*tome-sode*" (short-sleeves) or else "*tome-shin.*" When a *kamuro* was about to become a "*furi-shin,*" her master would first of all summon her parents and surety (*shōnin*) and hand over to them a *baishū-shōmon* (certificate of sale) in exchange for the ordinary *hōkōnin shōsho* (certificate of hire) which had been given them when the young *kamuro* was first engaged. The master would also hand over a certain sum of money to the parents, under the expressive name of *mi-no-shiro-kin* (money for the body), the amount of which depended on the beauty and accomplishments of the unfortunate girl. It would, however, sometimes happen that the astute parents of the girl had been in communication with a *zegen* (a professional procurer) prior to this event, and when they were summoned by the brothel-keeper they insisted on removing their daughter as the term of her enagement as a *kamuro* had expired: they then sold the girl, at a greatly advanced price, to another brothel through the agency of the *zegen.* This action of the girl's parents meant some loss to the original master, as he had to go to the trouble and expense of training another courtesan in all the tricks of the profession, whereas, if he had secured the *kamuro,* he would have had a girl who knew every little point regarding the business routine, and who was already trained and ready to commence her new duties. As the original contract was to employ the girl as a *kamuro*, the master was powerless to resist the wishes of the parents when the term of apprenticeship was up, so, as a precautionary measure against either future disappointment or dunning, the brothel-keeper, in many instances, purchased the child outright, and demanded a certificate of sale when he first engaged her as a *kamuro*.

Yarite.

(*Female Managers.*)

The duties of a *yarite* consist in watching everything which happens in a brothel, and includes the management of the courtesans and the due espionage of both the inmates of the house and their guests. Nowadays these women are called "*obasan*" ("auntie!") The *yarite's* room is generally situated in front of the stairs so as to be more convenient as a position from which the general affairs of the house can be observed. No person can fill this important post satisfactorily unless she be thoroughly well versed in the ins and outs of every matter pertaining to the Yoshiwara, and unless she possesses a fund of actual practical experience on which she can draw in an emergency. The *yarite*, therefore, are for the most part picked from the old veterans who have themselves served their time as courtesans. In the Ō-mise (first class house) the *yarite* are ensconced in their rooms, employing *shinzō* who play the role of aide-de-camps, while in the *komise* (small houses) they are accustomed to receive visitors themselves and recommend suitable courtesans. The *komise yarite* is indeed kept very busy, for she has not only to receive guests, arrange meetings, etc., but she has to watch the reception given to visitors by her girls, form an opinion of the visitors themselves, and attend to a hundred and one other things also. The *komise yarite* may be described as "cute," and there are mighty few things that escape the notice of these lynx-eyed old beauties! The *yarite* originated in the *furo-ya* (a sort of brothel) and their original title was "*kwasha*" (火車=a fire wheel). In the "*Kiyū Shōran*" (嬉遊笑覽) is a note to the effect that the meaning of *kwasha* was "to grasp" (*tsukamu*) which in former times was used in the sense of "buying" prostitutes: it also had the meaning of "making oneself familiarly selfish; and as the *yarite* made rules which her women were bound to obey, she often showed herself heartlessly selfish towards the courtesans, and hence the name of *kwasha*. The regular wages received by *yarite* were insignificant, but their real sources of income were tips received from guests and (by previous arrangement with their employer) commissions on the sums spent by guests. They invariably wore *maki-obi* (a girdle simply wound round the waist without being crossed at right angles at the back). In ancient times they wore a hood or cap over the *mae-gami* (a coil of hair above the forehead) and wore *maki-obi* of black satin. They received wages twice a year, viz:—about the middle of August (*chūgen*=15th day of the 7th month; the last day of the Feast of Lanterns) 2 *Bu* (*Yen* 5.00), and the end of December (*seibo* 3 *Bu* (*Yen* 7.50).

Besides, they charged a commission on the food and other things brought to the guests.

(In those days the rate of commission allowed to the *yarite* was 200 *mon* (20 *sen*) on every *Bu* spent on food by guests, and she levied 200 *mon* (20 *sen*) per guest on the tea-house concerned). Even to this day the "*obasan*" receives a certain percentage of commission, so she is fairly well off if she is employed in a popular and largely frequented house. In smaller house the visitors give the "auntie" a tip of 20 *sen* or 30 *sen*, and those who omit to propitiate the lady in this manner find that things are not made pleasant for them. In certain houses, however, a notice is posted to the effect that no gratuities are expected by the servants, that the proprietor is anxious not to burden guests with extra expenses such as tips, etc., and that patrons will be treated with all possible consideration irrespective of such presents. Sometimes a "complaint-box" is provided and hung up, and beside it is a notice, written in bold characters, setting forth the laudable intentions of the proprietor and requesting guests to make immediate complaint if they have been improperly treated, or if they detect any objectionable practices being carried on in the establishment. Practically, however, the prevailing customs of the Yoshiwara are so ingrained and hard to fight against that there is scarcely any visitor who has courage enough to lodge a complaint.

In ancient times it was the obnoxious custom for the *yarite* to administer corporal punishment to prostitutes who were accused of neglect of duty, and, taking advantage of their power, they often subjected the miserable object of their displeasure to very cruel and inhuman treatment. Happily, such practices have almost ceased since the principle has been recognized of according courtesans a reasonably full measure of liberty; but even in these enlightened days sinister stories are told regarding the harsh treatment of women in some of the lower class houses. No doubt the *obasan* greatly abuse their power at times, and this arises from giving them too much liberty and discretion in dealing with the inmates of brothels: they find themselves in a position to domineer over a number of other women (all of whom are practically dependent on the good-will of these female overseers) and, unless they happen to be exceptional persons, they are naturally apt to give way to their tempers and to show unfair partiality towards their subordinates, treating some kindly enough and others most cruelly. What with tips, squeezes, and lending money to the girls at usurious rates of interest, the *obasan* enjoy a fairly lucrative position.

The "Kutsuwa."

In the "*Yoshiwara-Daizen*" (吉原大全) it is stated that the custom of calling the proprietor of a brothel "*kutsuwa*" came into vogue when the prostitute quarter was situated at Yanagi-chō. The place was laid out in the form of a Japanese bridle-bit (*kutsuwa*=a bit: shaped like a cross moline within a circle) and the houses were built in that shape, so it became the fashion for visitors to call the brothels *kutsuwa*.

It is stated in the "*Ruishū-Sanyō*" (類聚纂要) that brothels were named *kutsuwa* (which in Chinese characters reads 亡八 and means "forget eight") because persons frequenting them were apt to forget the eight virtues, viz:—filial piety, brotherly kindness, loyalty, faithfulness, politeness, righteousness, integrity, and the sense of shame. In the Genna (1615-1623) and Meireki (1655-1657) eras the *kutsuwa* were called *kimi-ga-tete* (sovereign and parent: or "Prince of the Courtesans") owing to the fact that at the time of the opening of the Yoshiwara the *daimyō* and other notables used to call the founder of the quarter—Shōji Jinyemon—by that name. One never hears this term nowadays.

In the "*Yoshiwara-Enkakushi*" (芳原沿革誌) it is mentioned that *kutsuwa* (a "bridle bit" 馬銜) is another name for a brothel. Some say that a certain Hara Saburōyemon (who had formerly been a groom of the Taikō) having founded a brothel, the name of *kutsuwa* was given to it in commemoration of his old employment and the *kutsuwa* (bits) he had handled in bye gone days. Another account says that the prostitute quarter of Fushimi resembled the shape of a bridle-bit, and hence this name came into popular use. Still another version is given by the "*Nobunaga-ki*," (信長記) according to which a retainer of Nobunaga's, named Ōta Umanosuke, was once detected receiving bribes. This coming to his master's ears, the latter, who was of a humorous turn of mind, composed the following poem and sent it to the guilty henchman:—"*Zeni-gutsuwa hameraretaru ka Umanosuke? Hito-chikushō to kore wo iūran*"—"Have you been bitted and bridled with a bit made of money Umanosuke? We must call you a man-beast." (You have been gagged by a golden bit, you may therefore be described as a man-beast). In the Chinese characters, *kutsuwa* (亡八) meant "selfishness" or "covetousness."

Wakaimono.

(*Male Servants.*)

The "*Yoshiwara Shin-hanjō-ki*" (吉原新繁昌記) says:—According to the custom of the Yoshiwara, all men-servants in brothels were called *wakaimono* (young fellows), and this term was applied, in a most inconsistent manner, even to middle-aged or old men in the employ of these houses. The word is practically equivalent to "boy" as used by foreign residents in the East. There are different duties assigned to the *wakai-mono.* In the best houses they are divided into *mise-no-hito* ("shopmen"), *naka-don* (inside men), *toko-ban* (bed men), *chūrō* (overseers), *nezuban* (night watchmen—this duty is undertaken by all the men in turn), *furo-ban* (bathroom men), *shita-ban* (downstair men), etc. In the medium houses the *chūrō* are omitted, but in some of them another class of men termed *oi-mawashi* (overseers) are employed. In the case of most lower-class houses these grades are not known, or at least the division of labour is not so well arranged. In medium houses all the business is transacted by "*shop-men,*" "*inside-men,*" "*downstair-men,*" while in the lowest establishments, such as are to be found at Waru-gashi, Rashō-mon, and Fushimi-chō, a couple of men meet all the requirements of the brothel. It is also needless to say that there is a considerable difference in the number of servants employed according to the number of prostitutes kept by the various houses. The wages of these people range from 75 *sen* to 1 *Yen* per month (in 1899) which of course, would not be enough to keep them in clothes and food were it not for their perquisites and pickings. A "shop-man" (*mise-no-hito*), for instance, receives a squeeze of one *sen* per *dai* (a dish containing food) and one *sen* per each bottle—holding 1 *gō*—of *saké* consumed by guests, and besides 5 *rin* (½ *sen*) for each pair of boots or clogs of which he takes charge. [This fee for taking charge of foot-gear is deducted from the *agedai* of the courtesans.] There is another source of income which is by no means despicable. It is derived from the extortion—for no milder term seems adequate to express the meaning—of a small, or sometimes large, balance of change which is due to guests when the latter settle their bills. In the event of a bill amounting to *Yen* 1.90, for instance, if a guest hands over 2 *Yen* in payment, the courtesan, who is ready for the occasion, urges—nay almost compels—him to give the change (*tsuri*) to the servant. It may happen that this goes against the grain of the victim, but he generally yields to the pressure of the girl's persuasion for fear of being considered mean. This squeeze is called a *chōchō* (butterfly) and in some houses a collection of "butterflies" amounting to more than two or three *Yen* per night is netted by the astute *wakaimono*. It will be observed that these "butterflies" are caught by the courtesan, therefore if the *wakaimono* are not on friendly terms with the women they will not be successful in catching such nice fat *chōchō*.

According to the rules of each house accounts are kept either by the *mise-no-hito* ("shop men"), *nakadon* (inside men), or *yarite*. In every houses the proceeds arising from the sale of waste paper (*kami kuzu*) form part of the income of *meshi-taki* (the kitchen servants). Tips are naturally desired by all the servants of brothels, but the *yarite*, *shinzō*, and *nakadon* are the most frequent recipients of them, as their duties bring them into direct contract with guests. The *ōi-mawashi* (overseers) and *meshi-taki* (kitchen maids) have no share in tips other than those given under the name of *sō-bana* by visitors.

The powers wielded by the *bantō* (head clerk) of first-class houses are similar to those exercised by the masters themselves, and the respect in which they are held by the other servants almost equals that which is accorded to the employer himself.

For instance, a *bantō* generally comes down to his "office," so to speak, every evening about 6 o'clock and remains until midnight (*nakabike*). On his arrival at, and departure from, the brothel, he is attended by the *naka-bataraki* (parlor-maids ?) and other servants, all of whom treat him with the most profound respect. Any commission (i.e.—*kasuri* or "squeezes") gathered in prior to the departure of the *bantō* (this is before 12 o'clock p.m.) goes to him, but after that hour the "profits" are divided among his subordinates. The monthly revenue of a *bantō* of one of the best houses from this source is, generally speaking, not less than 50 or 60 *Yen*, and even in a medium or lower-class house it ranges from 12 or 13 *Yen* upwards to 20 or 30 *Yen*.

The *wakai-mono* are technically known as *gyū* and the origin of this term is explained in the "*Dōbō Goyen-ho*" (洞房語園補) as follows :—

In the era of Shō-ō (1652-1654) there was a brothel-keeper in *Fukiya-chō* named Idzumiburo no Yohei. In this house was a man called Kyūsuke who had been long employed in the establishment and was consequently experienced in the reception of guests. The man, who was an inveterate smoker, made a peculiar pipe out of a thick piece of purplish coloured bamboo tube to which was attached a mouth-piece and bowl, and he was so fond of this contrivance that he carried it round with him everywhere, sticking it in his girdle when not in use. He was hump-backed and short in stature, and when he went about smoking his long pipe the good folk of the place said he looked like the Chinese character *kyū* (及). The name was gradually transfered from Kyū-suke, an individual, to the whole class of attendants. First people spoke of going to "Kyū's" (及) place, and this nick-name afterwards became almost a general term for men-servants in brothels. The present word "*gyū*" is a corruption of "*kyū.*"

Hōkan and Geisha

In the Yoshiwara, *taiko-mochi* (*hōkan*) are called *otoko-geisha* in contra-distinction to female *geisha*. More generally they are called *tayū-shū.* At first they were divided into several classes, among them being *Uji* (Uji's school) *Sugano* (Sugano's school) *Ogiye* (Ogiye's school) and *Sukura-gawa;* their profession was to attend *sakê* parties and sing or play to amuse the guests. Gradually, however, they were forced to look after various affairs of their customers in order to buy the good-will of the latter. At present they have completely degenerated. In spite of the fact that the Yoshiwara is the veritable birth-place of the *hōkan,* those belonging to the quarter are far inferior to their contemporaries of the City proper in many respects. When a *hōkan* of the present day is called to attend a party of guests in a brothel, he enters the room holding a folded fan in his hand, and after saluting the guest who has called him snaps the fan he carries with a sharp clicking sound and expresses his obligation to his patron's companion in the stereotyped phrase—"*oiran maido arigatō*" (thank you madam for your constant favours). He then bows in turn to every person in the room, including other courtesans and *geisha,* his actual patron being disregarded for the time being. As soon as the party gets livened up from the effects of liquor, and the feasting has began to flag, the jesting and buffoonery of the *hōkan* waxes fast and furious and is accompanied by droll contortions and gesticulations, *ashi-odori,* *suteteko*, and even *hadaka-odori*.* These disgusting and highly suggestive antics of the *hōkan*, far from scandalizing guests, are received with great applause and appear to afford much amusement to all present. In the Yoshiwara, the most popular *hōkan* at present (1899) are Zenroku, Minchū, Hambei, Shōkō, and Heiki. The usual costume of a *hōkan* consists of a *haori* of black cloth having five crests upon it, and a *kimono* of a different coloured crêpe. According to the narrative of an old man, there were in the era of Tempō (1830-1843) two classes of *hōkan* named *zamochi* and *taiko-mochi*. The former were well versed in every branch of polite accomplishments including *kō-cha* (incense-burning and tea-ceremonial) *ikebana* (floral arrangement) *shikyoku* (playing various kinds of musical instruments) etc., and were generally called to parties given by nobles, gentlemen, and wealthy merchants. In private life they were admitted to the friendship of poets and literary men, and even in ordinary times wore crested ceremonial clothes. When attending their customers they wore a small wooden sword called a "*kami-ire-dome*" (pocket-book holder) and carried about them a sum of at least 25 *ryō* (about *Yen* 250) for the purpose of making payments on behalf of patrons, as it was not the custom to receive money from the latter on

ASHI-ODORI.

---

* *Ashi-odori* is shown in the wood-cut, *Suteteko* is a vulgar pantomimic dance, and *Hadaka-odori* a dance *in puris naturalibus*.

Geisha Dancing the "*Kapporé.*"

the spot. The ordinary *taiko-mochi*, on the other hand, were those who had no special accomplishments, but even these were more accomplished than their modern representatives. They were also colloquially termed "*no-daiko.*"

When a *hōkan* intends to enter the profession on his own account, he goes round to the various brothels and the tea-houses under the guidance of his teacher and fellow *hōkan* for the purpose of introducing himself and soliciting patronage. This proceeding is described as *hirome wo nasu* (to "advertise" oneself) and the larger the number of fellow *hōkan* who follow the debutant the greater the honour to the latter. On this day he requests the tea-houses or brothels with whom he is particularly friendly to recommend him to guests, and the latter are under a species of moral obligation to assist the beginner in this matter. In the "*Dōbō Go-yen*" (洞房語園) it is stated that men who entertained parties of persons, under engagement by guests, were called *taikomochi* (大鼓持 = a drum-holder). In the days of Ōta Nobunaga there lived in the city of Kyōto a man named Jige Yazaemon who was an expert player on the drum, and whenever he was called into the presence of notables to give a performance he used to beat the instrument while it was being held by one of his pupils, he himself being seated on a drum-shaped tub. Among his pupils was one named Idayū who was skilled in the act of holding the drum, and who was a great favorite of his master Yazaemon * * * For this reason, parties wishing to engage Yazaemon used to request his performance through Idayū. This state of things gave umbrage to other pupils of Yazaemon, so they spoke of him contemptuously as "that *taiko-mochi*" (drum-bearer). From that time, persons who endeavoured to curry favour by flattery began to be spoken of as "*taiko-mochi*" until the word become almost equivalent to "sycophant." Yazaemon was the founder of the "*Kwanzé*" school of drum-beating, and in consideration of his fame in this line he was allowed to sit even in the presence of high dignitaries. In the "*I-hon Kō-i*" (異本考異) portion of the "*Dōbō Go-yen*" (洞房語園) it is stated that the origin of the name *taiko-mochi* is as above related, and that to match this title prodigals (*hōtō-mono*=a dissolute person) were called *dora-uchi* (鉦打=bell/gong strikers). Of late years, entertainers of guests without special accomplishments have been termed "*no-daiko*" ("field-drums" or "rustic drums") and this name was apparently given them as a term of contempt. Nowadays, *geisha* of both sexes have come into existence and assist in the entertainment of guests and courtesans just like the *taiko*. In ancient times *taiko-mochi* were known as *taiko-shu*. The origin of the *hōkan* in the Yoshiwara may be traced to olden times. The "*Kuruwa Roppō*" (廓六法) says:—"*Taiko Naoyuki ga kuro no haori ni tate yotsume no mon-tsuki taru wo kite dote-bushi utōte uwate-sase ageya no sashi-gami ikutsu mo mochi, un-un*" (Taiko Naoyuki was walking along singing a song known as "*dote-bushi.*" He was wearing a black haori with a "*yotsume*" crest dyed upon it, and was carrying *sashi-gami* from *ageya* [to various courtesans]).

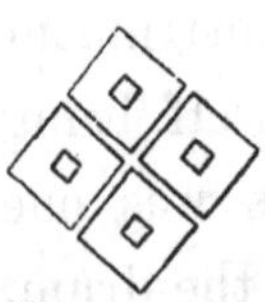

Yotsume no mon.

This refers to the state of a *taiko-mochi* being sent round by *ageya* to call women from brothels. Again it says:—"*Taiko-mochi Naoyuki wa Shōji no mon wo onore no mon to su* * * * (*Taiko-mochi* Naoyuki appropriated to his own use the crest of Shōji (Jinyemon) * * * *mon dokoro made o-ashi ni nitari* (even his crest resembled cash). These statements show that this particular *taikomochi* was greatly liked by the founder of the Yoshiwara—Shōji Jinyemon—but from the tone of the language employed we may infer that even in those days the profession was looked down upon as a mean one. About the era of Kwambun (1661-1672) *taikomochi* came into existence in the Moto-Yoshiwara, and Naoyuki was the most popular of *hōkan* at that period. In the era of Manji (1658-1660) Kutsuno Jiroyemon was the best known man, while in the era of Genroku (1688-1703) Higeno Mukyū, Bōzu Kohei, and Nishuban Kichibei were favorites. The last two were really actors, but they occasionally entered the Yoshiwara in the capacity of *taikomochi*, and the fact that they were patronized by Kinokuni-ya Bunzaemon is mentioned in different books. About the Meiwa era (1764-1771) a *taikomochi* named *Ippyō* was very famous. (It was to the house of this Ippyō that Hiraga Kyūhei went for the purpose of meeting the courtesan Hinadzuru).

Sometimes the *hōkan* were called "*kami*" owing to the fact that among the regular attendants of Kinokuni-ya Bunzaemon was a man named Kamiyui Chōshichi, a hairdresser by profession, who excelled in dancing the *gaki-mai* (hungry devils' dance) to the accompaniment of tunes which he whistled, and who was a great favourite with the Yoshiwara women. This individual, being a barber, was called "*kami*" (contraction of *kami-yui*=a hair-dresser) which of course was written 髮 ("hair") but after a time the word was corrupted into *kami* (神=a god) and perhaps this was why the name of *massha* (末社 a "small shrine") was applied to the attendants of wealthy men and now is used colloquially to mean a "jester" or "buffoon." The *hōkan* of the Yoshiwara is considered as below the female *geisha* in rank. In former times they lived outside the *kuruwa* and seldom made buffoonery their sole profession, but in the era of Meiwa (1764-1771) and Anyei (1772-1780) they gradually moved into the enclosure, licenses being granted to them by Shōji Jinyemon in which they were described as "*otoko-geisha*" (male *geisha*). By the 7th year of An-yei (1778) their number had reached twenty and they were recognized as a regular class of professionals. Since the establishment of the *kemban-sho* in the 8th year of the same era (1779) the *geisha* of both sexes were brought under its management, but so far as the *hōkan* were concerned the Government only knew and registered them as *dote-ninsoku* (embankment coolies) or *suibo-kata* (coolies provided to guard against flood) so the social status of these men may well be imagined. [At Fukagawa they were officially known as *amma* (shampooers), at Shinagawa as *tsuye-barai* (tipstaffs), at Naitō Shinjuku as *kera-bori* (insect-diggers)].

Since the Bunkwa and Bunsei (1804-1839) eras the singers of *Katō-bushi* and *Itchū-bushi* songs came to attend guests as *hōkan*. When called by notables or *samurai* they wore *hakama*, and, while entertaining the guests with various amusements, acted with civility, but in the presence of traders they discarded the *hakama*. Generally speaking these men were well versed in deportment and various accomplishments, and, as they were fit to move in the best society, they were often engaged by poetasters, dilettantes, lovers of art and letters, and wealthy people, more as friends and companions than as the mere mercenaries they are at present. Indeed they were such highly educated and accomplished men in so many respects that persons of higher social standing were in

Geisha, *Hōkan*, and Guest-period. 1800

no wise ashamed to have them for intimate acquaintances. At present the *hōkan* are looked down upon as belonging to a mean profession because they practice it as their sole means of earning a livelihood, whereas, in former times, it was individual taste rather than necessity which attracted persons to engage in this vocation. In order to make both ends meet, the latter-day *hōkan* grovel before and toady to their guests, and thus they have forfeited all title to the respect of the public. The story of the visit made to the Yoshiwara by Hōichi may be read in the light of revelations by one who was thoroughly familiar with the quarter. In the Bunkwa (1804-1817) and Bunsei (1818-1829) eras the hair of the *hōkan* was dressed in a style known as "*mame-honda*" (豆本田) and in the era of Tempō (1830-1843) in the "*ko-icho*" (小銀杏) style.

"*Mame-Honda*" style of dressing hair.

Gradually the *hōkan* have deteriorated, but the men themselves are not solely to blame, for had their guests been respectable people, and punctilious sticklers for etiquette, these entertainers would have been compelled to maintain a high standard as regarded accomplishments and to have conducted themselves in a decorous manner. The trouble first arose through permitting laxity in the manner of dress and allowing the men to appear without *hakama* in the presence of guests: as soon as an inch was granted an ell was claimed, and so matters drifted on until the *hōkan* had sunk down to the very low social status they occupy nowadays. In an Oriental country, at any rate, if you permit any impropriety or breach of etiquette in silence the result will always be far-reaching and disastrous! In the pre-Restoration days, the fee (*gyokudai*) of a *hōkan* was 1 *ryō* (about 10 *Yen*) for 4 hours (from 6 to 10 p.m.) and out of this 500 *mon* (50 *sen*) was deducted by the *kemban* (see that heading) as commission. In order to evade necessity of paying a commission to the *kemban, hōkan* were in the habit of promenading the quarter in the hope of catching sight of guests whom they might happen to know, and of thus being engaged without the intervention of the registry office. This was known as "*oka-dzuri*" (岡釣リ = land-fishing), and although the practice was known to the *kemban* that office simply winked at it. The present price of the *hōkan's* services is 10 *sen* per joss-stick, and generally he receives a gratuity of from 50 *sen* to 1 *Yen* (from these payments certain small squeezes are levied by the *kemban* and the tea-house). There are now two classes of *hōkan,* one called *jimae* and the other *kakae*: members of the former (*jimae*) carry on their profession independently, while those of the latter (*kakae*) live in the houses of their masters and in return for board, and the loan of professional clothes, divide their earnings with their *padrones.* In fact the system is identical with the women *geisha* system. Among themselves they use many slangy expressions such as "*O Chaya San*" (instead of "*hikite-jaya*"), "*Nesan*" (instead of *geisha*: this word is only used in reference to the older women, the rest being designated by their own proper names). Going to a party by engagement is called "*o zashiki*" (instead of *kyaku no seki ye deru*); a brothel keeper's private room "*Go nai-sho*" (instead of *rō-shu no kyo-shitsu*); courtesans "*oiran*" (instead of *shōgi*); etc.; etc. In the Yoshiwara the public women are supposed to occupy the first position as leaders of society, so they are never spoken of as *jōro* or *shōgi* by any professional men and women, but called by the more flowery and euphemistic name of *oiran*.* Any song in which the words "*Yoshiwara jōro-shū* (or *shōgi*)" occurs is sung altered to "*Yoshiwara oiran*," thus softening the expression and making the sound more agreeable and less offensive to the courtesans themselves. They also call a courtesan's room "*oiran no o zashiki*" (the august room of the *oiran*) instead of "*shōgi no zashiki* (courtesan's room). *Shinzō*, tea-house maids, etc., are spoken of by their respective names, and, generally speaking, the same is the case with female *geisha*.

---

* The following explanations of the origin of the word "*oiran*" are given:—

The "*Kinsei jibutsu-Kō*" (近世事物考 Reflections about modern things) says:—"The higher priced women of the Shin Yoshiwara are now called "*oiran*." The reason for giving them this name is that in the era of Genroku (1688-1703) the courtesans of the Yoshiwara all planted a large number of trees in the Naka-no chō (central street). About this time a *Kamuro* (female page) attached to a certain house called the "*Kishida-ya*" wrote a stanza of poetry which ran:—

"*Oiran ga itchi yoku saku sakura kana!*" which means in ordinary language "*Oira no ane-jōro no ueshi sakura ga ichi-ban yoku sakitari*" (The cherry-tree planted by my *ane-jōro* has blossomed more luxuriantly than the others).

This poem, which the little *Kamuro* so proudly wrote, is a proof that the word *oira* ("I," or in connection with *no* or *ga* "my" or "mine") had been corrupted to *oiran* in the Yoshiwara. It would therefore appear that the present word *oiran*, which is universally used, arose from the fact that the attendants of courtesans anciently spoke of them as "*oiran*" (*oira no ane*=my elder sister)."

The Dōbō Go-yen-ho 洞房語園補 says:—

"*Oiran* means "*ane-jōrō*" (elder-sister, or "senior," courtesan) or "my elder sister" in the vocabulary of the Yoshiwara. The word *oiran* is applied to a mild and gentle courtesan."

Another explanation is that the *oiran* were so beautiful that even when an old person (*Oi-taru mono*) met them he was apt to be excited, agitated, and half crazy (亂=*ran*) for the love of their pretty faces. Thus the word *oi*+*ran* (an aged person+excited and half crazy with agitation). The word "*oiran*" is written 花魁 (*hana-no sakigake*)

As female *geisha* are also controlled by the *kemban-sho,* their *samisen* boxes are placed out in a row at the office, each box bearing a paper label on which its owner's name is written in large letters. Only the Naka-no-chō *geisha* are registered in this establishment, and it takes no cognizance of *moguri geisha* (a *geisha* who carries on her profession clandestinely) or private *geisha* kept in smaller houses. In summoning a *geisha,* tea-houses send a maid-servant and brothels a *wakaimono* (man servant) to the registry office, and this messenger calls out— "——— *san* ——— *oiran no o zashiki desu*" (or translated freely "Miss ——— is wanted by guests in Miss ———'s apartments"). So thoroughly do the clerks in the *kemban-sho* know their business that no further conversation takes place, and the *geisha* is sent out forthwith: in most cases the clerks do not even enquire from whence the messenger has come as they generally are quick to recognize his or her identity, and at night a glance at the lantern of the applicant (which always bears a name or device) shows them the house to which the *geisha* is to proceed. If the *geisha* thus called has already been engaged, or is unable to attend to the call on account of sickness or other cause, an answer is

---

and means "the leader of flowers" (i. e.—the most beautiful of all flowers) because a beautiful woman may be compared to a flower, and *oiran* occupy the same position among other courtesans as the cherry does among other flowers.

The *oiran* is also compared in a poem by Senryū to the "*renge-sō*" (*Astragalus lotoides?* a small wild flower of a whitish pink colour closely resembling a lotus blossom in shape) when he says:—

"*Te ni toru na! Yahari no ni okê, Renge-sō.*

"Gather not the blossom of the *Renge-sō*. Better leave the flower blooming in the meadows."

This poem conveys a warning to young men not to choose wives from among the denizens of the Yoshiwara.

The word *oiran* appears in a famous satirical poem, as follows:—

"*Oiran no Namida de Kura no Yane ga mori.*"

"The tears of an *oiran* cause the roof of one's house to leak."

given to that effect. (In the latter case a toothpick is stuck in the *samisen* box to show that the *geisha* is not able to visit her guests). The servants of the *kemban-sho* (*kemban no ko-mono*) are employed in carrying the *geisha's samisen* wherever she goes. When a *geisha* is about to make her *début* she goes the round of tea-houses and brothels, accompanied by her employer (*kakae-nushi*) and comrades, distributing to each house towels or *sakê*-cups inscribed with her name. These calls are made by way of introduction and to solicit patronage (*aiko wo tanomi*), and (as is the case with a new *hōkan*) the larger the number of friends who are present on this occasion the greater the honour to the *geisha*. The "*shin-gao*" (new-face), as she is called, invariably wears on the day of her *début* garments made of silk crêpe (*chirimen*) dyed with three white crests on each of them. Her hair is dressed in the "*shimada*" style, her *obi* (girdle) tied in a bow called "*taiko-musubi*," and when she walks she turns back the skirt of her dress a little so as to allow a glimpse of her exquisite crêpe petticoat (*naga-jiban*) beneath. In case of the debutante being an *o shaku* (a young girl training to become a regular *geisha*) the style of her dress is left to her own choice, and on the day of her introduction she is called by some guest in accordance with previous arrangements made through a tea-house or brothel. If the young *geisha* has no engagement on this first night of her professional life it is considered as a great disgrace to her employer. It is a custom for the Yoshiwara *geisha* not to wear clothes bearing crests, except during the time of the

Shimada style of coiffure.

New Year's festivities and other time-honoured holidays and festivals, but to dress themselves in plain striped stuffs. On the "crest days" (紋日 = *mom-bi*. These are the *Go-sekku* or five national holidays, *tori-no-machi*, etc.) *geisha* are generally engaged, by previous appointment, by tea-houses, brothels, or by the request of some guests, and they therefore stop, during the proper hours, in the houses where they have been engaged, even though there be no guests to attend to. [On these particular days they don their crested garments for the nonce.] Should the *geisha* fail to keep her appointment, or not remain at her post during the regular time in accordance with established rules, she will be scolded by not only *kemban* but by the tea-houses and brothels, and it will be said about her:—"*Zuibun tare San wa zubora da ne!*" or *shitsurei wo shiranai*" ("Miss So and So is very neglectful isn't she?" or "She has no sense of propriety or courtesy").

The fees payable to a *geisha* are calculated at the *kemban-sho* by the number of hours her *samisen* box is away from the office. The fee is 12½ *sen* per hour (it was 2 *shu*—*Yen* 1.25—in the olden days) and the tip given (*tentō* or *shūgi*) generally 1 *Yen:* for younger *geisha* (*o shaku*) the fee is 10 *sen* per hour and the tip about 20 *sen*. At present there is a class of cheap *geisha* who charge the rate of a younger *geisha* (*o shaku nami no gyoku-dai* = a fee the same as that of an *o shaku*). A small percentage of the *geisha's* earnings is taken as commission by the tea-houses arranging the engagement. Some features of the old style of *geisha* are still retained among the singing-girls of the Yoshiwara. For instance, they wear a large *maru-obi* (a broad sash made out of a single piece of stuff folded lengthways once and sewn together at the edges, loosely tied and hanging down quite low) and a dress so long that it touches, and almost trails upon, the ground. The ancient styles of the coiffure are fast disappearing, their place being usurped by the *Ichōgaeshi* (or inverted maidenhair-leaf which requires no false hair, but consists of two tresses parted at the crown, made into rings, and gathered in at the top) and even the *sokuhatsu* (European style) style. Formerly the *shimada* was *en regle* and any other style was considered as impolite vis-a-vis guests. [Nowadays the ordinary *geisha* in the cities violate ancient customs in a hundred and one ways]. They also considered it stylish and "the thing" to go about barefooted and never, even in the coldest weather, wore socks, whereas of late years the *geisha* all wear *tabi*.

Ichōgaeshi style of coiffure.

It is stated that *geisha* first came into existence at Kyōto and Ōsaka in the 1st year of Hōreki (1751), but they were vastly different to those of the present day. Up to the eras of Shōtoku (1711-1715) and Kyōhō (1716-1735) nearly all the courtesans were skilled in the arts of singing, dancing, music, etc., and as they were equal to the task of enlivening parties with their performances there was no room nor necessity for *geisha*. Besides the fact that the courtesans were accomplished, it was the custom for the wives and daughters of brothel-keepers to play the *samisen* and dance for the amusement of guests: these were called *tori-mochi* (entertainers). Again, those *shinzō* who were versed in amusing arts such as dancing and music, were invited by guests to assist at parties, although no fixed arrangement was made with them. These things ceased at the end of the Hōreki era (1751-1763).

COURTESAN DANCING FOR THE ENTERTAINMENT OF GUESTS.—KWAMBUN ERA (1661–1671).

Formerly there was a class of female professionals called *odori-ko* (dancers), who not only gave exhibitions of dancing but even offered themselves as substitutes for the ordinary courtesans in order to eke out their means of subsistence.

In the 4th year of Hōreki (1754) regular *geiko* (kind of *geisha*) sprang into existence for the time, and the term *geisha* developed later on about the 11th year (1761). In the latter year, we read that in the "*Daikoku-rō*" (brothel), was a *geiko* named Toyotake Yasohachi, in the "*Ōgiya*" (brothel) a *geisha* named Kasen, in "*Tama-ya*" (brothel) two *geisha* called Ran and Toki respectively, while another *geisha* known as Mondo was engaged in the "*Iseya*" (brothel), etc. The *geisha* were experts in the *gidayū* (musical drama), *naga-uta* (lyric poetry or song), aud *bungo-bushi* (a style of song which originated in Bungo), etc., and, as their name implies, they were accomplished women. The proper sphere of the *geisha*, on the other hand, was to entertain parties by playing popular airs and singing popular "catchy" songs. When the *geisha* first came into existence—about the 10th or 11th year of Hōreki (1760-1761) they were employed by the brothels and lent to guests of the houses, but, as their popularity and number increased, they came to be engaged by tea-houses and individuals, or to start independently, and so gradually formed a separate and distinct profession. The liberty of action which they had acquired since they had set up independently soon degenerated into license, and it often happened that *geisha* not only sold their accomplishments but their charms as well: this led to the establishment of the *kemban-sho* by Daikoku-ya Shūmin in the 8th year of Anyei (1779) and the placing of *geisha* under proper control. Prior to the establishment of this *kemban-sho* the *geisha* were at liberty to go out of the great gate with guests, but subsequently this was strictly forbidden except to two *geisha* each day. Only on New Year's day and the 13th day of the 7th month (*Bon no jū-san-nichi*) were they free to pass out of the Yoshiwara irrespective of number, but even on those days their hours of liberty expired at 4 o'clock in the afternoon. We find it recorded that the rules were so stringently enforced that comparatively few *geisha* actually ventured outside the gateway even on the special days above mentioned. The *kemban-sho* further made strict sumptuary regulations prohibiting *geisha* from wearing unnecessarily fine clothes, believing that if these women were dressed too magnificently it might lead to their making easy conquests of the guests they met. The dress was limited to clothes of plain non-figured stuffs dyed with their crests, and collars of some white material (*shiro-eri muji no mon-tsuki*) while their coiffures had to be made in the "*shimada*" style ornamented with one *kōgai* (hair-pin), one comb, and one smaller hair-pin only. This style of dress is adopted even in these times on certain days called *mom-bi* (crest days). In order to make assurance doubly sure, *geisha* were generally recruited from among comparatively plain women so as not to set up a counter-attraction to the *oiran* or out-shine the latter, and in a party of guests they were not allowed to sit close beside the latter except in cases of sheer necessity. When a *geisha* was suspected of too much intimacy with a guest an enquiry was held by the *kemban-sho* people, and if they considered the suspicion to be well-grounded they would suspend the fair sinner from the exercise of her profession for the space of from one to three days and admonish her as to her future conduct.

Nowadays, *geisha* have perfect freedom of action in the matter of going out of the Yoshiwara, the only stipulation being that they are required to notify the *kemban-sho* of their purpose. Formerly, *geisha* licenses were issued by the *nanushi* but are now given by the *kemban.* In the *kemban* hung a number of wooden tickets bearing the names of *geisha* registered there, and as soon as a woman was engaged her ticket was taken down and hung up again with its face to the wall: this enabled the *kemban* people to tell instantly whether a certain *geisha* was "in" or "out." Three *geisha* made one "set" (*kumi*) and not less than three could be engaged: this was a precaution against allowing one girl to make herself unduly familiar with a guest, but now the "set" has been reduced to two *geisha* only. The hours of engagement were limited from noon to 10 p.m., and during that time 7 joss-sticks (*senkō shichi hon*) were supposed to have been consumed: the fee was fixed at 1 *ryō* 3 *bu* (*Yen* 17.50) and was divided between the *kemban* and the *geisha*, the latter receiving 2 *bu* 2 *shu* (*Yen* 6.25). The *geisha* also received a gratuity of from 2 *shu* to 1 *bu* (*Yen* 1.25 to *Yen* 2.50). In the Yoshiwara there were no *hakoya* (*samisen*-box carriers) the clerks of the *kemban* acting in that capacity: at night time these clerks carried lighted lanterns on which were painted the sign of the *kemban.*

On the 2nd day of the first month the ceremony of *hikizome* (first playing of the *samisen* in the new new year) was observed. After about 4 o'clock in the afternoon the *geisha* and *hōkan,* in groups of fives or sevens, went round to the various tea-houses and brothels in their holiday dress wishing the proprietors and inmates a happy new year, playing tunes of a felicitous nature, and soliciting future patronage. The tea-houses and brothels entertained these callers with *toso* (spiced *saké*), ordinary *saké*, and food. This custom of celebrating the *hikizome* still prevails.

In closing this chapter it may be of some interest to readers to note that the *Sakura-gawa* school of *hōkan* is the most influential in the Yoshiwara, and consequently many persons have concluded that this style is indigenous to the quarter : such, however, is not the case, for it originated in Fukagawa. Of late, several classes of amusements and many new songs, said to be in the *Sakura-gawa* style, have been introduced, but they do not seem to be particularly noteworthy.

The Europeanization of the Yoshiwara and the Introduction of Loochooan Courtesans.

The origin of the addition of *rō* (樓)=a two-storied or " high " house) to the names of brothels is traced back to the *Go-mei-rō* (五明樓) which was another name for the " *Ōgiya* " of the Shin Yoshiwara about the era of Temmei (1781-1786). In the pre-Restoration days no houses were allowed which exceeded two stories in height, but since the beginning of the *Meiji* (the present) era changes have been introduced into the architecture of brothels and several magnificent and commodious houses have been built in a hybrid European style. The *Tōkyō-kaikwa-hanjō-shi* (東京開化繁昌誌) states :—

" At the time of the Restoration, high and commodious buildings, such as had never been seen even in the mansions of nobles, were constructed in the European fashion, etc., etc." Illustrations of the *Kimpei-rō* and the *Go-sei-rō* in the European style are given.

In the "*Shin-Yoshiwara-Zensei-kurabe-Shōgi-hyōban-ki*, (新吉原全盛競娼妓評判記) published in 1870, is a passage which reads:—" Houses were built in the Western fashion and *many rare and delicate things were placed on the table*" (*sic.*)

The adoption of foreign costume by prostitutes was first introduced by the Yamada-rō of Ageya-machi in 1886, and later on this example was followed by the *Shin-Inaben-rō* and several other houses, but before long the new fashion fell into disfavour and was abandoned. When the "foreign craze" was at its height, the Yamada-rō provided foreign bedsteads for the women, and served up food in foreign dishes; but they never got so far as knives and forks, and although the plates were of a Western pattern one was expected to eat the viands with the cedarwood chopsticks provided!!! The *Yamada-rō* seems to be great on new sensations, for in 1889 that house engaged two or three Loochooan women as courtesans. This novel departure filled the house for a time, but before long the novelty wore off and the lovely Loochooans ceased to be an attraction.

Zegen.

(*Procurers.*)

There may be various causes which compel many an unfortunate girl to plunge into the "sea of trouble and bitterness" (*ku-gai*), and out of each the enterprising novelist and feuilleton writer has over and over again constructed a peg on which to hang his story, but, when all is said and done, *the* cause of causes is *poverty*. Nowadays, the police regulations are so stringent that it is virtually impossible for persons to traffic in human flesh and blood and sell their fellow-creatures, but in former times there were rascally scoundrels known as "*zegen*" who made a regular business of procuring, selling, and buying women. These infamous pimps not only extorted outrageous fees for their services but treated their victims in a most cruel brutal manner, and they even had the temerity to kidnap young innocent girls for the purpose of selling them to brothels. Even the officials of the *Bakufu* (Tokugawa Government) were startled out of their perfunctory method of doing things when they realized the danger these pestilent fellows were to the community, and in the 5th month of the 4th year of *Kwansei* (1792) the following notification was issued by the government prohibiting procurers from exercising their nefarious calling:—

> " Among those people living in this City who make it their " business to find positions for men and women desiring to " obtain employment are parties known as *zegen* or *naka-tsugi*. " The plan of action adopted by these individuals is to engage " women for a specified number of years at certain fixed wages, " although at the time there is in fact no opening offering. In " the written memoradums of agreement entered into, it is " provided that even should the women thus hired be employed " in such disgraceful or low positions as *meshimori* (lower class " prostitutes kept in inns under the guise of servants) menial " servants, or in any other capacities whatsoever, they shall " have no grounds for raising objections or complaints of any " kind on that account. Under these circumstances it is not " usual for *zegen* to keep women on their hands for long, and if " no suitable situation be found within a short time they sell " and transfer the girls to other *zegen* for a certain sum of " money. The *zegen* also prolong the period of service contract-" ed for with the result that the parents do not know when to " expect their daughters back. In this manner the whereabouts " of many women are lost, and their parents or relatives are " compelled to apply to the authorities to search for and dis-" cover them and cause their restitution. It is also reported " that sometimes *zegen* extort money from parties seeking " relatives, and from the proprietors of brothels, and thus

"matters are arranged and compromised privately without "referring them to the authorities. These practices are tanta- "mount to traffic in human beings and are highly reprehensi- "ble, therefore the profession of *zegen* or *naka-tsugi* is hereby pro- "hibited. This law is to be strictly observed."

In the official rules relative to deeds of engagement of courtesans issued in the 7th year of Kwansei (1797)—that is four years after the issue of the above notification—occurred the following clauses :—

"1.—When a brothel engages a new courtesan through the "medium of a professional (*kuchi-ire no mono*=a person who finds "situations for would-be employés, and employés for would-be "employers) full enquiries shall be privately instituted as to "whether the woman has been kidnapped or otherwise, her "birth-place, status, position, etc. Also as to whether she is a "real or adopted child of her reputed parents. Enquiries shall "also be made as to the status, residence, etc., of her surety. "These matters must be thoroughly investigated previous to "entering into a contract of engagement: the enquiries are to "be made through the medium of third parties and not from "the said middleman himself, and if the woman be actually "engaged the above-mentioned details shall be entered into the "*nanushi's* book. The term of engagement arranged must not "exceed twenty years.

"2.—The profession of *zegen* and *naka-tsugi* having been pro- "hibited in the 4th month of the 4th year of Kwansei (the year "of the "Ox") on the application of interested parties the "authorities rendered the following decision:—

"Whereas heretofore there have been numerous instances "of *zegen* and *naka-tsugi* having signed and sealed documents as "sureties for courtesans under the pretence that they were re- "latives of the women, it is hereby decreed that, on and after "the 5th month of the present year, when the period of service "has expired (as mentioned in the separate bonds of guarantee "handed to their masters) the ex-courtesans shall not be given "over to their sureties but to their own actual blood relations, "and it is further ordered that the proprietors of brothels are to "assist the time-expired women in the matter of placing them "in the charge of such actual blood relations as aforesaid.

"Should any *zegen* residing within the precincts of the "Yoshiwara receive applications direct from women seeking

"employment as courtesans, such *zegen* shall conduct the ap-
"plicants to a brothel for the purpose of introducing them to an
"employer. When engagements are finally concluded the *zegen*
"shall not (as formerly) seal the agreements inasmuch that he
"is only permitted to act as a mere introducer between the
"parties.

"3.—Should the number of middlemen in the Yoshiwara
"be limited, the profession would become a monopoly, and
"to prevent the selling and buying of the goodwill of
"the trade, as well as to prevent any dishonest practices, an
"agreement was lodged by each middleman with the *nanushi*.
"The latter has been in the habit of reminding the middlemen
"of the contents of this contract once in every month, and
"obtaining their signatures each time in proof of his having
"done so. Of late, persons plying a similar profession have
"appeared in the vicinity of the Yoshiwara, but have remained
"outside the enclosure. This is contrary to the notification and
"makes it difficult to exercise proper control over them, there-
"fore they shall be compelled to move into the Yoshiwara under
"pain of having the exercise of their profession suspended.
"Henceforth all persons desirous of carrying on the business of
"a middleman shall only be allowed to do so inside the gates of
"the quarter."

From the above it would appear that the profession was not altogether abolished, and that it was merely concentrated in the Yoshiwara for the purpose of enforcing a strict control over *zegen* and *naka-tsugi*. Even these regulations were relaxed in course of time, and by the era of Tempō (1830-1843) there were over ten houses carrying on the business of *zegen* in Tamachi, Asakusa, and Sanya. Among these, the most famous was the establishment of Ōmiya Sampachi, as he employed ten or more *kobun* (partly employé and partly protégé) who, in conjunction with the provincial *zegen*, freely resorted to the practice of kidnapping girls. These *zegen* sent agents into the country to buy, beg, borrow, or steal, women and girls, whom they brought back and locked up securely till the moment of their absolute transfer into the hands of brothel-keepers. How they maltreated the poor wretches whom they had kidnapped may be inferred from the fact that the owners of these "registry offices" were in the habit of stripping the girls absolutely naked every night, and hiding their clothes under their own *futon* (mattress) lest the unhappy victims should escape. When the women were about to be sold to the brothels with whom the men had made previous arrangements, they were nicely dressed in hired clothes (in order to make them appear to better advantage and thus enhance the selling price) and taken round as "goods on view." Then followed protracted negotiations between the parties interested, each haggling over the bargain like a fish-monger and a house-wife, the *zegen* trying to squeeze out as much money as possible from the intending buyer, and the brothel-keeper endeavouring to beat him down. At length the price would be settled to the satisfaction of both the buyer and seller, but even then there would generally ensue a struggle relative to the payment of *mizu-kin*, or rebate allowed to the buyer as a fund with which to provide the woman with an outfit. [Some people say that this word should be *mizu-kin* 不見金 = *money without seeing*) because the money was never seen by the parents but deducted immediately by the brothel-keeper). Another version says that is a corruption of *mi-tsu-ki-kin* (身付金=*money attached to the body*) because with this money the clothes and personal effects of the woman were supposed to be purchased. When a girl was sold as a prostitute, a certificate—called a *nenki shōmon* (年季證文)—was given by the parents to the brothel-keeper. It ran (freely translated) as follows :—

Name of the girl.....................

Age.............

This.........................(name) residing at.....................
daughter of.................you..............., owner of..............
brothel, agree to take into your employ for...............years at the price of...............ryō.

...............ryō you retain as "mizu-kin"................ ryō, the balance, I have received.

I guarantee that the girl will not cause you trouble while in your employ.

She is of the............... sect, her ancestral temple being the ....in .... street.

Parents' name .... (SEAL.)

Guarantor .... (SEAL.)

Landlord .... (SEAL.)

.................................*Name of "teishu."*

....*"joroya."*

It must be understood that many of these documents were "fakes" as regards the signatures of the parent and of the landlord of the parents' house. So long as some persons were found to act as the necessary parties, the papers were signed and stamped, and in exchange for such an instrument the *mi-no-shiro-kin* (price of the body) was paid over in hard cash on strictly business principles. The "parcel of goods" having been taken delivery of by the brothel keeper, the *zegen* appropriated 10 per cent as his commission, but besides that they generally managed to obtain further sums of money on various pretexts, including *hone-ori-kin* (money for labour performed) *ifuku no son-ryō* (hire of clothes), *makanai-ryō* (expenses for food and lodging), etc., etc. [In passing, it may be noted that in *zegen* circles a girl who had been kidnapped was known by the name of "*Inari*" (really the Goddess of Rice, but in popular supersition the fox-deity) which is perhaps the reason why people often call courtesans "*kitsune*" (foxes)].

As already mentioned, the Kwansei (1789-1800) notification prohibiting the improper selling of women by *zegen* had very little practical effect, but on the 2nd October, 1872 (2nd day of the 10th month of the 5th year of Meiji) the Japanese Government earned the everlasting gratitude of right-thinking persons by issuing Decree No. 295 which ordered the *unconditional* liberation of all prostitutes throughout the length and breadth of the Empire. This Decree reads, according to the official translation, as follows :—

"Whereas transactions involving the sale of persons and "their entire subjection to the will of their masters for life or "for a period are contrary to the principles of humanity, and in "consequence have been prohibited from olden times; and "whereas the actual condition of persons heretofore hired for a "term of years as servants, or in any other capacity, virtually "amounts to servitude, therefore all such transactions are "henceforth strictly prohibited.

"It shall be admissible for any persons to bind themselves "as apprentices for the purpose of acquiring practical training "in agriculture, trade, or art. Nevertheless the term of such "apprenticeship shall in no case exceed seven years, after the "expiration of which, such term may be prolonged with the "consent of both parties.

"In the case of ordinary servants or employés the terms of "service shall be limited to one year; and if the service be "continued after the expiration of that period the agreements "shall be renewed.

"The release of all prostitutes, singing girls, and other per- "sons bound to serve for any term of years, is hereby ordered, "and it is further directed that no suits relating to debts "incurred by, or on account of such persons, shall be entertain- "ed."

NOTIFICATION ISSUED IN OCT., 1872, (5th YEAR OF MEIJI) BY THE JUDICIAL DEPARTMENT.

No. 22.

(PUBLISHED BROADCAST.)

"Whereas on the second day of this month the Council of State issued a decree No. 295, persons are hereby notified relative to the same and are to bear in mind the following articles:—

Although the sale of persons has been forbidden from olden days yet persons are hired for periods under various names, but in reality this "hiring" constitutes a "sale" and it is considered that the capital of persons hiring prostitutes, singing girls, &c., is equivalent to stolen money, therefore should any person complain about the foregoing, upon investigation the whole of the money in dispute shall be confiscated by the Government.

As stated above, prostitutes and singing girls having lost the rights of human beings, they may likened to cattle (*gyū-ba ni kotonarazu*=they do not differ from oxen and horses.) There is no sense for human beings to endeavour to exact repayment from cattle!

Therefore no payment shall be demanded from prostitutes or singing girls for any moneys lent or debts due and in arrear hitherto, but it is provided that as regards transactions subsequent to the 2nd day of the present month, such prohibition ceases.

Persons who for money considerations cause girls to become prostitutes and singing girls under the pretext that such girls are their adopted daughters, are actually trafficking in human bodies, and will hereafter be severely dealt with."

[Since then, detailed regulations have been established relating to the profession of prostitutes and are still in operation]. The losses sustained by the brothel-keepers at the time of this wholesale liberation of women are said to have been simply enormous. The "*Tōkyō-Kwaika Hanjō-shi*" (東京開化繁昌誌) has the following under the caption of "*Liberation of Courtesans*":—"In the winter of 1872, all the prostitutes and *geisha* who had been engaged in the brothels and inns throughout the country were unconditionally set free * * * * Thousands of wretched women (whose lives might be compared to those of birds cooped up in cages) having been suddenly liberated, the confusion caused by the crowds of delighted parents and daughters who thronged the prostitute quarters beggars description * * * Notwithstanding the general rejoicing, owing to being in debt, or to other circumstances, a large number of these unfortunates were compelled to apply for new licenses and to continue their calling in the brothels which were now re-named *kashi-zashiki* (貸座敷 = a house with rooms to let)." From the above remarks the actual condition of affairs at the time may well be imagined.

The old fashioned style of *zegen* (procurer) have now disappeared, and most of the women desirous of becoming courtesans are hired through *yatoinin-kuchi-ire-jo* " (Registry offices for persons seeking situations). By law these registry offices are forbidden to negotiate such transactions, but it is well known that this prohibition cannot be enforced in practice. The brothel-keeper, or his substitute, attends to the engaging of women, and is always on the look out for " bargains." In the same manner that vultures swoop down to feast on the dead bodies of soldiers after a sanguinary battle, so these rascally fellows turn the misfortunes of others to their own profit by visiting localities which have been overtaken by terrible natural calamity. Earthquakes, fires, floods, and bad crops are the natural allies, of the brothel-keepers, as is proved by actual statistics. For instance, out of the present 3,000 inmates of the Yoshiwara fully 40 per cent. are natives of Gifu and Aichi Prefectures, and we know quite well that these localities have suffered severely from earthquakes, floods, and bad seasons of late years. It is said that when a particular district is visited by some serious misfortune the various brothel-keepers proceed to the spot in order to see what game they can bag at cheap rates.

The Dress of Courtesans.

Nowadays there is no fixed rule as to the dress of these women, and they dress themselves in accordance with the wishes of the brothel-keepers or according to the dictates their own taste. Thus we find some of the modern courtesans dressed in gold or silver embroidered brocades after the fashion of *oiran* of bygone days, others are clad in gaudy red crêpe (*hi-jirimen*) with embroidered collars, and wear gigantic satin sashes (*obi*) tied in front, while others again try and make themselves look younger and prettier by wearing *yūzen* stuff (generally silk crêpe decorated with various beautiful figures) purple satin collars and *maki-obi* (a narrow sash wound round and round the waist: this sash is not tied into a bow but the end is merely tucked in to hold it in place). Other women wear plain crested clothes, or imitate the style of *geisha* (singing girls) or of Court ladies, and others even go so far as to ape the (save the mark!) European style! In low-class houses a long loose robe (*shikake*) of striped stuff and an under garment (*naga-juban*) of mousseline (*merensu*) compose the whole stock of the wardrobe of a prostitute. At present a long loose robe (*shikake*) of black colour is only worn by the chief courtesans (*o shoku kabu*) of the best houses. Compared with the luxurious costumes of former years, the present holiday clothes of the women only correspond in quality to those of the ordinary every-day garments worn by their predecessors: from this statement the comparatively inferior nature of the present costumes may be inferred. It is the custom of prostitutes nowadays to wear clothes of striped material (*shima-mono*) when they are in their own rooms with intimate guests. In the *ō mise* (best house) after her introduction (*hikitsuke*) to a strange guest (*shokwai no kyaku*) the servants cry "*o meshi-kae*" (honourable change of garments), and immediately the courtesan goes to her room, changes her clothes, returns clad in a dress made of some figured material (*moyō mono*), and waits on the visitor during the feasting and wine-bibbing which follows. At the time of "*o hikê*" (honourable retirement, i.e.—the time to go to bed) she again changes her clothes for a costume of striped stuff. In the medium and lower class houses the women only change their dress once, and the material employed in their wearing apparel is exclusively crêpe (*chirimen*).

With regard to the sumptuary regulations relative to restrictions on the dress of prostitutes, among the five items of the notification given to Shōji Jinyemon by Honda Lord of Sado in the 3rd year of Genna (1617) it was provided that "prostitutes are forbidden to wear clothes with gold and silver embroidery on them; they are to wear ordinary dyed stuffs." This policy of enforcing simplicity of dress was adopted by the authorities at the time when the establishment of the old (Moto) Yoshiwara was permitted, and the courtesans therefore used to wear either plain *kenchū* (pongee?) or striped clothes: their *obi* (sashes) were broader than those of ordinary women, but never exceeded 4 *sun* (if this is cloth measure it will equal 6 inches English) whereas in those times the usual *obi* did not exceed 2 *sun* (say 3 inches English) in width. The sleeves also were much shorter at that time, but later on they were gradually made longer as the sumptuary laws fell into desuetude. Since the founding of the Shin Yoshiwara luxurious habits of dress gradually spread in the quarter, and bye and bye extravagance was carried to its utmost point. In the Kwambun and Empō eras (1661-1680) the *tayū* usually wore *rinzu* (figured satin) or *habutaye* (a superior kind of pongee) dresses. In the "*Dōbō Go-en*" (洞房語園) we read about the narrative of an old gentleman named *Muramatsu Shō-a* who said that in the era of Kwambun (1661-1672) a certain person met the *Tayū* Takao of Mi-ura-ya Dō-an's house in Kyōmachi and saw one of her new costumes: the lining was of pale blue silk, the face of the dress black *habutae*, and the whole garment so made as to be suitable for a man's wear. In the "*Saikaku Ichidai-Otoko*" (西鶴一代男), published in the 2nd year of Tenna (1682) it is mentioned that the clothes of some women were made of *shiro rinzu* (white figured satin) for underwear, over which were worn two dresses, the under one of scarlet *kanoko* (material dyed with minute white spots) and the upper one of pale-blue *Hachijo*-silk. These clothes were used when the wearers attended to parties of guests, the taste of the period demanding stuffs costly as regarded price but plain and simple in appearance as compared with the brilliant gold and silver embroideries and the velvets used in later days. In the Teikyō (1684-1687) and Genroku (1688-1703) periods it had become a general custom to use plain purple materials (*murasaki-mu-ji*) for the *shikake* (cloak). In the Hōyei era (1704-1710)—fifty years after the opening of the Shin Yoshiwara—magnificent embroidered clothes came into fashion, and in the era of Gembun (1736-1740), some thirty-years later, a courtesan named Shigasaki introduced the custom of wearing a broad *obi* (sash) she herself having worn one 33″ (*kujira* 2 *shaku* 2 *sun*) in width (*sic*). This sash was worn and tied in a style known as "*Karuta-musubi,*" and the woman who first set the fashion was known as "*Obi Shigasaki*" or "*Obi-gokumon.*" (The first means simply "Sash" Shigasaki: the second "Sash-exposing-a-criminal's head." The latter has a joking reference to the ancient custom of exposing the severed head of an executed criminal to public gaze: the sash was supposed to be so broad that only the head was visible above it.) Since then, a luxurious and extravagant tendency in the dress of courtesans manifested itself so strongly that in the 7th year of Kwansei (1795) the authorities again considered it necessary to impose restrictions on this rage for idle show: it was therefore announced that dresses should be of plain stuffs (according to ancient custom) and that *date-mon* (伊達紋 ornamental crests) should not exceed 6 *sun* (if ordinary measure=7.1586 inches: if "*kujira*"—cloth measure—about 9 inches) in diameter. The tide of luxury, however, could no more be stemmed by a mere notification than could the waters of the ocean be dammed by a man's hand, and in the eras of An-ei and Bunsei (1772-1829) the zenith of barbaric splendour was attained. Costumes of crêpe, velvet, figured satin, plain satin, *habutae,* etc., were freely used, while *obi* (sashes) were made of velvet, gold-brocade, silk-brocade, damask, etc. As to colours and patterns, these were chosen according to the taste of the individual courtesan and were by no means uniform. In a book called "*Nishiki-no-Ura*" (錦ノ裏 "Behind the Brocades") published in the 3rd year of Kwansei (1791) a very elaborate description of an elegant costume of the time is given. The upper garment consisted of white *nanako* dyed with purple clouds among which peeped out some tasteful pattern: every here and there were flowers embroidered in silk and finished by handpainting representing in vivid colours the four seasons, while the crest consisted of a wistaria flower sewn upon the dress with purple silk-thread. The underwear consisted of a figured satin garment bordered with plain brown *Hachijō* silk and embroidered with the same pattern in coloured silk, and of a lower girdle of claret-coloured figured satin lined with bright scarlet silk crêpe. As an instance of the beauty and costliness of the night-gown of a certain young miss, the "*Keisei-kai Shi-ju-hat-te*" ("Forty-eight methods of buying courtesans") mentions:—"The garment was of scarlet crêpe, "trimmed with purple figured satin and edged with gold and "silver threads so as to give the effect of waves breaking upon "the sea-shore, while her night-sash was of *kabe-chōro* (wrin-"kled silk.") In the eras of Bunkwa and Bunsei (1804-1829) the costumes were simply gorgeous. The pattern of the *shikake* or cloak generally represented a cloud with lightning and a golden dragon, or rocks with peonies, and a tiger chasing a butterfly; the embroidery being silver and gold. That the dresses of the "*jōro*" of these later periods were gorgeous, the paintings of Utamaro, Eizan, Kunisada, and others, clearly show. It appears that in those times there was a fixed rule in every brothel appointing the make, stuff, colour, and pattern of the dresses to be worn by the respective grades of women, and that this rule was strictly adhered to. No courtesan, therefore, was permitted to wear a dress unsuitable to her particular rank in the brothel, even though she could afford it, but nowadays the girls are at liberty to wear any clothes they choose and can pay for, especially if they are popular and beautiful women. There are various arrangements made as to defraying the expenses of dress in different brothels, and the clothes of modern *shōgi* are divided into *awase* (worn in May, June and October), *hitoemono* (worn in July, August and September), *wata-ire* worn (November to April,) etc., according to the season, in the same way as with ordinary persons.

Coiffures of the Yujo.

Although it is remarked in the "Yoshiwara Taizen" (吉原大全) "their hair even now is dressed in the "Hyōgo" "style after the fashion of the Hyōgo-ya brothel at Ōhashi, "Yanagi-chō," yet when we find no coiffure of this style in the pictures painted prior to the Tenna era (1681-1683) the correctness of the assertion may be doubted. Judging from ancient pictures of the "*Uki-yo-e*" school, it would appear that up to the era of Keichō (1594-1614) courtesans wore their hair hanging down the back, and that even in the era of Kwan-ei (1624-1643) they merely gathered it up on the top of the head in a very simple manner. It is mentioned in various books that in the era of Kwam-bun (1661-1672) a *tayū* named Katsuyama, living in the Yamamoto-ya in the Shin Yoshiwara, devised a method of coiffure, called after her, "*Katsuyama-magé.*" In the "*Dōbō Go-en*" (洞房語園) it says:—

> "About the period of Jō-o (1652-1654) or Meireki (1655-1657) "there was a *tayū* named Katsuyama in the house of Yamamoto "Hōjun of Shimmachi in the Shin Yoshiwara. Formerly she "had been a *furo-onna* ("bath-woman:" really an unlicensed "prostitute) in a bath-house (known as '*Ki-no-kuni-buro*'), kept "by a man called Ichibei, at Kanda in front of the Tango-den "(neighbourhood of the present Kiji-chō). When the *furo-ya* "(bath-houses) were abolished this woman returned to her

Types of Courtesans' Coiffures.

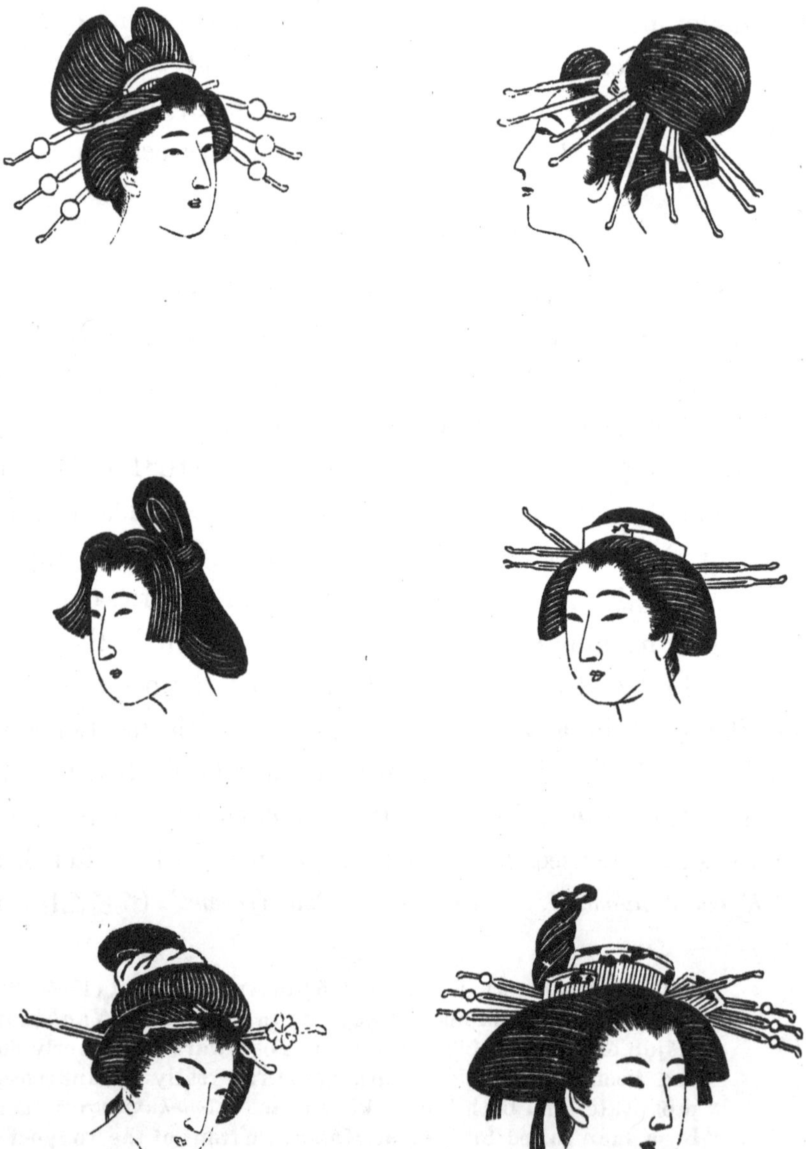

"parent's house, but appeared again as a *jōro* in the house of "Hōjun. Her hair was bound up in one ring and tied with "white *moto-yui* (cue cord) and this style still exists under the "name of *Katsuyama-magé*, etc., etc."

[The *Maru-magé* of later years is believed to have been evolved from the *Katsu-yama-magé.*] In the era of Tenna (1681-1683) *Hyōgo-magé* and *Kaisei-shimada* came into vogue. The *Shimada-magé* is said to have originated in the era of Kwan-ei (1624-1643) with a dancing-girl of Kyōto named Shimada Jinsuke. The *Keisei-shimada* resembled the present *Shimada* in nearly every respect. In the era of An-ei (1772-1780) the *Kinshōjo-bin, Utsusemi-mage, Nakabin, Hishidzuto, Yoko-hyōgo, Yamagata-tori-bin, Sogidzuto-musubi, Tate-hyōgo,* and other styles, came into fashion, and later the *Susuki-bin, Otoshi-barake, Tsutogiri, Sumi-Shimada, Adzuma-bin, Kai-nade-dzuto, Chasen-magé, Tsumi-hyōgo,* etc., came into vogue. By the era of Bunsei (1818-1829), however, of these only the *Tate-hyōgo, Shimada,* and a few others had survived. [At present the hair of the red bear (*sha-guma*) is used to form a tuft of false hair over which to spread the natural hair in making up a *Tate-hyōgo* coiffure: sometimes, although very rarely, it is used in dressing the hair in *Shimada* style]. It appears that in the Tenna and Teikyō eras (1681-1687) only vegetable oil was used in dressing the hair, and that *bin-tsuké* (pomatum) had not yet come into use. In the "*Go-nichi Mukashi-monogatari*" (後日昔物語) the statement of an old man born in the 3rd year of Empō (1675) is quoted to the effect that:—

"A certain old gentleman, who was ten years older than "my father, traversing an assertion by the latter that the hair "of courtesans was hardened by too much oil, said that such "was not the case in former years when the girls rubbed a "little thin oil on their heads: he also said that the hair

Types of Courtesans' Coiffures.

"remained in its natural state and did not show any greasiness "of appearance. The old pictures substantiate this assertion."

Moreover, in those days of comparative simplicity, the women used to dress their own hair. The "*Hyōkwa Mampitsu*" (萍花漫筆) remarks:—

"In ancient times it was considered a disgrace for courtesans not to dress their hair themselves, but of course it must "be recollected that there were no professional female hair-"dressers at that period; they were of later origin * * * In an "old document, said to be a certificate of a *yūjo* belonging to the "house of Idzumi Kankichi of Edo-chō, the following sentence "occurs:—'*This woman having been taught by her parents how to dress "her hair, and how to write, no concern need be felt on these points.* "There is a considerable difference between this certificate and "one of the present day."

According to the "*Kumono-Itomaki*" (蜘蛛糸巻), written by Kyōzan, a well-known writer, the professional female hair dresser came into existence at the end of An-ei (1772-1780) and therefore it was undoubtedly later than that period before the courtesans used to have their hair dressed by regular experts.

Referring to the style of hair dressing, the same authority says:—

"For about 20 years after the Temmei (1781-1788) era until "the era of Bunkwa (1804-1817) the style of hair-dressing of the "*oiran* was generally the *Tsumi-hyōgo*, but of late years this has "ceased to exist. The size of hair-pins, on the other hand, has "become larger than in former days, for in the Temmei period "they were very small and light and no person placed the "present artificial tortoise-shell (*bazu*) ornaments on her head. "As regards the style of hair-dressing, the *karawa*, *hyōgo*, *shimada*, *marumagé* (*katsuyama-mage*) and *shiitake*, came into "vogue in the order named."

For further information on the styles of hair-dressing, the reader is recommended to refer to the "*Reki-sei-onna-sōkō*

Types of Kamuro Coiffures.

(歴世女裝考). The woodcuts inserted in this section illustrate the principal styles of *coiffures* which have been adopted in the Yoshiwara from time to time.

Rooms of the Yūjo.

There is but little difference between the modern apartments (*kyo-shitsu*) of the *yūjo* and those of ancient times. The room in which a *yūjo* receives her guests is called the "*zashiki*," and generally contains about eight mats (*hachi-jō-jiki*), while the adjoining room (*tsugi no ma*) is a smaller private apartment containing perhaps three or four mats.

A Rainy Day in the Yoshiwara—within and without.

Some women have a third room placed at their disposal in addition, but this consideration is mostly granted to the "*o shoku*" exclusively.

Typical *zashiki* are cosy rooms fitted with the usual *toko-no-ma* (alcove) and *chigai-dana* (a recess with two shelves, one a little lower than the other, and each only reaching about half way across the width of the wall-space involved); in the former hang either picture or specimens of caligraphy (not always genuine!) by such noted artists as Chosanshū, Tesshū, Zeshin, Keishū, and others.* The rooms are prettily decorated, and furnished with cut flowers arranged in vases of Kutani porcelain; these flowers are changed according to the season. There will also be found musical instruments such as the *koto* (harp), *samisen* (banjo), *gekkin* (guitar), *ni-genkin* (a two-stringed musical instrument), etc.; numbers of sundry knicknacks, such as a shelf-ornament in the shape of a rabbit, made of imitation crystal, which is perched on a tiny cushion of daintily dyed crêpe; a hanging clock, a handsome mirror, a framed oil-painting; a small library of novels, magazines, theatrical notices, playbills, and other light reading matter designed to beguile the tedium of guests. On the *chigai-dana* (recess fitted with shelves by the side of the *toko-no-ma*) rests a deep lacquered tray (known as a *midare-bako*, in which are put the guests' garments) and other objects, while the room invariably contains a clothes-horse (*emon-kakê*) and

* Mr. Henry Norman says in the "*The Real Japan*":—"There is nearly always a large written and framed scroll in a conspicuous position, exhibiting some scrap of appropriate poetry tersely told in the complicated Chinese characters. One I was shown had the four characters *matsu kiku nao sonsu*, literally, "Pine chrysanthemum still are," *i.e.*, the pine and the chrysanthemum always preserve their charm, even in winter when other flowers die, and by implication, "My charms are everlasting, like the pine and the chrysanthemum."

a six-fold screen (*roku-mai-ori-no-byōbu*). In the private apartment is a shelf on which the *yūjo's yagu* (bed-clothes) are placed, and this is covered with a bright green *furoshiki* on which is dyed the ornamental figure of a vine (*karakusa*) and the name of the girl to whom it belongs. Below this *yagu-dana* (shelf) is a chest of drawers containing the wardrobe of the *yūjo*, while the other articles of furniture consist of a *naga-hibachi* (oblong brazier) on which is placed a kettle (*tetsu-bin*), a cupboard with a glass door (*garasu-do-iri no nedzumi-irazu*) within which *yō-cha-ki* (tea things) and *inshoku-no-gu* (eating and drinking utensils) are neatly arranged, a mirror-stand (*kyō-dai*), a cup used for gargling (*ugai-jawan*), a *mimi-darai* (a metallic or lacquer tub with a pair of handles or ears (used for toilet purposes), cushions (*zabuton*), and various other paraphernalia of a courtesan's room. The *zashiki* (rooms) are rented from the brothel-keeper by the *yūjo*, and are furnished at their own expense. The above is a description of a first-class house, and in the lower-grade establishments a girl (there called a *heya-mochi*) only possesses one room, or, at the most two rooms. In the better houses the rooms are known as *zashiki* (a "parlour") and in the lower-class houses as merely *heya* ("room"). In ancient days the *shinzō* had no rooms of their own, and it was the custom for all of them to sleep in the *ane-jōro's* room. There are also rooms called *myōdai-beya* (substitute rooms) which may be used by any of the women when they have more than one guest at the same time. In the lowest houses several guests and their girls are packed up together in one room, each couple being only sheltered from the gaze of the others by screens. This is known as *wari-doko* (割床="divided bed.") When a *yūjo* has not sufficient means

Courtesans Composing Letters to their Guests.

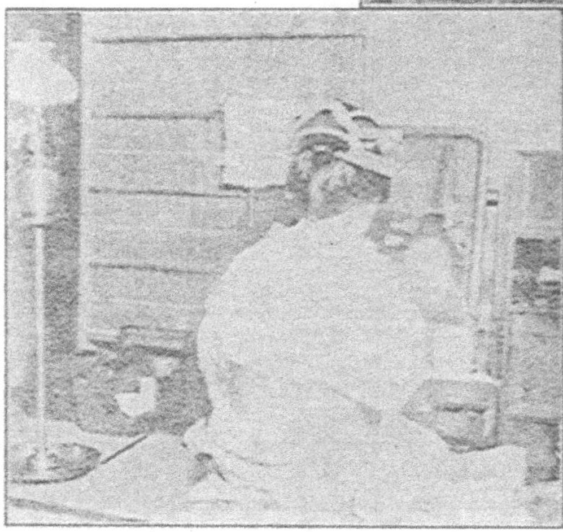

Courtesan making her Toilette.

to defray the expenses of furnishing and decorating her room, it is paid for in instalments, but in some cases an intimate guest will assist her by paying these expenses himself. The expenses of repairs to her *zashiki* and of the daily cleaning are also borne by the girl; the *sōji no chingin* (wage for cleaning) is paid direct to the *wakai-mono* (man-servant) who performs this office. The expenses which *yūjo* have to bear in this direction are very heavy, and according to the official rules issued by the authorities in the 7th year of Kwansei (1795) the girls were exempted from these burdens; but an ancient custom is not easily broken up, and the evil, being by no means thoroughly eradicated, has survived to these days. Unfortunately, in this profession, a pernicious custom exists of spending money lavishly, and should the *yūjo* show herself mean or stingy (or even moderately prudent) in her expenditure, this will cause her unpopularity, raise up a host of enemies, and make trouble for her in a hundred different ways; thus old customs cling to the Yoshiwara and defy the many earnest efforts made to root them out. It would appear that at the time when *yūjo* used to receive guests in *age-ya* there was no need to pay much attention to beautifying their own rooms, but as a matter of fact they were made very pretty because the *ki-jin* (貴人="nobles" and "honourable persons") would not enter *age-ya* and came direct to the brothels. The regular style of *futon* (mattress) used was a *kagami-buton* (*i.e.*—a *futon* the border of which is made of stuff different to that of the centre, making it look like a mirror in it's frame). In the best houses the borders were made of black velvet and the panels of red crêpe. Three of such *futon* (mattresses) were laid one upon the other and the pile formed a nice soft bed, but in the lower houses only two were used and these were made of inferior material such as *merensu* (*mousseline de laine*) or *kanakin* (calico): in the very lowest establishments only one was provided. The night gowns also varied in richness according to the class of the house. By the official rules issued in the 7th year of Kwansei (1795) fabrics mixed with gold or silver threads, silk brocades, or velvets, were forbidden to be used in making *futon*, and the number used was limited to three: these sumptuary regulations soon became a dead letter and utterly failed to effectively check the luxurious habits of the time. During the Meiwa era (1746-1771) a woman named Hinadzuru, belonging to the Chōji-ya, used a pile of five *futon* made of silk brocade, but this was quite unprecedented. When *yūjo* used to be called to visit guests in an *aye-ya* their night-clothes were carried with them on each and every occasion: these earlier *futon*, etc., are supposed to have been greatly inferior to the costly ones that came into fashion at a later period.

Tsumi-yagu no koto.

(The piling up and exhibition of bedding).

In the "*Ume-no-haru*" (by Kiyomoto are the words:—

> "A pile of as many as twenty of the rich floral brocade *futon*
> "and bedding which share the couch of Benten San."*

This passage refers to a custom known as "*tsumi-yagu*" which forms one of the leading features of the gay quarter: there are several songs and stanzas of poetry extant in which the splendid spectacle of a pile of magnificent brocade night-clothes and bedding is rapturously dilated upon in amorous

* Goddess of Love.

Arranging "*Tsumi-yagu*" (Exhibition of Bed-clothes) in the Kiōwa period (1801 to 1803).

(*After the Picture by Kitagawa Utamaro.*)

language. Vanity is an inherent attribute of the fair sex, and among the class of women to whom the *yūjo* belong "*the rage for competition, show and style*" has no limits, consequently they all vie with each other in the attempt to outshine their sisters in the matter of obtaining, and placing on exhibition, piles of gorgeous bedding. It is a matter of professional pride for the girls to make as lavish a display as possible, and in former days, when the *go-sekku* were approaching the *yūjō* would persuade one of her most intimate guests to undertake the financing of this expensive function, and so well did they play their cards that they often succeeded in inducing their infatuated admirers to disburse several hundred dollars to gratify a passing whim. Nowadays, the holidays known as the *go-sekku* are not strictly observed, therefore exhibitions of *tsumi-yagu* are made either at the time of cherry-viewing in the spring, the lantern festival in the autumn, during the first week of the New Year (*matsu-no-uchi*) or at the time of the *tori-no-machi* (see description under that heading) when the Yoshiwara is most frequented by crowds of sight-seers. Generally speaking, this display of bedding is confined to the *ō-mise* (best houses) or *chū-mise* (medium houses), but occasionally the women in smaller houses endeavour to proclaim, by means of *tsumi-yagu*, that all the world does not belong to their prouder sisters in the better-class establishments. As I have previously mentioned, in ancient times gold and embroideries were used in making up this exhibition of bedding, but now damask and crêpe are mostly employed. The present cost (in 1899) of a set of *tsumi-yagu* is from 100 to 200 yen: by using *yūzen* crêpe the price may be kept as low as 100 yen, but damask will amount to 200 yen, and if a person is extravagantly inclined there are no limits to the cost. As the *tsumi-yagu* set would be charged at an exorbitant figure if purchased from an ordinary *gofuku-ten* (drapery store) they are usually ordered from one of the regular contractors in the Yoshiwara. There is generally a tremendous amount of bargaining done before the price of the *tsumi-yagu* is finally settled, and it is said that when the negotiations are made by the brothel-keeper, that astute gentleman invariably dovetails into the figure charged a commission of about 20% (twenty per cent.) as an honorarium presented to himself for "valuable services" rendered. A set of *tsumi-yagu* consists of three *futon* and a large coverlet or quilt: if it be summer a mosquito net is added, and if it be winter a lighter coverlet. As a rule the colours chosen are very loud indeed: the older women prefer pale-blue for the lining, but the younger girls usually have the coverlets lined with red. The *futon* are made like a mirror in a frame, the centre panels being of the same colour as the linings of the coverlets: the collars of the latter are made of velvet. On the coverlet is worked in gold thread the crest of the guest who has presented the set as well that of the *yūjo* who has received it. A small (light) coverlet (*ko-yagu*) is generally wadded with the best *wata* (cotton wool), but in large coverlets (*ō-yagu*) and *futon* an inferior quality of wadding is used. When the set is quite completed, it is placed on a stand and exhibited just inside the entrance of the brothel, facing the door-way, so that everybody who passes is bound to see the show: and in order to further attract attention, the *tsumi-yagu* is labelled with a paper on which is written in bold letters the name of the lucky *yūjo* who owns it. On the day of this ceremony it is usual for the guest concerned to give a "*sō-bana*" (*a present made to all the inmates of a house*) of 5 yen, and a further sum of 5 yen as "*soba-dai*" (*cost of buckwheat macaroni*) to be partaken of by all the *yūjo* in the establishment. As it is not considered to be conducive to the good reputation of a woman to continue this exhibition of *tsumi-yagu* for too great a length of time, there arises the necessity for another ceremony called "*shiki-zome*" (commencing the use of the *yagu*). On this occasion the lady in question plays the part of hostess, and she is bound by custom to entertain the guest who has presented her with the set by giving him a feast and engaging at least a couple of *geisha* to enliven the proceedings. When a guest undertakes to provide a set of *tsumi-yagu* for his *innamorata* he must be prepared to spend on tips, and for various sundries, at least 50 yen over and above the cost of the bedding, and if he makes a *hikite-jaya* a party to the arrangement this will cost him another 10% (per cent.) commission. An exhibition of *tsumi-yagu* being considered something to be proud of, women who have no guests rich enough to render them the necessary pecuniary assistance occasionally go so far as to even borrow funds from the brothel-keepers and order a set of bedding for themselves, thus securing a fine advertisement and enhacing their reputation. It however sometimes happens that the girls find themselves unable to refund money thus borrowed, and are therefore compelled to dispose of the bedding they once so earnestly coveted: these circumstances have tended to place a number of second-hand sets of *tsumi-yagu* on the market, and it is a said that certain women who are vain enough to love empty show, but too poor to afford it, borrow these relics of extravagance on hire and exhibit them to the public gaze! But here let us be merciful and draw a veil over the doings of these unfortunate women, for it would be boorish and unmanly to further expose the weakness of frail humanity. [As to the origin of this custom, it appears that a *kōshi-jōro* of the Miura-ya (kept by Magosaburō) named Utanami, first introduced it in the era of Kwampō (1741-1743)].

"Sobana."

(All round "tips.")

A "*sōbana*" is a tip by a guest to all the servants of a brothel, and is shared in by the *yarite, shinzō,* men-servants, and bath-room attendants. It is usually given on a *mombi* (crest day: New year's day, the *go-sekku tori-no-machi* festival, etc.) and varies in amount according to the class of house: the sums given are regularly classified and divided into amounts of 2½, 3, 4, and 5 *Yen*, etc., as the case may be. When *sōbana* is given, the names of the donor and his lady friend are posted in a prominent place in the house: the larger the number of such posters, the greater is the honour to the woman in question. This custom appears to have been in vogue since ancient times, for the amounts fixed during the Kwansei era (1789-1800) were 3 *ryō* for a first-class house, 2 *ryō* for a second-class house, 1 *ryō* 2 *bu* for a third-class house, 2 *bu* for a lower grade establishment. When a *sōbana* is given, all the servants of the house come up to the room and kneeling down outside thank the guest for his present and clap their hands in unison.

"Shokwai"

(First meeting)

AND

"Mi-tate"

(Selection of women.)

The "*Zensei Kuruwa Kagami*" (全盛廓鑑) says that in the dusk of the evening, when all is chilly and lonesome, the

Introduction of Courtesans to Guests.

deep-toned curfew bell of Iriya sends forth a resonant and withal melancholy clang which depresses the spirits and fills the heart with a vague sense of gloomy sadness. Strange as the coincidence may be, just at the very time the solemn sound of the temple bell is reverberating over hill and dale, the women file into their cages (*misé wo haru*) in the brothel quarter, the "*flowers of the Yoshiwara bud and blossom*," and the whole *yūkwaku* becomes a scene of vivacious animation. These courtesans (who have practically fallen to the level of being regarded as so much merchandise awaiting buyers) sit for hours exposed to the gaze of the passers-by, decked out in all the splendour of coral and rare tortoise-shell hair-pins stuck around their heads like a saint's glory, and gorgeous in dresses of silk and gold and silver embroidery, the heavy cost of which weighs them down and forces them still deeper into the "*stream of debt.*" In days of yore it was customary for the women to enter their *misé* while the "*sugagaki*" was being played and bunches of clog-checks (*gesoku-fuda* = wooden tickets given to guests in exchange for foot-gear left in charge of attendants at the entrance) were being struck noisily against the floor. Among the *yūjo* the *o shoku kabu* (or proud leading beauty of the house) with painted face, rouged lips, and penciled eyebrows, sits lazily smoking her long red bamboo pipe, emitting faint blue rings of tobacco smoke from her mouth, pretending not to see the crowds of people swarming in front of the cage and yet—cat-like—furtively watching their every movement. While the other women are engaged in a whispered conversation about the personal appearance of on-lookers, the *o shoku* feigns to be absorbed in the perusal of a long espistle supposed to have been received from one of her numerous admirers, and every now and again she artfully allows a smile to irradiate her countenance as a token that she is reading a specially interesting sentence. Such a skilful Jezebel is sure to have some rich guests who keep her liberally supplied with funds: as a rule she will have no lover (*jōrō* 情郎 = a male paramour: sometimes read as "*ii hito*") to whom she must give pecuniary assistance, and generally speaking she will avoid *koke-kyaku* (young and impecunious guests) and *san-jaku-obi* (low class of loafers) as she would the pest. Rather slender in person, having a good contour of the nose, and possessed of bright eyes, if she cannot be called strictly beautiful she is at least very interesting and attractive. This "Dainty Iniquity" (as Kipling puts it) is always sure to be a perfect actress, and looks irresistibly charming as she talks with her sister *yūjo* in a whisper or as she gracefully bends her head and covers her face with her sleeves to stifle an apparently spontaneous burst of merry laughter and then quietly flirts with, and encourages, some likely guest who is gazing at her intently through the bars. The above is a rather lengthy description of a *yūjo* who is expert in the art of twisting men round her little finger and manipulating guests (*kyaku wo nekokasu*) according to the circumstances of the occasion. Those women who are worried by anxiety about private affairs will be seen to conceal their hands within the folds of their dress, to allow their heads to sink deeply into their *eri* (collar of a dress) in an irregular manner, to every now and then glance round the cage and up at the ceiling, or to otherwise reveal, by their fidgety and impatient demeanour, that they have something unpleasant on their minds. Those who act unreservedly and chat noisily

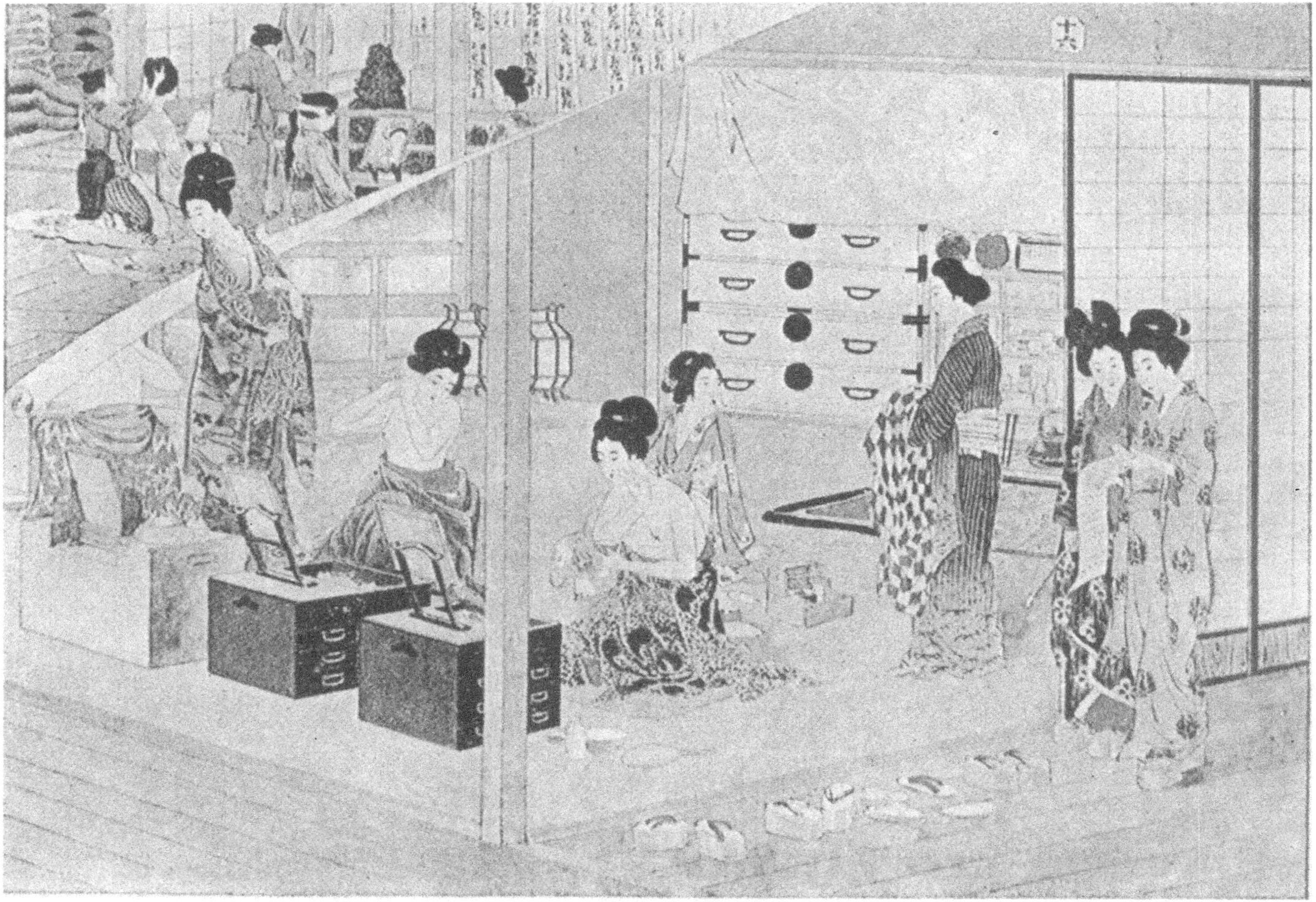

Courtesans making their toilettes.

with the other women are assuredly new to the life, and when they become familiar with guests they are unfeignedly sincere in their regard for those they like. The woman who sits out of the row sideways and listens to the ribald songs of the passers-by shows her fickle and forward disposition by treating all as fish who come to her net: she has sympathy with no man but as a matter of business policy and will bestow equal attention on all comers, no matter whether they be good-looking, bad-looking, or jealous as fiends. Those who are blowing the berry of the winter-cherry (*hōzuki*), making paper-frogs as a charm to attract the men for whom they are waiting, practising "*tatami-zan*" (divination by mat-straws) and playing other innocent little games, are generally new arrivals in the house who are willing to please their guests in every possible manner.

When a guest wishes to be accommodated with a "temporary wife," and enters the house to which she belongs, he is led by a *wakai-mono* to the *hiki-tsuke-zashiki* (introduction chamber). If he glances round the room he will perhaps find the alcove decorated with a large *kakemono* (hanging-picture) representing the rising sun and a stork, the ceiling painted with an enormous phœnix, and everything so spick and span that he will wonder whether he is in fairyland. Candles are now lighted, and a black-lacquered tobacco-box brought in. Next a set of three *saké*-cups are produced with which to perform (though nominally) the necessary nuptial ceremony called the "*san-san-ku-do*" in imitation of the custom observed at a real wedding. The girl then appears accompanied by her *shinzō* who plays the part of a go-between (*nakōdo-yaku*) for the couple by uttering the conventional phrases of "*anata*" and "*konata*," and the unholy "marriage" ceremony is finished. After this the *yūjo* retires to change her clothes, (*o meshi-kae*) and at the same time the guest is conducted to her apartments where the table is laid ready and a charcoal fire is glowing in an enormous brazier. This bright red, and almost incandescent charcoal fire, always reminds one of the ardent passion of the poor devil of a guest in the next room, who alone and waiting for his partner glows with all the rage of jealousy and intense longing! Food is served in dishes of enormous size, but the net contents of these platters are microscopic, so the "feast" amounts to little more than a mere show and is just sufficiently imposing to warrant being handsomely charged for in the bill under the title of "*On ryōri*" (the august repast). The chopsticks used are new for the occasion and are regular *wari-bashi* (a stick made of *sugi* wood with a split at one end, used as chopsticks by splitting it in two) but, alas! they too are soon prostituted to base uses, being used as snuffers to cut candle wicks, and even as tongs for the *hibachi* of a tenantless room!*

It is curious to note that when tea-house people offer a *sakê*-cup to the *yūjo* they invariably sit obliquely, partially turning their backs to the guest and never facing him directly. Perhaps this custom unintentionally betrays their secret intention of sitting on the visitor, squeezing him for all he is worth, and then kicking him out! The *yūjo* herself at the first meeting with a new guest is apt to look askant at the latter and "draw" him by occasionally gossiping about her "sisters-in-vice." Every now and again one may faintly hear the sound of a pipe being sharply struck against a bamboo spittoon

* *Mawashi-beya* 廻し房 is a kind of spare room in which a guest is accommodated when the *yūjo* he hires has another visitor in her own apartments.

Interior of a Brothel. 1. Nightwatchman (interior) on his rounds.
2. Time-keeper's office. 3. *Yūjo* arranging various matters with the "*yarite*."

in a neighbouring room: this is probably a signal that your neighbour is lonely and weary of waiting for his sleeping-companion, and you may make up your mind that he is craning his neck forward and straining his ears to catch the sound of her returning footsteps. It is said that a warrior awakens at the jingling of a horse's bridle-bit, but, under the above circumstances, the sound of a woman's sandaled feet shuffling down the passage appeals to the drowsy watcher with ten times as much force and braces him up like a powerful tonic. In Japan, however, men do not like to show themselves too "soft," and when the woman finally slides back the *shōji* (paper shutter) of the room her guest is almost sure to sham being fast asleep: this is called "*tanuki-neiri*" (badger-sleep). As the hour advances, the crowds of loafers (known as "*hiyakashi*") in the Yoshiwara gradually disperse and nothing, except the cries of peripatetic macaroni sellers ("*nabeyaki udon*") and blind shampooers ("*amma-hari*") and the dismal howling of impish mongrels disturb the stillness of the night; but even when comparative quietness has been restored, the guest's sleep has been so thoroughly broken that he remains tossing uneasily on his pillow longing for daylight. After a few hours of fitful slumber, which leave the wretched fellow even more fatigued than before, the eastern sky begins to glow with a faint rosy light, and with the dawn of day the great black crows in the neighbourhood awake and fly circling around, cawing loudly as if in mockery and derision. Jaded and exhausted by excess, and played out by reason of his night's debauch, the poor guest crawls wearily out of bed, feeling as limp as a dish-clout, and as a preparation for his return home proceeds to drag himself to the wash-stand and make his toilet. Oh,! what a face he sees reflected in the water—a drawn, distorted, and haggard face, with pale bloodless lips and sunken bloodshot eyes! And oh! the nausea resulting from undigested food and adulterated *saké*, the agony of "hot coppers," the racking headache, and the formidable bill—six feet long—which makes one's hair rise on end! Then the woebegone victim of his own asinine stupidity settles his bill and sneaks away from the presence of the *yūjo*, who comes to bid him farewell with the words—"*o chikai uchi*................" (please come again very soon), climbs heavily into a *jinrikisha* and is whirled away to his own residence, thoroughly agreeing in spirit with the words of the Vulgate:—"*vanitas vanitatum, et omnia vanitas.*"

"I-tsu-dzuke no koto."

(*Spending several consecutive days in a brothel.*)

The "*Zensei-Kuruwa-Kagami*" (全盛廓鑑) says:—"The act of remaining in a brothel for several days, owing to stress of weather or other cause, is known as *i-tsu-dzuke.*"

"O cha wo hiku" to iu koto.

("*Tea powdering.*")

It is remarked in the "*Dōbō Go-yen*" (洞房語園) that the term *o-cha wo hiku*, as applied to women of ill-fame who have no guests, is of ancient origin and should be considered as one of the peculiar idiomatic expressions of the Yoshiwara dialect: everywhere in prostitute quarters some special dialect is exclusively used, and this is more especially true of the Yoshiwara of Tōkyō. In the era of Keichō (1596-1614) the servants of the various tea-houses at Uji (near Kyōto) were

Guest Detained by "Love and Stress of Weather." Kiōwa period (1801 to 1803).

(After the Picture by Kitagawa Utamaro.)

practically unlicensed courtesans, and were in the habit of carrying on illicit intercourse with guests who patronized their establishments. These women employed their *leisure* time in pulverizing tea (*o-cha wo hiku*) for the tea-drinking ceremony, and in course of time this expression "*o-cha wo hiku*" came to be applied (as a slang phrase) to a courtesan who had no guests in consequence of her unpopularity. By and bye this phrase was brought up to Tokyo by natives of Uji and Kyōto and became one of the idiomatic expressions of the Yoshiwara. It is now used throught the entire Empire.

Shiki-zome no soba-burumai no koto.

(*Presentation of buck-wheat macaroni to celebrate the first use of night-clothes.*)

It appears to be a universal rule to present *soba* to all the inmates of the house whenever a *yūjo* uses her newly-made night-clothes for the first time. This custom is binding on all classes of women from the proud *oiran* down to the *nagaya-jōro*, but, practically, the lower class women are debarred from making an exhibition of night-clothes (either on their own account or by the assistance of guests) by reason of the expense involved: it may therefore be said that this ceremony is performed by women belonging to first (*ō-misé*) and second-class (*chū-misé*) houses exclusively. Originally this ceremony was only performed when the *tsumi-yagu* was used for the first time, but later it became a rule that when any new night-clothes began to be used—generally on New Year's day—buckwheat macaroni was to be presented to the inmates of her house by the *yūjo* to whom they belonged. This custom, which still survives, is called "*shiki-zome no soba-*

burumai." In the houses of ordinary people the spreading out of bedding and night-clothes in the day time is greatly disliked as unlucky, therefore, when a sick person recovers, the occasion is one of rejoicing and congratulation and is called *toko-agé* (removal of bed-clothes). In brothels, however, just the reverse idea obtains, the keepers rejoice to see the night-clothes used even in the day-time, their fervent wish being to have the bedding employed as much as possible because it bears an important relation to the prosperity of their "trade."

In different brothels different devices are adopted for the purpose of determining who shall be considered the "leading lady" of the house (*o shoku*). Some take the number of guests as a standard, others the number of *najimi-kyaku* (that is "regular guests") while others adopt the rather disgusting method of fixing the order of precedence according to the total amount of money spent by the guests of the respective women. In first-class establishments no such methods as the above are employed, and the rank of the women is determined by the number and value of their own night-clothes and those given by them to the servants of their own and other houses. The idea may be attributed to the great esteem in which night-clothes are held by both men and women in the Yoshiwara.

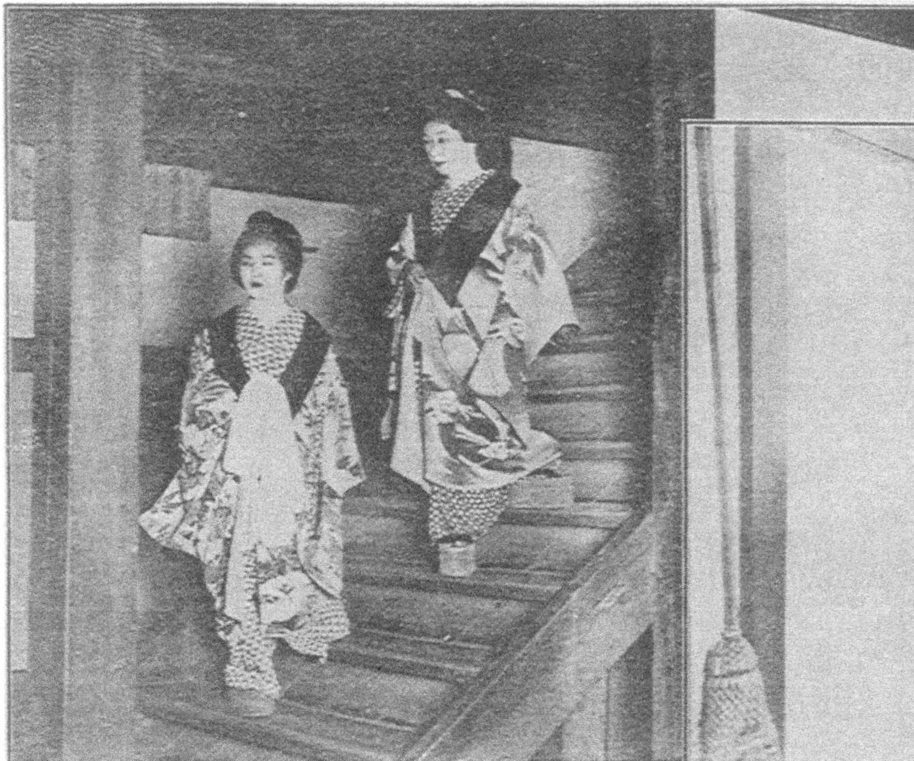

Courtesans on their "Rounds" visiting Various Guests at Night.

Courtesan entering a Guest's Room.

"Shashin-mitate-chō."

(Photograph albums for facilitating the selection of women.)

In lower-class houses the women are exhibited after nightfall, when the lamps are lighted, in the long narrow cages of the brothels, where they sit with powdered faces and rouged lips looking for all the world like so many motionless wax figures, and are, to all intents and purposes, set out for sale like ordinary articles of merchandise. Under these conditions, a would-be guest has the opportunity of making his selection very easily, for he has only to indicate the woman he fancies to obtain her company immediately. In the first and second-class houses, however, there is no such thing as a *hari-misé* (a " dressed shop-front ") and persons who intend to visit them must be introduced by a *hikite jaya:* the selection of the particular girl to be engaged is usually left to the discretion of the mistress of the tea-house, who of course does her best to please her patrons by choosing for them women likely to prove satisfactory.

Until about 1882 (15th or 16th year of Meiji) the photographs of all the inmates of houses were displayed in frames in front of the respective brothels, but now this plan has been abandoned, and albums containing portraits of the women belonging to first and second-class houses are provided in the *hikite-jaya* for the the convenience of guests. These books are called "*Shashin Mitate-chō*" (albums of photopraphs to facilitate the selection of women), and it is believed that the following specimens of prefaces will be interesting :—

Photograph-album of the *O-hiko-rō :—*

"The old saying '*if you wish to see flowers go to Yoshino*' "seems somewhat stupid considering that one can find any "flower which he desires to see if he goes to the Yoshiwara. "Nowadays, however, customs of ancient times are changing, "and the flowers no longer parade the Naka-no-chō. The flowers "which are shown to the public are limited to those which "blossom on the small fences, while the *oiran* (who may be "likened to the queen of all flowers) are concealed from the "public view in the privacy of their own chambers, and may be "compared to beautiful blossoms hidden from sight by a dense "mist. However, the practice of promenading in the Naka-no-"chō is too old a custom to be revived in these times, and so we "have hit upon the plan of grouping a bevy of belles into the "space of a small photograph-album, and leave our honour-"able guests to select the flowers their fancy may dictate, etc., "etc."

This preface winds up with a poetical appeal—quite untranslatable owing to puns on words—that the patronage of guests "may not be as short as the dream of a spring night," but as steady and constant as the bedding used in this house is thick and beautiful. [In Japanese the word "thick"—*atsui*—has a double meaning: it means "thick" as an antonym of "thin," and also "plentiful, liberal, and bountiful." It also has the sense of "excessively friendly" or "intimate," and is sometimes used to express the idea of "in love with."]

Photograph-album of the *Kado-ebi-rō*:—

"The Chinese character *kōzen* 紅髯=redbeard) may be also "read *kōzen* (浩然=resolute: firm) on account of the similarity of "sound, and the characters *kairō* (=海老 a shrimp. These charac-"ters also sound as "*ebi*") which is part of the name of this house "and resemble in pronunciation the letter *kairō* (偕老=becom-"ing old together and being buried in the same spot undivided "even by death. In the letters in use from times immemorial "are ideas not fully expressed. Individual selection may be "left to individual taste."

Guests making their toilettes preparatory to leaving the house.

Shōgi no nedan ai-jirushi.

(The signs or cyphers showing the fees of courtesans).

According to the "*Kyokutei-Zakki*" (曲亭雜記), written by the well-known novelist Bakin, the *tayū* were all represented by the mark ⧗ in the *saiken** (guide-books) during the Kyōhō era (1716-1735) * * * * At that time the price was 60 *momme* (10 *Yen*). A class of courtesans called *kyō no tayū* came into existence at the time, but dropped out of fashion without receiving much attention from the public. The various classes of women were represented by the following marks from the era of Kyōhō (1716-1735) to the Hōreki era (1751-1763) :—

⧗ Tayū : 井 Kōshi-jōro : 亽 Ni-nin Kaburo : 合 Yobi-dashi : ⏏ Tsuki-dashi : 仌 Zashiki-mochi : 仌 Kōkin : 仌 Bunkin : ◓ Chū-ya : ⊜ Ni-shu : ✕ Uchi-komi : Yama-sancha : Umecha : ㊄ Go-sun Tsubone : ● Nami-Tsubone and Ha-age-ya : ■ Chaya. By the 6th year of Gembun (1741) the fees of courtesans were stated in *Saiken* for the first time as follows :—

⧗ Tayū, 80 *momme* (*Yen* 13.33) ; 井 Kōshi, 60 *momme*, (10 *Yen*) : ヨ Yobidashi, 45 *momme* (*Yen* 7.50) ; ▲ Sancha (for day and night) 3 *Bu* (*Yen* 7.50) ; ● Bun, 1 *Bu* (*Yen* 2.50) ; ✕ 12 *momme* (2 *Yen*) ; ㊃ *Shi-sun :* ⊖ Nami-Tsubonė ; ∴ six tea-houses attached to the *ageya.* Since then matters have undergone various changes, but the following are the present (1899) cyphers used in the *Saiken-ki* :—

---

* The Yoshiwara Office publishes these guide-books at intervals. The books contain the names and fees of inmates of the various brothels.

			Yen. Sen.
(Iriyamagata hitotsu-boshi)		fee is	1.20
(Iri-yamagata)		"	.90
(Mitsu-yamagata hitotsu-boshi)		"	.60
(Mitsu-yamagata)		"	.50
(Futatsu-yamagata hitotsu-boshi)		"	.40
(Shiro-yamagata)		"	.35
(Yamagata hitotsu-boshi)		"	.30
(Yamagata)		"	.25
(Tsuji)	X	"	.20

San-gyō chōmen no tsuke-kata.

(*The system of book-keeping employed by brothels, tea-houses, and courtesans.*)

In former days there were no fixed rules as to the system of making entries in books kept by brothels and tea-houses, and, in consequence, considerable inconvenience was experienced by the authorities when they found it necessary to examine the accounts. In February, 1884, the "Controller of the Three Professions" fixed a uniform system of entries to be made in the account-books of brothels and tea-houses, instructing the proprietors of such establishments to adhere to the same in future. The system thus inaugurated in 1884 is still in force, and the following is a description of the ledgers, etc., used.

On the cover of a brothel ledger—right in the very centre—are written the words "*Kashizashiki Motochō,*" on the right "*Meiji nan nen nan gatsu nan nichi yori, nan nen nan gatsu nan nichi made*" (From the............day of............, to the............day of............, 189.....); and on the left the name of the house and its proprietor. The book is to consist of upwards of 200 sheets of *Nishi-no-uchi* or *Ōban-shi* (paper), and the following particulars are to be printed in it :—

1.—Name of the brothel.

2.—That the book is to be preserved for at least four years.

3.—That taxes are to be paid daily in accordance with the regulations.

4.—That in this book are to be entered in detail the names of every guest, names of the *shōgi* engaged, names of *geisha* called, names of the *hikite-jaya* concerned, the fees of *shōgi* and *geisha*, amounts spend by guests, advances made, etc. [These items may be expressed by signs (in cypher) but their total must be written in ordinary characters.]

5.—That in the first page of this book the signs (cyphers) to be used in a brothel in describing various items shall be shown, and that in case of alteration of such cyphers due notice shall be given to the manager's office.

6.—That besides this ledger the use of two memorandum books (one for the proprieter of the house and one for the *shōgi* herself) shall be allowed, but that such memorandum books shall be stamped with the stamp of the manager and be kept at least for one year.

7.—That the payment of taxes shall be made in accordance with this ledger, and that daily accounts shall be made up in the following form. (The monthly accounts shall be made up in the same manner.)

(*See over.*)

(ACCOUNT FORM.)

Number of guests ....

Number of women engaged ....

Total gross receipts.................... *Yen.*

ITEMIZED ACCOUNT.	*Yen.*	*Sen.*
Shōgi age-dai (Courtesan's fees)		
Sekiryō nan ko (Hire of rooms).............................		
Shu-kō-han ko-mono-dai (*Saké*, food and sundries)		
Geigi age-dai (*Geisha*-fees)		
Shūgi sono hoka tate-kae (Gratuities and advances)........		
Total receipts of the brothel.................		
Taxes due thereon..................		
Total receipts of the courtesans		
Taxes due thereon..................		
Total taxes due......................		

The foregoing rules are issued by the Metropolitan Police Board and are to be strictly complied with.

(Date)...........................

Controller of the *Shin-Yoshiwara.*

(The number of pages in this book are................)

The signs used in this book are as follows :—

○	Fee of courtesan ....*sen*
●	Ditto.
□	Ditto.
■	Ditto.
△	*Geisha's* fee ....*sen.*
	Food.

 Ditto.

 *Saké*, 1 bottle ....*sen.*

 *Saké*, 2 bottles ....*sen.*

EXAMPLE OF THE USE OF ABOVE CYPHER.

Date..................

Name of *hikite-jaya.*

 Name of guest.

" " courtesan.

  " " guest.

" " courtesan.

  " " guest.

" " courtesan.

Total..................

The above example shows that a party of three guests engaged three *shōgi* and one *geisha*, the latter having been employed during the burning of four joss-sticks (*senkō*). It also shows that they were supposed to have ordered three sets of *ō-dai* (large dishes) and one set of *nami-dai* (small-dishes) and consumed four bottles of *saké*. It is superfluous to give an example of the system of book-keeping employed in *hikite-jaya* because it is practically the same.

There is another small book (*te-bikae*) kept by each *shōgi* which is commonly known as the "*gyoku-chō*" and in which the number of her engagements is noted. As to the mode of entering up this *gyoku-chō*, there appears to be no fixed rule, but according to the regulations each *shōgi* must make up an account of her earnings every ten days and get the entry certified by the stamp of the brothel-keeper. This book must be kept as long as she remains in the business.

Mr. Norman, in his "*The Real Japan,*" observes with regard to the book-keeping methods of the Yoshiwara:—"It goes without saying that no Solomon could devise theoretical safeguards which would practically protect a girl under such circumstances from unscrupulous greed. For instance, every person in Japan has a private seal corresponding to a signature with us, with which all documents, even down to private letters, are attested, and to counterfeit or reproduce such a seal is forgery. Now the keeper of every *kashi-zashihi* is compelled by law to keep a big ledger in which all money transactions between himself and the *shōgi* are entered, and the *shōgi* is compelled to keep a similar smaller book in which the keeper makes identical entries, each of which must be attested by her private seal. This book is regularly inspected by the police with a view to prevent extortion, and it is expressly forbidden by law for the keeper to take away the girl's seal. On one occasion I visited the largest and best *kashi-zashiki* in the Yoshiwara in company with my official interpreter. The keeper was a sharp-looking woman of fifty, who had 45 *shōgi* in her house, which she had just built at a cost of 45,000 dollars. We were taking tea ceremoniously in her private apartments, and after a while I inquired if I might put a special question to her. "Certainly," she replied. "Any question?" "Certainly." "Then," I said to the old lady through my official interpreter, "will you be so kind as to show me some of the seals belonging to your ladies, that you have at this moment in your possession." She winced visibly and turned several colours, but after a minute got up without a word, trotted off and returned immediately with the private seal of a certain Miss Man, and I took an impression of it in my note-book, to her evident great alarm. This meant, of course, that she was in the habit of entering the accounts in all the books, attesting them herself with the seals of all her *yūjo*, and thus the police would be shown an immaculate record, while the *shōgi* themselves would never even see the books, or know with how much they were debited and credited from week to week."

By the way, a hypothetical specimen of the entries made in a book kept by courtesans is given in the "*Share-bon*" (洒落本) written by Jippensha Ikku—the ancient Mark Twain of Japan.

HOW A VISITOR'S BOOK SHOULD BE KEPT.

1st	●	(first)	Dearly beloved one. Oh! how I love you! come—do come! *Hamanoya.*
2nd	○ ●		Vexing and horribly irritating. *Kichisama.*
3rd	●		As he does not know my real mind it is very irritating. *Ryūsama.*
4th	●	(second)	Oh! you sickeningly ugly brute! Your face is like that of Heisaku the Octapus! *Sumiya.*
5th	●	(first)	The fellow looks just like Hachibei of Tamachi. (*i.e.* "*an ass.*") *Iseya.*
6th	○ ●	(first)	I love you! Come quickly! *Sumiya.*
7th	●	(first)	Yes you are handsome: if you want to come then come. *Minatoya.*
8th	○ ●		Ah! what joy and gladness! *Minatoya* (and) *Yasu Sama.*

Yūjo no hiki-fuda.

(*Brothel advertisements*).

Up to the 20th year of Meiji, both brothels and *hikite-jaya* were in the habit of freely distributing hand-bills for the purpose of attracting guests, but since then all classes of advertisements, having for their object the enticing of visitors to prostitute quarters, have been strictly prohibited by the authorities. Under these circumstances, it may prove interesting to reproduce some specimens of the old hand-bills issued by enterprising brothel-keepers in past times, and accordingly they are printed below.

[*Note.*—The first of these two hand-bills is dated the 5th month of the 1st year of Kayei (1848), the second the 5th month of the 1st year of Ansei (May 1854) and the third the 8th year of Meiji (1875). The last-named, unlike the others, was neither "antique" nor "refined" and was printed on foreign paper with regular foreign-style type, showing that the resources of civilization are pressed into every kind of service in this go-ahead country!]

Specimen No. 1.

It affords me much pleasure to know that my patrons are all doing well. By reason of your kind patronage and favour, for which I am extremely grateful, I have been enabled to continue the business of brothel-keeping for many years, but regret to observe that there are signs that the prosperity of the Yoshiwara is on the wane. The cause of this state of affairs may be attributed to the fact that evil practices have arisen in the houses of some of my confrères, who are carrying on their profession according to the dictates of their own fancies and entirely disregarding the regulations promulgated in the era of Kwanséi (1789-1800). For instance, a custom has arisen of paying to *hikite-jaya* as much as 300 to 350 *mon* (about 30 to 35 *sen*) commission for each 2 *shu* (*yen* 1.25) spent by a guest, or even of equally dividing between tea-house and brothel the amount of money spent by him, the consequence being that more than three hundred *hikite-jaya* have sprung into

(Terms "spot cash.")
遊女大安賣
(No introducer required.)
(*Filles de joie* for sale at very cheap prices.)

existence within the past few years. Under these circumstances, it follows as an inevitable consequence that the food and drink served to guests is allowed to deteriorate in quality, thus causing a general depression in our "trade." I have therefore hit upon a different plan of carrying on the profession, and decided not to receive any guests sent from tea-houses in future, but to conduct my business on cheap and expeditious lines at the "spot cash" prices mentioned below. Moreover I have engaged a large number of "*filles de joie*" who are guaranteed to afford satisfaction to guests in every respect, and I propose to pay scrupulous attention to the quality of *saké*, *food*, and *bedding*. I shall be greatly obliged if you will kindly inform your friends of these improvements introduced by me, and earnestly beg that you will favour me with a visit, either in the daytime or night-time, coming direct to my establishment without making your arrangement through a tea-house.

		(Hitherto.)	(Reduced price.)
1.	Women possessing *zashiki*	*1 Bu*	*12 momme* (*silver*)
		(*Yen 2.50*	(*Yen 2.00*)
2.	" " *heya*	*2 Shu*	*6 Momme* (")
		(*Yen 1.25*	(*Yen 1.00*)
3.	*Private geisha*..................	*2 Shu*	*6 Momme* (")
		(*Yen 1.25*	(*Yen 1.00*)

N.B.—We supply the "*Masamunê*" brand of *saké*, and our cuisine is fully equal to that of the leading restaurants.

Tips and gratuities to "lady friends" and *geisha* may be given according to the discretion of guests.

Positively no guest sent through a tea-house will be received or entertained.

(Date)

(Signed) MANJI-YA MOKICHI,
Sumi-chō,
Shin Yoshiwara.

Should any woman be found unsatisfactory another may be substituted.

Specimen No. 2.

Verbal Message.

I am exceedingly glad to know that my patrons are all in good health. I am also thankful that, owing to the long period of continued tranquillity and peace we are enjoying, I have been enabled to pursue my occupation undisturbed for many years. Wishing to introduce some novelty for the amusement of my guests, I have devised a new style of dance which is performed by my *yūjo* to the accompaniment of popular songs. This dance is something like that anciently performed by *shira-byōshi* (a kind of singing girl of the *Hetaira* type) and I am confident that it will prove a source of pleasure to my august patrons. Persons coming to my establishment, either through the medium of tea-houses or direct, will be treated with all possible courtesy and attention, and as regards the question of expenses the aim of my house will be to make my prices as moderate as may be compatible with doing everything conducive to the entertainment of guests. I hope that this new departure may be made known to the public at large, the members of which are respectfully solicited to visit my house in an unceasing stream (in numbers).

Hire of *yūjo*, and cost of *saké*, soup, *on-suzuributa* (a tray of cooked foods), *on-hachizakana* (fish served in dishes), and *mitsu-mono* (a set of three procelain vessels containing food).	3 *Bu.* (*Yen* 7.50)
Hire of *yūjo* and cost of *saké*, soup, a tray of cooked food, and *mitsumono.*	2 *Bu.* (*Yen* 5.00)
Hire of *yūjo* and cost of *saké*, soup, *kuchi-tori* (a side dish), and *mitsumono.*	1 *Bu* 2 *Shu.* (*Yen* 3.75)
Hire of *yūjo* and cost of *saké*, soup, side-dish, and *futatsu-mono.*	1 *Bu.* (*Yen* 2.50)
Hire of *yūjo* and cost of *saké*, soup, and *futatsu-mono.*	2 *Shu.* (*Yen* 1.25)
Per *geisha* and cost of one dish of food.	2 *Shu.* (*Yen* 1.25)

N.B.—For those who do not like *saké*, tea and *kuchi-tori* (a side dish of sweet food) will be served.

In force from the 10th day of the 5th month (cycle of the Tiger).

DAIKOKU-YA BUNSHIRŌ.
Yedo-chō It-chō-me,
Shin Yoshiwara.

Specimen No. 3.

Notice.

At the time of the establishment of the *Sangyō-kwaisha* (office of the "three professions") I was obliged, by reason of unavoidable circumstances, to transact the business of the office, and in consequence trouble arose between the brothel-keepers and owners of tea-houses. For a time it appeared as if the trouble had blown over, but apparently such is not the case, as I now learn that the tea-houses have combined and agreed not to send a single guest to my house. Far from being affected by their compact, my business is as brisk as ever, because, I depend on my patrons themselves and not on the tea-houses. Nor is this all, for when the three and twenty fair ladies (*oiran*) who belong to my house heard about the selfish decision of the tea-house keepers, they justly gave vent to their indignation at this attempt to interfere with their profession. They proposed that in future they and I should combine to increase the popularity of our house, and with this end in view I have been urged by the *oiran* to do all in my power to ensure the satisfaction of guests, while they on their part have promised to coöperate with me in order to convince the tea-house folk of the fact that the Yoshiwara would prosper without any *hikite-jaya* at all. What is meant by the resolution of the fair damsels it is for visitors to my house to explain. Accordingly I have decided on the following plan of action :—Firstly, to endeavour to curtail the expenses of guests to the lowest possible figure, and secondly, to see that every care is taken to ensure their pleasant entertainment. As to the females in waiting, their number will be further increased, and they will appear clad like the graceful *nakai* (waitresses) of Kyōto and Ōsaka. Care will also be exercised in the *cuisine* of my house, and certain dishes will be served without extra charge. These alterations will take effect on and after September 1st next, and it will then remain with you to test the truth of this announcement. I trust that these facts will become known far and wide, and hope to be favoured with your continued visits and patronage.

September, 1875.

KIMPEI DAIKOKU,
(*Kashi-zashiki* keeper)
Yedo-chō It-chō-me,
Shin-Yoshiwara.

Ageya no sashi-gami.

(*Summons to the "Ageya."*)

In ancient times a guest was unable to visit a brothel direct, but had to negotiate for the services of courtesans through the "*Age-ya.*" The "*Age-ya*" then issued a written request or "summons" (*sashi-gami*) to the brothel, nominating the woman desired. The bearer of these *sashi-gami* accompanied the courtesans both going and coming between brothels and "*Age-ya,*" and as soon as guests had finished their "spree" and left, the *yūjo* were sent back to their respective houses. In the "*Kwagai Manroku*" 花街漫錄) a specimen copy of the summons is given: the size is about 11″ × 5″ (actually 9 *sun* 6 *bu* × 4 *sun* 3 *bu*) and wording as follows:—

Specimen of "*Sashigami.*"

To Shōzaburō Esq.

As we have a guest to-day, we desire to engage the services of a courtesan belonging to your house named Tsumasaki during the day-time. I guarantee that my guest is not one of those persons who are "wanted" by the authorities, but a respectable party, and should anyone be found to allege anything to the contrary I am prepared to offer an explanation of the matter at any time or place. The above is written for future reference.

5th day of the 5th month.

(Signed.) KYŪYEMON. (Proprietor.) (SEAL.)

(Countersigned.) CHŌBEI. (Monthly Manager.) (SEAL.)

The above was issued iu the "*year of the dog*"—the second year of Tenna (1682)—and at that time Shōzaemon was the keeper of the "Kadomanji-ya" in Sumi-chō. Again, in the same book, (*Kwagai Manroku*) are given the following rules, relating to *age-ya*, which were in force in the Tenna era:—

1.—*Yūjo* shall not be detained after the departure of a guest.

2.—A man-servant shall be provided by the *ageya* for the purpose of escorting *yūjo* to and from the tea-house: such servant to be barefooted (*su-ashi.*)

3.—Should a courtesan be unwilling to attend any particular guest, the *yarite* (female manager ot a brothel) shall endeavour to prevail upon her to re-consider her decision, and, if the negotiation be successful, a summons shall be sent to her and the fee paid at the time of settling accounts. [In practice, the *yarite* had the option of deciding whether or not the guest should be accepted.]

4.—When a *yūjo* who had a previous engagement has been induced to attend to a later guest, the latter shall pay *shurai-gin* (an extra fee) to the tea-house which first engaged her. In case, however, of a substitute *yūjo* being chosen, no *shurai-gin* shall be paid, and if the original guest who had made special arrangements beforehand fails to appear, no room-rent (*zashiki-dai*) shall be charged.

Thus, when one wished to engage a courtesan in those times, he had to make a special arrangement in advance, fixing the date so as to avoid inconvenience, this agreement was termed a *ken-yaku* (兼約=a previous convenant). The act of inducing a woman to cancel a previous engagement in favour of a later guest was called "*morai*" (貰ひ=something received, (a gift), and when this was insisted upon, the successful bidder had to pay, besides the regular fee, an extra sum as compensation to the *age-ya* which was party to such previous engagement. This extra fee was the "*shurai-gin*" referred to in the above rules. The origin of the "*age-ya*" dates back to the

Moto-Yoshiwara, and by the eras of Tenna (1681-1683) and Teikyo (1684-1687) these establishments had reached the zenith of their popularity. Since the *sancha-jōro* appeared, the *age-ya* gradually declined until the 10th year of Hōreki, when they completely disappeared, leaving *hikita-jaya* in their place.

"Kuruwa-kotoba" or Yoshiwara Dialect.

It appears that owing to the Yoshiwara being a rendezvous of people from various parts of the country, there were a great many provincialisms spoken. This caused considerable inconvenience to persons visiting the quarter, and therefore, for the purpose of making the language used as uniform as possible, a kind of dialect known as the "*sato-kotoba*" (里言葉 language of the prostitute quarter) was coined, and all the prostitute were taught to speak it. The "*Hoku-jo-ryo Kigen*" (北女閭起原) says:—

> "When a woman speaks the Yoshiwara dialect it successfully conceals her awkward pronunciation, no matter from what distant part of the country she may have come, and stamps her as a regular denizen of the quarter. For this reason, study of *sato-kotoba* has been greatly encouraged."

It is, however, suggested by some people that the dialect was transmitted from Shimabara, Kyōto (a noted prostitute quarter) for under the "Shimabara" section of the "*Ukiyo Monogatari*" (浮世物語) reference is made to the popular *sato-kotoba* words "*kinanshita ka?*" (have you come?), and "*hayōinanshi*" (go quickly.)

According to ancient records, up to the period of Meiwa (1764-1771) the honorific irregular verb *masu* (to be), which is always used as a terminal in conjunction with other verbs, was corrupted to "*nsu*," therefore such words as *omoimasu* (to think) *gozaimasu* (to be: to have) and *mōshimashō* (to say, to be) were changed to "omoi*nsū*," "gozarin*su*," "moshi*n*shō," etc. From the end of Anyei (1772-1780) this again changed to "*isu*" and words like "*gozaimasu*" and "*omoimasu*" were pronounced "gozar*isu*" and "omo*isu*." At that period "*gozarimasu*" was often pronounced as "goza*nsu*," or even "oza*nsu*," and in the vulgar colloquial it was sometimes pronounced as "goz*ensu*" or "goz*ēsu*": accordingly "*nasarimasé*" (please deign to do) changed to "nasan*sé*," but in the Yoshiwara dialect this was further abbreviated to "na*nshi*. Thus instead of "*o kun nasai*" (an abbreviation of "*o kure nasarimasé*"=please do) and "*o agari nasaimashi* (an abbreviation of "*o agari nasaimasé*" =please come in: (or) please eat) were developed the words "o kun na*nshi*," and "o agan na*nshi*," etc. From the end of Kyōwa (1801-1803) until the Bunkwa era (1804-1817) "*masu*" and "*mashi*" changed to "*namashi*," and afterwards into *zansu*, *zaisu*, *zaimasu*, *ossu*, *osu*, *ariisu*, etc.

It also appears that in former times the various brothels had their own special dialects, but these, not being specially interesting, all the dialectical differences are omitted here.

A few examples of sundry sentences and expressions may be cited to give an idea of the language :—

Yoshiwara Dialect.	Modern Japanese.	English.
Nushi wa mada chaya ni iinsuka"	Anata wa mada chaya ni i-nasaru ka?	Are you still in the tea-house?
Kore wo o mi nanshi.	Kore wo goran nasai.	Please look at this.
Oide nasen ka e?	Oide nasaimasen ka?	Won't you go? (or) Won't you come?

Mō chitto shite mērin-shō.	Mō chitto shite mairi-mashō.	I will go (or "come") a little later on.
Uso-uso shimē yo.	Sawaijā ikenai.	Don't be excited.
Sonnara o tano-mō-shinsu.	Sonnara o tanomi mō-shimasu.	Well then I will leave the matter in your hands.
Sore wa tareshi mo sō de ozansu.	Sore wa dare demo sō de gozaimasu.	That is the case with everybody.
Sō ossēsu ga.	Sō osshaimasu ga.....	You say so but.......
Kurashinsu zo e.	Uchimasu yo!	I'll strike you!
O busharezansu na.	Baka ni suruna.	Don't try and make a fool of me.
Hagurakasu.	Age-ashi wo toru.	To catch a person tripping.
Sonna koto wa shirin-sen.	Sonna koto wa shiri-masen.	I don't know any-thing about it.
Yabo.	Fu-anai no hito.	A stranger who is un-acquainted with a place.
Sui.	Tsūjin.	An adept: a person posted up on all points; one who "Knows the ropes."
Yonde kiro.	Yonde koi.	Call him.
Hayaku oppashiro.	Isoide yonde koi.	Call him quickly.
Itte koyo.	Itte kuru.	I will go.
Ayobiyaré.	O aruki nasai.	Please walk (on).
Fukkobosu.	Kobosu.	To spill; To grumble,
Kechi na koto.	Warui koto.	A wicked thing.
Kosoppai.	Kosobaii.	Ticklish.
Unasaruru.	Osuwaruru.	To have the night-mare.
Daijin.	Fu-kyaku.	A rich guest.
Daté.	Daté.	Luxurious and ele-gant: a fop.
Hanka.	Nama-naka.	Impertinent and ped-antic.
Shara-kusai.	Nama-iki.	To pretend to be something that one is not. "Cheeky."
O kan.	Atsu-mono.	A hot object.
Tanabata.	Tama ni kuru kyaku.	An occasional guest.
Kuzetsu.	Chiwa-genkwa.	A curtain lecture.
Sashi.	Ai-gataki kyaku.	A guest with whom one cannot meet.

Nushi.	Iro-otoko.	A paramour.
O yukari sama.	Najimi kyaku.	A familiar guest.
Mukō no hito.	Yō-tashi akindo.	A Yoshiwara storekeeper.
Shirōto-ya.	Futsū no shōka.	Merchants and shopkeepers.
Go te san.	Go teishu.	The proprieter of a tea-house or hotel.
Okasan.	O kamisan.	The wife of the above.
Ani-san.	Musuko.	The son of the above.
Gebizō: Kurai-nuke.	Bōshoku suru hito.	A glutton.
Inasé.	Sugata no yoi hito.	A person with an elegant figure.
Shitta ka yō.	Bakarashii.	Ridiculous.
Jirettōsu.	Jirettō gozaimasu.	I am vexed.
Yō-zansu.	Yō gczaimasu.	All right: Very well.
Nan zansu ka?	Nan de gozaimasu ka?	What is it?
Kii-shita.	Kimashita.	Has come.
Dashi-kitte.	Arawasu.	To show (or) manifest anything.
Shinobi-komeru	Hisoka ni.	Secretly.
Samisen-ban.	Mise no samisen wo adzukaru *shinzo*.	*Samisen* keeper.
Nanto demo ii nanshi.	Nanto demo o ii nasai.	Say whatever you like (I don't mind).
Chotto mi nē!	Miyagaré.	Oh! just look at (hear) him!
Ii ame dakké nē!	(The same).	What good rain!*
Akire-kēru yo.	Akire-kaeru yo.	I am astonished.
Pochi-pochi.	Oiran ni kawai-gara-reta hito.	A guest loved by a courtesan.
Chaki-chaki.	Oiran ni niku-mareta hito.	The reverse.
Ki-fū.	Kiita-fū.	Pedantic style.
Shiwo-ya. / Enjirō.	Jiman unubore no hito.	A conceited fellow.

A saying in vogue about the Bunkwa era (1804-1817) was :—You can distinguish the Ōgi-ya by "*watakushi*," the Tama-ya by "*shitsukata*," the Chōjiya by "*zansu*," and the Matsuba-ya by "*osu*." This was said because of the peculiar

* Said by a courtesans to a guest detained in a brothel owing to rainy weather.

dialects, spoken in the respective houses, changed into *zansu, zaisu, ossu, osu, ariisu,* etc. The *sato-kotoba* has now entirely disappeared, but as many of the women come from the Western provinces, in the neighbourhood of Kyōto, it is common in the Yoshiwara to hear such words as "*anata itsu kiyaharimasu*" (when will you come?), "*sō dakka*" (is that so?), "*ahōrashii*" (nonsense!), etc.

Shōgi no okonau juho.

(Magic charms practised by the Yoshiwara courtesans).

The Yoshiwara inhabitants are all peculiarly superstitious people and great believers in omens, consequently they carefully avoid anything which may be construed as fore-shadowing ill-luck. The word *cha* (tea) is supposed to be unlucky because it occurs in the phrase *o cha wo hiku* (literally "*to pulverize tea,*" but idiomatically it is applied to women of ill-fame who are unpopular and means "*to be out of employment*") therefore it is carefully eschewed not only by courtesans but by *geisha* also.* The courtesans call "tea" "*agaribana*" ("going-up-flower": meaning a guest who is going up the stairs) or "*yamabuki*" ("yellow rose") or *Uji* (the name of a place) because the liquor of the infused tea is the colour of the *yamabuki* flower, and because Uji (near Kyōto) is a noted tea-district. *Geisha* speak of tea as "*o-de-bana*" ("august-going-out-flower") because this expression conveys the sense of their "going out" and gathering presents (*hana*) from guests. Sitting on the staircase is looked upon with aversion, as this is supposed to decrease the number of

* For the derivation of this phrase see page 118.

guests. When a cat, or a domestic fowl, passes through a room it is immediately caught and brought back to the direction from whence it came, because the local folk believe that the toleration of such an event will tend to make guests go away without stopping at the house. There are a great many silly superstitions of a similar nature in the Yoshiwara, and charms of all kinds are extensively practised. Every evening the *bantō* of each brothel says a prayer before the "*Engi-dana*" (the shelf of good luck: this was formerly furnished with emblems of *phallic* worship), a bundle of wooden clog-checks (to which a long rope is attached) is held up and struck several times against the floor of the house, and then an imitation of a rat's squeak is made while the *bantō* strikes a pillar of the house with his hand. This process is said to be a charm for attracting many guests. It would require a thick volume to contain a description of all these charms, therefore only a few of the principal ones as mentioned in the "*Shōbai Ōrai*" (倡賣往來), written by Jippensha Ikku, are given here.

Charm for attracting a person for whom one is waiting:—It is a most efficaceous method to stick an eel-skewer in the wall and pray for the advent of the party whose presence is desired.

Ditto (another method):—Fold a piece of paper so as to represent a frog, write the name of your guest on its back, stick a pin through it and put the frog where no one can see it: the person desired is sure to turn up. After his arrival, however, the pin should be removed and the paper frog thrown into the river.

Ditto (another method):—Cut a sheet of white paper to a size of 2 inches square, fold it in two, place it in a white envelope and address it to the desired guest. This charm is much in vogue in the brothels of Kyōmachi though it has not yet spread to Yedo-chō. In *Masurō* this charm has been especially successful.

How to ascertain whether an expected guest will come or not:—Draw out a thread from the end of a towel. If this feat be successfully performed the guest is sure to come, but if the thread breaks he will not turn up.

A peculiar charm. Take one equal part of *sakê*, vinegar, soy, oil, *ohaguro* (mixture for blackening teeth), water, and a handful of *tōshin* (wick of a lamp made from vegetable pith). Boil these seven ingredients together and add a piece of paper on which is depicted the private parts of your lover. Boil again for a short time, and the charm is sure to cure the man's fickleness.

At present nobody seems to be acquainted with the charms mentioned above, they have fallen into disuse nowadays.

Below will be found a description of charms now in vogue. These are most important occult secrets and should not be lightly revealed to the vulgar!

To attract a person. Write the first letter of the name of the person, together with the date of his birth, on a piece of paper. Paste this under a staircase on the third step from the bottom, but do it secretly so that nobody will detect it. If a person misses his footing and falls from this stairway the charm will certainly be effective.

Ditto. When there is any particular guest whom a courtesan wishes to call, a letter supposed to be addressed to him should be prepared, and on the cover should be written the words—"*Kogaruru kimi ye*" (To my beloved prince) and "*Go zonji yori*" (From—you know who). This missive must be dropped at a cross-way, and if it be picked up by somebody the charm will work.

Ditto. Take a sheet of *hanshi* paper and cut it in the style of a *noren* (curtain hung before a shop) and on each leaf write the Chinese character 狐 (*kitsunè*="fox"). Stick this on the inside of a cupboard or drawer so that nobody will know about it, and then offer up a prayer for the speedy advent of the person for whom you are waiting. When he arrives you must secretly remove the paper and throw it away.

Ditto. There is a game called *en-musubi* (marrying) which is played by making a couple of *koyori* (soft Japanese paper twisted into a string) and holding them in the middle while a person ties both ends together. The *koyori* are now stretched by pulling, and if they become entangled in the process the marriage is supposed to be assured. If you tie the paper strings which have been used for this purpose to a tobacco-pipe-stem, or to the mouth of a teapot, this will certainly cause the appearance of the party whose presence you desire.

Ditto. Seven paper-strings (*koyori*) are bundled together and held by the centre, while four of them are fastened at one end in pairs; the remaining three are also fastened, two with one string. Of the last two strings, one represents the girl's lover, and is to be marked as such. When all these strings are pulled, sometimes none of them get tangled, but now and then one of the three strings tied together may entangle itself with the others in a curious fashion. Taking this as the "boundary" the length of the remaining two strings should be compared, presuming the one that is marked to be the man and the other to be the woman. If the male string is longer it means that the man's love is deeper, and *vice versa.* When the paper strings have entangled themselves in an auspicious manner, such strings should be fastened to the end of the woman's *koshi-maki* (kind of waist-cloth) and they will prove to be an irresistible charm for attracting men. When the person longed for finally arrives, this *koyori* must be secretly removed and thrown away so as not to be detected by anyone. Should this once be forgotten, and the woman go to bed with her lover while the strings are still attached to her waist-cloth, the charm will lose its efficacy in future.

Ditto. The woman must concentrate her mind and think of the abode of her lover (if the street, number, etc. is not clearly known a hypothesis will suffice), the route to be taken in going there, and the distance. She must then imagine herself departing from her own house, and on her way to that of the lover, counting her steps as she goes. Then she will shortly suppose that she has reached her destination, that she has met with the man she was seeking, and that she is urging him to visit her in the evening without fail. After obtaining his consent she must mentally commence her return journey, going through the same process as she did on her outward journey. Of course all this labour of love is mentally performed, so that it may be done even in the presence of another guest without arousing the slightest suspicion in the minds of outsiders. This practice of telepathy is said to be startlingly effective in its results.

Ditto. Take a sheet of *hanshi* paper and from it cut out seven human figures, all joined together. Then fill in the eyes, noses, and mouths, but do not complete these in each figure:

let some be without a nose or mouth, or minus one eye, etc. On the abdomen of the central figure should be written three times the first letter of the man's name, and on the remaining six figures it should be written five times. The central letter on the central figure should be pierced with a needle in an upward direction, and all the figures should then be solemnly promised that if the desired party turns up, their organs shall be completed and that they shall be thrown into a stream and allowed to float away. The figures should then be pasted in a place where they will not be detected. In the event of the person whose presence is desired actually appearing, the organs of the figures should be completed, and then the paper men should be thrown either into the moat or the W.C.

Ditto. In the small hours of the morning, enter a room which faces the street and which is not usually occupied by anybody. Shut up the paper shutters (*shōji*) and place your sandals in the room with the bottoms upwards. Then pass through the room out into the verandah, place your hands in the the bosom of your dress and shutting your eyes repeat an old well-known poem three times in succession. If you then listen very carefully you will hear a human voice which, speaking in an undertone, will tell you whether "he" will come or not. This is a very doubtful charm!

Ditto. Write on a sheet of *hanshi* paper the well-known poem:—"*Konu hito wo Matsuo no ura no yū-nagi ni yakuya moshiwo no mi wo kogashi-tsutsu*" [this has been translated by Mr. F.V. Dickins (with a slight verbal alteration) as follows:—

On Matsuo's shore, our meeting place,
At dusky hour of night, I wait
My longed-for loved one to embrace;
Ah, why linger'st thou so late!
My ardent passion, than the fire
That heats the salt-pans, rages higher.

or "*Waiting for he who comes not with a passion fervent as the heat which bakes salt,*"] and at the end of the papers—"*Tare sama itsu made ni kuru yō ni tanomi-age-mairase-sōrō*" (I beg that Mr....... will come by ....(date)........) as well as the name of the God or Buddha which you usually worship. Stick this paper on the wall upside down.

Charm for attracting guests when "trade" is dull. Either burn a large *moxa* on the bottom of the wooden pillow you generally use, or tie two pillows securely together with an *obi* (sash) and fling them into an unlighted room. The charm is said to be extraordinarily effective.

Charm for attracting an unfaithful man. When you desire to see an unfaithful man for the purpose of upbraiding him for his insincerity, first write everything you wish to tell him and pour out all your wrath upon him in the letter. Then procure a frog, stick a needle in its back, and putting your letter before the reptile tell it to take the missive to the addressee, promising that if it be successful in conveying the letter into the man's sleeve-pocket the needle shall be extracted. The frog will assuredly deliver the letter into the man's sleeve-pocket, come back, and immediately die. The faithless one, finding the letter in his sleeve, will certainly visit you to seek an explanation of the mystery.

Charm to send away a guest. Take a *ko-yori* (a paper string or "spill") and with it form the shape of a dog. Place this on the wardrobe or mirror-stand in a room next to the one in which the guest is, making the paper animal face him. Ask the doggie in a whisper to quickly answer you whether the guest will go away or stop. It is said that this charm is so extraordinarily efficaceous that a guest who is thinking of taking his departure goes away forthwith, while one who wishes to stay immediately expresses his intention of renewing the engagement and prolonging his visit.

Ditto. If the end of the underfold of your waistcloth or "petticoat" (*koshi-maki*) be tied in a knot the guest will leave immediately.

Ditto. Wrap up a small quantity of luke-warm ashes in a piece of paper and place the packet under the night-clothes (bedding) of the guest near his feet. He will immediately go away.

Ditto. Stand a broom on end in the room next to your guest's room, and laying out a pair of sandals before it, say in a whisper—"There now, *do please* go away quickly." The guest will leave at once.

How to know whether "he" is coming or not. This charm is a somewhat indelicate and disgusting one, but it runs as follows :— In the small hours of the morning enter the W. C., carry ing a piece of red paper and a box of matches. Light the paper by means of a match and glance down into the W. C. pan, and you will see the face of the person you are thinking about appear mysteriously. If the face is smiling your relations are at an end, and you must resign yourself to the situation; but if, on the other hand, it betrays signs of anger, the man will visit you ere long. When the charm has worked, put out the light and throw the remains of the paper down the W. C. If you accidentally drop the burning paper on the face of your ghostly visitant a scar is said to be left on the face of the real man.

To ascertain about the health a of man. Very early in the morning enter an unoccupied room which contains eight mats. Take a broom with you, dress it up with clothes as if it were a person, then tie an *obi* round its supposed waist, and cover the head with a towel after the fashion of *hōkamuri.* Now place a letter addressed to your friend in the bosom of the figure, instructing the dummy to deliver the missive to the addressee, obtain a reply from him, and place same in a certain specified drawer. Then stand the dressed-up broom in a corner of the room against the wall, and without looking back quit the chamber. Sometimes the broom topples over by itself without there being a puff of wind to cause the fall. If it falls down the charm will work, a reply be found in the drawer mentioned, and you will receive news of the person about whom you wish to know. (This is an exceedingly doubtful charm.)

How to read a man's mind. While your guest is asleep, crawl secretly out of bed very early in the morning, and getting a single sandal from the W. C. get into bed again without awakening the man. If the guest is sound asleep, rub his chest very gently with this sandal and at the same time ask him his read mind towards you. He will, under these conditions, answer, as if in a dream, any question you may put to him, and thus unbosom all his secrets. When the charm is completed, you must return the sandal to its original place, and coming back go to bed again.

To call in money. If you have asked a guest for money and failed to obtain it, dress a broom up with clothes like a human figure, and standing it upside down complain to it of the non-fulfilment of promises just as if it were a human being: then knock the figure down, telling it to bring the money without fail on the following day. This will cause the man to dream of your indignation at his breach of promise and he will visit you forthwith, bringing with him the necessary money.

To arrest the menstrual flow. Before retiring at night, float some *tōshin* (pith wick of a lamp) or ashes on water and drink the mixture. This is said to be wonderfully effective in arresting the courses.

Some Queer Japanese Superstitions.

1. If the ears are ticklish it is a sign of a lucky event about to happen. In the morning the right ear and in the evening the left ear tickles.
2. Sneezing denotes :—

   Once,—Some person is secretly praising you ;
   Twice,—Some person is backbiting you ;
   Thrice,—Some person is in love with you ;
   Four times,—You have caught a cold.
3. Cramp in the leg is cured by plucking out a straw from the matting of the room, slightly wetting it with saliva, and rubbing it on the forehead while repeating the formula—"*Shibire Kyō ye noboré!*" (Cramp, go up to the Capital !).
4. He who puts parings of human nails, or hair from a human head into the fire, will go mad.
5. To dislodge a bone which has stuck in the throat, stroke the throat thrice with any ivory instrument and repeat the formula—"*U no nodo, u no nodo*" (Cormorant's throat, cormorant's throat).
6. To cure a corn on the foot. Previous to mentioning anything about it to another person rub it thrice with the natural oil which exudes from the side of the nose.
7. How to tell the sex of a child yet unborn. After obtaining a charm (for ensuring safe delivery) from the temple of Kwannon (Goddess of Mercy) at Asakusa, if the paper within the packet is red the child will be a girl, and, if green, a boy. It is also said that if on the morning of the first day of the month of parturition a male visitor arrives the child will be a boy, but, if a female visitor, a girl.

   When the combined ages of a married couple can be divided by three without leaving a remainder, a girl will be born, but if there is a remainder a boy will be born.

   If the yet unborn child shall have been conceived in one year and its birth be due in the following year, the ages of the parents should be added together, one year added to the number resulting, and then the total should be divided by three.

   If a pregnant woman asks her first-born child (whether boy or girl is a matter of indifference) "*Mame ka adzuki ka?*" (Ordinary bean or Adzuki bean?) and the child answers "Ordinary bean" a girl will be born, but if the answer is "Adzuki bean," then a boy will be born.

8. If you wear a basket on your head by way of a hat you will become dwarfed in stature, and if you tread in horse-dung you will become tall.
9. Dust in the eyes may be removed by closing the eyes and licking the upper lip for a short time, or by spitting thrice and repeating the formula "*Gomi, nara dero ; suna nara tokero!*" (If dirt go out; if sand melt!)
10. When you meet a person suffering from opthalmia, and he stares at you, if you do not stare back you will catch the disease.
11. When you meet a funeral procession you should conceal your thumbs or else your parents will die.
12. Should a woman wash her hair on the "day of the Horse" (*Uma no hi*) she will go mad.
13. A person who is not sensitive to tickling is the child of an illicit lover.
14. If one allows the nail of his little finger to grow, he will not be forgetful.
15. If one removes the skin excretions (*aka*) from his navel (*heso*) he will catch cold.
16. Method of curing toothache:—

    Place a piece of white paper on the floor, put both your feet upon it close together, and draw the outline of the feet. You have now a shape on the paper approximating to a human face. In this draw eyes, nose, and then draw a representation of a set of teeth in the mouth. Then paint the representation of the aching tooth quite black, and the two next teeth slightly black, fold up the paper in eight folds, drive a nail through the same and then throwing the paper into a river let it drift away down stream.

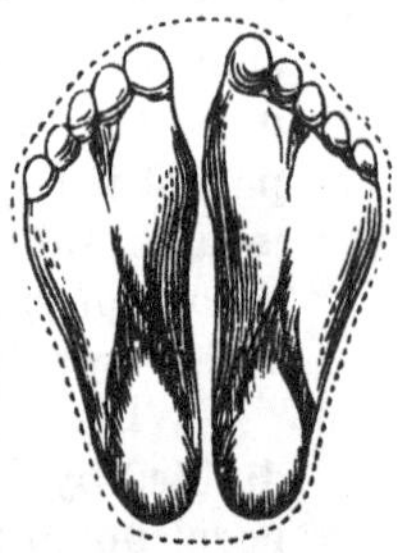

17. To cure a corn on one's foot. Draw upon it three times the character 鳩 (*hato*=pigeon) and then thoroughly smudge out the character. (Perhaps the idea is that the pigeon eats the corn!)
18. If one allows wax to collect in the glands of the ears his memory will be improved.
19. To cure ringworn (*tamushi*). Draw on the affected part the character 鴫 (*shigi*=snipe) or else 南 (*minami*=south) and then thoroughly smudge out the writing with black ink. (It is said that when the character 鴫 (*shigi*=snipe) is used the idea

is that the snipe will eat up the *tamushi*—ringworm. This arises from a play upon the words used. *Tamushi*, if divided, becomes *ta mushi*, and phonetically may mean 田 (*ta*=a ricefield) + 虫 (*mushi*=an insect). It is well-known that snipe (*shigi*) devour the insects (*mushi*) in the rice-fields (*ta*) and thus the superstition.

20. If you dream of eating anything you will catch cold the following day.
21. When a woman has trouble in suckling her child owing to the flow of milk being scanty, she should draw a picture of a *namadzu* (cat-fish) on a piece of paper, and stick this paper on a Kōshin-dō (shrine of the Kōshin). This is a sovereign remedy and will certainly ensure a full flow of the lacteal fluid.
22. If a woman washes her hair when she has the monthlies, she will die of a burning fever.
23. To cure the hiccoughs, fill a tea-cup with hot water or tea, and on the top of the cup place a pair of chopsticks cross-fashion. Then drink a mouthful from each of the four divisions thus formed, and after each mouthful be sure not to forget to mention the name of some bridge. You must however be careful that the word bridge (*hashi*) appearing in the name is not changed in the combination by reason of euphony. For instance Same-ga-hashi (Shark's bridge) Naka-no-hashi (Middle bridge) Ō-hashi (Great bridge) Ichi-no-hashi (First bridge) will do, whereas Nippon-bashi (Japan bridge) Kyō-bashi (Capital bridge) will not do because the word *hashi* (bridge) undergoes a phonetic change in the combination.

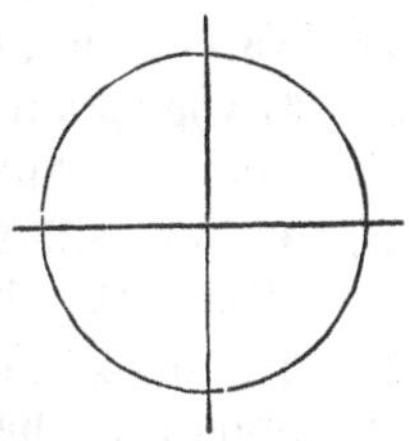

24. To cure a wart. Wrap a spider's web around it, or go to a grave-yard and apply water from the oldest grave-stone. Another method is to rub the wart gently with an *adzuki* bean and then bury the bean in the earth placing a heavy stone or tile upon it. If this bean does not germinate and sprout the wart will disappear. Still another method is to stand by a *sanshō* (*Xanthoxylon piperitum*) tree, and to gently stroke the tree, repeating the formula "*ibo utsuré, ibo utsuré!*" (Wart be transferred, wart be transferred!). This last method is eminently efficaceous.
25. In order to hasten menstruation thread a needle with red thread and stick it into the wall of the W. C. In order to

prolong the courses, step over three *adzuki* beans or over the bank-like paths dividing the fields. To swallow an *adzuki* bean is also efficaceous.

26. If one places a mushroom on his navel, and keeps it there, he will not become sea-sick.

27. In case of many persons having had illicit intercourse with a woman, and it is not certain who is the father of the child, if the placenta be placed on a lacquered tray and examined it is said that the father's crest (armorial bearings) will appear.

28. If one goes to sleep early on the night of the *Kōshin*, a boil will form on his buttocks.

29. If you shake your legs you will become poor.

30. If you break wind your tongue will turn yellow for a little while.

31. If you cut your nails at night you will be bewitched by a fox.

32. A woman who has curly hair is lecherous.

33. Talk about your own death and you will live to a good old age.

34. If your front teeth are wide apart you will soon be separated from your parents.

35. If you tell falsehoods your tongue will be plucked out by *Emma* (the King of Hell).

36. If a person bleeds at the nose or eyes when climbing a high mountain he is a wicked man.

37. To cure ring-worm rub the effected part with *ame* (a kind of syrup made from malt), stick this *ame* on the branch of an *e-no-ki* (*celtis sinensis*) and go straight away without looking back.

38. To cure a stye (*mono-morai*). If it has grown on the lower eyelid, you must receive some *nigiri-meshi* (boiled rice rolled up into a ball-like shape) from a person in an inferior station in life and eat the same: the *nigiri-meshi* must be received from outside of the window, the giver being inside the room. If the stye be on the upper lid, the *niyiri-meshi* must be obtained from a person who is your social superior.

Or, stroke the affected spot with a *miso* (bean-sauce) strainer and reflect half the bottom of the strainer in a well: when a cure is effected reflect the whole strainer in the well.

Or, rub a comb until it becomes warm by reason of the friction, and then touch the stye with the same.

39. If you kindle a fire in front of the entrance of your house (*Kado-guchi*) on the occasion of the *Shōryō-matsuri* (the festival

celebrated in commemoration of dead relatives on the 7th day of the 7th month—old calendar) and tread on the ashes, your legs will become strong. If your light your pipe by this fire you will not suffer from coughs.

40. He who shaves off the hair from his legs will not be able to run swiftly when he runs away.

41. If a small boil or pimple forms within your nostrils, a child will be born in the house of some relative.

42. If you glare fiercely at your parents, you will become squint-eyed (*yabu-nirami to naru*).

43. Strike a person on the chest and you will not survive three years.

44. If you have *te-midzu* (water for washing the hands) thrown over you, you will die within three years.

45. If you hang up over a *midzu-game* (water-jar) a straw snake (*mugiwara no ja*) such as is purchased by *Fuji-mōde* (pilgrims to Fujiyama) on the first day of the sixth month (old calendar), the inmates of your house will not suffer from fever. If you preserve the tongue of this straw snake it will be efficaceous as a febrifuge if boiled in water and the resulting liquor swallowed by a feverish person.

46. If a child has been bruised, and is in pain, if he repeats the formula—"*Chichin pui-pui, go yō no on takara*" (This cannot be translated into English) the pain will disappear.

47. If a pregnant woman drinks *saké* (Japanese rice wine) and eats the flesh of a sparrow together, the child to which she gives birth will be lewd and immoral (*impon*).

48. In order to determine the sex of a fœtus, look at the *jijikké* (soft hair growing on the nape of the neck) of the child born previously, and if it is bent to the left the child will be a boy whereas, if to the right, a girl.

49. If a pregnant woman happens to touch her own skin while beholding a conflagration, the child to which she gives birth will be found to have maculæ (*aza*) on the corresponding part of its body. If however she happens to be carrying a mirror in the bosom of her dress the child will escape being thus marked.

50. Should two pregnant woman live together in the same house, one of them will either die together with her child, or have a miscarriage.

51. If a child plays with fire he will urinate the bed.

52. If one spits into the W. C. he will go blind.
53. If you press down a person's shoulder, your own stature will become short.
54. If you throw *te-midzu* (see No. 44) over a person you will have a child born without hands.
55. If the soles of your feet become ticklish you will become poor.
56. If you urinate on an earth-worm your penis will swell up and become inflamed, but if you subsequently wash any earthworn with water the swelling will subside and the inflammation disappear.
57. If you go to sleep with your hand on your breast you will be disturbed by dreams.
58. If when you have "the hiccoughs" you repeat thrice, without taking breath, the formula—"*Ebisu sama no omori-mono nusunde Kuiyasen ka!* (Haven't you been stealing and eating the things offered up to Ebisu Sama?*) you will be cured.
59. When many circular and wave-like lines or wrinkles (*udzu no makitaru shiwa-suji*) appear on the finger-tips, one becomes skilful at doing everything.
60. If the great toe of a person's foot is shorter than the next toe, then he will be more prosperous than his parents.
61. Persons whose eyebrows are close together are short-lived.
62. If you stick a piece of paper, on which is written "*Chinsei Hachirō Tametomo Kō on yado*" (The sojourning place of Chinsei Hachirō, Lord Tametomo), on the door ot the house, small-pox will not enter.
63. If you dress a small-pox patient in red garments the attack will be but slight. The imp of small-pox is pleased with the sight of red garments and deals gently with the wearers.
64. If you write "*Hisamatsu rusu*" ("Hisamatsu is not at home") on a piece of paper, and stick it on the door of the house, you will not catch "*o some kaze*" (influenza). [The origin of this saying is that in the good old times there lived two lovers, the man being named Hisamatsu, and the woman O Some. *Ergo*, when Hisamatsu is not at home, O Some does not enter the house, whereas if he were in she would enter to meet him.]
65. If previous to going to bed you repeat the following three times, you will awake the next morning at any hour you choose:—

* God of wealth and guardian of markets

Hono-bono to *Akashi no ura no* *Asa-gari ni* *Shima-kakure-yuku* *Fune wo shiso omou* *	Gazing upon the beautiful scenery of the coast of Akashi, and faintly seeing the fishing boats going out to fish in the grey light of the dawn, I feel a sense of regret when the white sails of the tiny crafts disappear from sight behind the islands in the distance.

[This poem was composed by Hitomaro, one of the *Sanjū-rok-ka-sen* or thirty-six famous poets of Japan.]

66. When a white spot forms on the finger-nails, one's stock of clothes will increase.

67. If you are guilty of unfilial conduct you will get a *sasakure* (hang-nail.)

68. If a stye has formed on your eyelid, go to the house of another person and ask for food. Eat the food given you and the stye will disappear.

69. If a child be conceived on the night of the *Kōshin*, he will turn out a robber. ["*Kōshin is a deification of that day of the month which corresponds to the 57th term of the Chinese sexagesimal circle.*" *Murray's Hand-Book for Japan.*]

70. When you are suffering from *kusa* (a kind of cutaneous eruption), draw the character 馬 (*uma*=horse) upon the affected spot and it will then heal up.

71. If you desire not to beget any more children, when you name your last child you should introduce the character 留 (*tomé*=to stop; to stay) or 極 (*kiwa*=to come to an end; a limit). This method is most efficaceous.

72. To protect a child from having convulsions. Hang up together to the ceiling (1) a toy basket, (2) a toy umbrella, (3) a *papier maché* dog (*inu-hariko*), all of which things must have been purchased in the *naka-mise* (the row of shops leading up to the gate of Kwannon Sama) at Asakusa.

73. To protect a child from whooping-cough (*hyaku-nichi-zeki*). Take a piece of white cotton (*shiro-momen*) one *shaku* (15 inches) square, and wrapping therein one *gō* (1.2706 gills) of salt, tie the whole up with red silk thread and then hang the package up to the ceiling of the *doma* (the small unfloored court at the entrance of Japanese houses.)

---

* This will not bear translation. The idea is conveyed as explained by a poet-friend.

74. To protect a child from *natsu-boshi* (a kind of prickly heat). Place one of the first fruits of the egg-plant (*hatsunari no nasu*) in a tea-bag and suspend from the ceiling.

75. If a woman sweeps and cleans out the W.C. her labour will be easy in child-birth.

76. When a person finds that his children die and that he cannot rear them, it is a good plan to abandon the next child born, watch until some person picks it up, and then reclaim it. This will ensure the child's subsequent health and it will grow up safely. It is also a good plan to use the character 捨 (*suteru*=to throw away) when composing the child's name, or else to call him "Aguri." If one constructs a *tōba* out of the wood of a *keyaki* (*Zelkowa acuminata*) tree, using it upside down so that the grain points downwards, and erects it by the grave of the last child who died, children born subsequently will grow up safely. [As *tōba*, or *sotōba*, is a long, narrow, and thin wooden table on which is inscribed Sanskrit characters quoted from the Buddhist sacred books, this term is derived from the Sanskrit word *stupa*="a mound."]

77. If an infant not yet weaned has two lines on the back of the thigh between the buttocks and the knee, the next child born will be a girl. If only one line be visible the next child will be a boy.

78. An old saying runs—"Don't cut your nails on the day of the Hare (U), Swine (I), Serpent (Mi), or Goat (Hitsuji), or the tears on your sleeves will never dry up," (Japanese use their long flowing sleeves in wiping their tears away) and in consequence of this maxim, people do not like to cut their nails on those days: they also dislike to cut their nails at night (*yo-dzume*), or when about to go out (*de-dzume*).

79. If on the day of the Dog (*inu no hi*) a pregnant women makes an *iwata-obi* (the bandage worn by pregnant women after the 5th month until confinement), her delivery will be painless.

80. If you stumble and fall down in a graveyard you will die within three years, and if you are wounded the scar will not heal up.

81. If you fall down at San-nen-saka (three years hill) in San-nen-machi (three years town) in Kōjimachi district, you will not live three years.

82. To cure toothache. Wrap a piece of paper round the top of one of the piles of the sluice near Same-ga-hashi in Yotsuya district, and then tie it on with *midzu-hiki* (a fine paper cord used for tying up presents.)

83. If you wash your face with too hot water wrinkles will appear very soon. If you hang up a wet towel on a rack without smoothing it out, your face will soon become wrinkled.

84. If you pull out one of the soft hairs on the back of the neck (*jijikké*) this will stop bleeding of the nose.

85. If you do not put out fire with your foot you will never have a calamity or loss by fire.

86. If you bury pen and ink (*fude-sumi*) with the placenta (*ena*) the child will become a skilful penman, and if a fan be buried also, the child will rise in the world.

87. If you allow your nails to grow too long you will catch cold.

88. The child always dislikes (has an aversion towards) the particular insect that first passed over the place where the placenta (*ena*) was buried. (If the first insect to crawl across was a caterpillar, the child will always feel a creeping horror when he sees one in after years).

89. If you sit down on a seat which has just been vacated by a person, you will fall out and quarrel with him unless you tap the seat thrice before sitting down.

90. If a man and woman visit the shrine of Benten Sama (in Enoshima) together, their connection will be severed.

91. Fan the palms of your hands and your whole body will become cool.

92. If after giving birth to a child the stomach is aching obstinately, burn an old tea-bag and eat the ashes. This will cure the pain.

93. If you dream of being cut down (wounded) by a person, it is a sign that you are going to make money.

94. To prevent the spead of infection in case of fever, wrap up some horse-dung in a piece of paper and place the package under the mattress on which the patient is lying.

95. If the palms of the hands itch you will receive money; if the backs of the hands itch you will disburse money. When the sole of the foot itches, go straight home and scratch it and you will certainly escape the impending evil.

96. If you have contracted *hayari-me* (epidemic opthalmia), you can cure the disease by the following method. Get a *tsukegi* (old-fashioned sulphur match), write on it "Yamme ō-yasu-uri" (Diseased eyes for sale cheap), and throw it away, together with 10 *Mon sen* (1 sen present coinage), at a place where cross-roads meet.

97. If you suffer from earache (*kara-mimi*) you can cure yourself by applying water to the ear from the oldest grave you can find.

98. To care ague (*okori*). Write down the patient's name and age on a piece of paper and throw the same into the river from Jinnoi-bashi at Fuku-tomi-chō in Asakusa district.

Yoshiwara "Pot-pourri."

The following items are given in the "*Yoshiwara Ō-kaga-mi*" (吉原大鑑=The Great Mirror of the Yoshiwara) under the heading of "*Sho-yaku Hyaku-monogatari*" 諸譯百もの語) One Hundred Miscellaneous Tales).

Things which are long: The *Nihon-dzutsumi;* a dispute between lovers; the *magaki* song at night; the night to a guest who has been jilted by a *yūjo.*

Things that are short: Night of a lovers' meeting; the first letter from a *yūjo* to a strange guest.

Things one would like to see: The Diary of a *yūjo;* sincerity in a prostitute; a square egg; the false letters of a *jōro*, and the end of a heartless courtesan.

Things one would like to hear: The name of a *yūjo's* secret lover; the whispers of a courtesan.

Things that are funny: Apologies of a guest who has offended a *yūjo;* a guest who bestows too much attention on a *kamuro* (young female page).

Things that are enjoyable: A long sojourn of an intimate guest at a brothel; secret lover; love-quarrels between sweethearts.

Hurried things: A *saké* cup that is *not* offered to a guest by the courtesan of his choice on the occasion of their first meeting; feigned sleep on the morning of the guest's departure; conversation about one's acquaintances; the crest on the clothes of a courtesan made by a rival guest.

Pleasant things. Spiritedness of a courtesan; a sprightly *jōro.*

Quiet things. The possession of a courtesan's room at the first meeting; a *tayū* who has come down to be a *kōshi-jōro.*

A clever thing. A demand for gratuities by means of broad hints.

Clumsy things. Squandering too much money in a tea-house; going into a *sancha* restaurant in the rain; demand by an unpopular courtesan to be engaged on a holiday.

Things for which one is sorry. A fire on the night of a lovers' meeting; for a courtesan to unknowingly receive counterfeit money from a guest as a present.

Comfortable things. A snowfall on the night when one stays in a brothel; a hood that is put on the head from behind.

Offensive things. The night-sweat of a *jōro;* warming the bowl of a tobacco pipe by a woman before the guest is well acquainted with her; the coarse skin of a guest; the relative one meets on his way to the Yoshiwara; a guest who doesn't clean his teeth.

Things which are soiled. The nostrils of a guest; the tobacco-box of a slovenly courtesan.

Laughable things. A party of *jōro* all of whom have their collars covered with paper to prevent soiling their clothes; sudden showers of rain which drench sightseers in the Yoshiwara; demand for a night-garment by an unpopular *jōro.*

An unsightly object. The day-time slumber of a *jōro* with her mouth wide open.

Annoying things. Frequent visits of other *jōro* to the room where their comrade's guest is staying; whispering in the ear of a guest by a courtesan at their first meeting.

Cruel things. Expiry of the term of engagement of an unpopular *jōro;* corporal punishment of a *kamuro* by her *ane-jōro.*

Detestable things. The physiognomy of a *yarite;* talk about rude things by a prostitute; the indiscretion of a *gyū.*

A hopeful thing. A woman who redeems herself.

Foolish things. Respectable *samurai* who visit the Yoshiwara; elderly visitors to the Yoshiwara; a drunkard who cannot control himself.

Contemptible things. A guest who keeps away from a brothel when accounts have to be settled; one candle for a company of three persons; a *jōro* who slavishly obeys a *yarite;* a lantern which is used for two rooms conjointly.

Things for which one waits impatiently. An agreement to wait until the expiry of the term of a *jōro's* engagement; bed-time on the occasion of a first meeting.

Apparently reliable things. The address of a *jōro's* parents as told to her guest; the infant name of a *jōro.*

Unreliable things. The tears of a *jōro* when she inflicts a curtain lecture on her guest.

Dai-ya no koto.

(Cook-houses of the Yoshiwara.)

In former days the present "*Dai-ya*" (cook-houses) were called "*Ki-no-ji-ya*" owing to the fact that a man named Oda-wara-ya Ki-ue first established such houses. Originally only the smaller brothels were supplied with food from these *dai-ya*, but now-a-days all the brothels, irrespective of size or grade, draw their foodsupply from the cook-houses. These *dai-ya* supply every conceivable kind of food, be it *sushi* (a fish and rice roll, *kwashi* (cakes), *soba* (buck-wheat macaroni), *midzu-gwashi* (fruit), or what not; and according to the quantity of food, dishes are divided into three classes, viz:—*Nami-dai* (ordinary dish), *Dai-shō* (medium-sized dish), and *Ō-dai* (a large-sized dish). These sizes are charged out at 25 *sen*, 37½ *sen*, and 50 *sen* respectively, but the *dai-ya* are said to supply brothels at one third of the above prices, and if that be so then the latter earn a profit of two-thirds of the selling price to guests! The *rule* is to make a prompt cash payment on delivery of food, but as a matter of fact a wooden ticket, bearing the sign of each brothel, is given in exchange for *dai-no-mono* (food brought in) every time it is brought in, and payment is made the following day. It is stated by "those who know" that there are some brothels which have a debt of several hundred *Yen* to the *dai-ya*. There are a great many *dai-ya* in the Yoshiwara, but those which usually supply first-class brothels are "*Koi-matsu*" of Ageya-chō Ni-chō-me; "*Yao-kyū*" of the same street; and "*Matsu-no*" of Sumi-chō. In counting the number of *dai-no-mono*, the auxiliary numeral "*mai*" is used: thus "*nami-sammai*" (ordinary three flat things) means three ordinary dishes of food. This is generally abbreviated to simply—"*nami san*" (ordinary three) etc., and the auxiliary numeral eliminated. An ordinary dish, with a bottle of *saké* thrown in, is known as "*ichi-mai ippon*" [one (dish) and one bottle.] Sometimes a guest orders food merely for the good of the house, and under these circumstances will be asked:—"What will you take?" He will no doubt reply:—"*Nan demo ii yo*" ("Anything will do") and so the cook-house is instructed to send in a *demo-dai* (a dish of "anything": *demo* is a contraction of *nan demo*="anything") which means that there is no particular choice on the part of the customer.

By the way, there is, in the "*Shōbai Ōrai*" (倡賣往來) by Ikku, an item which shows a bill of fare in a *dai-ya* a hundred years ago. It is as follows:—"The bill of fare of the "*Ki-no-ji-ya*" consisted of:—

Kimpira-gobō.	Chopped burdock-root fried in *goma* oil.
Teri-gomamé.	Dried young sardines roasted and boiled in sugar and soy.
Aramé.	Arame sea-weed (*Capea elongata.*)
Aburage.	Bean-curd fried in oil.
Ko-zakana nitsuke.	Small fishes, boiled.
San-kai.	Various fishes and birds.
Suzuri-buta.	A nest of boxes containing sundry foods.
Tamago.	Eggs.
Kuwai.	"Arrow-heads."
Kama-boko.	The flesh of fish hashed, seasoned with a little *saké* and salt, rolled around a stick and baked.
Kawa-také.	River-mushroom.
Tsuke-warabi.	Salted fern-shoots.
Hachi-zakana.	Fish served in dishes.
Karei.	Sole-fish.
Nibitashi shin-shōga.	Fresh ginger-roots (boiled.)
Domburi.	A porcelain bowl containing food.

Fuki.	*Petasites japonicus.*
Yaki-dōfu.	Roasted bean-curd.
Su-gobō.	Root of the burdock in vinegar.
Udo.	Japanese asparagus (*Aralia cordata.*)
Renkon.	Lotus roots.
Ika.	Cuttle-fish.
Nishi-sazai-kinome-age.	Conch flavoured with the young leaves of the *sanshō* plant.
Suimono.	Soup.
Musubi-gisu.	*Sayori* fish tied in a knot.
Hamaguri.	Clams and vegetables.
Senyō.	A kind of soup.
Umani.	Any food cooked in a mixture of soy, *mirin*, sugar, and the shavings of dried bonito.
Taimen.	Food made of vermicelli mixed with the minced flesh of the *tai* cooked.
Ankake.	A kind of soup, containing *tōfu* or arrowroot.

etc., all of which foods are suitable for those persons who stop in brothels for several consecutive days.

Famous Things of the Yoshiwara

ALSO

Peddlers, Hawkers, and Beggars.

Takemura no sembei.	Rice and flour cracknels of Takemura.
Sanya-tōfu.	Bean-curd of Sanya.
Kobu-maki.	Rolled seaweed.
Shiso-maki.	Rolled *shiso* leaf.
Tsuke-na.	Pickled greens.
Ni-mame.	Boiled beans.
Nameshi.	Green rice.
Maku-no-uchi.	Boiled rice balls.
Dengaku.	*Tōfu* baked and covered with sweetened *miso*.
Mugi-meshi.	Boiled wheat.
Aoyagi-sushi.	*Sushi* of Aoyagi.
Kanro-bai.	"*Kanro*" plum.
Hakuro.	"*Hakuro*" sweet-cake.

O-kagura.	"*O-kagura*" buckwheat.
Kabasho-dango.	Rice dumplings of Kabasho.
Shinowara-dango.	Rice dumplings of Shinowara.

These things were very popular (even outside the Yoshiwara) from the An-ei (1772-1780) to Bunsei (1818-1829) eras, and the "*Dote no kin-tsuba*" (a cake made in the shape of the guard on a sword-hilt), was well known even after the Restoration. There is still one store which deals in this time-honoured cake, and it is as popular as ever.

The *meibutsu* (famous things) at present are the following:—The cuisine of the Kaneko restaurant; the *kama-meshi* (iron-pot-rice) of Horikawa; the *tempura* (fried fish) of Hamada; the *kabayaki* (roasted eels) of Ōtsune; Matsumo-*zushi*; *shiruko* (rice-cakes with a sauce of red beans and sugar) of Takaoka; *Ki-no-ine-meshi* (rice boiled with soy); *kwashi* (cakes and confectionery) of Futaba-ya; the *saké* of Okuda; the photographs of Katō; the bath-houses of Ageya-chō and Kyōmachi; the patent medicines of Nakane and Konishi; the *ezōshi* (coloured pictures) of Sanuki-ya; the *komamono* (fancy goods) of Nori-ya; the *zōri* (sandals) of Hishi-ya; etc.

Above all, the cooking of Kaneko is well known, and greatly esteemed, not only in the Yoshiwara but even outside the quarter as well. The construction and decoration of every room has been carried out in exquisite taste, and the furniture of the house is at once rare and costly: moreover, there is a fine bath-room in the restaurant, and, as everything is thus arranged comfortably for guests, many visitors to the Yoshiwara patronize the "Kaneko," and go there accompanied by the *yūjo* they have chosen as their companions.

In the streets are to be found vendors of rice-dumplings

(*dango*), boiled red-beans (*ude-adzuki*), fruit (*midzu-gashi*), *oden* (a kind of dumpling) *saké* (rice-wine); *sushi* (rice-cakes plastered over with fish or sea-weed on which vinegar has been sprinkled) etc., and crowds of miscellaneous hawkers and quacks, including *tsuji-ura* sellers (*tsuji-ura* are small pieces of paper on which are printed poems or mottoes: these are wrapped in cracknels made of rice (*sembei*) or put among parched-peas as a pastime), newspaper sellers, fortune-tellers (*uranai-sha*), *nattō*-sellers (*nattō* is a kind of food made from boiled beans), sellers of the *tōfu* (bean curd) of Komatsu-bashi, sellers of *fūki-mame* (cooked and sweetened beans), blind shampooers (*amma*), female hairdressers (*onna kami-yui*), washermen (*sentaku-ya*), messengers, etc. Then there are *shinnai-bushi* singers (*shinnai-bushi* is a style of popular song originated by a man named Tsuruga Shinnai), *Kapporê*-dancers, singers of *hayari-uta* (popular songs), *ahodara-kyō* (reciters of comic imitation of Buddhist sacred writings and prayers), and flute-players (*shaku-hachi*). Beggars swarm in front of the smaller brothels early in the morning and ransack the remnants of food left over by guests from the previous evening: the sight of these hordes of dirty unkempt beings, clawing at and hungrily devouring the broken victuals, is a sight at once sad and disgusting.

The Examination of Licensed Women at the Hospital for Venereal Complaints.

In September 1867, a hospital for the treatment of venereal diseases of prostitutes was established in Yokohama for the first time in the history of Japan, and subsequently similar institutions were established at Kōbe and Nagasaki. This measure was adopted by the *Bakufu* Government owing to the representations made by an Englishman—Dr. Newton, R. N.—who, in spite of much opposition from prejudice and ignorance, succeeded in converting the authorities to his views after a long struggle. At first the physical examination of prostitutes was limited to the three ports of Yokohama, Kōbe, and Nagasaki, but in September 1871 the measure was applied to the women at Senju. The vital importance and value of such inspection not being understood by the public at large, the courtesans regarded the system with strong aversion, and they accordingly began to remove away from Senju to other quarters which were as yet free from the objectionable measure. This anti-inspection movement so seriously interfered with their business that the brothel-keepers were eventually forced to apply to the authorities to suspend the system, with the result that it was abolished in April 1872. In June 1873, however, the Tōkyō Municipal authorities again established physical examination offices, one being opened in each of the following six places:—Yoshiwara, Nedzu, Senju, Shinjiku, Shinagawa, and Itabashi. Examinations were made several times a month, and women who were found suffering from venereal diseases were sent to the hospital at Atagoshita for treatment. This was the first instance of a Lock hospital in

Tōkyō, but since then similar institutions have sprung into existence in different parts of the country.

In October 1888, physical examination places were established in the Yoshiwara and five other *yūkwaku* by the authorities, but in July 1889 these were abolished, and the brothel-keepers were ordered to fit up a hospital at their own expense: since that time the Lock hospital in every prostitute quarter has been maintained by the parties locally interested.

In the "Regulations of the Lock hospital of the Shin-Yoshiwara," which obtained official sanction in June 1889, we find the following:—

> "This hospital shall be known as the "*Kubai-in*" (Hospital for stamping out syphilis) and shall be established on the ground allotted for the purpose of providing against fire.
>
> This hospital shall be devoted mainly to the treatment of prostitutes who are suffering from venereal diseases, and shall be conducted on the system pursued in the former Police Lock hospital.
>
> There shall be a separate ward in the hospital in which prostitutes who are suffering from diseases other than syphilis may be treated.
>
> The hospital shall have one chief physician and five assistant physicians, one chief pharmaceutist and two assistant pharmaceutists, four officials to attend to miscellaneous duties, two clerks, and ten female nurses.
>
> The director and sub-director of the brothels shall supervise the monetary affairs of the hospital, and the appointment and dismissal of the chief surgeon and the members of the staff of the hospital shall be subject to the approval of the Metropolitan Police Board.
>
> As to the mode of maintenance, and financial arrangements, etc., of the hospital, these matters are provided for in a separate set of regulations."

[The rules relative to various details such as govern admissions, wards, etc., are omitted.]

The above extract will furnish some idea of the working

of a Lock hospital, and as to the question of maintenance the following particulars may be interesting.

Buildings, furniture, and surgical instruments.......	15,000
(This was defrayed from the reserve fund of the brothels).	
Working expenses per month	969
This is met as follows:—	
By levying a contribution of 1 sen per diem on each prostitute and reckoning the number of women as 2150...	645
By charges made to patients of 9 sen each with an average of 120 patients per diem..................	324

Generally speaking, the hospital is maintained in this manner, but when there is a deficit in its revenue this is made good by an appropriation from the reserve fund of the brothels (*kashi-zashiki no tsumi-tatekin.*)

As the number of prostitutes in the Yoshiwara is about three thousand women their physical examination cannot be effected in a single day; the quarter therefore is divided into districts to facilitate the process of inspection.

The regular examination days, and the inspection districts, are as follows:—

Monday:	Kyō-machi It-chō-me;
Tuesday:	Kyō-machi Ni-chō-me, and Sumi-chō;
Wednesday:	Ageya-chō, and Yedō-chō It-chō-me;
Thursday:	Yedo-chō Ni-chō-me.

Of course special examinations are made when necessity arises.

According to the latest investigations, the result of examinations showed the average rate of infected persons to be over 6 per cent. The annexed figures for 1897 may prove interesting, but it must be borne in mind that they can only be considered as comparatively reliable. The results of examinations of course depend very much upon the strictness of the doctors in attendance, consequently every prostitute quarter varies in its stated percentage of infected cases. In 1898 the percentage of disease rose to as high as 5.58 average as against 4.73 average in 1897. This difference has been caused by the more thorough inspection instituted by the present surgeon in charge—Mr. Doi.*

Results of Medical Inspection.

1897.

Month.	Number of inspections.	Number of infected cases.	Proportion per 100.	Number of guests entertained.
January	9,515	340	3.573	135,356
February	9,383	372	3.965	98,981
March	11,137	381	3.421	107,842
April	9,879	476	4.816	130,524
May	9,956	425	4.278	109,769
June	11,062	466	4.212	99,398
July	10,066	597	5.930	106,527
August	10,656	618	5.799	99,441
September	10,648	611	5.738	100,870
October	9,651	506	5.242	115,961
November	10,792	613	5.679	119,403
December	11,065	456	4.121	101,596
Total	123,810	5861	4.733	1,335,668

There were about 2900 to 3000 women in the Shin-Yoshiwara, and therefore each *yūjo* must have entertained, on the average, between 415 to 460 guests during the year.

* *Vide* further statistics in appendix.

Mu-sen Yū-kyō.

(*Going on a " Spree " without having any money to pay for it.*)

Mu-sen yū-kyō, or going on a gay frolic without being possessed of the necessary means, is locally known in the Yoshiwara as "*Ebisu-kō*" or *Hōritsu* (" Law "). The former term has been brought into use because the majority of those who intentionally go " on the spree " without money attire themselves in the gab of wealthy people and so resemble the God of Wealth (*Ebisu*), who is much *en evidence* at the festival of "Ebisukō" (in honor of the God of Wealth), although in reality they haven't a " red cent " (*bita-ichi-mon*) with which to bless themselves when the time for squaring up accounts comes. The latter term has been coined owing to the fact that a large number of law (*hōritsu*) students have been guilty of swindling, but they generally contrive to evade their liabilities by means of ingenious arguments and managing to force their victims into committing technically illegal acts of which they take mean advantage and which they use as a weapon against creditors. As a matter of fact, the brothel-keepers sometimes find it impossible to appeal to the police, and are often forced to " grin and bear " their losses in silence owing to the " cuteness " and sophistry of the " *hōritsu*." It is not uncommon for men belonging to the *shokunin* (artisan) class to enter a brothel under the influence of liquor without consulting the state of their purses, and consequently

Ebisu (The God of Wealth).

to find themselves confronted next morning with a long bill which they cannot settle. These fellows are taken in hand by professional "fixers" (*shimatsuya*=one who "fixes up" and settles matters) called "*uma-ya*" (horse-houses) who undertake to collect the bill on commission. The "fixers," or "*uma-ya*," send a messenger, known as an "*uma*" (horse), home with such defaulting guest, and this "*uma*" will dog the foosteps of the debtor until the latter pays his bill. Cases have however been known where the guest conducted a "horse" (*uma*) to a certain house, which he pretended was his own, entered on the pretext of obtaining some money, and walking through quietly, slid out of the back-door and escaped. But even when a guest temporarily escapes in this way, he is generally detected, and then, if he can't pay, the "*uma*" levy a squeeze of 50 *sen* per day on their victims.

The "*Ebisu-kō*" plan of having a "good time" gratuitously is made a kind of profession of by some rascals, and it is said that in Tōkyō there are several societies or bands (*kumi* or *gumi*) of expert swindlers in this line. Thus there are the Hongo-gumi, Kanda-gumi, Shitaya-gumi, Shiba-gumi, Fukagawa-gumi, etc., each *kumi* taking its name from the district to which it belongs. There is also a special *kumi* called "*Daruma-gumi*," because its members have the figure of Daruma tatooed on their forearms, and carry on their fraudulent operations in a delightfully free and easy manner. The figure of Daruma is supposed to represent the celebrated prince

(*Daruma.*)

and priest of Southern India—Dahma. This holy patriarch sat for nine years in profound abstraction till his legs fell off, therefore he is described in Japanese as "*o ashi no nai*" ("being without any august legs") but this, by a pun on the words, can be understood as "being without any august cash." Considering that the members of this "*Daruma-gumi*" never pay for anything, the "trade-mark" they have adopted is certainly very appropriate! Among the members of these beautiful societies, the act of evading payment of bills is known as "*Kipparai*" (*Kipparau*=to cut right through an obstruction) or "*Nakaseru*" ("to cause to weep").

Yoshiwara-gayoi no Jinrikisha.

(*The jinrikisha traffic of the Yoshiwara.*)

The use of *tsuji-kago* (palanquin) by the general public was permitted from the Genroku era (1688-1703), but the number of these conveyances in Yedo was limited to one hundred only! People, therefore, were in the habit of visiting the Yoshiwara on horseback. [The name of a street in the Yoshiwara—Uma-michi (Horse-street)—testifies to the fact that horses used to pass to and from the quarter.] Later on the palanquin traffic increased, but with the appearance of the Meiji (present) period, *kago* dropped out of fashion.

The *jinrikisha*-men who ply between the Yoshiwara and Uma-michi are called among themselves "*yonashi*" (an abbreviation of *yonabe-shi*=night-workers), owing to the fact that they sleep during the day-time and go to work at night. The best known *jinrikisha* houses ("*Ban*" 番) in the neighbourhood of the Yoshiwara are called:—"Tatsu-shin," "Hage-gumi," "Honchō-ban," "Dote-gumi," "Misawa," etc. The men belonging to these houses come out to pick up fares about dusk, and fortified with a "helmet of *saké*" chase after any likely pedestrian, accosting him with the words:—"*Danna, naka madé ikaga desu?*" ("Master, how would you like to go as far as the Yoshiwara?"). At first these knights of the *jinrikisha* demand an exorbitant fare, but reduce the same, after some haggling on the part of the would-be riders, to about 15 *sen* per *ri*. As soon as the man has settled terms, he will probably exclaim "*oi kita! hora yo!*" (almost untranslatable) and picking up the shafts of the vehicle start off as fast as his legs can carry him, brandishing his lantern (they call it a "*kamban*" among the jinrikisha fraternity) as he speeds along. A coolie who aims to secure a tip will probably ask his customer "*Danna, dochira ye tsukemasu ?*" ("Master, to which house shall I take you ?") and if the reply is "*Nani,*

Jinrikisha ("*Kuruma*") with puller and pusher (*atōshi*).

ō-mon de yoroshii" ("Oh, just put me down at the great gate") the rider is probably only bent on a stroll through the Yoshiwara for the purpose of sight-seeing. If, on the contrary, a fare replies "*Emon-zaka de orosē*" ("Put me down at Emonzaka"), he is generally a cowardly fellow who is desirous of protecting himself from the *jinrikisha*-puller's demand for additional payment by means of the close vicinity of the police-box on the hill.

When two *kuruma-ya* are employed—one as an *atōshi* (pusher) or *tsunappiki* (extra puller in front)—three times the single fare is usually demanded because one of the men must return without a vehicle, and cannot therefore pick up a fare on his way back. The *atōshi* or *tsunappiki* has to waste his time in going home, whereas the man who has his *jinrikisha* with him can generally earn something by picking up a fare on his return journey.

When a *jinrikisha*-man has brought a guest to a brothel or tea-house he is usually given a tip of from 20 to 30 *sen*, which is paid by the house and afterwards charged to the guest. There is also a body of *jinrikisha*-coolies known as "*mōrō-shafu*" ("shady" *jinrikisha*-men) who are invariably very bad characters. Sometimes these rascals have an arrangement with certain of the lower-class brothels (*bori-ya*=greedy and covetous houses) to inveigle country-folk into their dens and thus make improper gains. Among the *mōrō-shafu* there have been desperate scoundrels who even dared to go the length of taking fares to lonely places and there robbing them

Jinrikisha ("*Kuruma*") with puller and "*tsunappiki*"

of valuables and money after the fashion of highwaymen, but, owing to the stringent police system, as well as the control exercised by the jinrikisha-men's guild, these evils have been greatly diminished. As regards the slang used by the Yoshiwara *jinrikisha* coolies, there seems to be but little difference between it and that employed by outside *jinrikisha*-men.

Their method of counting is as follows:—

YOSHIWARA SLANG.	ORDINARY JAPANESE.	MEANING.
Oji	*Is-sen*	1 sen.
Jiba	*Ni sen*	2 "
Yami	*San sen*	3 "
Dari	*Shi sen*	4 "
Genko	*Go sen*	5 "
Ronji	*Roku sen*	6 "
Seinan	*Shichi sen*	7 "
Bando	*Has-sen*	8 "
Kiwa	*Ku sen*	9 "
Dote	*Jis-sen*	10 "
Furikan	*Ni-jis-sen*	20 "
Yari	*Ni-jū-go-sen*	25 "
Furi or "*Hansuke*"	*Go-jis-sen*	50 "
Ō-yari or *Ensuke*	*Ichi yen* or *Ichi mai*	1 yen.

Other slang words abound, but we have not space enough to give more than a few examples:—

Yaka. Being in a hurry (*Isogu koto.*)

Yanagi. Not being in a hurry (*Isoganai-koto.*)

Kaidashi. This word is used to express the idea of a *jinrikisha*-man taking a fare to a certain place at a very cheap rate with the object of securing a better fare on his return journey.

Aibako. (*Ni-nin-nori no kuruma*) A jinrikisha to seat two fares.

Monde-yuku. The act of changing half-way when two *jinrikisha* are being pulled in company and one contains two people and the other only one person.

Terashi. (*Rōsoku*) A candle.

There is a funny story told relative to the introduction of jinrikishas, and the consequent falling into desuetude of palanquins. A certain guest asked his "lady friend" in a brothel if she could tell him what sign was most used on the lanterns of *jinrikisha*-men: she promptly replied "*Yamagata ni ka no ji ga ō gozaimasu*" ("Mostly the shape of a mountain ᄉ with the *katakana* syllable "*ka*"— カ —"). She was thinking of the signs used to denote the different classes of prostitutes (*vide* page 123) and mistook the characters 人力 (*jinriki*) for the sign ᄉ and the syllable カ. It appears that in those early days the names of districts or guilds were not painted on the lanterns, but merely the two characters 人力 (*jinriki*), and hence the comical error!

Sanya-uma da-chin-dzuke.

(The cost of hiring horses to and from the Yoshiwara.)

The "*Kinsei Kisekikō*" (近世奇跡考) says that in the olden days young bloods who frequented the Yoshiwara used to travel to and fro on horse-back. It was also a fashion of the period to consider everything white to be tasteful. Thus the craze went so far that people fancied white horses, white sword-hilts, white leather *hakama* (loose pantaloons), white sleeves, and white everything else. In a book called the "*Ko-uta Sō-makuri*" (小唄總まくり)—published in the second year of the Kwambun (1661-1672) era—the following scale of charges for horse-hire is given:—

The "*Sanya-uma.*"

Guests going to the Yoshiwara. (*From an old print.*)

From Nihon-bashi to the gate of the Yoshiwara. Ordinary charge........	200 *mon* (20 *sen*)
Ditto, with a caparisoned white horse, and two footmen singing the "*Komuro-bushi*" song........................	348 *mon* (34 *sen* 8 *rin*)
From Iida-machi to the gate of the Yoshiwara. Ordinary charge	200 *mon* (20 *sen*)
Ditto, with a caparisoned white horse, and two footmen singing the "*Komuro-bushi*" song.......	348 *mon* (34 *sen* 8 *rin*)
From the Asakusa gate to the gate of the Yoshiwara. Ordinary charge........	132 *mon* (13 *sen* 2 *rin*)
Ditto, with a caparisoned white horse, and two footmen singing the "*Komuro-bushi*" song........................	248 *mon* (24 *sen* 8 *rin*)

The above proves the taste of the period for white horses, and besides this there was a song in vogue in the Meireki era (1655-1657) which described the graceful appearance of a man of rank visiting the Yoshiwara on the back of a white steed.

Byō-chū oyobi In-shoku no koto.

(Of the sickness of prostitutes and of their meals.)

Generally speaking, every *yūjo* possesses a room in which she lives irrespective of the fact of whether she has visits from guests or otherwise; but, in some houses, when a prostitute falls sick, she is not allowed to remain in her room, and is sent down to the *ō-beya* (large apartment) for treatment: this room is known among the inmates of the brothel as "*yosé-ba*" (place of gathering).

In a courtesan's apartment is to be found every cooking utensil necessary in the preparation of a meal, and therefore many of the girls take their meal in their own room, merely getting boiled rice up from the kitchen and preparing other articles themselves.

In some houses however, all the inmates have dinner together in the kitchen, and so there is an old saying—" *Yūjo wo nabe-kama nashi no shotai-mochi* " ("*Yūjo* are like householders who are possessed of neither pots nor pans.") In the Kajita-rō the *yūjo* used to make their servants boil rice for them in their own rooms over charcoal fires.

Hike no koto.

(Closing hours in the Yoshiwara.)

Mention is made in the " *Yoshiwara Ōkagami* "(吉原大鑑) that the *hikê* was fixed at 10 o'clock, but afterwards this was considered too early, and no clapping of *hyōshigi* (a pair of wooden blocks which are struck together as a signal) was made at that hour. The great gate (*Ō-mon*) was shut at 10 o'clock, but the *kuguri-do* (a small low door cut in a gate) was left open so as to permit ingress and egress. When the hour of midnight struck, (then called *kokonotsu-doki*), the *hyōshigi* were clapped together four times, and the place was finally closed up.

Kō-chō no koto.

(The next morning.)

In the " *Yoshiwara Ōkagami* " (吉原大鑑)—referred to in the preceding chapter—it says that " *the parting and return home in the morning is called* " *Kōchō* " (後朝), but in ordinary Japanese the parting of two lovers in the morning is idiomatically termed " *Kinu-ginu no wakare.*"

Hiru-jimai Yo-jimai no koto

(The day and night engagements of courtesans.)

The " *Yoshiwara Ōkagami* " (吉原大鑑) also says that there were formerly two kinds of *shimai* (仕舞 here the word means "engagement") viz:—*Hiru-jimai* (day engagement) and *Yo-jimai* (night engagement.)*

Raku-seki no koto.

(The removal of names from the register of the Yoshiwara.)

The "*Yoshiwara Ōkagami*" (吉原大鑑) says:—

There are three kinds of *rakuseki*. One is to leave the Yoshiwara at the expiry of the term of engagement (*nenki aki*); the second is to be redeemed by a guest before the term of service has expired (*mi-uke*); the third is to be redeemed by parents (also *mi-uke*). When a woman is discharged by her master, owing to the expiry of her term of engagement, she receives back from him her contract (*shōmon*) of service and goes away after bidding farewell to her friends and acquaintances. At the same time a check or pass (*tegata*), couched in the following terms, is given to the woman to serve as a token of her right to pass out of the great gate:—

Courtesan..........(name)..........belonging to the house of ....(name)........

Her term of engagement having expired, she is to be handed over to her relatives outside the quarter, therefore please allow her to pass throught the great gato without fail.......... (Date)..........

(Signed) HEADMAN. (SEAL.)

To SHIROBEI, Esq.

Great gate.

But although a woman may be fortunate enough to escape the bitterness of this living death, and succeed in reaching the outside world again, yet she has violated the virtue of chastity, wasted the flower of her youth in vicious living, and as she is unaccustomed to attend to the proper duties of women her future prospects are anything but cheerful and reassuring.

Generally, the term of engagement is supposed to expire when a prostitute reaches the age of 25 years, but as a matter of fact the girls generally remain until they have reached the age of 27.

* *Shimai* is changed into *jimai* after "*hiru*" and "*yo*" for the sake of euphony.

As for the *mi-uke* (redemption by a guest), it is a vastly different thing to the *nenki-aki* (expiry of term of engagement) as it not only relieves a woman from years of disgusting and painful servitude, but it may enable her to attain to a life of comparative ease and luxury. Under these circumstances, *mi-uke* is earnestly desired by many a prostitute, and although in vulgar novels certain girls are made to decline the offer of *mi-uke* by some rich guest, because they have lovers to whom they have pledged themselves to marry on the expiration of their term of engagement, such occurrences in real life are extremely rare. Far from dissuading a guest from purchasing her freedom, the average *yūjo* will positively importune him to take her out if he manifests his intention of doing so. When a guest wishes to redeem a woman for whom he has taken a fancy, and whose affection he desires to obtain, he mentions the matter to the brothel-keeper, who in turn communicates with the girl's parents, and as, of course, the latter can raise no reasonable objection, the *mi-uke* is forthwith arranged. The redemption-money (*mi-no-shiro-kin*), and all the debts of the girl, are paid by the guest, and her contract of service (*mi-uri shōmon*="document-of-the-sale-of-the-body") is returned. In the proceedings that follow, the brothel-keeper plays the part of a parent to the girl. To her friends *sekihan* (red rice : rice boiled with red beans) and other food is distributed, while presents of *seki-han* and *katsubushi* (smoked bonito) are made to the tea-houses of the Naka-no-chō to celebrate the occasion. Farewell tips are also given to the *geisha* (singing girls), *hō an* (jesters), and *wakai-mono* (men-servants), with whom the guest is acquainted, and a splendid banquet is held in the room where he has so often disported himself. On this occasion, the girl who has been redeemed, and her erstwhile fellow *yūjo*, assemble, and *geisha* and *hōkan* are invited to enliven the dinner. After the feast is over, the couple are escorted by a troop of men and women as far as the *ō-mon* (great gateway), where palanquins (*kago*) are waiting for them, and amidst a chorus of good-wishes and "*sayonara*" (good-bye!) enter these conveyances and ride away.

Further, there are two kinds of *yūjo*, known as "*zegen-tsuki*" and "*zegen-nashi*," or those who were sold by parents direct, and those who are sold through the medium of procurers (*zegen*). Those who are sold direct by parents (*zegen-nashi*) are easier and less expensive to redeem, whereas the *zegen-tsuki* (sold through procurers) are not so, as the *zegen* often purposely try to increase the debts of such women, or to secretly prolong their term of engagement, thus throwing obstacles in the way of their redemption by a guest.

Gwaishutsu oyobi tōbō.

(Exit and flight from the Yoshiwara.)

The *Yoshiwara Ō-kagami* (吉原大鑑) says that the going abroad of prostitutes was prohibited at the founding of the Yoshiwara, and only *tayū* were occasionally allowed to attend the Hyō-jō-sho (Supreme Court) to wait on officials.

In the case of a "jōro" being summoned before the "*machibugyō*" she was accompanied by two *wakaimono*, the master of the brothel, five wardsmen ("*go-nin-gumi*") a representative of the "*nanushi*" and her "*yarite.*" The latter made a small present to the attendants of the "*bugyō*" that they might spread a mat for the "*jōro*" to sit on, and the "*jōro*" remained silent while the "*yarite*" answered the questions of the judge.

Once in every Spring, all the inmates of the brothels used to go out to either Ueno, Asukayama, or Mukōjima, to see the cherry-blossoms, and on these occasions they spent the day in drinking *saké* under the cherry-trees, and amusing themselves by dancing and other pastimes. The custom of the *tayū* appearing at the Hyō-jō-sho ceased about the era of Kwan-ei (1624-1643), and that of cherry-blossom viewing also dropped out of fashion after the Bunsei era (1818-1829). Even after this latter date, sick prostitutes requiring the treatment of a physician outside the Yoshiwara, or those who wished to go to their master's villa (*rō-shu no bessō*) for the benefit of their health, were allowed to pass through the gate. If the parents of prostitutes who lived at Asakusa, and in its neighbourhood, were dangerously ill, they were allowed to visit them by the special permission of the *rō-shu* (brothel-keeper), but even in these cases the women were passed out under pretext of sickness, and a passport was given to them by the *nanushi*, as follows :—

> Courtesan........(name)........employed by.........(name)........, who is under my management, being sick, is sent out of the great gateway (*ō-mon*) to visit Doctor.........(name).........accompanied by her master. She is to be allowed to pass the gate without fail.
>
> (Signed)...........................
>
> (*Nanushi* (SEAL.)

To SHIROBEI ESQ.,
Great Gateway.

A woman thus allowed out of the Yoshiwara would perhaps have looked out of her *kago* (palanquin) as she was borne along through the streets, and wondered at the novelty of her surroundings. Then she might have become impatient, owing to her anxiety after her parent's health, and urged the *kago-ya* (bearers) to hurry forward. Arriving at her parents' house she would perhaps have found her father, seriously ill, lying in squalid wretchedness, and have been met by her poor old mother who, taking her daughter's hand in her own, might have been overcome with deep emotion and wept bitterly. Then came long consultations about the future, and the day of grace began to draw to a close, for it was a rule that courtesans out on leave had to return to the Yoshiwara before 5.30 p.m. By and by the sad and solemn tones of the temple bell at Asakusa would give her warning that her time had expired, and urged on by the *yarite* (an old brothel hag), whom she had perforce brought with her, she rose and bade farewell to her weeping parents, and re-entering her *kago* was carried back to her life of gilded misery well-nigh blinded by an agony of helpless tears.

Although the rules relating to the passage of the *ō-mon* (great gateway) were as above, there were some prostitutes who attempted to run away from the Yoshiwara, owing to an irresistible desire to see their lovers, or being heavily in debt. When such an event happened, the brothel-keeper concerned sent out men on all sides to trace the absconding woman, or applied to the police office (*mem-ban-sho*) for her capture, and as detectives were immediately set to work to ascertain her whereabouts, nearly all runaway women were caught and ignominiously brought back to their masters. When an absconder was brought back, she was censured for her ill-considered step by the master, *yarite*, and *bantō*, and all the expenses incurred in connection with her detection and capture were added to her debt: this had the effect of prolonging the term of her servitude in the brothel. Sometimes private punishment was meted out to her by the master if he thought she deserved it. When an elopement was attempted twice or thrice in succession, the woman in question was generally re-sold to one of the prostitute quarters outside the Yoshiwara through the agency of a *zegen* (procurer): this practice was called "*Kuragae*" (change of saddles). It is said to have been the custom that when the keeper of a brothel outside the Yoshiwara was in treaty for the purchase of a "*kuragae*" prostitute, he sent his *bantō* to the house to which she belonged as an ordinary guest. The *bantō* spent the night with her, and the *mi-no-shiro-kin* (price-of-the-body) was settled according to his report.

Yūjo byō-shi oyobi jō-shi no koto.*

(Of the death and double-suicide of courtesans.)

The *Yoshiwara Ō-kagami,* (吉原大鑑) says that as the life of a courtesan is generally spoken of as "*the painful world*" (*Ku-gai* 苦界) its really painful nature may be well imagined. Not only does a woman who has fallen into this unhappy position become a mere plaything to gratify the lusts of immoral men, but her freedom is so curtailed by circumstances that she cannot even sleep and eat independently, and therefore often has her constitution ruined owing to her irregular mode of eating and drinking. Others fall sick by reason of excessive anxiety over monetary affairs, and others fall a prey to loathsome and, perchance, virtually incurable diseases.

When a first-class prostitute (*jōtō no yūjo*) was sick, if the master of the brothel had been to much expense in procuring her, he would spare no pains to cure her illness, and if the matter was serious the woman would be removed to the master's villa, (which was situated, perhaps, in the vicinity of Imado or Sanya), for treatment. Such an invalid would be closely attended by a *kamuro* (female page), and sometimes the master himself went to some temple to pray for her recovery. If, however, the *yūjo* happened to belong to a lower class, and was not particularly popular, the attitude of the brothel-keeper would be entirely different, and the treatment of the girl would be simply entrusted to some quack doctor, the poor creature being meanwhile thrust into an out-of-the-way gloomy room where she would pine away unseen by the other inmates of the house. When her condition was considered very precarious, the master, in order to avoid the trouble and expense

* Also see appendix.

involved at death, used to summon her parents and hand the sick woman over to them together with her *shōmon* (document of engagement). When a *yūjo* died in a brothel the matter was reported by the monthly manager (*tsuki-gyōji*) of the Yoshiwara to the *nanushi*, and the latter summoned her parents or surety to take delivery of her corpse. In the event of the home of her parents being far away, the remains of the *yūjo* were interred by the brothel-keeper in the Dōtetsu (general burial place) on the bank in the presence of her surety. This place was also known as the "*nage-komi*" (the "throwing-in-place"). There is an old poem illustrating the sad future which is in store for some unfortunate *shōgi*: it runs:—

> "*She is hurried to the grave in a pauper's coffin, with but one solitary little maid to mourn her.*"

Alas! this description was only too true in many cases.

Besides natural death, there were many *yūjo* who committed suicide, together with their sweethearts, owing to various reasons, among which the most powerful were either their inability to live together in conjugal felicity with each other, or their pecuniary embarrassments. Such double suicides had been known as *shinjū* (心中 "the inside of the heart or mind), but about the era of Kyōhō (1716-1735) Judge Ōoka Echizen-no-Kami, (who is regarded as the Japanese Solomon), gave it out as his opinion that the word *shinjū* (心中) if read reversed would make *chūshin* (中心=loyalty) and that it was absurd to call the double suicide of a man and woman, owing to love affairs, "loyalty". He therefore ordained that this kind of suicide should be called "*aitai-jini*" (相對死="death by mutual consent") and that word was accordingly adopted.

The late Mr. Koidzumi Yakumo (Lafcadio Hearn) in his "*Glimpses of Unfamiliar Japan*" (Vol. 1.) gives an extremely interesting example of *shinjū*, as follows :—

"There lived in ancient times a *hatamoto* called Fuji-eda Geki, "a vassal of the Shōgun. He had an income of five thousand "koku of rice,—a great income in those days. But he fell in love "with an inmate of the Yoshiwara named Ayaginu, and wished "to marry her. When his master bade the vassal choose between "his fortune and his passion, the lovers fled secretly to a farmer's "house, and there committed suicide together."

"The sad occurrence was commemorated in a popular song "which ran:—

"*Kimi to neyaru ka, go-sen-goku toru ka?*
"*Nan no go-sen-goku kimi to neyo?*
"Once more to rest beside her, or keep five thousand koku?
"What care I for koku? Let me be with her!"

According to the *Tōto Ko-fun-shi* (東都古墳志=Record of ancient tombs in the Eastern Capital), the Jōkan-ji (浄閑寺) temple of Minowa, Shitaya district, was the burial ground of the *yūjo* of the Yoshiwara. When the secret prostitutes of the City of Yedo were transported into the Yoshiwara, they were called *baijo*(賣女="sold women"). Originally the bodies of these women, and other secret prostitutes, were interred in the burial ground of this temple only, but later on it became the custom to bury their remains elsewhere, as also those of regular *yūjo*. The book goes on to say :—

"In these burial places are to be found many graves of *yūjo* "who committed suicide with their paramours. On the tomb-"stones are to be found engraved the descriptions of the swords "with which they killed themselves, as well as their names and "ages. There is something so weird and uncanny about these "horribly pitiless records on the grey lichen-covered monuments "that the blood of a sightseer runs cold and he becomes so "nervous that he leaves the gloomy spot with the intention of "never visiting it again."*

* During the Genroku (1688 1703) and Shōtoku (1711-1715) eras, "*shinjū*" or double suicides of guests and "*jōro*" became so common that the jōroya were forced for the sake of self-preservation to expose the bodies of both the man and the woman on the

Shin Yoshiwara no Bodaiji.

The Cemetery of the Shin-Yoshiwara).

The *Jōkan-ji* temple at Minowa, and the Dōtetsu on† the bank (the Nihon-dzutsumi), were formerly the fixed burial places of the Yoshiwara *yūjo* who died during their terms of service and who had no person to take charge of their remains. Since the Restoration, however, the regulations of the prostitute quarters having been altered, the burial of a *yūjo* in these cemeteries is a rare occurrence.

The grave of the famous Taka-o of the Mi-ura-ya, and that of Usugumo, are both in the Dōtetsu cemetery. The grave of Usugumo is known as *neko-dzuka* (the-mound-of-the cat). October the 25th, 1893, having fallen on the 233rd anniversary of the death of Taka-o, a grand religious service was held in this temple and was attended by large crowds of people belonging to the Yoshiwara.

On the grave of Taka-o is written :—

Samu kaze ni	Alas! poor maple leaves
Moroku mo kutsuru	which are crushed and scat-
Momiji kana !	tered by the cold winds.

Karitaku no Koto.

(The temporary prostitute quarter.)

The *kari-taku* means the establishment of a temporary place for carrying on business when the Yoshiwara is com-

Nihombashi for three days. The *eta* or "outcasts" then buried them, and writing their story, read it about the streets of Yedo. The burial of those who committed "*shinjū*" was the burial of dogs. Their hands and legs were tied together, and the bodies were wrapt up in straw matting and thrown into a common grave. The people of the jōroya believed that this would prevent the ghosts of the dead haunting the house where they died, the superstition being that animals had no ghosts.

† Now called the "*Kō-gwan-zan Saihōji*," situated at No. 36, Shōden-chō, Asakusa district.

pletely destroyed by fire. When such a disaster occurs, the brothel-keepers apply to the authorities for a permit to establish a *kari-taku,* and their application is said to be granted forthwith, even in case of only partial destruction of the quarter by fire.

The Yoshiwara has been enjoying comparative immunity from fire for quite a long period, but as late as 1862 (May 29th) more than half of the brothels in the quarter were burnt to the ground, and a *kari-taku* was established in the neighbourhood of Fukagawa. During the time that the business is carried on in a temporary quarter, rules and usages are not adhered to very strictly by the brothels, and sometimes, under the pretext of aiming at simplicity, even tea-houses are allowed to carry on the profession of brothel-keeping. Under these circumstances, more money flows into the pockets of the brothel-keeper than in ordinary times, and the trade usually becomes brisker than previously, owing to a larger number of guests being attracted by the novelty of the altered conditions. When therefore the Yoshiwara is not prosperous, and trade is dull, the brothel-keepers not unnaturally wish for the establishment of a *kari-taku.* In the 2nd year of Kei-ō (1866), while the *kari-taku* was established at Monzen-chō, Fukagawa, an application was forwarded to the authorities by a certain brothel keeper, offering the payment of 10,000 *ryō* per annum if they would give permission to leave the "temporary quarter" there permanently: the application was rejected. The "*kari-taku*" practice originated in the third year of the Meireki era (1657) when the brothels of Fukiya-chō were swept out of existence by the memorable conflagration of that year, and pending removal to the Yoshiwara, temporary brothels were established at Imado, Sanya, and Yama-no-shiku by means of renting ordinary houses.

After that time, whenever the Yoshiwara was destroyed by a fire, a temporary quarter was established for from two hundred to three hundred days, either at Ryōgoku, Nakadzu, Takanawa, Fukagawa, Asakusa, Namiki, Hanakawado, etc. The temporory brothels established in the second year of Kōkwa (1845) were scattered here and there in twenty different streets, viz:—*Yamakawa-chō, Ta-machi, it-chō-me, Ta-machi, ni-chō-me, Sanya-machi, Asakusa-machi, Shin Torikoye-machi, it-chōme, Shin Torikoye-machi, ni-chō-me, Shin Torikoye-machi, san-chō-me*, in front of the *Hachiman On-yado:* (in *Honjō* district); *Rokushaku-yashiki, Kaneyashiki, Nagaoka-chō, jit-chō-me; Hachirobei-yashiki; Matsui-chō, it-chō-me*, and *Irie-chō;* (in *Fukagawa* district); *Eitai-ji-Monzen-chō, Naka-chō, Higashi Naka-chō, Yamamoto-chō, Matsumura-chō, Tsukuda-chō, Tokiwa-chō, ni-chō-me.* In *Hanakawado-machi* and *Shōden-chō* (*Asakusa*), Tamaya Sanzaburō, and twenty-one other well-known brothels, were carrying on their business under special charter (*tokkyo*) received from the authorities.

The official instructions issued at the time of the establishment of temporary brothels were not uniform by any means, as they were drawn up to suit special circumstances, but an idea of such notifications may be gained by perusing the following transcript of one issued in the 6th year of Kwansei (1794):—

> Owing to the destruction by fire of the Yoshiwara, the carrying on of the profession in temporary houses is hereby allowed, provided that the Keepers strictly conform to the following conditions:—
>
> (1). The clothes worn by the *yūjo* shall not be such as to be strikingly attractive.

(2). No *yūjo* or *kamuro* is to be allowed outside the houses, and this applies even to being outside the houses to which they may actually belong.
Even inside the houses, they shall not be permitted to appear in the front second-storey or in the windows in such a manner as to attract passers-by.

(3). So long as the business is carried on outside of the regular quarter, everything shall be done in a quiet and unobtrusive manner, and no such displays as are allowed in the Yoshiwara shall be attempted nor permitted.

The following description of a *Kari-taku* is given in the "*Yedō Hanjō-ki*" (江戸繁昌記 Records of the prosperity of Yedo):—

"A temporary brothel has, as a rule, very limited accommodation, its capacity being only about one-tenth of that of the proper permanent building in the Yoshiwara, while the influx of guests is ten times larger than usual. Under such circumstances the beds of several guests are packed into one room, and simply divided off by means of screens: this kind of sleeping accommodation is called *wari-doko* (a divided bed). The beds are so arranged that sometimes one's feet are in juxtaposition with another person's head and *vice versa.* Inside the screens may be heard the voice of a *yūjo* chattering to her guest and flattering him with complimentary speeches such as:—'Ever since our first meeting my love for you has become an ardent passion, and my whole soul yearns for your presence. There may be days when the raven will cease its cawing, but never a night when I fail to dream of you, my prince!' * * *

"'Within the fortification of screens to the left you can faintly hear a guest whispering to his *yūjo* that if she loves him he is willing to redeem her and take her away. * * * In front, the guest would appear to be a student, as he is reciting some Chinese poems from the Tōshisen. By and by his *yūjo* begins to wonder what he is talking about, and asks him: 'What magical words are you uttering, and what is that *chōmen* (account-book) you carry with you?' 'Alas! what an ignorant woman you are!' the guest retorts, 'these are famous Chinese poems which you would do well to remember' * * * At the back is a guest who has been deserted by his *yūjo* and who, finding it impossible to remain passive, is having frequent recourse to yawning and stretching. * * * Somewhere in the room is a gentleman who has been carousing too freely, and although he is so top-heavy that he cannot stand up, he objects to lying down and going to sleep. He is apparently so beautifully boosy that when he struggles hard to arise from his couch his legs give way under him and he sinks back huddled up in a heap. Disappointed, but not discouraged, at his inability to get up, the groggy veteran begins to express his maudlin sentiments in a loud grumbling voice, venting his indignation one moment and laughing at imaginary objects the next. Shortly afterwards he will endeavour to relieve the monotony of existence by starting to sing *Kiyari* (firemen's songs) in a shrill falsetto tone with all the force his lungs are capable of, but every now and then breaking down and finishing off with an inarticulate mutter or drunken gurgle.

"All of a sudden the lovely noise ceases, as his companion *yūjo*, fearing that his continued bawling may disturb other guests, tries to gag the singing inebriate, persuades him to lie down quietly and go to sleep, covers him over with the bed clothes, and thus extinguishes him for the balance of the night * * * Now, one guest, who has been sound asleep under the influence of liquor, suddenly wakes up and starts off to obey the calls of nature, but in the semi-darkness he comes into contact with the wall of screens surrounding him. Then he gropes around in order to find an outlet, but failing, owing to his muddled condition, to discover his geographical position, he commences to angrily demand the reason of his supposed imprisonment and to threaten that if he be not instantly released he will smash everything in the house. No reply being forthcoming, the pot-valiant young man kicks out savagely at the screens around him, knocking them down on the top of those sleeping beauties within and rudely dispersing their pleasant dreams; and then, giving way to a paroxysm of maniacal rage, he makes a furious attack on the remaining screens, throwing them round and down in every direction, thus disclosing some very interesting sights in various parts of the room. This proves too much for the nerves of the other guests, and a general stampede ensues, the whole position being accentuated by the hysterical cries of *yūjo* and shouts of 'fire,' etc."

From this description it is evident that ordinary houses temporarily transformed into brothels must have been interesting places to visit, especially when crowded with guests, and that many comical and amusing scenes must have been enacted within their walls. It is just because the *kari-taku* presented so many novel and funny features that persons were tempted to go crowding into them.

Dochū no koto oyobi tsuki-dashi no koto.

(*The procession of yūjo and the first appearance of "recruits" in the Yoshiwara*).

The procession, or promenade, of *yūjo* has been considered as, *par excellence*, the most splendid spectacle and important ceremony of the Yoshiwara. Once in the earlier years of *Meiji*, and once again in 1887, when the cherry-blossoms were in full bloom, this wonderful procession took place, but since then no attempt has been made to revive the time-honoured custom. Even on the two occasions referred to, the affair was not carried out in strict accordance with the ancient style, but in a far simpler fashion.

The best account of this procession of *yūjo* ever written is given in Mr. Henry Norman's "*The Real Japan*," and it is therefore quoted here.

> "The most extraordinary spectacle of the Yoshiwara takes place for a few afternoons at five o'clock three times a year, when the flowers in the long street gardens are changed. First in spring comes the pink glory of the cherry-blossoms; then in summer the purple of the iris; then in autumn the hundred colours of the chrysanthemum, the national flower of Japan. When the new flowers are planted the *yūjo* pay them a state visit. From each of the principal houses half a dozen of the most beautiful are chosen and arrayed in gorgeous clothes, their hair dressed monumentally, combs three feet long stuck in from side to side, and then they are mounted upon black lacquered *geta* or pattens a foot high. When they are ready to start a score of servants accompany them; two or three precede them to put the crowd away; one holds the hand of each *yūjo* upon either side, and solemnly and very slowly, a step a minute, the wonderful procession moves

round the garden. Other processions issue from the houses and meet and pass, and by and by the whole main street of the Yoshiwara is packed with an open-mouthed crowd, over whose heads the faces of the processionists can be seen here and there.

"The walking upon the tall heavy *geta* is itself an accomplishment and girls are specially trained to it. One foot is put out a little way and planted firmly, then the other *geta* is lifted by the toes tightly grasping the strap which passes between the first and second toes, and swung round in front of the other and across it. The first is then lifted and placed on the other side of the second—exactly in fact like a skater doing the outside edge. The Japanese call it *hachimonji ni aruku*—' figure of eight walking.' It is difficult to give in words an adequate notion of the extraordinary effect of this procession. The costly and gorgeous clothes of the *yūjo*, silks of marvellous richness, and brocades blazing with scarlet and gold; the exaggerated bow of her *obi* tied in front (the courtesan is compelled by law to distinguish herself in this way),* the pyramidal *coiffure*, the face as white as snow, the eyelashes black, the lips vermillion and even the toe-nails stained pink; the men-servants respectfully holding the tips of her fingers on each side and giving as much heed to every step as an acolyte might give to an aged Pope, her several women-servants walking solemnly behind: a footman pushing back the crowd and another removing every twig or dead leaf from her path; her slow and painful *hachimonji;* her stony gaze straight before her, half contemptuous and half timid; the dense and silent crowd; the religious aspect of the vicious ceremony,—all these go to make a spectacle apart from anything one has ever seen—an event outside all one's standard of comparison—a reminisence of phallic ceremonial—a persistence of Priapus.

In the "*Yoshiwara Taizen*" (吉原大全 *The Complete Book of the Yoshiwara*) reference is made to the effect that

"The term *dōchū* (道中 a journey; travelling) meant the going out "of a prostitute to an *age-ya*, or to promenade in the Naka-no-chō. "It was used in the sense of travelling to a distant part of the "country because, for instance, when a *yūjo* of Yedo-chō started "out to go to Kyō-machi she was supposed to be going on a "journey.

"It requires some considerable training to enable a *yūjo* to "make a *dōchū* as it is a most difficult thing to lift the lower por-

* Formerly this was the case, but now the *obi* is tied in front merely out of deference to old custom. The ancient sumptuary regulations have been abolished long ago.

"tion of her clothes in such a manner as to move with graceful
"dignity.

"Though there are no *age-ya* to be found at present, the cus-
"tom is still preserved, and the appearance of *yūjo* in the
"Naka-no-chō is called the *dōchū.*"

In the days when there were *age-ya* in the Yoshiwara it was the custom for a *tayū* to go out to the *age-ya* to which she was called to meet her guest, and on these occasions she was escorted by her *shinzō, yarite, kamuro,* and *wakaimono.* With reference to this subject, the *Dōbō Go-en* (洞房語園) says that

"In the Moto Yoshiwara (prior to its removal to the present
"site), *yūjo* used to be carried to *age-ya* on the backs of servants
"when it rained. These men-servants (called *roku-shaku*), by plac-
"ing their hands behind their backs made a seat, by means of
"their palms, on which the *tayū* sat—or rather knelt—carefully
"wrapping her underwear around her feet and leaving her outside
"dress hanging loosely down. The *tayū's* hands were not employ-
"ed in holding any part of her bearer's body, but engaged in ad-
"justing her garments, etc. From behind, a servant covered her
"with a long-handled oil-paper umbrella, and in this position the
"*tayū* is said to have looked very stylish."

Since the removal of the old brothel quarter to the present Yoshiwara, it is said that *tayū* sometimes went out to *age-ya* riding in palanquins, as this was considered to be a convenient mode of transit.

In the "*Dōbō Go-en I-hon Kō-i*" (洞房語園異本考異) it is stated that

"Up to the era of Keichō the ladies of noble families were
"usually borne on the backs of men-servants in rainy weather,
"palanquins being but every seldom used. These ladies wore a
"kind of veil-like hood (*katsugi*) on their heads, and on the backs
"of the bearers were fastened wooden rests on which the women
"could sit. The custom of prostitutes being carried on the backs
"of men-servants appears to have arisen through a desire to ape
"the higher classes.

Courtesans being carried to *age-ya*—*vide* pages 192–193.

"Since their removal to the Shin Yoshiwara, palanquins were "often used, but later on were dispensed with, and *yūjo* preferred "to walk to their destination even in rainy weather * * * As stated "above, better-class *yūjo* went out in palanquins when the weather "was rainy, or the roads dirty, but *shin-zō* used to walk, wearing "sandals called "*tsume-kakushi*" (nail hiders): these *tsume-kakushi* "were more particularly in use in the Mi-ura-ya of Kyō-machi."

The reason that the promenading of *yūjo* became one of the most splendid spectacles of the Yoshiwara in later days was because (though the women ceased to pass to and from the *age-ya* after the disappearance of the latter) they used to be in the habit of showing themselves gorgeously apparelled in the Naka-no-chō and holding an exhibition of themselves in the tea-houses there. The custom of the *dōchū* is therefore a relic of a prevailing fashion of those times.

As already stated, a *yūjo* who went out walking in rainy weather was covered by a long-handled umbrella held over her head from behind. This umbrella was usually employed by persons of gentle birth, but its use by *yūjo* was permitted on the supposition that the latter were Court ladies.*

To see the procession of a *yūjo* at night passing through the brilliantly lighted streets surrounded by her *shinzō*, *kamuro*, *yarite* and *wakaimono*, proceded by a great lantern emblazoned with her crest, and followed by a crowd of tea-house and *funa-yadō* people each carrying a lighted *chōchin*, was a very imposing sight indeed, and one which probably was unique of its kind and without a parallel in any other country.

In ancient times all *yūjo* wore sandals, but later on a woman named Fuyō (in the employ of Hishiya Gonzaemon of Sumi-chō), who was an open-handed extravagant person and

* This involves a pun on the words *jōro* (女郎 "a harlot") and *jōro* (上臈 "a lady in waiting attached to the court.")

fond of ostentatious display, began to wear *koma-geta* (a kind of matted clog) even on fine days. The charming manner in which this woman minced along on her *koma-geta*, artfully disclosing the scarlet lining of her clothes as she walked, and the general grace of her demeanour, evoked universal admiration. Imitation, it is said, is the sincerest form of flattery, and the people must have been very much fascinated with Fuyō's *koma-geta*, for they all began to gradually imitate this style of foot-gear, until it became the popular fashion of the Yoshiwara. On New Year's day, and on other holidays, no *koma-geta* were used by the women belonging to the house of Matsubaya Hanzaemon of Yedo-chō, and it therefore seems that even at this period something of the simplicity of old-time customs was retained, and that the community had not as yet fallen into the luxurious habits of later days. The extravagance manifested in wearing apparel used in promenading appears to have reached its climax about the 11th year of Kwansei (1799), for it is mentioned in the "*Kyaku Monogatari*" (客物語=written by Samba—a noted humourous writer), that the outer garment was of deep blue coloured satin, the skirt being embroidered with a pattern composed of lobsters: the underclothes were of green coloured *mōru* (a kind of thick cloth woven with raised figures) secured by a *shigoki* (loose girdle) of grey-coloured satin lined with red crêpe. The hair was done in the *Hyōgo-musubi* style and was ornamented with two combs and eight hair-pins, this having been the regular custom of the time.

In the Bunkwa (1804-1817) and Bunsei (1818-1829) eras the *shikake* (loose robes) worn when promenading were either black or green in colour and were, as a rule, richly embroidered in gold and silver thread and silk thread of various hues. The patterns most in vogue were *unriū* (dragons and clouds), *hiriū* (flying dragons), *gan-ka no botan* (peony flowers below a rocky cliff), *mō-shi kyō-hon* (raging lion), etc ; and the general effect of these gorgeous embroideries, glittering with gold and blazing with all the colours of the rainbow worked in harmonious blendings, was indeed striking and unique. Under the *shikake* were worn three white *rinzu* (figured satin) *kosode* (one over the other) each bearing five large crests dyed upon them.

Their manner of walking was known as *uchi-hachi-mon-ji*, because each step was taken with the toes pointed inwards (*uchi*) like the Chinese character (*monji*) eight (*hachi* 八). There are but very few persons who now understand this Style of walking. Later on, the custom of wearing *geta* (clogs) was introduced by the *yūjo* Fuyō, (already mentioned) who was vainly fond of finery, as she initiated the practice of wearing three-legged *geta* with straw sandals attached to them. There were certain fixed ceremonial dresses which were worn according to the season, and special costumes for the New Year's holidays and the 1st day of the 8th month. It is stated in the *Kita-zato Bun-ken-roku*(北里聞見錄) that on the 3rd day of the 1st month of the 11th year of Bunkwa (February, 1814) among the *yūjo* who were out walking in their brand new *geta* and magnificent gala dresses, astonishing the spectators with the dazzling splendour of their gay apparel, was a woman named Ariwara (belonging to the house of Tsuru-ya Ichisaburō of Kyō-machi It-chōme) who became the centre of attraction owing to the novelty of her costume. She wore robes made in imitation of those worn by certain military officers of the Imperial Court (*Ō-uchi bu-kan*). From the waist upwards the material was of a pale blue tint and on it were embroidered three corded lines in silver thread. On the left shoulder was embroidered a bundle of *kiri-fu no ya* (arrows winged with the spotted feathers of a falcon) worked in gold, silver, and coloured threads. This upper garment represented the *naoshi* (a kind of robe worn by nobles). The lower portion was dyed a deep purple and embroidered with *yatsu-busa no fuji* (eight-petalled wistaria flowers) in silver: this apparently was intended for *sashi-nuki* (a kind of silk trousers worn by warriors.)

Her *obi* (girdle) was of crimson worked with elaborate embroideries in gold, silver, and coloured threads. Her hair was done in the *karawa* (*osa-fune*) style. The whole " get up" was that of a Court warrior, and it is said that the idea of dressing herself in this manner occurred to Ariwara owing to her family name being similar to that of the noted warrior and poet of ancient day—Ariwara Narihira Ason. This instance of the extravagant nature of a *yūjo's* dress in those days is merely given to illustrate the quaint costumes adopted, and the lavish manner in which the women spent their money in their endeavours to show themselves off in novel and costly habiliments. It is curious that notwithstanding the magnificence of their costume the *yūjo* ceased to wear *tabi* (socks) in the Kwansei (1789-1800) and Bunkwa (1804-1817) eras, although they had worn them prior to the Tenna era (1681-1683). In ancient times the *tabi* were of leather, stained purple.

When an *ane-jōro* (elder-sister-harlot) initiated her *imōto-jōro* (younger-sister-harlot), and allowed her to appear in the *misé* for the first time, the act of thus furthering the interests of the younger woman was called *tsuki-dashi* (to push out and forward). It was the bounden duty of an *ane-jōro* to arrange everything connected with this *tsuki-kashi* ceremony at the request of the brothel-keeper, and this act of duty was known as "*o yaku.*"

The *tsuki-dashi* proper lasted for a week, and during that time the debutante, accompanied by her *ane-jōro*, used to promenade the streets of the Yoshiwara by way of introduction, in the same manner as if she were performing a regular *dōchū*. Every day, both the debutante and the *ane-jōro* appeared in different costumes. The hair of the *ane-jōro* was done either in the *Hyōgo*, *osa-fune*, *sage-gami*, or *shimada* styles, but the coiffure of the debutante was invariably made in the *shimada* style. [Since the advent of the Meiji era this custom has disappeared, but according to the narrative of a person who once saw such a ceremony, the debutante wore *yellow* clothes, and the clothes of her retinue of *yarite*, *kamuro*, and *wakai-mono*, were all of a similar hue].

During the week of introduction, the new-comer was engaged by her fellow *yūjo* in turn, and to the latter presents were made by way of reciprocity.

The expenditure involved in connection with the appearance of a new *yūjō* was roughly estimated at from 300 to 500 *ryō*. Then there were expenses connected with the *tsumi-yagu* (bedding), usually ordered from "*Dai-maru*" and "*Echigo-ya.*" Of course in all these matters there were wheels "within wheels," and, although the *tsuki-dashi* expenses were nominally defrayed by the *ane-jōro*, as a matter of fact the latter tapped the pockets of her guests to meet the bill. Generally an *ane-jōro* would have a number of admirers who could well afford to be generous, such as officials of the Government treasure godowns, weathly *saké* merchants of Shinkawa, etc., and on these occasions the astute lady would not fail to wheedle out of them all the cash she wanted. The classes of *yujo* who anciently participated in promenading were the *Chusan* and *Yobi-dashi*, and though the system of going to *age-ya* when called by guests no longer existed, the women continued to walk in the Naka-no-chō after dusk for the purpose of showing themselves to the spectators and as a means of attracting guests. The procession was preceeded by a couple of firemen (*tobi-no-mono*) carrying a *kanabō* (an iron staff fitted with rings), which they struck on the ground as they walked, producing a sharp metallic jingle and thus warning the crowds of the approach of the *oiran*.

With them walked a *wakaimono* (man-servant), lighting the way with a big lantern (*dai-hari*) on which was emblazoned the crest of the *yūjo*. The *yūjo* herself walked slowly along escorted by two *furi-shin* (*furi-sode shinzō*), two *kamuro*, one *banshin* (*ban-tō-shinzō*) and six *wakaimono*. They never returned the same way they went out: it was a rule that when a procession walked on the right side of the street on its way out, it should return on the left side. While the procession moved, the proprietors of tea-houses came out to the front of their establishments, saluted the passing beauty, and urged her to sit down and rest there; but she would merely smile graciously and walk on, placidly smoking her handsome pipe the while. *Yūjo* were formerly well-trained in their special manner of walking in procession, and though they wore very high clogs, accidents but rarely happened. To stumble was considered a sad disgrace, and if a *yūjo* accidentally tripped up in front of a tea-house custom demanded that she should enter the establishment and entertain all the inmates at her expense. The sight of a lovely and bewitching *yūjō* clad in rich silk brocades glittering with gold and polychromatic tints; of her wonderful pyramidal coiffure ornamented with numerous tortoise-shell and coral hair-pins so closely thrust together as to suggest a halo of light encircling her head; and her stately graceful movements as she swept slowly and majestically through the Naka-no-chō, must indeed have appeared magnificent and awe-inspiring to the uninitiated. Indeed we are told by ancient writers that the spectacle fairly entranced the country-folk and "robbed them of their very souls", and from such remarks we may gather that these processions of *yūjo* were by no means conducive to the elevation of the moral tone of the crowds of persons who flocked to see the Yoshiwara with gaping mouths and upturned eyes.

Yomise "Suga-gaki" no koto.

(*The night exhibition and the suga-gaki.*)

In view of the approaching "mixed residence" of foreigners in the interior, it is said that the authorities are contemplating the advisability of interdicting the present custom of exposing *yūjo* in "cages" to public view; and that Susaki will be the first prostitute quarter to discontinue this somewhat scandalous practice. Even as it is, the exhibition of *yūjo* in cages is not openly recognized except in the Yoshiwara and a few other *yūkwaku*, so the probability is that is will be discontinued ere long, even without the interference of the local governments. While many have no sympathy with the "*hai-shō-ron*"* movement which found a good many supporters in Japan a few years ago, it is their profound conviction that the prostitute quarters should not be made a show-place, that display for the purpose of the attracting attention should be discouraged, and that reverence for humanity and common chivalry should forbid even the semblance of anything approaching the public exhibition of unfortunate women, however low they may have fallen. At the present time, the majority of the Japanese public do not seem to see anything shocking or strange in the sight of hundreds of gaudily attired courtesans sitting in rows exposed to public view as living "samples," and this tends to bridge over the sharp line of demarcation which should exist between the *demi-monde* and honest women. This again leads to a good deal of freedom and license of speech, and permits the doings of *yūjo*, and the libertines who support them, to be unblushingly chronicled in newspapers and indelicately alluded to in novels. Then again, at the time of the festival of the "*Tori-no machi*," the various *yūkwaku* are crowded by a vast multitude of sight-seers including thousands of young persons of both sexes: this means that very young and perfectly innocent boys and girls are so accustomed to the strange scene that they see no indelicacy in it, and so they grow up knowing far more about these matters than is good for them. To Europeans and Americans it is a strange sight to see family parties, including modest young girls, wending their way through the crowded streets on the night of the *Tori-no-machi*, buying various knick-knacks and gazing at the painted beauties in their gorgeous dresses

* Movement in favour of the abolition of licensed prostitution.

Modern Courtesans exposed "on view" in their cages.

of glossy brocade and glittering gold. It is certainly opposed to foreign ideas to take one's young daughter sight-seeing in a prostitute quarter!

The chief objection to the public exhibition of handsomely dressed women is that it tempts youths who might otherwise remain chaste, and attracts them to the brothel-quarters. It is true that it is a boy's nature to wish to see all unusual spectacles and pageants, and so long as they exist he will certainly make it a point of going and feasting his eyes upon them. If the authorities decide to prohibit the present system of "showmanism" it will mean that men will be obliged to enter the houses in cold blood for a definite purpose, and not be exposed to the temptation of being drawn in by the sight of a pretty face exposed as "on sale." The authorities would also be well advised to absolutely forbid any kind of public *fête* or festival from being held within the precincts of *yūkwaku,* to have the gates strictly guarded as of yore, and to refuse admittance to either women or boys unconnected with the brothels. This would be a blow to the "business" for a time, but it would result in a healthier moral tone among the rising generation, and do good in the direction of diminishing, if not preventing, the serious and far-reaching troubles and entanglements which occasionally involve young men in great distress and lead them on to commit actual crimes to gratify either their own salacious desires or the whims of the "scarlet women" with whom they are infatuated.

While the quarter was still situated at the Moto Yoshiwara the "profession" was carried on in the day-time exclusively, but when, on the 9th day of the 10th month of the 2nd year of Meireki (24th November, 1656), Ishitani

Shōgen (the *Machi-Bugyō*) gave permission for the removal of the brothels to the present sites, the carrying on of business at night was also sanctioned.

This proving far more convenient for visitors who were not willing to be seen by others entering the quarter, the number of day-guests gradually dropped off, and at length nearly everybody came to visit the Yoshiwara after dark exclusively. In this manner, the brothels obtained the privilege of carrying on their "trade" both in the day and at night, and the fees of courtesans (*age-dai*) were divided into "*night*" and "*day*" fees. Each one of these fees was known as a *kata-shimai* (half engagement). When the "day" hours were over, a large lantern (*andō*) was hung out in front of every brothel, and thus a distinction was made between "*day* and *night*". The *Dōbō Gō-en I-hon-kōi* (洞房語園異本考異) says that :—

> The reason why the profession of brothels was prohibited at night during the era of Tenna (1681-1683) was because that period was immediately subsequent to great internecine strife. Later on, in the case of the Yoshiwara only, this restriction was removed, and since that period the occupation has everywhere been carried on at night. In the Yoshiwara for instance (as in other quarters), "day work" became merely nominal owing to the simple reason that there were but very few guests in the broad daylight.

The "*Yoshiwara Taizen*" (吉原大全) remarks :—

> The "day" was from noon until 3 P.M. and the "night" from 5 to 10 to o'clock P.M. Apparently finding that 10 o'clock P.M. was too early to close up the "shops", some genius hit on the pleasant fiction of causing the watchmen to strike their *hyōshigi* (wooden clappers) announcing the hour as 10 when in reality the temple bell was striking midnight. This originated the terms "real 10 o'clock" and "nominal 10 o'clock".

At night-fall (about twilight) a small bell (*suzu*) was rung before the shrine (*kami-dana*) at the entrance of the house, and at the same time the *yūjo* appeared in the *mise* (cages) and the "*shinzō*" of the house struck up an air called "*sugagaki*" on the *samisen*. This performance seems to have been a relic of the times when harlots were skilled in singing and dancing.

It is stated in the *Yoshiwara Taizen* (吉原大全) that while the Moto-Yoshiwara was in existence some short songs were sung to the accompaniment of the playing of the *sugagaki*. The following are examples :—

> "Willow tree—forked willow tree—on the road-side!
> Prithee tell me whither thou wilt incline thy drooping branches when swayed by the breeze?
> I trow 'twill be towards the gentleman you love!"
> "Who is he that breaketh off a branch of yon willow tree on a calm Spring day ?
> He is a gallant who rideth on a white horse."

The singing of these songs was continued even after the removal of the Yoshiwara, but was dropped after the era of Kwansei (1789-1800). It also appears that the songs varied according to the house, but that gradually matters became simplified until the songs ceased and the *samisen* was merely tinkled by the private *geisha* of each brothel, as a pure formality. Even the playing of *samisen* ceased prior to the advent of the Meiji era (1869—).

In the *Nishiki-no-Ura* (錦の裏) written by Kyōden, published in 1791, a "*Furishin*" is made to say :—

> "Who was in charge of the samisen last night? The koshimoto (a little maid) is complaining that she can't find the *bachi* (plectrum)."

This was because it was the duty of the *shinzō* to play the *sugagaki* every evening, and each one of them took charge of the *samisen* alternately. Up to the An-ei period (1772-1780) *shinzō* sung some *naga-uta* or *Bungo-bushi* and played the *koto* or *samisen*, and, when the *shinzō* happened to be a favorite, people came out in front of the neighbouring houses to hear her sing. This custom was of a comparatively later origin and was observed by some houses.

Now-a-days, just prior to the appearance of *yūjo* in their "cages", the *gyū* strike a bundle of wooden clog-checks (*gesoku-fuda*) against the floor, and, while slapping the pillar of the entrance door with the palm of their open hand, imitate the squeaking of a rat. The hour this charm is performed corresponds to that at which *sugagaki* was played in former days. *Sugagaki* seems to have been evolved and developed from the tunes of *koto* music, because one authority states that "*sugagaki*" means the playing of certain *koto* airs without any accompanying song. In ancient times a blind musician made a departure in the direction of playing *koto* music on the *samisen*, and this was handed down in the Yoshiwara as "*sugagaki*".

During the Genroku era (1688-1703) "*Ni-agari sugagaki*," "*Yedo sugagaki*" and "*Sanya-sugagaki*" came into vogue owing to their suiting the tastes of fashionable persons.

There is a *kiyomoto* song entitled "*Hokushū*" in which reference is made to the *sugagaki*, and the prosperity of the Yoshiwara at that time vividly described.

Daijin-mai no koto.

(Dancing of millionaires.)

This style of dancing was most popular in the Yoshiwara during the Shōtoku era (1711-1715). The songs which were sung as a kind of accompaniment to this dancing are said to have been composed by a comic actor named Nakamura

A Street Scene in the Yoshiwara a hundred years ago.

Copied from a drawing by Kitagawa Utamaro.

Kichibei (commonly known as Nishiban). Kichibei, being an expert singer of *ko-uta* (light songs), was present at many *saké* parties given by rich people, and entertained the guests so well with his singing and dancing that he became very popular. According to a certain book of songs, however, it is claimed that the songs were composed by a man named Seisai, but as the same book states the songs were composed during Gembun era (1736-1739) the identity of the composer is extremely doubtful. If these ballads were really written during the *Genroku* (1688-1703) and *Shōtoku* (1711-1715) eras, it is inconsistent that the names of Kibun* (紀文) and Naramo* (奈良茂) should appear in the verses!

Some people allege that the ballads were the result of literary efforts on the part of Kibun himself, but this seems rather apocryphal inasmuch that the name of Kibun is mentioned in them, and he would hardly compose songs about himself!

However, we may be well content to leave various antiquarians to quarrel over musty documents and ancient books, and content ourselves with knowing that the ballads *did* eventuate in some way or other, and that *somebody did* compose them. The following extracts are made from the "*Dai-jin-mai Kō-shō*" (大盡舞考證) and will give an idea of the songs, but it must be borne in mind that the translation is very free owing to the crudeness and vague character of the original text and the virtual impossibility of reducing the words into intelligible English.

The treasures of the Shin-Yoshiwara are hidden by the back of a palanquin. Passing through Shim-machi, Ageya-chō, Uki-hashi, Komura, and Yatsuhashi, one comes out into the Shitaya streets, sees the small cherry temple of Tōyeizan (Uyeno park)

* Millionaires.

and the Toraren temple of Kinryū-zan (Asakusa temple). The thing which is praised and admired here is the long flowing haori of Kōhei-bō. Then you know Confucius said, ha! ha! whosoever worships us, ha! ha! will certainly be dragged to the wicked place, ho! ho! (Chorus:—" Ho-ho-hon, ho-ho-hon-non, ho-hon-yo ho-hon-yo no notamawaku wa, soto senya soto senya ariya chin na.)

Ha ha! ho ho! It is a felicitous omen of this tranquil reign that the waves of the four seas are undisturbed ha! ha! ho! ho! Look at the *Daijin-mai* (dance).

(*Next* "*Daijin*"): The origin of the *kuruwa* (prostitute quarters) is that Yuge no Dōkyō, by Imperial command, founded a *kuruwa*. On account of guests flocking in (*kuru* 来) and their hearts being softened (*wa* 和) it has been named "*kuruwa.*" Ha-a! ho-ho! Look at the *Daijin-mai* (dance).

(Next "*Daijin*"): The five streets of the Yoshiwara have been named because Yedo-chō has "*en*" (affinity) with Yedo city: Fushimi-chō has affinity with *fushin* (*fushin* suru=to build); all difficulties having been overcome Sumi-chō was built, Shinmachi opened, and the bustling Kyō-machi established.

(*Next Daijin*): The title of *tayū* originated when the first Emperor of Shin was out a hunting and encountered a heavy rain-storm. His Majesty then sought shelter under a small pine-tree, when the branches of that tree miraculously extended and the leaves spread out and locked together so closely that the Emperor was completely protected from the elements. For such virtues the pine and the bamboo are felicitous. Ha-a! ho-ho! Look at the *Daijin-mai* (dance).

(*Next Daijin*): As to the beginning of guests, though the people may know nothing about Corea or China, everywhere in Japan they know the name of Kinokuni-ya Bunzaemon (Kinokuni Bun-za). The Donsu Daijin ("Damask" millionaire) rivals him and redeems Kichō of Miuraya. Five rolls of red damask together with the cost of cotton-wool lining he sends to Ogiya Hanshi. He also presents a dagger valued at 25 ry which is still preserved as a treasure by Hanshi. Ha-a! ho-ho! Look at the *Daijin-mai* (dance).

(*Next Daijin*): As the next *daijin* we must mention Master Naramo. He redeemed Ura-zato who was well-known at Shim-machi as the leading belle of the Kagaya. He placed her in a mansion specially built for her reception at Kuroe-chō, Fukagawa, and the name of the mansion was "Mokusan Goten". The *hōkan* (jesters) in attendance on her were Itchō, Minbu, and Kakuchō, while her female servants were O Man, O Kin, and O Yō. Koshirō,

Zenroku, Kichibei, and Seigorō attend her in various capacities. But oh! what a change of taste, however, that this *daijin* should again redeem Arashi Kiyoji! Ha-a! ho-ho! Look at the *Daijin-mai* (dance).

(*Next Daijin*): The day-break on a Spring morning as sung by Seishōnagon (noted poetress) is interesting. Being attracted by the tinkling notes of *sugagaki*, crowds flock into the Yoshiwara dressed in their holiday clothes, to visit the girls for the first time in the New Year: so the *kuruwa* becomes lively, and men walk about stretching their necks like herons.

The *tayū* and *kōshi* prosper and the *sancha* and *baicha* also become popular, their voices echoing like the twittering of singing birds. The great houses of Yamaguchi and Miura are famed for their wealth and prosperity, and indeed they are the famous things of Sumichō. Ha-a! ho-ho! Look at the *Daijin-mai* (dance.)

(*Next Daijin*): Yamamoto no Hōjun is a well-known resident of Shimmachi, *Kago-guke* (the feat of passing though a hollow cylinder of basket-work) of Tsunokuni is the famous thing of Sumi-chō, the Tosa smoked bonito sold by Temmaya is that of Ni-chō-me, and Hishidaya Matayemon is said to be a descendant of Shōji Jimbei. Look at the *Daijin-mai* (dance.)

(*Next Daijin*): The beginning of Sin-goza must be attributed to Iseya Jūbei. He redeemed a well-known *ūjo*—Katsuyama—belonging to Ōmatsu-ya of Ni-chōme. *Yukata-mono* (people belonging to respectable *samurai* families) is the commencement of Shin-goza. Ha-a! ho-ho! Look at the *Daijin-mai* (dance.)

(*Next Daijin*): As to the beginning of *yubi-kiri* (finger-cutting) it first took place between the leading *yūjo* of Tsuta-ya, named Fujishiro, and Totsuno Yohei, and then the practice gradually spread until it took place between Hana-Murasaki of Ōbishiya and Takayasu Hikotarō. Ha-a! ho-ho! Look at the *Daijin-mai* (dance).

(*Next Daijin*). [Here the text is so obscure that nothing can be made of it.]

As to the tunes played when the *Dai-jin-mai* was danced, these have been explained by Mr. Ōtsuki Jōden and by the widow of the late noted painter Naga-aki Anshun. (This lady was formerly a *geisha* in the Yoshiwara called O-Hata, and is well versed in music as well as the ancient customs of the

Yoshiwara: she lives at 42 Shōden-chō, Yokochō, Asakusa, Tōkyō). These songs are said to have usually been sung and danced by the *hōkan* before guests during the New Year holidays.

Daikoku-mai no koto.

(*Daikoku-mai* dancing.)

The custom of performing this *Daikoku-mai* dance has now completely disappeared in the Yoshiwara.

According to the reply given by Shichizaemon, manager of the dancing, and also a subordinate chief of beggars (*hi-nin kogashira*) to an enquiry made of him by the *nanushi* of the Yoshiwara in the 12th month of the 13th year of Tempō (January 1843,) there was, during the Genroku era (1688-1704), a subordinate chief of beggars, named Manjirō, living at the creek-side of Nihon-bashi, and this Manjirō was very proficient in the art of singing popular songs. One day he picked up a mask (representing the god Daikoku) floating in the creek, wore it, and danced comic dances in the Yoshiwara to the strains of the samisen played by his friend Shichizō. This was the origin of the *Daikoku-mai*. Shichizō (or Shichizaemon), who furnished this information, was a lineal descendant of the *samisen*-player Shichizō. The "*Dōbō-Goen*" says that in the first month of each year *Daikoku-mai* dancers came into the Yoshiwara, performed various antics, and entertained people with their buffoonery and comic imitations of things and persons.

They used to frequent the Yoshiwara from the 2nd day of the first month of the year until the first "horse day" (*hatsu-uma*) in the second month. After that the "*Daikoku-*

kagura" players frequented the Yoshiwara. The *Daikoku-mai* dancers, however, visited the Yoshiwara on all principal holidays, especially on the bean-throwing day (*mame-maki no hi*) in the twelfth month and the last day (*ō-misoka*) of the year. These players were great favourites with many of the *yūjo*, and considerable money was given to them by the latter. It is said that a good many secret love passages took place between the *yūjo* and these dancers. In the whole of the Yoshiwara only Kado Tsutaya at Yedo-chō, Ni-chō-me, made it a rule of the house not to grant admission to the *Daikoku-mai* dancers. Prior to this, puppet dancers (*ningyō-tsukai*) also frequented the Yoshiwara, but since the appearance of the *Daikoku-mai* dancers their visits ceased.

INTRODUCTORY SONGS OF THE "DAIKOKU-MAI."

"In the morning of New Year's day, facing the lucky direction of the compass, Daikoku-ten smiles as benignly as the *fuku-jusō* (Adonis amuraisis.)

Like the rising sun flows a spring of *toso saké* and crysanthemum *saké*. The *kamuro* crysanthemum emits the odour of youthful fragrance. Various species of oranges, including that of the *ukon*, and also the cherry-tree of *sakon* are planted in the gardens and covered with a purple hood. Look at the *Daijin-mai* dance! Look at the *Daijin-mai* dance.

On the head of the *jōro* are hair-pins with the figures of storks which live a thousand years, and others having the flowers of the plum and cherry carved upon them. The spectacle of the fairy-like *kamuro* promenading may well be compared to the flowers which are blooming in advance of the season. Who are the happy guests who come to this paradise at the beginning of the year? Look at the *Daijin-mai* dance! Look at the *Daijin-mai dance.*"

After having sung these introductory songs, the names of the most popular *yūjo* were read out in a kind of doggerel verse. When performing, the *Daikoku-mai* dancers wore some of the clothes given to them by their patrons or *yūjo* (some of these clothes were quite costly, being made of crêpe) and held a fan in their hand. They wore a hood known as *Daikoku-dzukin*, and the ceremonial *kamishimo*. The presenting of fine clothes to these people by *yūjo* was for the purpose of buying their goodwill. The "*Kiyū Shōran*" (嬉遊笑覽＝"Laughing-Pleasant view of Games and Pastimes") remarks that such people as Hidenji, Shinokasho, Kōgai, and others who imitated the style of the god Daikokuten, put on a mask and hood, and at the beginning of the New Year went around in every part of the city singing new songs: they were also called "*Daikoku-mai*." It appears that the *Daikoku-mai* originated in the *Sagi-chō* (ceremony observed on the 15th day of first month (o.s.) which consisted in burning, near the house, the pine, bamboo, *shimé*, etc. used as New Year's decorations). Reference is made in the "*Seken Munasanyō*" (世間胸算用) to the effect that in the neighbourhood of a certain person lived a man whose profession appears (though it was not, judging from the property he possessed) to have been a kind of public entertainer. He pawned the *eboshi* (cap worn by nobles) *shitatare* (long silk robe) and a long sword at the close of the year in consequence of having his profession changed to that of a *daikoku-mai* dancer who required only a cheap mask and a hammer made of paper. In the preface of the *Ebisu-Kyoku-Shū* (夷曲集) it is remarked that the abilities of the Daikoku are—firstly, he sits on bags of rice, secondly he smiles benignly, and thirdly he puts all the

Daikokuten.

luck and wealth in the bag he carries * * * The "*Gaen Suikyō-shū*" (雅筵酔狂集) also says that compared with the picture of the Daikoku with his fan, and sitting on five bags of rice, the fan is rather novel contrary to the conventional five bags of rice. Next, the "*Kenjo Shinshō*" (賢女心粧) referring to the description of the slums of Kwato (Kyōto) says that the living of a family is made by the husband getting money by the favour of Awashima Dai-Myōjin, and the wife by wearing the mask of O Fuku (O-Kame) * * * In Yedo, occasionally beggars come round imitating the style of Ebisu and Daikoku, but the times of their visits are not fixed except in the Yoshiwara."

From these fragmentary accounts it would seem that the *Daikoku-mai* was a kind of dance which degenerated until it was performed by beggars, wearing the Daikoku hood like the *manzai*, in front of every house. For a long time the Yoshiwara was free from their incursions, but the custom was resuscitated during the Kei-ō era (1865-1867) though in an altered form as far as their personal appearance was concerned. The latter day dancers of the *Daikoku-mai* were attired, like the *Dai-kagura* men in black clothes with crests upon them, and white *hakata-obi* : the skirts of their *kimono* were lifted up (*shiri-hashi-ori nite*) and fastened by tucking the ends into their *obi*. They even powdered their faces, imitated the voices of well-known actors, and did other similar things. Though all these men were of the *eta* class there were many handsome fellows among them and these were great favourites with the Yoshiwara women. A story is told of the daughter of a tea-house keeper at Tamachi called Minoya who eloped with one of these *eta* class dancers. At that time *eta* (leather dressers) were greatly despised in Japan, and under serious legal disabilities which prevented them from having any intercourse with other people, so the matter was at length brought before a Court of Justice and eventually this led to their being expelled from the Yoshiwara altogether.

There are now very few people—even in the Yoshiwara —who know much about these latter day *daikoku-mai* dancers.

Dote-bushi no koto oyobi Hayari-uta.

[*Dote-bushi (songs) and popular songs*].

Nowadays, a visitor to the Yoshiwara usually hurries there in a *jinrikisha*, drawn by a couple of agile and sprightly young fellows who rush along like the wind, brandishing their lanterns and giving vent to unearthly yells as they run. In former days, in contrast to the present time, a visitor rode slowly to the quarter on the back of a white horse caparisoned in white and red, the animal being led by two *mago* (grooms) who sang *komuro-bushi* in turn as they walked. The charges from Nihon-bashi to the *Ōmon* (gate-way) were 348 *mon* (34 *sen* 8 *rin*) including the fee for singing!

There were in the *Genroku* (1688-1704) and *Teikyō* (1684-1687) eras many popular songs such as the *nage-bushi, tsugi-bushi, magaki-bushi, kaga-bushi* of Uji Kagajō, *tanzen, numeri-uta, rōsai,* etc. In the beginning of Kwambun (1661-1673) a song called the "*Dote-bushi*" (embankment song) came into vogue, its name being derived from the fact that it was generally sung while people walked on the embankment. The words were about as follows:—

> "Though it is such an out-of-the-way place, yet when I think of the place of your abode it is dearer to me than a gallery of precious jewels. Pray do not laugh at me in not paying heed to what others may think or say. Rumours may spread."

The "*Dōbō Goyen*" (洞房語園) says that the above mentioned *dote-bushi* was composed by an old man named Odaka Josuisai who lived at the foot of Matsuchi-yama. This old gentleman was also accredited with having written many other popular *dote-bushi* songs which were sung by men belonging to the associations (*kumi*) of *otoko-date*, such as the Roppō-gumi, Sekirei-gumi, Yoshiya-gumi, Kanabō-gumi, Daishō-jingi-gumi, Tōken-gumi, etc. It is said that three of these songs remained popular up to the 2nd year of Bunkwa (1805), and that two of them ran as follows :—

> "Yesterday was a jolly day, but somehow or other to-day seems gloomy. Shall we send for *Wadadsumi* (sea deity) or *Shusubiin* (?). There is something much better than these. What is it? We have left behind the fruit of an egg-plant painted with *beni*. Where? It was drawn somewhere at the *funa-yado*. Set your wits to work Bekuzō: have you no good ideas about the matter? I have none, absolutely none. I have no concern at all in the matter. The path of love, after all, is a weary one. Last night when in the Yoshiwara I learned a popular song, but I cannot remember either the beginning, middle, nor end of it.
>
> Thinking I might forget it, I got it written down, but even the paper on which it was written I left at the entrance of my house. It is just the same with justice and reason. It is by no means amusing."

There are only a few people who know whether the notes of these songs still remain in the miscellaneous songs of to-day. The air of the "*Yoshiwara Suzume*" seems to have been derived from the *dote-bushi*, owing to the composition of Hara Budayū who from his infancy used to recite these songs and attained great proficiency in singing them as he grew up. The preservation of the *dote-bushi* note to this day—after the lapse of two centuries—must be attributed to him.

In a light song in vogue in the Yoshiwara about the era of Kwambun (1661-1673), which was also popular even outside the quarter, it is said :—

"The shaven-pated *taiko-mochi* (jester) K hei, wearing a long *haori* (over garment), goes strutting round the place."

In a song sung by *hōkan* about the same period are the words —"It being very lonely we looked out at the brothels. In another direction the tinkling of *samisen* and the sound of merry voices is heard. Who are these ladies wearing broad satin or damask *obi?* Let us ask their names. Who are they? They are Taka-o, Usugumo, Shibazaki, Tsushima, Yatsuhashi, Karasaki, and Yoshino. After having seen these beauties, our wives looked like the ghosts of Suzuki-chō. Having fed and clothed them, and left them at leisure, the beauty of these courtesans excels the celebrated cherry-blossoms of Yoshino. Well, well, I met with a remarkably lovely damsel. I rushed upon her with my javelin and we wrestled together right valiantly, then I pretended to be in my cups, and went round annoying everybody in the same manner as the plant-louse injures and vexes the azalea.

Do you support your parents? I am a night watchman: if you have compassion upon me pray speak to me. If possible give me your help.

The simpleton who has been jilted by the girl he fancies screens his face with a *haori.* Is there any girl who will become his partner? No doubt but that some *Kendon* (low class strumpet) will be found for him; *taiko-mochi* will negotiate for him."

The fact that during the era of Kwambun (1661-1673) visitors to the Yoshiwara rode there on the backs of white horses, having the leaders of the animals sing the *komuro-bushi*, is well-known to the general public. The *komuro-bushi* songs were generally sung by the horse coolies on the Tōkaidō when they were carrying the baggage of *daimyō* passing to and from Yedo. Originally the songs appear to have begun in Mikawa province, and since the emigration of the people of that province to the East, when the Tokugawa family moved to Yedo, they resided in Mikawa-shima, Toshima-gōri, Musashi Province, and the songs gradually spread among their descendants. The most popular one is: "*How pretty are the beautifully dyed reins of the horses which go up and down carrying baggage! It is the habit of the* mago (*horse-leaders*) *to accompany the sound of the horse-bells by singing in a loud voice—'When one passes through Yoshida, somebody dressed in a long-sleeved garment of* kanoko *beckons him from the second story.'*"

The notes of these songs are still remembered by some persons. Singers of *komuro-bushi* in the old days may be compared to the people who go round the brothels nowadays singing ribald songs, *hōkai-bushi*, and *hayari-uta*.

Annals of a Year.

The "*Yedo Kwagai Enkaku-shi*" (江戸花街沿革誌=Annals of the "Flower quarters" of Yedo) says that it will be interesting to mention the chief regular events which occur in the Yoshiwara—some of which still survive—all the year round.

Early on the morning of New Year's day—about 4 o'clock—the bath-houses in Ageya-chō and Sumi-chō sent men round the five streets of the Yoshiwara calling out that the baths were ready, so the *yūjo* arose while it was still dark, took their baths, and spent much time over their general toilet and dressing. By and by an announcement would be made by the *yarite* summoning the *yūjo* to assemble in the *hiroma* (廣間 large room) where the master and mistress of the house were sitting, and here the employers and employed exchanged congratulations and wished each other a happy new year. On this occasion the company partook of *toso* (spiced *sakê*) and the keeper of the brothel made presents to the inmates of his house; to each *yūjo* two dresses of silk crêpe, to each of the *shinzō* and *yarite* two dresses of *tsumugi* (pongee), to each of the *kamuro* a dress of cotton on which was dyed the pattern of pine-trees. After this ceremony was over, the *yūjo* returned to their own apartments and exchanged the compliments of the season by going to each others' rooms and paying formal calls. In the afternoon the first promenade of the year (*hatsu-dōchū*) took place, the *yūjo* going through the Naka-no-chō and making New Year's presents of sets of *sakê* cups to the tea-houses. Each *sakê* cup was inscribed with the crest of the *yūjo* presenting it, and each set was packed in a tiny box of *kiri* (paulownia) wood on which was written the *yūjo's* name and the name of the house to which she belonged. There was no special rule as to the style of the clothes which had to be worn by *yūjo* on the occasion, but it was an invariable custom that each *kamuro* attending her should carry a large battle-dore (*ō-hago-ita*) handsomely decorated with *oshi-e* (a picture made by pasting on a board pieces of thick paper wrapped with cloth of various colours). Generally speaking, the most splendid decorations were to be seen outside the tea-houses of the Naka-no-chō. In front of the entrances were hung *ao-sūdare* (green bamboo blinds), above the lintel of the door posts they hung lobsters (boiled red) and placed *mochi* (rice cake); and over the whole was fixed a *kōmori-gasa* (umbrella) bearing the signs of the respective houses, the latter being intended to ward off rain and protect the objects below. In front of every brothel larger New Year decorations were placed consisting of branches of pine and bamboo, among the

Courtesans about to visit their friends on New Year's Day. Period of Kiōwa (1801 to 1803).
(After the Picture by Kitagawa Utamaro.)

dark green leaves of which were hung bright fragrant oranges. In the case of the smaller houses in the side streets the decorations were usually confined to what is called *senaka-awase no matsu-kazari* (pine decorations set up back to back), thus making a double decoration with a space of about three feet between the two. (This custom is said to be observed even now). No *yo-misé* (night exhibition in cages) was held on New Year's day.

On the 2nd day of the 1st month the bath-house keepers again made the same announcement as they had the previous day. With the first cawing of the crow (*ake-garasu no koe to tomo ni*) the dealers of shell-fish thronged the quarter and cried their wares for sale in loud voices. Everyone who bought the *hamaguri* (clams) purchased them only from the men who were entering the quarter, and not from those who were going out and back, as it was not considered lucky to buy from departing vendors. The fishmongers, however, were smart enough to head off their patrons, and entering the gate they walked up the street shouting away until they arrived at the end of the thoroughfare. Then they quietly sneaked back to the gate and started afresh. This practice was repeated several times until the artful fellows had contrived to secure all the business in sight, and the simple buyers were happy in the belief that they had bought *hamaguri* from fishermen who had only just arrived in the Yoshiwara.

After this day guests began to arrive in increasing numbers, and, according to the charming little custom in vogue, *yūjo* used to entertain their visitors with *toso* (spiced *saké*) and make them presents of fans, towels, *hanshi* (paper) and other trifling articles.

The wife of a brothel-keeper always made a point of coming out, dressed in ceremonial clothes, to congratulate every guest on the New Year, and at this season the food served to patrons was better and more varied than usual. On this day, wives of the tea-house-keepers returned the congratulatory visits of the *yūjo*, going from room to room for that purpose.

From the 2nd day, until the end of the 1st month, as well as on the first horse-day (*hatsu-uma*) of February, and on the 8th day of the same month, the *Daikoku-mai* dancers came to every brothel and the *yūjo* vied with each other in giving them tips.

Only Tsuta-ya of Yedo-chō formed an exception to this rule, as it was the habit of that house not to grant admittance to the dancers.

On the 7th day the *nanakusa-no-iwai* (ceremony when a soup compounded of seven kinds of greens is eaten on the 7th day of the first month) was performed, and on the 11th day came the ceremony of opening store-houses for the first time in the year (*kurabiraki*). On the 14th followed the *toshikoshi*,* while on the 15th, 18th, and 20th there were some further ceremonies observed. The date of celebrating the *Ebisukō*† was not uniform, and each brothel had its own methods. In ancient times it was a universal custom to observe this ceremony twice a year, viz—in January and October. In the era of Bunsei (1818-1829) the ceremony in the 1st month became greatly

---

* *Toshi-koshi.* The ceremony of scattering parched peas about in an occupied house to drive out evil spirits, crying aloud the while "*fuku wa uchi, oni wa soto,*" (good fortune is within, and devils outside). This ceremony is also known as "*mame-maki*" (bean throwing) and "*oni-yarai*" (casting out devils.)

† A fête in honour of the god of trade and industry.

curtailed, and finally the Ebisukō was only observed in the 10th month.

The *yūjo* did not all appear in the cages until the 20th of the 1st month, so the night aspect of the Yoshiwara did not resume its normal appearance until this date. The *saruhiki* and *dai-kagura** began to pour into the Yoshiwara from the 1st day of the 2nd month: on the night of the first "horse day" the front of every brothel in the first and seconds wards of *Yedo-chō* and of *Kyō-machi* was illuminated by a large lantern on which was written the names of the *yūjo* in the house. Votive offerings of red rice, fried bean-curd, and fruit were made to the family shrines of the god Inari.

Many of the *yūjo*, accompanied by their guests, visited the four temples in or near the quarter dedicated to Inari Sama,† viz.—Kurosuké Inari, Akashi Inari, Kai-un Inari and Enomoto Inari. *Kagura* dances‡ were performed in the Jishimban (guard or watchman's office) at Yedo-chō Ni-chōme, and all was bustle and confusion in the Yoshiwara. The following day the brothel keepers contributed to the shrine of Inari the large lanterns which had been hung before their establishments the previous evening. On and after the 3rd day of the 3rd month cherry-planting (*hana-ue*) com-

* *Saruhiki.* One who goes about getting money by leading a monkey who performs tricks.

Dai-kagura. A kind of dance performed in the streets by boys wearing wooden lion-head masks. Also called "*Shishi-mai*"

† *Inari.* Goddess of rice (written with the two characters 稻荷 = "*rice bearing*"). *Inari* is sometimes spoken of as the "fox-deity," but the foxes appear to be mere guards to the temples dedicated to the Goddess. There is more or less confusion as to the sex of Inari as sometimes "she" (*sic*) is represented as a bearded man!

‡ *Kagura.* An old Japanese dance which may yet be seen in the grounds of certain temples. The performers wear masks and quaint gowns of real or imitation damask. The *kagura* mentioned above was probably a profane invention of a comic nature.

menced.* Cherry-trees were planted on both sides of the streets of the Naka-no-chō, and these drew a multitude of sight-seers who gazed with delight on the delicate pink and white blossoms which smothered the branches in a rolling mist of fairy-like florescence. The origin of this custom is mentioned elsewhere.

In April the cherry-blossoms had already fallen, green leaves had appeared on the trees, and everything foretold the rapid approach of Summer. Towards the end of this month fire-fly dealers (*hotaru-uri*) began to perambulate the Naka-no-chō, exhibiting their luminous wares as if in mockery of those who scorched their bodies in the fire of lust and dissipation!

On the 5th day of the 5th month the *yūjo* changed their winter clothes for those of summer, and used to present new summer dresses to *shinzō* and *kamuro*, but it seems that the cost of these latter was defrayed by guests of the house out of compliment to the *yūjo* with whom they were acquainted. There is a comic song which runs:—" *Those guests who ran away during the last days of the old year, and returned in the Spring, have again fled on account of the utsuri-gae* (change of garments)." It is rather laughable that the *yūjo* themselves would tease guest by reciting these lines. On this day, as on New Year's Day, the *yūjo* visited the tea-houses of Naka-no-chō to wish them the compliments of the season. Later on, it became a custom to plant iris blossoms in the quarter, after this day, as a means of attracting visitors. After the beginning of the *doyō* season in June, *yūjo* made

* *Third month.* It must be remembered that this was April according to the present calendar.

presents of fans to their familiar guests, and to tea-houses, as a token that they solicited continued patronage at the hands of their friends.

On the 7th day of the 7th month the festival of the weaver was celebrated in the quarter by *yūjo* tying branches of bamboo (with white fans, on which poems were written, fixed to them) before their doors. Even the inmates of smaller brothels observed this time-honoured custom. In some houses the keepers, acting on the advice of guests, took advantage of the opportunity to make a display of rare curios and furniture, and consequently the Yoshiwara was thronged with visitors.

On the 10th day the festival of the Asakusa Kwannon took place. This day was called the "*shi-man-roku-sen-nichi* (46,000 days) the idea being that he who visited the temple on that day performed as meritorious an action as if he made a pilgrimage there on 46,000 occasions, and consequently it follows that one visit to the Asakusa Kwannon on the 10th day of the 7th month ensured the pilgrim a life-long blessing from Buddha.

This festival attracted crowds of people to the Yoshiwara and "trade" boomed up on account of the large number of visitors seeking "blessings"! From the dawn of the 12th day until 9 o'clock on the following day the stalls of dealers in articles necessary for celebrating the festival of the dead were erected between the *Ō-mon* and *Suidō-jiri*. This festival was called the "*Kusa-ichi*" (Grass-market). Toilet articles and toys were also sold on this occasion. On the night of the 13th day no guests were received, and the *yūjo* roamed about the quarter, as they choose, in groups of threes or fives. In their rooms the *i-hai* (a wooden tablet bearing the posthumous name of dead persons) of their parents were placed on their wardrobes and before these improvised altars *yūjo* offered tearful prayers from acheing hearts. A Japanese stanza says :—

> *Ushi uma no tsunagare-nagara nagare-keri, chiisai toki wo hanasu keisei.*

"Courtesans separated from their parents in early childhood and drifting over the sea of life tethered together like dumb driven cattle."

On the 15th day the *yūjo* paid another complimentary visit to the tea-houses, in the same way as they were wont to do on New Year's Day. From the last day of the 6th month, and during the 7th month, while the "Feast of Lanterns" continued, the *hikite-ja-ya* (tea-houses) of the Naka-no-chō hung lanterns, generally square in shape, inside and outside their houses, but on the 13th and 14th this practice was suspended and after the 15th new lanterns were substituted. The lighting of *bon-dōrō* (memorial lanterns) during the *bon* (feast in memory of the dead) is a universal custom in Japan, and originally lanterns of various shapes were used in the Yoshiwara. But since the lighting of a special kind of lantern in the 7th month of the 13th year of the Kyōhō era (1728) in memory of the third anniversary of the death of Tamagiku of the Manji-ya, the pattern has become more uniform aud the custom more general in the quarter.

On the 1st day of tho 8th month (*hassoku*) the *yūjo* went in procession through the Yoshiwara wearing *shiro-muku no kosode* (wadded clothes of white silk). In ancient times *yūjo* wore lined clothes (*awase*) of dyed stuffs on the *tango no sekku*

Gathering of Courtesans at the "*Hassaku*" (1st day of the 8th month).

(*After the Picture by Kitagawa Utamaro.*)

(the festival of the sweet flag celebrated on the 5th day of the 5th month) and similar clothes of white silk on the 1st day of the 8th month. One year, in the beginning of the *Kwambun* era (1661-1672), it happened to be extraordinarily cold and a *yūjo* named Yūgiri (evening mist) belonging to the Sōgyoku wore wadded clothes on the 1st of August, thus making a departure from the established usage. Her costume attracted universal attention, and she looked more beautiful and happier in it than the other women, who appeared chilly and uncomfortable in their lighter garments. Two years later, on the 1st day of the 8th month, all the *yūjo* turned out in wadded clothes in spite of the fact that the season was unusually warm, and henceforth this costume was generally adopted. Another version attributes its origin to the fact that during the Genroku period (1688-1703) a *yūjo* named Takahashi, of the Tomoeya, went to an *ageya* in response to the invitation of an intimate guest, despite her illness, attired in her night-garment of white wadded silk. This version of the origin of the custom is of doubtful authority. During the same period a *yūjo* belonging to the Myōgo-ya, named Ōshū, used to promenade wearing clothes of white silk on which were depicted human skulls and *susuki* (*eularia japonica :* " reed-grass ") painted in India ink, greatly surprising spectators with her extraordinary taste. On the 14th, 15th, and 16th, the ceremony of " viewing the moon " (*tsuki-mi*) was observed. On those nights *sambo* (wooden stands) were stood out and loaded with dumplings, chestnuts, beans in pods, sweet potatoes, persimmons, lespedeza blossoms (*hagi*), eularia grass (*sususki*), aster blossoms (*shion*), etc., as offerings to the moon. They also set out vessels filled with sacred wine, and burnt altar-lamps in her honour.

In the rooms of the *yūjo* were set out artificial representations of the seven kinds of autumn flowers to represent an autumnal field, or a *sudare* of glass was hung in front of the shelf by way of ornament. At first liliputian (boy) actors, and puppet showmen, etc, were called into brothels to give entertainments on these nights, but later on this custom disappeared. During the greater part of the eighth month, commencing on the 1st day, the festival of Kurosuke Inari was celebrated, and the Yoshiwara then presented a very lively spectacle in consequence of the exhibition of cars, filled with dancers and musicians (*neri mono*), which were drawn about the streets. Up to the Bunkwa era (1804-1817) bamboo branches were set up on either side of the *ō-mon* (great gateway) and *shime-nawa** were hung upon them. Throughout this month *yūjo* who were proficient in singing and dancing took part in *niwaka* † dancing for the amusement of the general public whenever the weather was fine.

The first day of the 9th month being considered a day of good omen (*kashin*) every brothel celebrated it in an appropriate manner. On the 9th day of the same month, another day of good omen, called the *chōyō no sekku*,‡ chrysanthemum blossoms soaked in *saké* were eaten. This custom was borrowed from China.

On the 12th, 13th, and 14th, moon-viewing parties were held as in the previous month, and those guests who had been

* *Shime-nawa.* A rope with tufts of straw or of cut paper at fixed intervals, hung before shrines in order to sanctify the place within. It is a relic of the straw-rope which *Futodama-no-mikoto* stretched behind the Sun-goddess to prevent her returning to the cave after *Tajikarao-no-mikoto* had pulled her out and thus re-illuminated the universe which had been plunged into darkness.

† See special chapter on this subject.

‡ *Chōyō no sekku* The 9th day of the 9th month (o.s.); a festival day of the chrysanthemum.

present at a party on the eighth month were under obligation to again take part in this second observance, as the *yūjo* evinced much aversion to *kata-mi-dzuki* (a partial moon-viewing). The second "moon-viewing" was known as (*nochi no tsuki-mi*). In the 9th year of Bunkwa (1812) chrysanthemums were planted in the Naka-no-chō for the first time: this was repeated several times in succeeding years but, probably owing to the show not being sufficiently interesting to draw any large number of fresh guests, it was eventually abandoned as too expensive a practice.

On and after the first "wild boar" day of the 10th month the big braziers (*ō-hibachi*) were brought out in every brothel, and summer clothing was changed to that of winter. The festival of Ebisukō fell on the 20th day, and banquets were giving throughout the quarter: the *yūjo* had a holiday on this occasion, but some of the most popular of them were accustomed to invite certain familiar guests as they were proud enough to consider it rather a disgrace to allow such an interruption of the exercise of their profession.

The *hi-busé*, or "fire preventing festival" took place on the 8th day of the 11th month, when oranges were scattered about the gardens of the *jōroya* and scrambled for by children. On this night, lanterns were lighted throughout the Yoshiwara. On the 17th and 18th, what was called the *Aki-ha-matsuri* (festival) took place. In front of the large street lamp at Suidō-jiri, dealers in various articles erected temporary sheds for the sale of their wares, and the neighbourhood was crowded by *yūjo* and other people. On every "day of the bird" in this month all the gates of the Yoshiwara were thrown open, and the *Tori-no-ichi* festival was held in the quarter. On this night large numbers of persons thronged the quarter and formed an immense and surging crowd. The origin of the *Tori-no-ichi* festival is stated in another chapter.

On the 8th day of the 12th month "*kotohajime*", or New Year's preparations, began, and on the 13th was the regular *susu-harai* or general house-cleaning, but, as a matter of fact, the *susu-harai* was generally finished earlier than that date. The 17th and 18th days of the 12th month being "market days" (*ichi*) of the Asakusa Kwannon, a larger number of persons than usual visited the Yoshiwara, and the brothel keepers sent men to the market to purchase paper images of Daruma which they placed on the main pillars of their houses for good-luck. After the 20th, the making of *mochi* (rice-cake) commenced at each house, and firemen from Minowa, Kanasugi, Sanya, Imado, and vicinity, came to render assistance in pounding the *mochi* of those brothels which usually patronized them. In return for this assistance, the *yūjo* were in the habit of giving these firemen new *hanten, momohiki* and *tenugui* as presents of the season. This custom is said to have been originated by Chōzan of Chōji-ya during the Hōreki era (1751-1763). The following verses of a song while pounding *mochi* may be of interest:—

"I can hear your voice but cannot see you. You are really like a cricket that chirps in the field."

"If you live in Owari while your wife lives in Mino, you will naturally long for the latter province even though there be no rain."*

"Even a ship which is slowly sailing on the sea quickens its speed if beckoned by a courtesan."

From the 20th day of the 12th month the night exhibition of *yūjo* ceased for the year in the best houses, and even

* This is a pun on the name of Mino province and the Japanese word for straw rain-coat (*mino*).

Preparing "*Mochi*" (Rice Flour Cake) for the New Year in the Yoshiwara. Period of Kiōwa (1801 to 1803).
(*After the Picture by Kitagawa Utamaro.*)

the other brothels followed this example after the 20th day.

From about the 22nd day of the 12th month, until the 7th day of the 1st month, a hole was dug in the open space within the brothel entrance, and in this a fire was kindled by *shinzō* and *kamuro*. This hole was called *niwa-gama* (garden furnace), and the custom of lighting a fire in such a position was observed until the èra of Bunkwa, when it gradually fell into desuetude.

The above were the principal events in the life of *yūjo* in former days, but besides these there were days called *maru-bi* and *mom-bi:* on these days guests were obliged to pay the *agedai* for both day and night, although their stay might be limited to only one of those two general divisions of time. The *marubi* included the first seven days of the first month, also the 14th, 15th, and 25th days—in all 10 days. The *mom-bi* (crest-days) consisted of the five *sekku* days (as mentioned in an earlier part of this book) and they were so named because there were five crests dyed on ceremonial clothes. Some people pronounced this word *mono-bi*.

By the era of Kyōhō (1716-1735) the number of the *mom-bi* had greatly increased and reached ten every month, but then they gradually decreased and there are only three or four observed at present.

Naka-no-cho no Hana-ue.

(Flower-planting in the Naka-no-cho.)

Every year, on and after the 3rd day of the 3rd month (old style), notice of the opening of the flower season (*hana-biraki no fuda*) is posted at the *ō-mon* (great gateway), and in the middle of *Naka-no-chō* fences of green bamboo are constructed within which are planted blooming cherry-trees. The commingling cherry-blossoms, blending together into one dense mass of soft fleecy rolling cloud which braids the trees with visible poetry and transforms the avenue into a veritable fairy bower of pink and white florescence, the dazzling glory of the electric lights, and the flashing brilliance of thousands of crested lanterns, makes up a sight which baffles description and must be seen to be appreciated. The garish splendour and blazing radiance of the Yoshiwara at this time is such as to have earned for it the appropriate name of *Fuyajō* (不夜城= "Nightless castle").* Besides the actual flowers, artificial is added to natural beauty, and curtains with a cherry pattern dyed upon them are hung up in the second story of the tea-houses. There they gently wave in the soft spring zephyr, beckoning the passer-by alluringly and enticing him to exploit the secrets of dreamland which they veil so cunningly and suggestively. Of late years plum-trees are planted in the second month, iris in the 5th month, and chrysanthemums in the 9th month (old calendar), and on one occasion the figures of well-known actors made of chrysanthemum flowers—the work of the noted Yasumoto Kamehachi—were also shown. But of all the flowers planted none can equal those of *Naka-no-chō* "*Yo-zakura*" ("night-cherries") which have become famous throughout the length and breadth of Japan, and whose praises have been sung in song and told in story generation after generation by enthusiastic poets and writers during more than fifteen decades.† The origin of flower-planting was that in the

* Or "Nightless City," the title of this book.

† This paragraph of course refers to the inmates of the Yoshiwara.

Courtesans and Guests viewing the Cherry-blossoms in the Naka-no-chō. Period of Kiōwa (1801 to 1803).
(After the Picture by Kitagawa Utamaro.)

second year of *Kwampō* (1742) cherry-flowers in pots were exhibited in front of the tea-houses, and this having been noised about the city of Yedo, multitudes of persons visited the Yoshiwara nightly in consequence. The Yoshiwara people were not slow at taking the hint, and the following year several hundred cherry-trees were planted at Naka-no-chō.

Later, in the 2nd year of En-kyō (1745), cherry-trees were planted between the *ōmon* and Suido-jiri, bamboo fences being built around and bright lanterns being lit under them to enhance the effect. This departure attracted a large number of persons to the quarter.

In those times the expense of the enterprise was fixed at 150 *ryo* every year, 40 per cent being paid by the *Kembansho*, 40 per cent by the miscellaneous traders in the Yoshiwara, and 20 per cent by the tea-houses. The subscriptions were made in the shape of daily or monthly deposits by those interested, and it appears that this practice is still in vogue.

In front of the tea-houses on either side of the street curtains dyed with fantastic designs were hung, and in the front rooms red carpets were placed, these practices being observed even at the present day.

In ancient times, *kamuro* and *shinzō* were allowed to visit Ueno, Asuka-yama, Mukōjima, and other places to view the cherry-blossoms during this month; and another holiday was taken by the inmates of brothels, including *yūjo*, *wakaimono*, etc, who spent a day in giving *saké* parties and viewing the blossoms in the *Naka-no-chō*. One year the following song was composed by Ki-no-kuni-ya Bunzaemon and Kikaku conjointly :—" *Like silvery haze the cherry-blossoms reflect the setting sun; they are like a mountain strewn with golden flowers.*"

The prosperity of the Yoshiwara was at its zenith at this period, and the quarter was counted as one of the places in Yedo which was "worth a thousand *ryō* per day."

Tōrō no koto.

(*Lanterns.*)

At present, in the month of August every year, a large lantern, on which is a painting from the brush of some well-known artist, is exhibited in the centre of the Yoshiwara at *Naka-no-chō* for the purpose of attracting people. Besides this show-piece, revolving and other lanterns of various shapes and designs are hung in front of the tea-houses and lit up nightly. Under these circumstances many persons—not excepting women—flock into the Yoshiwara to witness the brilliant spectacle, and many a prodigal is induced to squander money there by reason of the lanterns which apparently only serve to dazzle his eyes and obscure his reason instead of enlightening him and guiding his footsteps. The general style of lantern is vertically long but narrow in breadth, it being made of silk stretched on black-lacquered frames. It is supported by a pair of cedar poles covered with an *ichimatsu shōji* by way of a roof. Each house is provided with a pair of these lanterns, one facing the street and the other the interior of the building, so that one can be seen from either side: this arrangement has nullified the old saying "*tōrō wa ura kara miro, niwaka wa mae kara miro*" ("*look at the lanterns from behind and the niwaka dance from the front*"). One writer observes that as late as the 20th year of Meiji (1887) the lanterns placed in front of tea-houses faced the streets, and were therefore only seen to

Illuminated lanterns in the *Naka-no-chō*

Illuminating Tea-houses with Lanterns in the Kiōwa period (1801 to 1803).
(After the Picture by Kitagawa Utamaro.)

advantage by pedestrians, while actual guests who went up into the second story of a tea-house had to content themselves with looking at the rear of these lanterns. The present day fashion would seem to be of very modern origin indeed. After the 10th year of Meiji (1877) the tea-houses in the Naka-no-chō hit upon the novel idea of putting up white cloths at the entrance and making displays by means of magic-lanterns, but as this made the Yoshiwara practically a dark world it occasioned great inconvenience to the guests. From time to time the tea-house-keepers have shown themselves very ingenious in getting up new schemes to attract visitors, and on one occasion they displayed an artificial moon on a screen so contrived as to show the movement of clouds flitting across its face: all these displays are reckoned as making up one of the notable events which take place in the Yoshiwara yearly.

According to the old custom, every year, from the last day of the sixth month to the last day of the seventh month, *bon-dōrō* (lanterns erected at the festival of the dead) were shown by all the tea-houses in the Naka-no-chō, but they were not exhibited in front of the small brothels in side streets as at present. The exhibition was suspended on the 13th and 14th days, and after the 15th day new lanterns called *ni no kaeri-dōrō* were substituted. The lighting of lanterns in the 7th month of the year, during the festival of the dead, was a universal custom in Japan from olden times, and therefore lanterns of various shapes and sizes were used in the Yoshiwara also. The "*Yoshiwara Taizen*" (吉原大全) says that one summer a popular *yūjo* named Tamagiku was taken suddenly ill, and that after lingering for a little while she passed away at the beginning of the 7th month.

In order to console her spirit, and as a sacrifice to the manes of the dead, the tea-houses who had been friendly with her hung up before their doors lanterns which were called "*kiriko-dōrō*" (a lantern of a cubical form with its corners squared). This illumination attracted considerable attention and drew many guests, so "business" flourished exceedingly that season, and accordingly in the following year (1716) the practice was followed by all the tea-houses. About that time an expert in fancy hand-work, named Ha-ryū, made a prettily contrived fantastic lantern which he gave to a certain tea-house, and this drew a large number of interested and admiring spectators. In this connection a story is told to the effect that on the 4th day of the 7th month of the 1st year of Gembun (10th August, 1736) a teacher of the *samisen*, named Kayei, who lived in Ageya-chō, held a service in his house in memory of Tamagiku and at the same time a new tune named *midzu-chōshi* (水調子) was played. In the room were hung a number of lanterns bearing the *kaimyō* (posthumous name) of Tamagiku, and every guest was presented with one on his return home. As it was considered as unlucky to have lanterns inside the houses bearing the Buddhistic name of a dead person they were hung up outside the tea-houses. [It is said that on the lower part of these lanterns lines of a green colour were traced.] A request to be allowed to exhibit these lanterns was preferred by the tea-houses to the monthly managers of the Yoshiwara, but as the latter refused their consent the tea-house keepers carried out the idea without obtaining permission. Dōjo of Yedo-chō, and Tamaya Dōkaku, who were then monthly managers, were greatly enraged at the independent action of the tea-house-keepers, and struck down the lanterns

Night scene in the Yoshiwara during the "*Feast of Lanterns*."

of Sumiyoshi-ya and three or four other establishments. The matter was however settled up quite amicably by the tea-house-keepers apologizing, and the authorities granting permission, so after the next year the lantern show commenced and has been continued down to this very day, though the religious aspect of the observance has been completely lost sight of. In former days it seems that besides the lantern show, acting by boys, circus-feats, juggling, etc, took place, but they ceased later. In some years the lanterns displayed have been very fine artistic creations, bearing pictures painted by well-known painters; and anyone who saw the Yoshiwara between the middle of July and the middle of August 1886 will never forget the historical drawings of Hōnen and Eitaku then exhibited on the lanterns.

"Niwaka" Dancing

The performance of "*Niwaka*" dancing is considered to be one of the most interesting features in the life of the Yoshiwara. It consists of a kind of dramatic representation given by the professional buffoons (*hōkan*) and singing girls (*geisha*) of the quarter, and it takes place about August or September each year. When this comic dance takes place the performers visit all the tea-houses giving an exhibition of their buffoonery, and it is said that this entertainment is given in return for the patronage all the members of the troupe usually receive from *chaya* (tea-houses) and *kashi-zashiki* (brothels). During the continuance of the "*Niwaka*" dancing wooden railings are put up on both sides of the Naka-no-chō for the purpose of demarkation, and in front of the tea-houses lanterns shaped like *asagao* ("morning glory"), bearing the respective house names, are hung up and lit. On either side of the *Ō-mon* are placed a pair of very large lanterns (*takahari-chōchin*) on which are written the letters 全盛遊 (*Zensei-asobi* = Magnificent Entertainment). To carry out this dance involves considerable trouble and much preparation, and the very first step which has to be taken is to obtain the permission of the police authorities. After official sanction has been granted preparations are commenced, and the *hōkan* and *geisha* all repair to the manager's office where they draw lots as to whether they shall take part in the first fifteen days' performances or the second fifteen days' dances.

Those older *geisha* who undertake the "lion" dancing and "*kiyari*" songs draw special lots for that purpose, but unless a *geisha* is a masculine looking woman she will not be admitted into this company, and admittance is earnestly desired by many of the professional singers who compete strenuously for the honour. The performance of "lion" dancing and "*kiyari*" singing is limited to the first half month, and the *geisha* who are picked out for this coveted company are experts in their line: those who are new to the quarter give way to their predecessors in order of precedence. When their order has been fixed, by means of lots, a dozen women are formed into a troupe, and for ten days the "*hiyari*" is practiced from morning till evening. For many years a man named "Kichi" (who was also known in the Yoshiwara by the nick-name of of *Chigeinei no Kichi San*) acted as a teacher of the "*Kiyari*" songs, but at present one of his pupils, named Chō is undertaking the task of tuition. The mode of training is for the first half dozen *geisha* to start a song and the remaining half dozen to follow them under the direction of the teacher.

The "*Niwaka-odori*" (Dance) in the Kiōwa period (1801 to 1803).
(*After the Picture by Kitagawa Utamaro.*)

The dancers of dramatic representations also place themselves under a teacher and train continuously for ten days. It is agreed between the performers that during the training period they will not respond to the invitation of any guest, and no one has ever been found to infringe this rule. It is also a custom—if we may be allowed to mention a mere gastronomic detail—for the performers to eat *unagi no domburi-meshi* (boiled rice and pieces of roasted eels served up in a deep bowl) at tiffin every day during of the period of rehearsal.

The dramatic representations played by the company include several new pieces, and the training of the dancers is confided to Hanayanagi Jūsuke. This man was born and brought up in the Yoshiwara, and so the duty of directing the dances is entrusted to him. It appears that new pieces are specially written by playwrights at the request of Jūsuke, and that all such productions are of a comic nature, because the *hōkan* generally aim at exciting the hearty laughter of spectators by means of droll extravaganzas. When the training is finished a grand dress-rehearsal is given in one of the tea-houses, and on this occasion the proper costumes are worn. This dress-rehearsal is known as *nari-mono-iri* (鳴物入リ). Then what is known as *kwai-sho-iri* (會所入リ) takes place in the *kensa-jō* (檢査場=inspecting office), each person entering the room in the order determined by drawing lots. The singers and musicians who participate in the meeting are all professionals. The *shishi-ren* (獅子連="lion" party) goes into the office first, as it is considered the most important part of the company. At this stage the police make an examination of the persons in the building, as nobody is allowed to enter it unless possessed of a special ticket.

On the first day of the "*niwaka*" dancing the *kwaisho* (office) sends out people with a drum (*shitaku-daiko*), which is beaten as they perambulate the Naka-no-chō), to announce the performance. If the weather be rainy, or the roads muddy and slushy, no performance takes place; when this is decided no drum is beaten and no lantern is hung before the *Ō-mon* (great gateway). The "lion" party (*shishi-ren*) and the *niwaka no ya-tai* (a kind of car, fixed up as a stage, on which the "*niwaka*" dance is performed) are started out from a certain fixed point at 7 o'clock in the evening, and go up and down the Naka-no-chō every night: if the car and the party go up the left side of the street this evening they will come down the opposite side to-morrow evening, and the show ends at 11 o'clock each night, when its members are recalled to the office. A "*niwaka*" stage-car consists of a wheeled stage about 18 feet square and proportionately high, and it is so made as to be separated into two sections, each of which is fitted with its own wheels. The stage is fitted up like a regular theatre, provided with scenery painted on silk and paper, and lighted by means of lanterns.

This stage-car is brought to a standstill just between two tea-houses in order that the performance may be equally well seen by both from their upper floors: the idea of placing the stage in such a position was originated by dancing-master Hanayanagi, whose great experience taught him that this scheme was the best for everybody concerned. Next come the *geisha* who play the *samisen*, riding in a car fitted with benches made to accommodate them.

To the left and right of the benches uprights are placed and covered with lattice-work *shōji*, curtains of white and red colours are stretched across the top, and the whole car is lighted by means of three lanterns.

Then follows a *soko-nuke ya-tai* (a bottomless car), which is a kind of square paper-box, without cover or bottom, in front of which is hung a *yoko-naga no andō* (a horizontal lantern) on which is written the names of players, singers, dancers, and the name of the owner of the car. Inside this car are placed the *hayashi-kata* (orchestra). The coolies who drag these cars from place to place are usually hired (through a contractor) in the vicinity of Matsuba-chō, Asakusa district, and are paid daily by the owner of the cars. The costumes of the *geisha* who play the *samisen* are of grey crêpe (dyed with their crests) trimmed at the bottom of the skirt with scarlet crêpe, white collars, black satin *obi*, and white socks. Their coiffure is in the *Shimada* style, and it is kept in place by a hair-pin decorated with the design of *susuki* grass.

The older *geisha* attire themselves even more strikingly than the younger girls, and make use of loud colours—such as blue and scarlet—in their costumes, thus attracting considerable attention by the incongruity displayed. The male players and singers wear blue cotton clothes dyed with their respective crests. The *geisha* who take part in the "*kiyari*" dress their hair after the manner of the top-knot style of men, intentionally spreading out their forelocks, and the whole get-up is like that of of a *teko-mai* dancer. They wear three or even five *jiban* (loose shirts) a *hara-gake* (a cloth shield for the abdomen) and an upper garment called a Yoshiwara-gaku. The right arm and shoulder is thrust out of the *jiban*, on which latter an elaborate design is usually dyed.

The girls all compete among each other in the matter of dress, and the result is that some exquisite patterns are adopted. They wear fine leggings, blue cotton *tabi* (socks) and straw sandals, while across their breasts, depending from the right shoulder, dangle silver chains to which are attached little *kake-mamori* (hanging charms): in their hands they hold fans (with black lacquered frames) on which are painted peony flowers, and besides these they carry *teppō-chōchin* (cylindrical lanterns) on which some of the girls boldly and unblushingly inscribe the names of their paramours. This custom was started in 1894 and led to a good deal of amusement, as their friends solemnly imposed upon both the girls and their sweethearts a mock fine of ten *sen* as a punishment for publicly advertising such love affairs! Thus equipped, they sing the *kiyari* to the sound of the drum as they move on. A drummer, a wooden-block striker, a drum-carrier, and another person who carries the "lion's head" mask, accompany the party. When one *kiyari* song is finished the leader lifts his fan as a signal for the *hyōshigi* to be struck, and the company moves on to the next house after shouting a farewell "*o yakamashū*" ("we've troubled you greatly"). The beginning and finish of the female, as well as the male *niwaka*, is announced by the striking of *hyōshigi*. In former times what was called the "*amefuri niwaka*" (*niwaka* after rain) was in vogue. After the rain had cleared, men went about the tea-houses performing impromptu farces which often elicited applause by the ready wit displayed, but this practice has now ceased. About 10 o'clock an announcement is made by the *kwaisho* people that a recess will be taken, and forthwith all the members of the company stop to drink tea which is provided

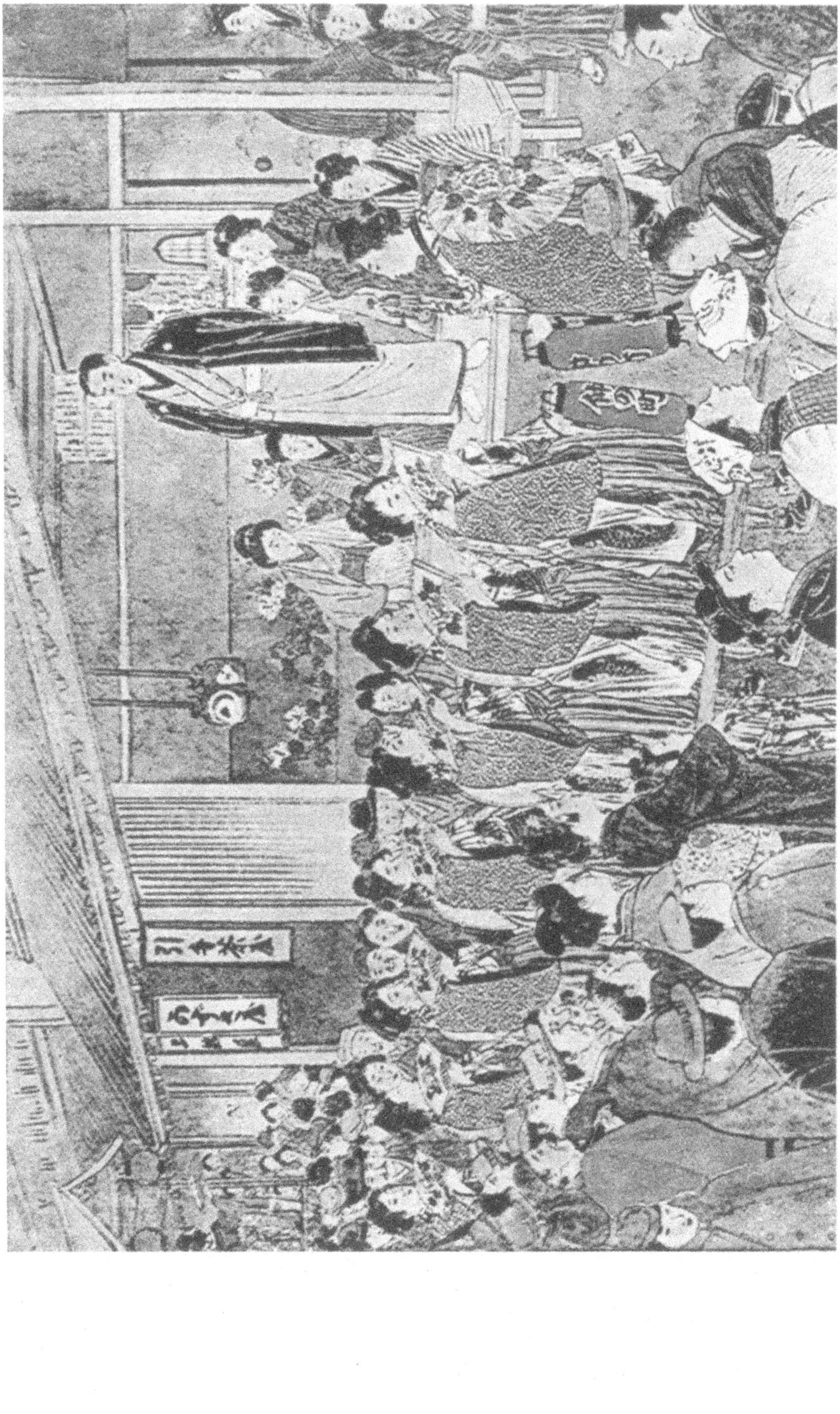

by the house in front of which they may happen to be: on this occasion they also eat such food as may have been sent as presents by intimate friends among the *yūjo* or their guests. During the period of these performances the company is open to engagement only in the day-time, and after 11 o'clock at night, as at the latter hour the public entertainment is finished. When the company receives a notice of engagement from a tea-house, the paper on which such notice is written is fastened on to the hair-pin of the leading geisha after being numbered, and after 11 o'clock the whole troupe go around to the tea-houses by whom they were invited in the order of the arrival of such notices. Needless to say, the company is elated in proportion to the number of these notice-papers. In ancient days the entertainments were often kept up through the night owing to the large number of engagements made.

On the first night of the *niwaka* the company's engagements are generally arranged in advance, for the reason that it is considered a disgrace to have no such appointments on the opening day. When the company obtains tips and gratuities from guests in tea-houses, etc., all such monies are divided among the persons taking part in the entertainment, not forgetting even the coolies. The engagement fees of the *niwaka* company are charged at the rate of 12½ *sen* per *geisha* per *joss-stick* (*ip-pon*) for each guest, and a tip of 20 *sen* each is also expected. Of course these rates are for first-class *geisha* only, and the fees of other inferior *artistes* are proportionately lower.

Strictly speaking, the company should go through its performances for the benefit of each contributing guest separately, but as a matter of fact the more convenient method of performing before several guests collectively is adopted. The *niwaka* entails considerable expense on the *geisha* taking part, and the means of defraying it are too often raised by yielding to the immoral desires of guests who are positively repulsive to them in every respect.

During the performance of the *niwaka*, every tea-house engages firemen to attend to miscellaneous duties, and the *kwaisho* people wearing *hakama* (bifurcated petticoat), and carrying lanterns, constantly go round through the streets to see if everything is in order. The "*wakai-mono*" ("young-men") of the Naka-no-chō are also out on duty with lanterns (called *daihari*), and iron staffs to prevent overcrowding by the spectators. The *dai-hari* carried by these men are placed in front of the tea-house by which the company has been engaged while the dancing is being performed: these great lanterns are intended as signals.

All the expenses connected with the *niwaka* are defrayed by the brothels, tea-houses, etc.

Originally *niwaka* meant an impromptu farce, but about the era of Tenna (1681-1683) the character was changed though the meaning remains practically the same. The "*Kiyū Shōran* (嬉遊笑覧) says that the *niwaka* seems to be an imitation of the Gion festival of Kyōto, and the festival cars (*nerimono*) of Shimabara and Sumiyoshi. It originated in the festival of the Kurosuke Inari which took place in the 8th month of the 19th year of Kyōhō (August 1734) on the occasion of that deity obtaining the title of *shō-ichi-i* (first rank.) Owing to this fact, until recently, whenever a *niwaka* dance took place, a bamboo tree, bearing leaves, was set up on either side of the *Ō-mon* (gateway) and a straw rope was hung across in order to sanctify the place within: this practice has now ceased. From the 1st of this month the festival of the Kurosuke Inari at Suidō-jiri took place, festival cars were drawn about the streets, and the Yoshiwara was much crowded by sight-seers. The custom of erecting bamboos at the *Ō-mon* (above referred to) appears to have been in vogue until the Bunkwa era (1804-1817). Again, from the 1st day of the 8th month the *yūjo* who were proficient in singing and dancing performed *niwaka* dances for the entertainment of the public every fine day for thirty days. The origin of this dance is stated to have been the visit of young *yūjo* to the Mazaki Tenjin in the 4th year of Meiwa (1767) but anyway, judging from the style of the present *niwaka*, the dancing in the Meiwa era appears to have been the origin of this dance.

Mention is made in the "*Kwagai Yenkaku-shi*" (花街沿革誌) that in a picture of *niwaka* dancing drawn in the era of Meiwa (1764-1771) was written:—

> "Ōtsuye shosagoto hayashi kata, ō-deki, ō-deki!" (Dramatic representation of the *ō-tsuye* musicians, splendid, splendid!). A drawing of a car-stage and of an elevated *shōji* was depicted, and around this wistaria flowers were hung: inside were the musicians.
>
> The *geisha* O Ishi, O Kume, O Yuki, and O Nami, who wore clothes with long sleeves, and *hōkamuri* (handkerchief covering the head and cheeks) played the *samisen*. *Yūjo* Taneko (of Shinkana-ya) and Masuno (of Ō-Ebisuya) also in long-sleeved clothes and lacquered hats danced bearing wistaria flowers in their hands. Next there were lantern bearers of Kyōmachi It-chōme which were acted by more than ten *kamuro*. The five leading *yūjo* were dressed in five-fold robes and red *hakama*, wore *yōraku* (crowns) upon their heads and held *hishaku* (sceptres) made of *hinoki* wood: in their hands. As the women walked along they were kept carefully covered by means of a special umbrella held over their heads from behind.

In the programmes of *niwaka* dances given in the Kyōwa era, (1801-1803) as well as in the pictures of the Bunkwa era

(1854-1859) are to be seen men playing a farce before the railings of a brothel. At that period no stage car was used, but the pantomimic dance was performed in the open, the players being made visible by means of candles placed on stands in front of the persons taking part in the performance. The players appear to have been gifted with a considerable fund of ready wit and humour, as nearly every word and gesture excited roars of laughter from the lookers-on. The latter day *niwaka* seems to have been derived from the dancing of *yūjo*. The famous "lion-dancing" and *kiyari* songs which form the chief feature of the *niwaka*, were originated during the Ansei era (1854-1859) by a *geisha* named O Ichi, who was very popular in her day by reason of her being an expert in these matters. It is stated that in the year 1898 the *niwaka* scheme was abandoned owing perhaps to the fact that the result to the Yoshiwara was not commensurate with the large outlay involved in getting up the entertainments, but on making a careful investigation we find that the police authorities declined to sanction the dance even for half the usual time. The proprietor of one of the largest establishments states that he and his *confrères* are greatly concerned about this attempt to abolish such an old custom, and that a supreme effort will be made to obtain the sanction of the police to produce the *niwaka* as usual. His argument was that such an exhibition is not inimical to the morals of the public, and that persons who visit the Yoshiwara go there with the express purpose of amusing themselves with such spectacles!

Crowds Visiting the "*Tori-no-machi.*"

Tori-no-machi.

(The fete of *Ōtori no Kami.*)

On the days of the fowl, in the month of November every year, the festival of *Ōtori-no-kami* is celebrated at the various places in Tōkyō where the "Eagle" shrines are located. On these occasions great crowds of people visit the Yoshiwara, as the most popular "market" is held in Ryūsenji-machi, Asakusa Tambo, close to the quarter.

These are the red-letter days for brothels and their inmates, and, as a rule, nearly all the *yūjo* are engaged by previous arrangement with their guests. It is considered rather a disgrace to *yūjo* to remain long on exhibition in their cages on such holidays. Popular women give ocular demonstration of their popularity by the means of *tsumi-yagu*, and *geisha* usually obtain promises of engagement from some guests beforehand.

The three gates besides the Ō-mon, which are kept shut except on the *Tori-no-machi* days and in case of fire or other emergency, are thrown open from early morning for the admission of the general public. The traders erect their stalls at the back of the Examination House (*kensa-ba*) as far as Suidō-jiri, and *yūjo* appear in the cages even in the day-time. At night the bustle and confusion of the Yoshiwara becomes intensified.

Tipsy rascals "three sheets in the wind" stagger along the streets or swarm in front of the brothels, thickly bawling out unseemly ditties, while some *yūjo* may be heard calling to would-be guests in their broad *patois*. The great crowd surges hither and thither like the eddies of the ocean, and the confusion well-nigh defies description; but, paramount above all, here, there, and everywhere is the ubiquitous blue-coated little policeman with sword, spectacles, lantern, and note-book, uttering his warning cry of "*koréya! koréya*" ("that'll do now:—move on") and overawing the *profanum vulgus* with the majesty of the law visible and incarnate.

Yoshiwara Nana-fushigi.

(The Seven Mysteries of the Yoshiwara.)

Contrary to the "Seven mysteries" of Echigo, Suwa, Honjō, etc, all of which consist of weird ghost stories or really inexplicable mysteries, the "*nana-fushigi*" of the Yoshiwara are most innocent and amusing in their nature: they are as follows:—

1.—Though the gateway, or great entrance door, is called the Ō-mon (great gate) there is no *genkwan* (entrance porch) within.

2—Though the moat around is called a creek (*kashi*) there are no boats visible.

3.—Though one of the wards is called *Sumi-cho* (corner "ward" or "street") it has no corner.

4.—Though the introducing houses are called "*cha-ya*" (tea-houses) yet they sell no tea.

5.—Though the servants in the brothels are called "*shinzō*" (young woman) most of them are old women.

6.—Among the *wakaimono* (literally "*young men,*" but here meaning "men-servants") are many bald-headed individuals.

Outside the Yoshiwara Lock Hospital on "Inspection Day."

7.—Although the old women in the brothels, are called *yarite* (遣リ手="*givers*") they really give nothing but take all they can get.

Such are the "Seven mysteries" of the Yoshiwara, but the greatest mystery appears to be the fact that they should have been accepted as mysteries at all.

Yoshiwara no Kyō-ka.

(*Comic Poetry.*)

Among the many witty and epigrammatic stanzas which have been composed by well-known literary men, the following have been selected as interesting and characteristic :—

"The sight of snowy evening at the Ō-mon is so beautiful that no man is fool enough to leave the Yoshiwara satiated." (*Yomo Akara*).

"On a calm Spring evening, when the women of the quarter enter their cages, it seems as if flowers were being scattered in the Yoshiwara by the bell announcing night fall. (*Yoma Akara.*)

"Though visitors may change, the *mikaeri yanagi* (looking-back willow tree) is ever green, and flowers perennially scarlet." (*Kyokutei Bakin*).

"Even without asking the question it is known that the *miyako-dori* ("oyster-catcher") lives in the Sumida river : the person I long for lives in the Yoshiwara." (*Santō Kyōzan*).

"If the wind could be kept out by shutting the *Ō-mon* (great gateway) the expenditure of a thousand *ryō* would not be begrudged for the sake of the flowers." (*Magao*).

"When one is intoxicated the same thing is repeated —'the flowers are blooming in the Yoshiwara : in the Yoshiwara the flowers are blooming'." (*Shoku Sanjin*).

"In the Yoshiwara a visitor's life is prolonged by means of the bells of "*hikê yotsu,*" which is struck later by two hours than the bells of the outside world." (*Shoji Nariyuki*).

"All the guests being tethered to the blossom-laden cherry-trees are led into the Yoshiwara as horses are put into harness together." (*Moto no Mokuami*).

"It is the season of flowers and Yoshino will find itself outrivalled by the "*oiran*" blossoms of the Yoshiwara." *Tegara Okamochi.*

Yoshiwara Kwai-rok-ki.

(Chronology of fire disasters in the Yoshiwara).

In the 12th month of the 7th year of Kwan-ei (January 1631) fire broke out at Hatchōbori and burnt out Negichō, Hasegawa-chō, and Tomizawa-chō.

On the 14th day of the 12th month of the second year of Shōhō (30th January, 1646), after a lapse of 16 years, fire broke out at Owari-chō, and the Yoshiwara was burnt. The progress of the flames was checked at Hasegawa-chō, at Ōmondori. This fire was known as the "*Sakueymon kwaji.*"

In the 9th month of the 3rd year of Sho-ō (October 1654), after the lapse of 19 years, fire broke out at Kirigashi and the Moto Yoshiwara was burnt.

On the 18th day of the 1st month of the 3rd year of Meireki (2nd March, 1857), after the lapse of 13 years (something seems to be wrong in this calculation?) fire broke out in the Hommyō-ji temple, Maruyama, Hongo, and the greater portion of Yedo, including the Moto Yoshiwara, was burnt.

The following are the disasters which have occurred since the removal of the Yoshiwara to the present site:—

A Fire in the Yoshiwara.

On the 7th day of the 12th month of the 4th year of Empō (10th January, 1677), after an interval of twenty years, fire broke out in a bath-house, kept by a man named Ichibei, at Kyō-machi-gashi, and the Yoshiwara was burnt.

On the 27th day of the 11th month of the 5th year of Empō (21st December, 1677) fire broke out in the house of Hanaya Ichibei, Yedo-chō *ni-chō-me,* and part of the street where the fire originated was burnt. Rain was falling heavily at the time.

In the 4th month of the 5th year of Meiwa (May 1768) fire broke out in the brothel at Yedo-chō kept by Yotsume-ya Zentarō, and the Yoshiwara was burnt down after an interval of ninety-two years.

On the 23rd day of the 4th month of the 8th year of Meiwa, (5th June, 1771) fire broke out in the house of Umeya Ihei and the Yoshiwara was burnt after an interval of four years.

On the 29th day of the 2nd month of the 9th year of Meiwa (1st April, 1772) fire broke out in the Daitan-ji temple, Gyonin-zaka, Meguro, and the Yoshiwara was burnt after an interval of two years.

On the 30th day of the 9th month of the 1st year of Temmei (15th November, 1781) fire broke out in the houses of Aburaya Yasubei, Fushimi-chō, and Yedo-chō *ni-chō-me* of the Yoshiwara was burnt after an interval of ten years. One account says that this fire originated in the Kadaya, Fushimi-chō, and that eleven houses in Yedo-chō *ni-chō-me,* ten houses Naka-no-chō, and ten houses at Fushimi-chō were burnt.

On the 16th day of the 4th month of the 4th year of Temmei (3rd June, 1784) fire broke out in the house of Maru-ebi-ya, and the Yoshiwara was burnt after an interval of four years.

On the 9th day of the 11th month of the 7th year of Temmei (18th December, 1787) fire broke out in the tea-house kept by Gorobei, Sumichō, and the Yoshiwara was burnt after an interval of four years.

On the 2nd day of the 4th month of the 6th year of Kwansei (1st May, 1794) fire broke out either in the brothel known as "Choji-ya" or in the house of Juzo (they stood close together) and the Yoshiwara was burnt after an interval of eight years. Tamachi (in Asakusa) was also burnt by this fire, sparks carried by the wind having ignited the residences there.

On the 23rd day of the 2nd month of the 12th year of Kwansei (18th March, 1800) fire broke out in the house of a farmer named Tsunasa Jinyemon, of Ryūsenji-mura, Shitaya district, and the Yoshiwara was burnt after an interval of seven years.

On the 21st day of the 11th month of the 9th year of Bunkwa (24th December, 1812) fire broke out in the compound of sheds belonging to Zenshichi (chief of beggars), and the Yoshiwara was burnt after an interval of thirteen years. This fire spread as far as Yama-no-shiku, and Tamachi (*ni-chō-me*), Asakusa.

On the 3rd day of the 5th month of the 13th year of Bunkwa (29th May, 1816) fire broke out in an unoccupied house owned by Shin-ebi-ya Kichisuké, (a brothel-keeper) at Kyō-machi *it-chō-me*, and the Yoshiwara was burnt after an interval of five years. The office of Sahei (a *nanushi*) at Yedo-chō *ni-chō-me* escaped the general holocaust. This conflagration spread as far as Ryūsenji-machi, Asakusa.

On the 26th day of the 1st month of the 6th year of Tempō (23rd February, 1835) fire broke out in the brothel kept by

Matsugoro, Sumichō. and the Yoshiwara was burnt after an interval of twelve years.

On the 19th day of the 10th month of the 8th year of Tempō (16th November 1837) fire broke out in the house of Gentaro (who was the father and guardian of the proprietress of a small brothel at Yedo-chō *ni-chō-me*) and the Yoshiwara was burnt after an interval of three years. The office of *nanushi* Nizayemon, at Yedo-chō *it-chō-me*, and the small houses in the back alleys, were not destroyed.

On the 5th day of the 12th month of the 2nd year of Kōkwa (2nd January, 1846) fire broke out in a brothel kept by Kawatsuya Tetsugoro, at Kyō-machi *ni-chō-me*, and the Yoshiwara was burnt after an interval of nine years. The office of *Nanushi* Sahei at Yedo-chō, *ni-chō-me*, that of *nanushi* Niyemon at Yedo-chō *it-chō-me*, and that of *nanushi* Rokuroyemon at Kyō-machi *it-chō-me*, however, were not destroyed.

On the 2nd day of the 10th month of the 2nd year of Ansei (11th November, 1855) a destructive earthquake occurred, and all the houses in the Yoshiwara were demolished by shaking or burning after an interval of eleven years. Numerous lives were lost.

On the 29th day of the 9th month of the 1st year of Manen (12th November, 1860) fire broke out in the house of Kinoji-ya Tetsujirō (at the *kashi* in Yedo-chō *ni-chō-me*) and the Yoshiwara was burnt after an interval of six years. The house of *nanushi* Jinshiro, at Kyō-machi, *it-chō-me*, was saved.

On the 14th day of the 11th month of the 2nd year of Bunkyū (3rd January, 1863) fire broke out in the house of Shimidzu-ya Seisuké (Kyō-machi, *it-chō-me*) and the Yoshiwara was burnt after an interval of three years. The fire spread to Gojikken-machi. The houses of *nanushi* Jinshiro and of Kaneko Hambei (at Kyō-machi *it-chō-me*) were saved.

On the 26th day of the 1st month of the 1st year of Genji (5th March, 1864), after an interval of three years, fire broke out in the store-house of a brothel (Ōguchi-ya Bunzayemon) of Yedo-chō *it-chō-me*, and all the houses in that street were burnt. The brothels on the creek-side of Ageya-chō were saved, and also some houses in Kyōmachi *it-chō-me*. On the 23rd day of the 9th month of the same year (23rd October, 1864) fire broke out in a tobacconist's shop in Yedo-chō *it-chō-me*, and six houses were destroyed.

On the 11th day of the 11th month of the 2nd year of Kei-ō (17th December, 1866) after a lapse of three years, fire broke out in a small brothel named Ō-Masu-ya (in Yedo-chō *it-chō-me*) and a portion of the Yoshiwara was burnt.

On the 28th day of the 5th month of the 4th year of Meiji (28th May, 1871) fire broke out in a paper-dealer's store, named Sanya Matsugoro, (in Kita Fushimi-chō) and the greater part of the Yoshiwara was burnt. The houses along the creek at Yedo-chō *it-chō-me*, Ageya-chō, and Kyōmachi *it-chō-me* were saved, as was also the "*Kado-ebi*."

On the 11th day of the 11th month of the 6th year of Meiji (11th November, 1873) fire broke out in the house occupied by Kobayashi-ya Rui, No. 25 Kyō-machi *ni-chō-me*, and this street, and Yedo-chō *ni-chō-me*, were completely demolished. In the vicinity of the *Ō-mon* two tea-houses (the "Ōmori-ya" and "Yagata-ya") only were saved. Some houses in Tamachi *ni-chō-me*, Yama-no-shiku, and Shōden Yokochō, were burnt in consequence of being set on fire by flying sparks.

On the 12th day of the 12th month of the 8th year of Meiji, at noon (12th December, 1875) fire broke out in the kitchen of the house of Nakamura Chōbei (Sano Tsuchi-ya) No. 25, Yedo-chō, *it-chō-me,* and in consequence Yedo-chō, *it-chō-me* and *ni-chō-me,* Sumichō, Ageya-machi, and Kyōmachi *it-chō-me* and *ni-chō-me* were burnt. Besides these the fire destroyed some houses in other parts of the Yoshiwara.

On the 2nd day of the 1st month of the 11th year of Meiji (2nd January, 1878) after an interval of four years, fire broke out in the house of Nakamura Chōbei (Iseroku) Yedo-chō *it-chō-me,* but it was extinguished after consuming the building in which it originated. The cause of fire was kerosene oil.

On the 23rd day of the 1st month of the 24th year of Meiji (23rd January, 1891), after an interval of seventeen years, fire broke out in the house of Kobayashi Kyūtarō ("Kobayashi-rō") No. 19, Kyōmachi *ni-chō-me,* and at Sumi-chō; forty-six houses were completely, and five partially, burnt. At Kyōmachi *ni-chō-me* thirteen houses were completely, and two partially, burnt. At Yedo-chō *ni-chō-me* two houses were completely, and nine partially, destroyed.

On the 4th day of the 4th month of the 26th year of Meiji (13th April, 1893) at 7.30 p.m. fire broke out in the third story of Irita Yoshitarō ("Baiman-rō") No. 31, Ageya-chō, and some forty-five houses were completely, and nine partially, burnt at Ageya-chō, Yedo-chō *it-chō-me,* and Kyōmachi *it-chō-me.*

The latest destructive conflagration in the Yoshiwara occurred at 4.30 a.m. on March 15th, 1896. It was started at the rear of the tea-houses *Shin Kirihan* and *Kanetama-ya* (which were situated on the border of Yedo-chō *ni-chō-me* and Sumi-chō) and quickly spread to Yedo-chō *ni-chō-me,* Naka-no-chō, Sumi-chō, and even to the outside of the *Ō-mon.* Altogether 139 houses were destroyed. In this fire a *yūjo* named Koiginu, 24 years of age, belonging to the "Kawachi-rō" (Sumi-chō) was burnt to death, her way of escape having been cut off by smoke.

A man-servant of the "Tanaka-rō" was also asphyxiated to death on this occasion.

Furi-sodé Kwaji.

(*The Great Fire of Meireki.*)

The following interesting legend is an almost literal translation of a popular Japanese tradition.

It seems that on the 18th day of the 1st month of the 3rd year of Meireki (2nd March, 1657), a fire broke out in the Honmyō-ji (temple) at Maru-yama in Hongo, which raged through the City of Edo during three days and three nights, burning everything before it. The number of persons who were burnt to death was over 108,000 souls, and tradition says that from ancient times to the present day no fire has broken out which can be even compared to this conflagration, and indeed that it is impossible to express in words the extent of this terrible and sad calamity. On enquiring about the origin of the fire, it appears that at the end of the Spring in the 2nd year of Meireki, when the cherry blossoms were blooming, the daughter of a certain Hatamoto who resided in the neighbourhood of Banchō, was taken in company with some neighbours to see the flowers at Ueno. At that time the young page of a certain temple was passing by the Sam-mai-bashi (bridge) at Hirokōji in Ueno, and was seen by the young lady who was going in an opposite direction. The youthful page was a fine handsome young follow, and the girl, on glancing carelessly at him, noticed he was a youth of about sixteen or seventeen years of age, and was wearing a black *haori* (a kind a loose overcoat) with long sleeves (*furi-sodé*) on which was dyed a pattern composed of water-wheels (a favorite Japanese design). His *hakama* (loose trousers) were made of striped brown material, and as he walked along with his swords (the scabbards of which were decorated with a flower design) thrust straight down in his belt, he looked like the ancient pictures of Narihira, or of Minamoto-no-Mitsu-uji, when they were children, at the time of their first admittance to the rank of knighthood. Then she wondered how anyone could surpass this youth, for his lips were red as the reddest of blossoms, his eyebrows arched and beautiful, his hair black and glossy, and his head in front showed the signs of the rite of *gembuku,* while his front hair was parted in the fashion of those times: and altogether he looked very prepossessing with his fair complexion which laughed at the driven snow, and his fresh appearance which seemed to be striving to emulate the beauty and fragrance of the fullblown flowers. As he passed the young lady, the long sleeves of his garment brushed against her dress, her heart was spontaneously affected, and she fell in love with him after a single glance. Although they were going in opposite directions, she could not help glancing round and wondering whether it was a man or a god that she had seen, and, as she gazed after him, her first love developed like the blossoming of the buds of the cherry flowers. However, as she had persons with her, she went on with them, although she was loath to be parted from her lover. Then she went on to Ueno with her friends, but, although she looked at the cherry-blossoms and sat there amongst them on the matting laid out for the accommodation of guests, the form of the youth she had seen kept dancing before her eyes, and the laughter and gaiety of the crowds assembled became very annoying to her as she sat wrapped in gloomy thought.

That day she returned home and thought—"I wonder who he can be? I know not where he lives and I have no means of tracing him. However much I may pine for my loved one my power of will is not powerful enough to reach to him and thus fulfil my desires. I think myself that I am foolish, but although I strive to banish my thoughts as vain and silly, yet I cannot for a moment relieve my heart of its trouble." Thus time passed wearily for her, and the days and months flew by until it had become the season of the summer rains, with its intermittent showers. Her thoughts were melancholy and she did not even have her hair dressed, but allowed it to fall dishevelled over her shoulders. She had been taken sick sometime previously, and therefore her parents were very anxious about her. One day her father, addressing her mother, said—"On thinking over the matter of our daughter's illness very carefully, she drinks no medicine and she dislikes the doctor, and there is something about it which I cannot understand. From what I heard accidentally the other day from a neighbour, it seems that at the time of viewing the cherry-blossoms our daughter met some young gentleman at Mihashi and she cannot forget about him. I don't know who he was, but it seems that he was a very handsome youth. I have heard that at that time she spoke about the young man to her friends, but I did not think anything about it, and yet it appears that our daughter returned home and from that time she has been moping and miserable. Lately her sickness has increased, and become very serious, and she is wasting away and looks wretched. If you will quietly sound her on the subject she will probably tell you the facts of the case." Being thus addressed the wife spoke quietly with her daughter that evening about the matter, but she only buried her face in her pillow and made no reply. In a short time however, she thought that after all now things had come to such a pass there was no use in concealing anything further, so she told everything saying—" At the time of flower-seeing this Spring —&c, &c,—." Then she went on to confess the whole matter to her mother, while her eyes were streaming with tears, and as she cried and fretted in a half apologetic manner she looked very miserable and pitiful, and she finished by imploring her mother, with averted face, not to laugh at her. Then the mother drew nearer to her daughter and asked her in a low gentle voice—" Do you know the name of the young man and his residence? Have you heard something about it?" But her daughter raised her head and replied— " I had no means of knowing his name or residence. The only thing I remember is that he had on a garment on the sleeves of which there was a pattern, and I am thinking lovingly about him." The mother nodded and said—" Well then, if I have a dress dyed with the pattern which you then saw, and place it at the side of your pillow, it may give you some comfort and relief." On hearing this the daughter seemed very happy, and the parents enquired minutely about the pattern and the colouring of the water-wheel design, then they consulted together and calling in their regular dyer made no agreement about the price but simply hurried him up saying "Please be quick and dye this at once." So, without any waste of time the material was very prettily dyed, and they hurried up the tailor likewise, making him work night and day until the garment was finished. They were indulgent parents and had reared their child very tenderly, so that this trouble caused their hearts to become as black as the black *ko-sodê* they had ordered. The pattern was composed of water-wheels in the midst of waves, and they revolved and revolved until at last they caused disaster and calamity to the world. The parents brought this garment quickly and showed it to their daughter, who, when she had seen it said "Indeed that's it, that's it!" and feeling as if she had ascended into Paradise, she clasped the dress in her arms and appeared like a demented creature. Then after four or five days had elapsed her illness became more and more severe, and she soon expired, still clasping the *ko-sodê* to her bosom: and as she thus lay in death, holding this garment in her arms, the sight was indeed a most pitiable and touching one. Well, after her death the parents had to part with their child, and the funeral took place with the usual rites in the burial ground of the "Hommyō-ji" (temple) in the district of Hongo. As to the dyed *ko-sodê*, as the poor girl had loved it so dearly, they put it on her coffin as a *kakemuku* (pall) and sent it forth to the temple. Sometime afterwards, the priests of the Hommyō-ji sold the garment to their regular second-hand clothing store, and during the ninth month of the same year this figured dress was again brought to the temple covering a coffin as a *kakemuku*, but the priests paid no particular attention to it, and again sold it off to the second-hand clothing store as usual. Again the identical figured garb was sent in as a *kakemuku* (pall) from a certain parishioner at daybreak on the 18th day of the 1st month of the 3rd year of Meireki (2nd March, 1657), and as this was the third time the same garment had been sent into this temple, it attracted the eyes of the *nasshō* (the priest who transacts the business of the monastery) and *bansō* (assistant priest) who thought—"How miraculous! There must be something mysterious in this event, and it is certainly no mere chance-work that this *ko-sodê* (long-sleeved garment) should have come round three times in succession to our temple"—and they told the Father Superior of their impressions. The Father Superior, after pondering the matter for a short time, said—"It is indeed a very important case. It is exceedingly mysterious that the garment should have passed through the hands of our parishioners not once but twice and thrice, and it is more mysterious that the deceased persons have all been young girls. I will myself interrogate the *seshu* (person who orders everything relating to the funeral) about the matter." Thus, prior to the funeral service, he interviewed the *seshu*, and enquired about the history of the *ko-sodê* (long sleeved garment). The *seshu* answered—"I am deeply ashamed by reason of your enquiries in that way, but our daughter went out one day to the neighborhood of Asakusa on certain business, when she saw this garment hung up in the shop of a certain cast-off-clothing dealer, and she was importunately anxious to get it. We bought it according to her earnest desire, and from that very night she was taken ill with a raging fever and not only that, but she talked deliriously like a lunatic, tightly embracing the garment the while. All my family together endeavoured very hard to take the garment away, but she would not allow it to be removed. Since then she became thinner and thinner and finally expired." The priest nodded to the speaker and then related in detail all about the mysterious garment, and how it had come into the temple twice before as a *kakemuku* (pall) from two of their parishioners. The *seshu* (person ordering the funeral) on hearing this story was struck with terror and said—" Then, if you should sell this *ko-sodé* again this time, the same calamity will fall upon another unfortunate individual. This is not my wish, and I think it will be proper to put it on the fire and burn it up after the funeral ceremony is finished." The Father Superior nodded several times and replied—" Indeed that is the wisest course,—yes—yes." Then after the funeral ceremony was over, and the people all gone, the priests brought out a brazier of three feet square in order to burn the garment, and crumpling up the *ko-sodé* they cast it on the fire, all chanting the prayer in chorus " *Oh let the souls of the three women quickly enter into Paradise. We adore thee Oh blossom of doctrine!—thou salvation bringing book of the wonderful Law!*" Immediately after they had flung the garment into the flames a sudden whirlwind arose which came sweeping from the North, blowing up sand and dust to such an extent that in an instant the sky was entirely blotted out by a cloud of grit and dust, which threatened to envelope the whole universe with a darkness as black as a raven's wing. The people in the temple looked at each other in horror, saying in their agitation that this was no chance event, when suddenly at that very moment, the burning garment spread out and was carried by the wind high up into the inner side of the lofty ceiling of the main chapel. The bystanders had no time to exclaim more than "Oh!" before the main chapel and the priests' dwelling were one mass of flame, and the fire was burning up furiously until it became at length the origin of a great disaster. Such was the origin of what is known as the *furi-sodê-kwaji* (Long-sleeved garment fire) of Hongo, Maruyama, Hommyōji (temple), which consumed nearly the whole city and which still remains upon the lips of the people to the present day.

Mei-gi ryaku-den.

(Brief sketches of the lives of famous courtesans.)

Taka-o.

The first Taka-o flourished in the period of the former (*moto*) Yoshiwara, and was called Myōshin Taka-o. She was also known as *Ko-mochi Taka-o* (*child-bearing Taka-o*) as she used to promenade attended by a wet-nurse who carried the child of which she had been delivered.

The second Taka-o was known as Daté Taka-o.

The third Taka-o was "Saijō Taka-o" who was redeemed by one Saijō Kichiyemon (a ratainer of Kii Chūnagon) and taken by him to his native province (Kii). Another account says that she was redeemed by Saijō Kichibei, a gold-lacquer painter at the Shōgun's Court.

The fourth Taka-o was called "Asano Taka-o." It is said that she was redeemed either by Asano Iki-no-Kami or Asano Inaba-no-Kami, both of whom were *daimyō*. According to the list of *daimyō* published in the 4th year of Meireki (1658), Asano Iki-no-Kami seems to have been the grandson of the well-known Asano Nagamasa.

The fifth Taka-o was called "Midzutani Taka-o." She was redeemed by Midzutani Rokubei, a banker to the Prince of Mito. Later she eloped with a servant of Mizutani—an old man 68 years of age. Then she married Handayū Ryō-un, and next became the concubine of Makino Suruga no Kami (a *daimyō*), but she again eloped with one of the latter's attendants named Kōno Heima. Next we see her as the wife of a hair-dresser at Fukagawa, then the wife of an actor named Sodeoka Masanosuke, and then that of an oil dealer at Mikawa-chō. The career of this much-married woman was brought to a close by her sudden death in the street in front of the Dai-on-ji temple.

The sixth Taka-o was called "Da-zome Taka-o," and was redeemed by a dyer named Jirobei. She is said to have been a very beautiful woman who surpassed all her predecessors except the fifth, (whose immoral behaviour we have just noticed) to have been a skilful writer (one of the necessary accomplishments of a lady) and to have been of a quiet and gentle disposition. With her lady-like accomplishments and graceful manner she was fitted by nature to become the wife of a gentleman of position, and yet she married Jirobei although the latter was not only in humble circumstances but noted for being a rare specimen of ugliness. The strange union, however, proved a great success as the pair lived on most happy and affectionate terms. The history of their marriage was briefly as follows. Jirobei, who was a dyer working in his master's shop, one day went out to the Yoshiwara with his comrades to see the promenading of *yūjo.* On this occasion he first saw his future wife, and, being greatly struck by her beauty and graceful demeanour, he thought if he could only approach her the one wish of his whole life would be gratified. At that time, however, the engagement of so superior a *yūjo* by a common artizan who made a hand-to-mouth living was, of course, out of the question and Jirobei felt desperate. The matter preyed on his mind to such an extent that when he returned to his master's house he looked so melancholy and depressed that his appearance attracted the attention of his employer. Unable to conceal his secret, he unbosomed himself to his master, and the latter encouraged him to work diligently and save money enough to engage the *yūjo*, as it was, after all, only a matter of money. For more than a year Jirobei worked very hard both by day and night, and by dint of great economy managed to save enough cash to pay the *age-dai* of a *yūjo* of Taka-o's class. The very moment that he had sufficient money he hurried off to the Yoshiwara, as he feared that should he wait too long the object of his love might be redeemed by somebody and thus be lost to him for ever. Entering the quarter dressed in his workman's attire, and looking dirty and uncouth with his unkempt hair and stubbly beard, he experienced considerable trouble in approaching Taka-o, but finally he succeeded in meeting her and disclosed everything without reserve. Her woman's heart was greatly moved by this proof of loving sincerity, and she finally promised to marry him when her term of engagement expired. This promise she afterwards faithfully redeemed, and Jirobei then opened a dyer's shop on his own account in the city, and became very prosperous in after years. It seems that Jirobei was not a success as a dyer as he was unskilful in the technique of his trade, but his business prospered on account of the many people who patronized his establishment in order to catch a glimpse of the famous and romantic beauty.

It is not on record as to who redeemed the seventh Taka-o. Some persons mistake the seventh for "Sakakibara Takao." In the Mi-ura record the sixth is erroneously mentioned as the "Sakakibara Takao." The eight and ninth appear to have had successful careers in the Yoshiwara, but they were apparently not redeemed by people of note as no record exists on this point.

The tenth Taka-o seems to have appeared in the Yoshiwara either in the 13th or 14th year of Kyōhō (1728 or 1729).

The eleventh Taka-o was redeemed by Sakakibara-Shikibu-Tayū, daimyō of Takata, Echigo province, who enjoyed an income of 150,000 *koku* of rice per annum. With the retirement of this lord she accompanied him to his clan headquarters (Takata): after his death she became a nun and died at the age of thirty and odd years.

Hana-ōgi.

The *Yedo-Kwagai-Enkahushi* says that the brothel-keeper named Ōgi-ya Uyemon was a pupil of Katō Chiin, well versed in the composition of Japanese poems, and favourably known by his literary name of *Bokuka* (墨河="Inky River"). Among the inmates of this gentle poetaster's house was a *yūjo* named Hana-ōgi who was very popular at that time. About the 6th year of Kwansei (1794) she escaped from the Yoshiwara and lived with a man with whom she had contracted intimate relations, but she was soon detected and brought back to her master's house. She then refused, on the plea of illness, to act as a *yūjo* any more and no persuasion had any effect upon her.

Finally the master of the house composed a poem to the effect that :—

> "Notwithstanding the careful attention given to the plum-tree by its care-taker in order that its flowers may not be injured the wind increases in violence."

and showed it to her. Hana-ōgi, bursting into tears, and touched by the kindness of her master, instantly composed another poem which read :—

> "The plum-blossoms that tightly closed themselves in order not to be shaken by a merciless wind may be found in bloom next Spring."

From this time she changed her mind and her popularity returned. The *Kinsei Shogwadan* says that Hana-ōgi, a *yūjo* of the Ōgi-ya, Yoshiwara, not only had poetical tastes and was well versed in the art of penmanship but was a most filial and dutiful daughter towards her aged mother. Though her literary accomplishments were well-known and recognized, her filial piety was not so widely known, and the author of the *Kinsei Shogwadan* says "filial piety ought to be prized above all other things. It is a rare quality among women who sell their bodies for prostitution." In the case of Hana-ōgi, her filial piety having been noised abroad until her fame reached even to far away lands, a Chinese scholar, named Hikosei, who visited Nagasaki on board a trading-ship, happening to hear about her sent her a letter of eulogy written in the style of a Chinese poem. The composition, which was characterized by beautiful and imaginative thought, may be freely translated as follows :—

> "You, who are the leading courtesan of a superior house of pleasure, are richly gifted by Heaven with a hundred various graceful accomplishment most excellent in woman. I, being a

stranger and sojourner from a far-off land, must sail away without beholding your charms, but I shall long for you while tossed upon the bosom of the boundless sea. There is in Yedo a famous courtesan, named Hana-ōgi, who not only is of unsurpassed beauty, but is well versed in literature. This lady has an aged mother at home whom she adores, and to whom she blindly devotes herself as a filial child is bound to do. I have sojourned in Nagasaki for a decade and have known many women at once beautiful and possessed of poetic tastes, but never have I heard of a courtesan acccomplished in literature and likewise distinguished for her filial piety.

"Having heard your story—Hana-ōgi—I wish to personally visit you, but this being impossible I compose a poem and send it to you."

(Signed) Shokei Hi-ko-sei.

It appears that Hana-ōgi was a pupil of Tōkō Genrin (a poet), and often composed both Chinese and Japanese poems. Three of her compositions run as follows:—

1.—The name of Hana-ōgi ("Floral Fan") does not suit the person who bears it, and is comparable to the case of a rough woodman who has an uncommon and ludicrously fine name.

2.—Though the autumnal moon is shining, the countenance of him upon whom I gazed for the last time in the days of Spring vanishes not from my mental vision.

3.—The moon shines so brightly and magnificently upon the trembling surface of the river that the shadow of a man who is handling ropes in a boat may be clearly discerned.

It is said that this noted courtesan wrote the Chinese character 鳴琴 (*meikin* "tinkling harp") and after framing the paper presented it to the *Ishi-yama-dera* (temple) where it was hung in the *Genji-no-ma* (room).*

* The monastery of *Ishi-yama* was founded in 749 by the monk Riō-ben Sūjō, at the command of Shōmu Tennō. It was destroyed by fire in 1078 and rebuilt a century later by Yoritomo. The present *hon-dō* (main hall) was built by Yodo-Gimi, the mother of Hideyori, towards the end of the 16th century. The little room to the right of the *hon-dō*, known as *Genji-nō ma*, is said to have been occupied by the famous authoress Murasaki Shikibu during the composition of her great romance, the "*Genji Monogatari.*" *Ishiyama-dera* is famous for the beauty of its maple-trees in autumn. (Murray's Hand-Book of Japan.)

Tamakoto.

In one of the poems of the famous Bashō it is said :—

"The pine-tree of *Karasaki* is more obscure than the flowers."

This poem is considered to be written in praise of the virtue of the evergreen solitary pine-tree which is inferior to the flowers on a cloudy night. Tamakoto may be favourably compared to this pine-tree of Karasaki (which is a universally recognized symbol of virtue), as she is described to us as "*a model of sincere, charitable, and charming womanhood, whose graceful manner and delightful conversational power lifted her high above the other women of her class.*" Owing to these unique and sterling qualities she became the most popular of all the courtesans of the Yoshiwara. The custom of depositing a leaf of a "*naki*" tree in the back of the handle of the mirrors used by ladies in making their toilettes, was inaugurated by Tamakoto. It was afterwards followed by many ladies of high rank. In feudal days the sword was called "the living soul of the *samurai*," and a lady's mirror was also considered as equally precious and important to her. The depositing of a leaf of the "*naki*" tree in the mirror handle appears to have had a religious significance, as the *naki* tree is said to have been the sacred tree of the shrine of Idzu Dai-Gongen, in Hakone, Idzu province. It was believed that the Hakone Gongen was the deity who supervised the carrying out of promises made between the sexes, and therefore the *naki* leaf placed within the mirror handle was equivalent to a pledge to the gods that the owner of the mirror would be faithful to men and never utter a falsehood. While she was yet in the prime of life Tamakoto fell sick and returned to her parents' home, where, in spite of everything done to restore her to health, she departed this life and "*set out on her journey to the unknown world*" in the 25th year of her age. During her life this accomplished woman composed a lyric song entitled "*The Sorrowful Butterfly*" which was afterwards set to music by Ranshu and sung in loving memory of the gentle authoress.

Katsuyama.

In the employ of Yamamoto Sukeyemon, of Kyō-machi ni-chō-me, was a *yūjō* named Katsuyama who, though a *san-cha-jorō*, was a gentle and kindhearted woman, accomplished in the art of composing Japanese poems and very æsthetic in her nature. Once, on the occasion of the celebration of *Hina-matsuri* in the third month of a certain year, a well-known poet of that age—Ransetsu—happened to be in Katsuyama's room and witnessed her preparations for the festival, and he wrote the following stanza:—

"*It is pitiable to see a barren woman celebrating the Hina festival.*"

This is in allusion to the fact that the doll-festival (*Hina-matsuri*) was originally inaugurated for the purpose of celebrating the birth of children and of manifesting a desire to have a succession of lineal descendants to perpetuate the family name. *Hina* means young birds newly hatched from the eggs, and in feudal times child-bearing was considered of such great importance that barrenness was a sad disgrace and formed a legitimate ground for divorcing a wife. A courtesan, in consequence of her unnatural life, and the physical strain to which she was subjected, was supposed to be incapable of conceiving, and hence Ransetsu's lament that a woman of of Katsuyama's goodness and beauty should be condemned to celebrate a festival which amounted to a mere mockery of her unfortunate position.

Though a courtesan, Katsuyama was a sincere and worthy woman, an earnest and devout Buddhist, possessed of refined tastes which made her a lover of the beautiful, an adept in floral arrangement, and an accomplished writer. She also seems to have been gifted with an inventive genius, for she devised an unique style of hair-dressing which was so simple and unaffected that it speedily found favour with every class of women, not excepting the ladies of the *daimyōs'* courts, the latter adopting this *coiffure* almost universally. It is still known as the "*Katsuyama magé.*" A very pretty story is told which illustrates the kindness of heart that characterized Katsuyama. There was a certain *bugyo*, named Kaisho, who was on intimate terms with the fair damsel and who was so infatuated with her goodness and beauty that he spent considerable sums of money in the purchase of rare and costly articles for the purpose of affording her pleasure. On one occasion he sent her a silver cage, fitted with a golden perch, containing a beautiful Corean bird, known as a *hiyo-dori* (brown-eared bul-bul). When he sent her this present he remarked that it was impossible to buy such a bird with money, and that he had only obtained possession of the pretty warbler owing to his position and influence as a *bugyo*. Katsuyama was delighted to receive the kind gift of her friend, but after she had exhibited it to the inmates of her house she took the cage into her own room and addressed the feathery inmate in the following words :—

"Sweet little birdie, there may be those who envy your position living in a cage decorated with gold and silver and being petted by people, but I, my birdie know that the thoughts which fill your mind are quite opposite to those others attribute to you; I have lived for many years in the Yoshiwara like a bird in a cage and can sympathize with your situation. I too have lived in a golden cage and am arrayed in gorgeous robes, but I know that a person deprived of freedom is like Ōshokun* for whom jewels and flowers had no attraction and who felt as if living in Kikaigoshima (Devils' Island). Judging by my own feelings I can imagine the sorrow of you, birdie, for be you ever so well treated and carefully tended you will flutter against the bars of your cage and long to fly away and be at liberty under the blue sky of Heaven just as I long to return to my dear native place."

So saying, Katsuyama took the beautiful bird from its cage and allowed it to fly away. If this had happened in the time of Kenkō Hōshi (the priestly author of the celebrated *Tsurezure-Gusa*) he would assuredly have praised her kindly deed in the same manner as he did a similar act of Kyōyū in his well-known book of jottings.

Segawa.

The second Segawa of the Matsuba-ya of Yedo-chō ni-chō-me (Yoshiwara) was redeemed by the master of E-ichi-ya (an establishment in the vicinity of Ryōgoku-bashi), and the third Segawa by a blind musician named Toriyama. The second Segawa lived on affectionate terms with her redeemer, but by and by she fell sick and lay helpless for a long time in spite of everything which her doctor could do. Some person having suggested that if she were named after an animal she would recover, Segawa changed her name to Kisa, (archaic term for "elephant") and tradition says that after this she

* Wife of an ancient Chinese King who was held by the enemy as a hostage in a foreign country.

was gradually restored to health under the treatment of a certain Doctor Kitayama Gian. While Segawa was still in the Yoshiwara she sent a letter, written in a beautiful hand, to her intimate friend Hinadzuru (of the "Chōjiya") on the occasion of the latter leaving the Yoshiwara in consequence of having been redeemed by a guest. The letter was a model of Japanese feminine writing, and ran as follows:—

"It is with feelings of the utmost satisfaction and delight that "I hear you are to-day going to quit the "house of fire" (*Kwataku* "火宅) of this Yoshiwara for ever, and that you are going away "to live in a cool and more congenial city. I cannot find words "adequate to the task of expressing my envy of the promising "future which awaits you at your new residence. Moreover, "according to the principles of divination, your nature has affinity "with wood while that of your husband has affinity with earth. "This is an excellent combination of the active and passive prin-"ciples of nature, for the earth nourishes and protects the wood "(tree) as long as it lives. This is indeed a good omen and augurs "well for your future prosperity and happiness, and I therefore "again congratulate you on the felicitous and promising union "you have made."

Usugumo. (Faint Clouds.)

In the Genroku period (1688-1703) Usugumo was one of the most popular of the Yoshiwara courtesans and ranked next to Taka-o in this respect. She was an exceedingly beautiful woman, graceful and slender as a willow-tree, and moreover she was versed in all those polite accomplishments the acquirement of which is necessary to a Japanese lady. On the 15th day of the 8th month of a certain year she was holding a "moon-viewing" party with her guest in the second story of an "*age-ya*" and was busily composing or reading Japanese and Chinese poems while enjoying the ravishing splendour of the full harvest moon which hung like a glittering silver mirror in the cloudless autumnal sky. Presently thin clouds appeared on the horizon, and gradually spreading themselves over the heavens screened the moon from view. In the adjoining room a *Kōshi-joro* named Matsuyama ("*Pine Mountain*") was also holding a moon-viewing party with her guest, and this woman, not being on good terms with Usugumo ["*Thin* (or '*Faint*') *Clouds*"] maliciously remarked:—

> "The thin clouds are insolently hiding the beauteous moon from public gaze."

Hearing this but ill-veiled sneer directed at herself by means of a clever play upon the words "*usu-gumo*" [*faint* (or *thin*) *clouds*] Usugumo, unable to control her temper, replied with cruel directness:—

> "Those thin clouds which now obscure the moon may appear to be blots on the sky above us, but after all they are but transient and will soon drift away. The pine-crowned mountain (*Matsuyama*) yonder on the contrary looms up dark and forbidding in the landscape and permanently obstructs the best view of the orb of night."

Discomforted by this spontaneous and fitting answer, Matsuyama coloured up and immediately retired from the party. Usugumo was well-known for her ready wit and cleverness in repartee, and the above incident proves that her reputation was well deserved.

Usugumo possessed a beautifully furred cat which she was accustomed to take with her whenever she went out promenading, the animal being carried by one of her attendant *kamuro*. Strange to say, whenever Usugumo went to the lavatory her pet followed her without fail, and this fact having become well known among the inmates of the house it gave rise to an idle whisper to the effect that the cat was in love with its owner! The proprietor of the "Miura-ya" (to which establishment Usugumo belonged), hearing of this story, one day caused the cat to be fastened to a pillar and awaited the result. On seeing Usugumo going into the lavatory, however, the cat became desperate, and biting through the rope with which it had been fastened attempted to rush after its mistress, leaping clean over a pile of kitchen utensils which stood in the way. As it flew along, one of the cooks gave the animal a blow on the neck with a sharp kitchen knife, completely severing poor pussy's head from her body. Usugumo, who had been in the lavatory, being frightened by the noise and commotion came hurriedly out and was much distressed to find her cat dead, but she noticed that although the body remained the head of the unfortunate animal had disappeared. On an examination of the lavatory being instituted, the missing head of the cat was discovered with its teeth tightly closed in a death grip on the throat of a great snake which was writhing in the throat of impending dissolution! Then the mystery of the cat's constant attendance on its mistress was fully explained, as the people saw that the unhappy animal, knowing of the snake's existence, had followed Usugumo for the purpose of protecting her from injury, and had died in her defence. When the story of the cat's faithfulness became known everyone bewailed pussy's sad fate, and in order to atone for the cruel treatment to which it had been subjected the animal was buried in the family cemetery of the house. Kikaku's poem to the effect that:—

> "The cat of Kyōmachi was wont to play between it and Ageya-machi"

seems to refer to Usugumo's pet.

In former days the grave of this loyal creature was pointed out at Ageya-chō, but nowadays the site of the monument has been forgotten owing to the frequent occurrence of fires in the Yoshiwara.

Ōsumi.

Though Ōsumi was comparatively lower in rank than Shiragiku of the "Yamagata-ya" and Karyū of the "Hyōgo-ya", she was a very popular courtesan and more sought after than they. One day she was suddenly taken ill, and her malady increasing in severity she could get no rest even at night. When, worn out with fatigue she finally succeeded in dropping into a fitful slumber, she shrieked and groaned in an agony of terror, while the cold sweat poured in a profuse stream from her quivering frame. Her symptons were so dreadful that the other inmates of the brothel felt their blood run cold as they gazed on her drawn and terror-stricken countenance and heard her awful cries of fear, but they did their best to alleviate her sufferings and attended her assiduously. Curious to relate, the women who nursed the unhappy sufferer found an immense toad at the side of her couch, and although they flung the loathsome creature away several times it would immediately return and squatting down by the bed would sit gloating over the patient—a portentous and revolting watcher!

At length, notwithstanding the efforts of her attendant physician Ōsumi wasted to a skeleton and finally died of the dread disease which had seized upon her, but to the last she uttered the most ghastly and blood-curdling cries and in her delirium expressed a sense of the most awful terror pursuing her to the grave.

It is stated that a certain priest had been in the habit of frequently visiting Ōsumi, and having fallen in love with her tried his best to win the fair courtesan for himself, but failed owing to her having a paramour. The latter had squandered his parent's money in riotous living and had been driven out of his home on that account. Ōsumi, in order to aasist her sweet-heart in distress, pretended to be deeply in love with the priest referred to, and by this means inveigled the recreant "Servant of Buddha" into supplying her with considerable sums of money, all of which she promptly gave to her secret lover. One dark night, the deluded priest was foully murdered on the banks of the Nihon-Zutsumi, and it is said that his troubled spirit sometimes passed into the body of a frog which sat haunting the bedside of Ōsumi, and at other times took possession of the body of *kamuro* and in a hollow sepulchral voice expressed his resentment to the heartless woman who had allured him to death and perdition.

Ko-murasaki (Little Purple).

(*The second of the name.*)

The name of this courtesan is known throughout the length and breadth of Japan, and the fame of the fair girl has been spread even to Western lands by means of a story entitled "*The Loves of the Gompachi and Komurasaki*" given in Mitford's "Tales of Old Japan".

She is regarded as a specimen of feminine faithfulness as exhibited by women of her class. She was proficient in the art of literary composition, wrote a beautiful hand, and was well versed in all those other graceful accomplishments which were considered necessary to ladies in this country. It is said that she was the authoress of a popular song called the "*Yae-ume*" (The double-blossomed Plum) which ran as follows:—

> "I am like the azalea which blossoms in the meadows, pluck my flowers ere they fall and are scattered.
>
> "I am like the firefly in the field which lights up the bank like a pine-torch. However impatiently I may long for you and pine to meet you I am like a bird imprisoned in its cage and cannot fly away, and my inexpressible sorrow makes me brood in melancholy."

The touching story of the loves of Ko-Murasaki and Shirai Gompachi is as follows:—

> "About two hundred and sixty years ago there lived a young man named Shirai Gompachi who was the son of a respectable *samurai* in the service of a *daimyō* in the central provinces. He had already won a name for his skill in the use of arms, but having had the misfortune to kill a young fellow-clansman in a quarrel over a dog, he was compelled to fly from his native place and seek refuge in Yedo. On arriving at Yedo he sought out Bandzui-in Chōbei, the chief of the *Otokodaté* (Friendly Society of the Wardsmen of Yedo) and was hospitably entertained and protected by that famous wardsman. One day Gompachi went to the Yoshiwara for the first time in company with Tōken Gombei, Mamushi Jihei and other protéges of Chōbei, and this visit was the cause of his undoing. While watching the gaily dressed courtesans promenading in the Naka-no-chō, escorted by their male and female servants, Gompachi's attention was drawn to a famous beauty who had recently made her début in the Yoshiwara.
>
> "It was a case of mutual love at first sight, and from that time the handsome young man went daily to the Yoshiwara to visit Ko-Murasaki. As was usual with a frequenter of the quarter, Gompachi, being a *rōnin* and without any fixed employment, had no means of continuing his dissipation and at last when his stock of money ran out he commenced to resort to robbery and murder for the purpose of replenishing his purse.

"Blinded and infatuated by his love for Ko-Murasaki, he continued his wicked course of life and kept on slaying and robbing, but at length he killed a silk-dealer on the banks of Kumagaya and robbed the unfortunate man of three hundred *ryō*, and this act subsequently led to his arrest and execution as a common felon at Suzugamori ("Bell Grove") near Ōmori which was the execution ground in the days of the Tokugawa Government. When Gompachi was dead, Bandzui-in Chōbei obtained the remains from the authorities and interred them in the burial ground of the Boron-ji Temple at Meguro. Ko-Murasaki, on the other hand, was redeemed by a certain wealthy man after her lover's death, but on the very night of her redemption she escaped from her benefactor's house and after spending the night somewhere she repaired the next morning to the temple where Gompachi lay buried.

"First she thanked the priest in charge for his kind consideration and care for the soul of the departed, made an offering of a bundle of costly incense-sticks and ten *ryō* to the temple, and placed five *ryō* in the hands of the priest asking him to expend the money in erecting a stone monument over Gompachi's grave. After this she went out into the burial ground and offered prayers over the tomb of her loved one, and committed suicide by means of a dagger she had brought with her for the purpose. When the chief priest of the temple—Zuisen Oshō—heard what had happened he reported the sad event to Bandzui-in Chōbei, and the latter soon came to the spot bringing with him the parents of the unfortunate girl.

"Unhappy in their lives, in death at least they were not divided, for the body of Ko-Murasaki was buried in the same grave as that of Gompachi.

"Beside the tomb was planted an orange-tree with two branches as a symbol that the two sleepers had entered into their eternal rest in perfect and mutual accord, and over the grave they erected a stone monument on which were engraved the respective crests of the couple—a *sasarindō** in the case of Gompachi and a circle containing two (井) characters in the case of Ko-Murasaki. The names of the dead pair were also inscribed on the tombstone, and the words "*Tomb of the Hiyoku*" added. The monument remains to this day, and by it stands another bearing the following legend:—

"In the old days of Genroku, she pined for the beauty of her lover, who was as fair to look upon as the flowers; and now

* A family badge in the form of a tuft of five overlapping bamboo leaves with their apexes spreading downwards, and surmounted by three little flowers.

beneath the moss of this old tombstone all has perished of her save her name. Amid the changes of a fitful world, this tomb is decaying under the dew and rain; gradually crumbling beneath its own dust, its outline alone remains. Stranger! bestow an alms to preserve this stone, and we, sparing neither pain nor labour, will second you with all our hearts. Erecting it again, let us preserve it from decay for future generations, and let us write the following verse upon it:—"*These two birds, beautiful as the cherry-blossoms, perished before their time, like flowers broken down by the wind before they have borne seed.*"

While Gompachi was in prison the following letter was sent to him by Ko-Murasaki :—

"*I am looking upon the rare flower which you sent to me only the other day, as if I were gazing upon your countenance. I am extremely distressed to learn that you find yourself placed in such an unpleasant position, and am inconsolable at the thought that your unhappy plight has been caused by myself. I hear it stated that there is a god even in the leaf of a flower and so I solemnly appeal to this deity to witness my unaltered faithfulness and constancy towards you, come what may.*"

The above document is still in existence and is known as the "*Hana-kishō*" ("the Floral Vow"). It is often quoted to show how Ko-Murasaki loved her sweetheart and how faithful and true she was towards him in the day of adversity.

Even to-day people think kindly of the sorrows and constancy of the beautiful courtesan and keep her memory green in song and story, and still pious folks burn incense and lay flowers before her grave and say a prayer for the souls of the ill-fated couple. A popular song expresses the feelings of the Japanese people towards Ko-Murasaki when it says :—

"*Who shall say that courtesans are insincere? Let him visit Meguro. Let him see the Hiyoku-zuka which bears silent but eloquent testimony to a courtesan's fidelity!*"

Kaoru (*Fragrance*).

Kaoru was an exceptionally beautiful woman and was the leading courtesan of the "Tomoye-ya." A certain enthusiast has left a record of the impression made upon him by this belle in the words—"Everyone who gazed upon her lovely countenance and noted her charming and graceful mien was intoxicated with the joy of her presence and remembered the story of the historical Chinese beauties Rifujin (李夫人) and Seishi (西施)." Once, one of her familiar guests brought her a water-vessel containing four or five much prized gold fish of a species known as *Ranchō*.

Kaoru and the other inmates of the house were greatly delighted with the beautiful gold-fish, and surrounding the vessel looked eagerly into it, quite forgetting in their excitement that they were neglecting their visitor. By and by the guest became weary of waiting, and to beguile his tedium he edged his way into the group of on-lookers to see what was going on. He perceived a maid-servant, under the directions of Kaoru, taking the gold fish out of the vessel one by one and placing them on the cover of the latter. This proceeding aroused his curiosity and he enquired the reason, saying—

"Why do you take the fishes out of their element? None of them are dead!" Kaoru blandly replied—"The fish seem quite tired, so I am giving them a rest by making them lie down on this cover."

The guest was dumbfounded at this marvellous exhibition of unadulterated ignorance and burst into laughter. This story may seem to reveal most crass ignorance and a wonderful depth of idiotic stupidity; but in those days such an exhibition of want of information on common topics was greatly appreciated in Japan, for it was supposed to betray maiden-like innocence of the world. At any rate, it is said that Kaoru's guest was so struck with her simplicity that he became more attached to her than ever after this event. There is another highly disgusting and somewhat Rabelaisian story narrated about Kaoru which is supposed to show the affection (*sic*) in which this charming courtesan was held in the Yoshiwara. A party of reckless young bloods were holding a *saké* party one night, and the liquor was flowing freely, when suddenly some stupid individual dared any person in the assembly to swallow the contents of a large cup filled with pepper. Flushed with wine, and ready for any devilment, another human ass immediately accepted the challenge and volunteered to undertake this feat of horrible gormandizing. First the enterprising idiot drank a cupful of *saké* and then proceeded to gulp down the pungent preparation, but no sooner had he swallowed the first mouthful of pepper than he fell down writhing in terrible anguish, his eyes starting from his head, and his countenance revealing the tortures of the damned in the burning hell. Naturally a scene of great confusion followed this occurrence, the party was sobered up by the untoward event, and a doctor was immediately summoned to treat the patient. This disciple of Æsculapius was apparently as well posted about medical affairs as an ordinary coolie, for he was at his wit's end to know how to treat the case. However, something had to be done to keep up the reputation of the "faculty," and the worthy leech gravely prescribed human fæces as a medicine possessed of remarkably curative properties! This abominable prescription frightened the attendants, and they decided to ask the patient for his opinion on the matter. The latter, being unable to speak, seized a brush and wrote down on a piece of paper—"If I must perforce take the horrid dose, *I prefer* * * * * * * * * * * *"!!!

Kokonoye (*Nine-folded.*)

Kokonoye was the name of a well-known courtesan who was possessed of considerable literary ability. Her story is a sad and withal interesting one as it reveals the vein of illogical reasoning traversing the unnecessarily severe and inhumane judgments of the Japanese judicial authorities in ancient times. It appears that Kokonoye had been in the employment of a certain respectable citizen of Tōkyō as wet-nurse for his infant son. By and by the child grew older, and one day while playing, he got drawn into a quarrel with one of his comrades. Words soon led to blows, and the boy inflicted an injury on his little playmate which caused the death of the latter. The dead boy's parents, indignant at the deed, complained to the authorities and the case came on for hearing before Ōka Echizen no Kami who was renowned as a great jurist in the olden days. The Solomon-like Judge decided that both the little prisoner and Kokonoye were alike guilty. He said that the boy had actually committed homicide, and that the nurse had been an accessory to the crime inasmuch that she had failed to exercise proper control over her charge. The boy was therefore sentenced (due consideration being had for his tender years) to be sent to a monastery and trained as a priest, while the unfortunate nurse was condemned to a life of shame in the "Sea of bitter misery" (the "Yoshiwara") for a term of five years. Kokonoye was accordingly sent to the Yoshiwara and was there engaged as a courtesan in the "Nishida-ya" at Yedo-chō, It-chō-me. Another account says that this woman originally belonged to the family of a Kyōto citizen, but that owing to her lewd conduct she was sent to the Yedo Court for trial and there sentenced to perpetual service as a courtesan in the Yoshiwara. That she was a woman of literary and poetical tastes some of her compositions testify; especially one poem in which she feelingly refers to her native place, her banishment, the three great duties of women, and the five obstacles against women attaining the joy of Nirvana. Years rolled by, and, on account of her age, Kokonoye was no longer able to retain the popularity which she had originally enjoyed. Accordingly in the Kyōhō era (1716-1735) the *nanushi* and elders of Yedo-chō proceeded to the Court and prayed for the commutation of Kokonoye's sentence on the ground of her age, but the petition was rejected. On hearing this the poor woman was overcome with the most bitter grief, and composed a poem which may be translated thus:—"Alas! I am doomed to live in a place far from my parents' home, and to ladle up for ever the water of the never-ceasing stream of the Sumida river." On reading this sad poem the *nanushi's* pity was intensified a thousand-fold, and with moist eyes be brought the lines to the officials of the Bugyō-sho and again begged the writer's liberty. Greatly moved by this expression of hopeless misery, the authorities were graciously pleased to show their clemency to the unfortunate courtesan, and readily granted the *nanushi's* second petition.

Kinokuni-ya Bunzaemon.

In the Empō era (1673-1680) there lived, in the vicinity of Nakabashi, Yedo, a man named Bunzaemon. This individual was a person of very humble extraction, but aided by his native shrewdness he managed to amass an enormous fortune in a comparatively short time, and the extravagance of his expenditure furnishes the theme for many a strange story to be found in Japanese novels. The true narrative of Bunzaemon's life has probably never been written, as every version appears apocryphal and more or less tainted with a strong vein of fiction, but perhaps it will be interesting to peruse the following story which is no doubt as true as any other told about the whimsical *parvenu*. One year Bunzaemon purchased, at a very insignificant figure, a large quantity of vegetable marrows, fruit of the egg-plant, etc., which had been used as votive offerings at the festival of the dead (*shō-kyō-matsuri*) in the seventh month. These various vegetables he pickled in a mixture of salt and rice bran and held in stock until such time as he could dispose of them. In the same year a most destructive fire broke out in the city, and as this caused a considerable rise in the market prices of commodities, Bunzaemon was able to unload his large stock of pickles at an enormous profit. With the money thus realized he immediately started out to Kiso in Shinano Province in order to buy lumber. For the purpose of making the simple country folk think him a rich and generous person he purposely and ostentatiously showed great liberality in giving the children in the neighbourhood gold coins as playthings. This plan succeeded admirably, and before he left the district he found himself the owner of a large tract of valuable forest land on which stood an immense quantity of timber. Later on the timber merchants of Yedo poured into Kiso to replenish their stocks which had been exhausted on account of an extraordinary demand caused by a great fire. To their astonishment and disgust they found that every available forest had already been secured by the astute Bunzaemon, and under these circumstances they were compelled to relinquish their quest and return to Yedo, where they purchased the necessary lumber from him at a considerable advance over cost. Not only did he make an enormous profit over the lumber speculation, but he made a fortune in contracting for the erection of mansions for *daimyō* who had been burnt out in the fire. Up to this time he had been residing in an obscure corner of the city with his aged mother, but now he blossomed out as a merchant prince and started a large firm at Ko-ami-chō, employing an army of clerks and servants. The firm-name adopted was "Kinokuni-ya," and thenceforth the proprietor of the concern was known as "Kinokuni-ya Bunzaemon." He then purchased a comfortable house for himself and his mother at Isshiki-chō, Fukagawa. Having once amassed a substantial capital, Bunzaemon's prosperity increased with the rapidity of the glorious rays of the rising sun. One larger contract after another fell into his hands, and among other orders he secured were those for rebuilding the Gokoku-ji temple (at *Ko-ishi-kawa*), the family mausoleums of the Tokugawa Shōguns, etc. After the completion of the latter contract Bunzaemon entertained in princely style all the Shōgunate officials connected with the work. Excursion boats were engaged, and the officials went out on the Sumida-gawa (river) accompanied by many popular professional entertainers, including Hanabusa Itchō, Nakamura Kichibei, and Shinkō. After enjoying their picnic, the party proceeded to the Yoshiwara, each man wearing a reed hat (*ami-gasa*) in accordance with the prevalent fashion. Bunzaemon was very fond of a style of song called the Handayu-bushi and took lessons in the same from the actor—Yedo Handayu. The latter had a great weakness for gambling and at one time lost everything he had, including his marionettes and their clothes, so he was unable to continue his performances and he got into every low water. Hearing of Handayu's misfortunes, Bunzaemon gave him two thousand *ryō* in exchange for a written promise never to indulge himself in gambling again, so the actor was able to redeem his puppets and effects and resume his business. At the beginning of the same year, Bunzaemon, in accordance with his usual practice, visited the Yoshiwara followed by a large number of professional entertainers, and made minute enquiries as to how much it would cost to engage the whole place to the extent of closing the great gate and refusing admittance to outsiders. The reply was that 2,300 *ryō* (*Yen* 23,000) would work the oracle, and Bunzaemon immediately concluded the bargain, had the gates closed, and held high revel with the whole population of the quarter at his heels.

In the 11th year of Genroku (1698) he secured the contract to construct the temples at Ueno, and large sums of money flowed into the great merchant's coffers. On this occasion again Bunzaemon invited the Government officials concerned to go out with him on the river Sumida, and he engaged a number of minor poets and actors to bear them company and enliven the proceedings. The party set out from the Kanda-gawa and landed on the other side of the Sumida-gawa to pay a visit to the Inari Shrine at Mimeguri, the day being enlivened by a display of fire-works, etc. It happened that year that there had been a great drought in the land and notwithstanding the prayers offered for rain not a drop fell. When Bunzaemon and his companions visited the shrine (called "*Mimeguri-no-Yashiro*") one of the farmers noticed that Kikaku (a famous poet) was among the company, and addressing the latter begged that he would compose a poem so touching that it would move Heaven to send rain upon the earth and thus gladden the hearts of all living things. The farmer pointed out that there was a precedent for this course as Ono no Komachi (a celebrated poetess in past times) had been successful in persuading the gods to grant a similar boon by means of a poem. Kikaku modestly disclaimed being able to control the elements, but he went into the shrine, prayed, and then wrote down :—

Yūdachi ya	"Oh send a shower of rain, if thou art
Ta wo mimeguri no	indeed the God who supervises the harvest,
Kami naraba.	for thou knowest the sad state of the fields."

This poem he offered up to the shrine, and tradition states that Heaven was so pleased with the production that rain commenced to fall very shortly afterwards and the whole earth was gladdened by the refreshing showers and cool breezes. Kikaku having performed this pious and laudable act, the whole party went to the Yoshiwara and for the second time the gates of that gay quarter were closed by virtue of Bunzaemon's money. Once, three rich men from Ōsaka and Kyōto visited Bunzaemon in order to make his acquaintance, and he entertained them most hospitably, offering them every luxury and pleasure that his enormous wealth could command. In the course of conversation one of the visitors expressed his belief that any man could procure the love and favour of a courtesan if he only possessed money: this statement rather offended Bunzaemon but he dissembled his real feelings and later on promised the three visitors to take them to the Yoshiwara on the following evening. Meanwhile, Bunzaemon sent four of his people to Ōtsuya Sanshirō in the Yoshiwara and made arrangements with him to engage every courtesan and tea-house in the place and to buy up everything that a visitor to the quarter would require: in short, the closing of the great gateway (*ō-mon*) was carried out in a more general and thorough way than ever before. The following day the three wealthy men from the West arrived at Imado-bashi in boats, accompanied by Bunzaemon and a gay company, and were received by the tea-house people, geisha, hōkan, etc., all of whom wore clothes given to them by Bunzaemon and bearing his crest. Bunzaemon now led his guests through Naka-no-chō and the other streets of the Yoshiwara, both sides of which were lined with courtesans, *shinzō*, *kamuro*, and other inmates of the quarter who had turned out in large numbers to welcome him. He then entered the "Ōtsu-ya" tea-house and from there proceeded to an *age-ya* called "Owari-ya" where he held a great banquet. The three rich men from the West now wished to send for courtesans to attend them, but to their great astonishment they were informed that as everything in the Yoshiwara had been bought up by Bunzaemon there were neither any women to be had nor eatables to be procured. The visitors protested most indignantly at this treatment and spoke about their wealth and possessions, but the words fell on deaf ears, and finally the crestfallen trio had to trudge away on foot owing to the fact that Bunzaemon had taken care to engage all the available boats and palanquins beforehand. It appears that these three men were very much incensed in consequence of the trick Bunzaemon had played them, and that they consulted together with a view to "getting even" with him. It seems, however, that they were not successful in hitting upon a suitable plan and that they eventually slunk away home " with their tails between their legs."

Although Bunzaemon caused the great gateway to be closed on three occasions, this is not all he did. There are many interesting stories told about the extraordinary life which this extraordinary man led and the various pranks he played. For instance it is stated that he would at times fling showers of golden coins about to be scrambled for by the persons present, and there is a curious story told about his extravagance in competing with another rich man, named Naramo, when the two attempted to vie with each other in prodigality and luxury. There is also a tradition which mentions the magnificent banquet given by Bunzaemon in the Naka-no-chō on the occasion of a snow-viewing party.

THE LAW RELATING TO BROTHELS *

NOTIFICATION No. 40. Issued by the Metropolitan Police Board, Tōkyō, 7th July, 1896 (*Meiji* 29 *nen* 7 *gwatsu* 7 *ka.*)

Notification No. 12 containing regulations relative to the control of brothels (*kashi-zashi*), introducing tea-houses (*hiki-te-jaya*) and courtesans (*shōgi*) issued by the Metropolitan Police Board in March 1889 (*Meiji* 22 *nen* 3 *gwatsu*) is hereby amended and revised as follows: The new regulations are also to be enforced in *Nishitama-gōri*, *Minamitama-gōri* and *Kitatama-gōri*, and should the provisions of this notification conflict with those of previous notifications the latter shall become null and void from the day that the present regulations are put into force.

* For latest regulations, see appendix.

REGULATIONS.

For the Control of Brothels, Introducing Tea-houses, and Courtesans.

Chapter I.

Brothels and Introducing Tea-houses.

Art. 1.—The business of brothel-keeping, or the keeping of *hikite-jaya* shall only be carried on in places approved by the Metropolitan Police Board, and no new establishments will be permitted outside of the *yūkwaku* (a place set apart for prostitute houses).

Art. 2.—Persons desirous of opening a brothel (*kashi-zashiki*) or *hikite-jaya* shall send in a petition to that effect to the Metropolitan Police Board through the Police Station having jurisdiction, and obtain a license: the same formality shall be observed should it be desired to change the seat of the business. The petition shall contain the following particulars :—

(*a*). Place of registration, position or rank, place of residence, surname and personal name, age.

(*b*). Name of the *kashi-zashiki* or *hikite-jaya.*

(*c*). Seat of the business.

(*d*). Drawing (plan ?) of the building in which the business is to be carried on. (Arrangement and size of rooms, and the width, number, and position of staircases must be stated).

Art. 3.—When it is proposed to erect buildings to be used as *kashi-zashik* ior *hikite-jaya*, and the height is to exceed three stories, a petition, to which plans and detailed specification of the construction are annexed, shall be submitted to the Metropolitan Police Board through the Police Station having jurisdiction, and permission obtained to carry out the work. In the case of buildings not exceeding two stories, only drawings need be annexed to the information to be given to the Police Board in the manner herein provided. When rebuilding or repairing, the same formalities shall be observed.

Every house (containing room space up to 30 *tsubo*) used as a *kashi-zashiki* or *hikite-jaya* must have at least two staircases of four feet in width, and another staircase shall be added for every additional 30 *tsubo*.

ART. 4—After the permission mentioned in Art. 3 is obtained, and the buildings have been completed, the Police Station having jurisdiction shall be notified and the premises inspected, and the said buildings shall not be used until the Police authorities have sanctioned same.

ART. 5.—Should the keeper of a *kashi-zashiki* or *hikite-jaya* be found infringing these regulations and thereby endangering public safety, committing offences again public morals and good order, or lending his (or her) name to others, the license shall be withdrawn or the business suspended.

ART. 6.—Should the keeper of a *kashi-zashi* or *hikite-jaya*, without reasonable cause, not commence business within three months of the date of receiving a license, or cease to carry on the same for a period of upwards of one year, said license shall become null and void.

ART. 7.—Two or more *kashi-zashiki* or *hikite-jaya* are not permitted to carry on their business in partnership.

ART. 8.—When a change occurs in the place of registration, position, rank, residence, or name of the keeper of a *kashi-zashiki* or *hikite-jaya*, when the name of an establishment is altered, when a change of guardianship takes place, or when business is relinquished, suspended, or commenced, the Metropolitan Police Board shall be notified through the Police Station having jurisdiction within three days of the date on which such change occurs.

Art. 9.—When a license is applied for through a guardian, or when a change of guardianship takes place, a certificate relative to the guardian's status must be annexed, such certificate being signed and sealed by the head man of a town, village, or district.

Art. 10.—Keepers of *kashi-zashiki* and *hikite-jaya* shall display before their establishments a signboard as follows, on which shall be clearly inscribed their names and the names of their houses, and at night they shall exhibit a lantern bearing a distinguishing sign.

3 ft.

Name of the house.
Brothel
(or *Hikite-jaya*)
Keeper's name.

8½" in:

Art. 11.—Keepers of *kashi-zashiki* and *hikite-jaya* shall prepare two books marked respectively "A" and "B." In "A" shall be entered the receipts of the house, and in "B" shall be minutely recorded the name, residence, profession, age, appearance, and style of clothes worn by each guest. Each and every time new books are opened they shall be inspected and sealed by the Police Station having jurisdiction, and after being used up they shall be preserved during a period of five years. Should said books be damaged, destroyed or lost, the Police Station having jurisdiction shall be notified within three days and the cause stated.

ART. 12.—When keepers of *kashi-zashiki* or *hikite-jaya* engage or discharge *employées*, the names of such *employées*, together with particulars as to residence, registration, and age, shall be minutely written down and notified to the Police Station having jurisdiction within three days.

ART. 13.—When in the course of their business, keepers of *kashi-zashiki* or *hikite-jaya* wish to engage assistants, they shall only engage persons who are possessed of "*employées pass-book*" mentioned in Art. 43.

ART. 14.—When keepers of *kashi-zashiki* or *hikite-jaya* afford lodging to females, this fact is to be notified to the Police Station having jurisdiction within twenty-four hours.

ART. 15.—Keepers of *kashi-zashiki* and *hikite-jaya* shall observe the following provisions :—

(*a*). Refreshments not actually ordered shall not be served or forced upon guests, neither shall they be urged to eat and drink against their will.

(*b*). Passers-by shall not be urged to enter and divert themselves ; keepers of houses shall not make arrangements with *jinrikisha*-men with the object of enticing customers, and persons shall not be persuaded to visit establishments by means of public advertisements, etc.

(*c*). Pupils of schools wearing the badges of their respective schools, and boys under sixteen years of age, shall not be permitted to enter and divert themselves.

(*d*). When a person wishes to see a guest, his (or her) request shall not be denied, and it is forbidden to conceal the presence of such guest so enquired for.

(*e*). In case of taking in pledge any articles belonging to a guest as guarantee for payment of his account, the guest shall be conducted to the Police Station having jurisdiction and the sanction of the Police authorities obtained.

ART. 16.—When special orders are given by Police Stations relative to the control of their business, keepers of *kashi-zashiki* and *hikite-jaya* shall observe the same.

ART. 17.—With regard to acts performed in the course of business, even although same be performed by members of their families or *employées*, the keepers of *kashi-zashiki* and *hikite-jaya* cannot plead non-liability.

ART. 18.—When it is proposed to plant flowering trees, to hold exhibitions of dancing or buffoonery, to hang up lanterns (*tōrō*), or to do anything else in the streets, a petition shall be lodged to that effect with the Police Station having jurisdiction, giving full particulars and permission be obtained. It is however provided that no such displays will be permitted outside the boundaries of *yūkwaku*.

ART. 19.—Keepers of *kashi-zashiki* shall not allow bedizened and bedecked courtesans to be seen by passers-by in the streets outside *yūkwaku*.

ART. 20.—In dealing with courtesans, keepers of *kashi-zashiki* shall treat the girls fairly, do all in their power to reform them, advise them to return to a virtuous course of life, and shall not cause them to squander money recklessly.

ART. 21.—Keepers of *kashi-zashiki* shall cause the courtesans in their houses not to infringe the regulations relative to physical examination, and when the women are ill shall at once cause them to receive medical advice and treatment.

ART. 22.—Keepers of *kashi-zashiki* shall hang up in a place where it can be easily seen by the courtesans a copy of the regulations with *hira-gana* written against the (Chinese) characters.*

ART. 23.—In the event of a courtesan infringing these regulations, information shall be given to the Police Station having jurisdiction, but the keeper of the *kashi-zashiki* shall not attempt to enforce an observance of the same by private arbitrary measures.

ART. 24.—When courtesans wish to enter another brothel, to give up the life of prostitution, to rest for a time from the exercise of their profession, or to visit some place outside the quarter, the keepers of *kashi-zashiki* shall not raise objections except on reasonable and valid ground.

ART. 25.—Whenever a courtesan absconds or returns, information is to be immediately given by the *kashi-zashiki* keeper to the Police Station having jurisdiction.

ART. 26.—Keepers of *hikite-jaya* are forbidden to allow guests, courtesans, or singing girls to lodge in their establishments.

ART. 27.—Keepers of *kashi-zashiki*, *hikite-jaya*, and courtesans shall form guilds within each of their respective districts, shall draw up rules and regulations, and obtain the sanction of the Metropolitan Police Board to the same through the Police Station having jurisdiction. The same formalities shall be observed when it becomes necessary to amend or change these rules.

ART. 28.—Guilds shall elect a Director and Sub-Director and obtain the approval of the Metropolitan Police Board of the persons elected through the Police Station having jurisdiction. Should the parties elected be considered as unsuitable for the position, the authorities may order another election or special election.

* *i. e*—Written in a very easy style so that even illiterate women can read the same.

ART. 29—Only males of not less than full twenty-five years of age, and who have been carrying on the business of *kashi-zashi* keeping or of keeping *hikite-jaya* for a period of not less than two years in the district, shall be eligible for election as Director or Sub-Director.

ART. 30.—The term of office of Directors is full two years, but after the expiration of that period they may be re-elected.

ART. 31.—When amendments or alterations of the regulations relative to *kashi-zashiki*, *hikite-jaya*, or courtesans are made, or when (Police) instructions are received, the Directors shall duly notify the members of their respective guilds.

ART. 32.—Directors shall affix their seals to petitions and notifications made by *kashi-zashiki* keepers, keepers of *hikite-jaya*, and courtesans.

ART. 33.—In addition to those duties determined in these regulations, matters which require the attention of Directors are specially provided for elsewhere.

CHAPTER II.

Courtesans.

ART. 34.—The profession of a courtesan shall only be permitted in *kashi-zashiki.*

ART. 35.—A woman who wishes to become a courtesan must send in a written petition for a license to the Police Station having jurisdiction. The petition must give the following particulars, and no woman under 16 years of age will be licensed.

(1). Document of consent signed and sealed by applicant's father or mother, or by her nearest relative if she is an orphan. The paper must state period of service contracted for and the amount of cash loan received.

(2). Certificate of registration from City, Town, or Village Office (name, age, birth-place, residence) and certificate of an impression of the legal seal of father, mother, or relation.

(3). Previous record of applicant.

(4). Agreement with the *kashi-zashiki* keeper in whose establishment she resides.

(5). Reasons for wishing to become a courtesan.

(6). Her assumed name (*nom de guerre*) and her fees.

(7). Term of applicant's engagement.

(8). Certificate of health given by medical inspector.

Art. 36.—Courtesans must reside in *kashi-zashiki*. When a courtesan wishes to change her house she shall petition the Police Station having jurisdiction to the effect and obtain permission. The petition shall be jointly signed by the keepers of both the *kashi-zashiki*. In this event documents mentioned in paragraphs 4, 6, and 7 of Art. 35 must be annexed, and should the house to which she proposes going be situated within the jurisdiction of another Police Station the petition shall be forwarded through the Police Station of the former jurisdiction.

Art. 37.—Should any change occur in the registration, position, name, professional name, or fees of a courtesan, or should she abandon the life, cease for a time, or commence, practising her profession, the Police Station having jurisdiction shall be notified within three days.

Art. 38.—When courtesans or other *employées* are engaged or discharged notification shall be made in accordance with the provisions of Art. 12.

Art. 39.—When courtesans received special instructions from a Police Station relative to the control of their profession they shall observe the same.

ART. 40.—Courtesans shall undergo physical examination in accordance with special regulations.

ART. 41.—Courtesans may not leave their *kashi-zashiki* except for the purpose of visiting the graves of their fathers or mothers, for nursing their grandfathers, fathers, mothers, uncles, aunts, brothers, or except when there is an occasion of rejoicing or mourning in connection with such relatives. They may, however, leave their houses so long as they remain within the boundaries of the *yūkwaku.*

When they go out of the *yūkwaku* they must obtain the sanction of the Director through the keeper of their *kashi-zashiki*, must wear ordinary female clothes, and must be accompanied by a person from their houses.

ART. 42.—When under the circumstances mentioned in Art. 41 it is necessary to lodge in some place outside the *yūkwaku*, or when it is necessary to receive medical treatment outside the *yūkwaku* for diseases other than those contemplated in Art. 2 of the regulations relative to the physical examination of prostitutes, the Police Station having jurisdiction shall be duly notified and permission obtained. Such document of notification must be signed by the courtesan and the keeper of her *kashi-zashiki*, and in case of sickness a doctor's certificate shall be annexed.

CHAPTER III.

Employées.

ART. 43.—Persons desirous of becoming *employées* of *kashi-zashiki* or *hikite-jaya* must prepare an "*Employées Pass-Book*" in the required form, and get the same stamped with the "Inspection stamp" of the Police Station having jurisdiction over such *kashi-zashiki* or *hikite-jaya.*

ART. 44.—In this "*Employées Pass-Book*" shall be entered particulars as to registration, position, rank, residence, name, and any changes relative to the same; the name of the employer, date of engagement and discharge, length of service; whether the owner has ever been punished by the authorities, how often, and for what offences.

ART. 45.—Each and every time changes such as are provided for in Art. 44 occur (with the exception of punishments inflicted by the Police authorities) the owner of the book is to enter particulars of the same and get the Police Station having jurisdiction over the *kashi-zashiki* or *hikite-jaya* to stamp the entry with the "Inspection stamp."

ART. 46.—Should an employées pass-book be damaged or lost the Police Station having jurisdiction over the *kashi-zashiki* or *hikite-jaya* shall be notified of the circumstances within three days: another book must be provided by the applicant and stamped by the Police authorities.

ART. 47.—When a person ceases to be an *employée* of a *kashi-zashiki* or *hikite-jaya* he (or she) is to apply to the Police Station which stamped the pass-book and request that the "Inspection stamp" be cancelled.

ART. 48.—When a person infringes the provisions of these regulations, or is considered to have committed improper acts in connection with his duties, the "Inspection stamp" in his pass-book may be cancelled.

ART. 49.—*Employées* of *kashi-zashiki* and *hikite-jaya* shall observe Arts. 15, 20, and 22 of these regulations in the performance of their duties.

CHAPTER IV.

Penal Provisions.

ART. 50.—Persons who have infringed Arts 2 to 4; 7 and 8; 10 to 16; 18 to 26; 31; 36 to 43; 45 to 47; and 49 shall be punished by detention of not less than one day and not exceeding ten days, or by a fine of not less than five *sen* and not exceeding one *yen* ninety five *sen*.

In addition to the foregoing, there are a great many detailed regulations governing the social evil, among which may be mentioned :—

Police Department Notification No. 22 *re* the physical examination of prostitutes. (Issued March 1894.)

Police Department Instruction No. 18-*a* prescribing method of physical examination of prostitutes. This is an instruction to the examining surgeons and to it is annexed specimen forms of reports to be made. (Issued April 1894.)

Police Department Instruction No. 38-*a*. Instructions for the practical enforcement of the regulations *re* Introducing tea-houses (*hikite-jaya*), brothel (*kashi-zashiki*), and prostitutes (*shōgi*). Gives forms of reports, books to be kept, etc. (Issued November 1896).

Police Department Instruction No. 42-*a* addressed to all Police Stations having jurisdiction over brothel quarters. This Instruction demands :

1. That information *re* suspicious characters must be given to the police. When visitors resemble the circulated descriptions of persons "*wanted*" by the police and advertised for with a picture.
2. Information must be given *re* persons who possess money or valuables manifestly unsuitable to their station in life, and *re* persons who are spending money recklessly.
3. Information must be given *re* persons possessed of swords, firearms, or other lethal weapons, and whose conduct is suspicious.

4. Information must be given about persons who remain in brothels for upwards of three days consecutively.
5. Information must be given when guests entrust or give to courtesans money or effects. (Issued December 1896).

Police Department Instruction No. 43-*a*, addressed to all Police Stations having jurisdiction over brothel quarters. Contains seven articles *re* the position of the Department *vis-à-vis* the *Kashi-zashiki*, *Hikite-jaya*, and *Shōgi* Guilds. (Issued December 1896).

There are also a great many detailed provisions intended to protect the women, among which may be mentioned one reading :—

"Should the keeper of a brothel endeavour to cause undue expenditure of money, or without valid reason try to interfere with the women desiring to reform, it is forbidden by law; and he can neither by law or under agreement, ill-treat the women cruelly or unfairly, therefore should anything like this occur, the women shall complain to the policeman on the beat or to the Police Station."

The laws are fair to a certain extent if carried out in the spirit in which they have been framed, but it is needless to say that the inmates of the Japanese brothels are entirely subjected to the will of their keepers, and although as a rule the girls are not inhumanely treated, they are to all intents slaves, just as much as if they were chained to the galleys. It is *not law, but custom* which keeps them there, and there is many and many an innocent victim driven to these devilish institutions by customs which exalt profligate fathers and beastly brothers into authoritative beings for whom every sacrifice should be made—even that of chastity. To say a woman has sacrificed herself for the sake of her relations covers everything among the lower and more ignorant masses, and the only thing which would be effectual with these model fathers, mothers, and brothers, would be a thorough horse-whipping each and every time a case crops up; or better still, the cat-o'-nine-tails laid on by an expert until they howl for mercy. The efforts of the Japanese Government to abolish the evil of this servitude have been vigorous, but custom—that law of fools—has been too powerful, and the regulations are infringed indirectly in many ways, chiefly however owing to the frantic opposition to reform raised by those numerous parasitic hangers-on who attach themselves to the prostitute quarters, and, while leading a lazy and mischievous life, manage to suck sustenance from the earnings of defenceless women. The position of the Government is clearly demonstrated by the text of the laws and notifications, *but no Government can eradicate an evil if not backed up by the people*, and at present the number of persons who have intelligently considered the question is very small indeed.

The Penal Code, promulgated July 1880, Art. 425, provides three to ten days' imprisonment, or a fine of 1 yen to 1 yen 95 sen, as a punishment for secret prostitution, or lending premises to persons for the purpose of assisting such secret prostitution.

To enable the reader to judge of the severity of the treatment which the Government in olden times meted out by way of punishment, annexed is a proclamation made by Ōoka Echizen-no-Kami, the famous Governor of Tokyo, dated Kyōhō, 7th year, 8th month, 16th day. (26th Sept., 1722).

"Whereas secret prostitution has been prohibited in the Wards of this City, and whereas it appears that the practice has been carried on in an audacious manner, it is hereby ordered that henceforth secret prostitutes shall be treated as follows:—

"1st.—The person harbouring secret prostitutes will be ordered to yield up to the Government his ground lot, furniture, house, and godown, and the woman offending shall herself have her furniture seized, and for the space of 100 days shall be manacled with irons, and committed into the custody of the responsible parties in her Ward, an officer being detailed off to visit the house every other day to inspect the seal on her manacles.

"2nd.—The owner of grounds and houses in which secret prostitution takes place, shall be held in the same penalties even although he is not living on the premises, but only represented by a care-taker. The care-taker shall have all his furniture seized, and shall be manacled for a period of 100 days, during which period he will be committed into the custody of the responsible parties in his Ward, and every other day the bonds shall be examined and the seal inspected.

"Three days after this date the appointed officials and Yoshiwara authorities will proceed to search for persons carrying on illicit prostitution, and if those persons are apprehended they will be dealt with as stated above.

"Persons harbouring offenders may be punished with banishment or death, and moreover the members of the Ward who are responsible for the parties may be likewise punished in accordance with the foregoing. Now therefore take notice, and let this be published throughout the City."

Again in 1875, the Police Department issued a notification. dated the 27th January, and numbered 23, as follows :—

"Persons practising secret prostitution and the keepers of secret houses used for that purpose, shall be punished as follows:—

Principal or Accessory	First Offence	Fine not exceeding 10 yen or 2½ months' imprisonment.
	Second Offence	Fine not exceeding 20 yen or 5 months' imprisonment.
Keeper of the House	First Offence	Fine not exceeding 15 yen or 3 months' imprisonment.
	Second Offence	Fine not exceeding 50 yen or 6 months' imprisonment.

The following is the text of a form of contract used at Susaki. It is practically the same as that used in the Yoshiwara :—

一金　　　　借用金高

内譯

金

金

右借用金ニ對シ貸座敷ト結約スル證書謄本左ノ如シ

結　約　證　書

一金

但シ利子ハ一ヶ月ニ付元金ノ百分一トス

右ハ自分義無據事情有之親戚承諾ノ上貴殿方ニ於テ娼妓稼業致候ニ付前書ノ金額正ニ借用致候處確實也然ル上ハ自分稼高所得ヲ以テ返金ノ目的トナシ左ノ項々結約仕候

一 揚代壹個金　　ト定メ内金　　ヲ自分所得トシ此内ヨリ小遣金
　ヲ引去リ殘金　　ハ前記借用金元利償却可致ニ付日々稼高ニ應シ計算ノ上
　御受取可被下候事

二 稼業中金圓時借致候トキハ本金ニ拘ラス當月ノ稼高所得ヲ以テ直チニ返金可致候事

三 洲崎病院入院中ノ食費ハ自辨可致ニ付本金ニ拘ラス退院當月ノ稼高所得ヨリ御引去リ可被下候事

四 時借及入院食費トモ當月ノ稼高ニテ返濟難相成トキハ本金ニ結込ミ第一項ニ依リ御計算可被下候事

五 營業ニ關スル自分所有品ハ借用金ノ抵當ニ差入置候故ニ他ヘ持出シ又ハ賣入賣却致間敷候事

六 稼業年限明治　年　月　日ヨリ明治　年　月　日マテハ必ス貴殿方ニ於テ稼業可致若シ年限内廢業又ハ稼換致候トキハ即時借用金元利皆濟可致候事

七 病氣ニ罹リ稼業難相成トキハ醫師ノ診斷ニ任シ擅ニ休業又ハ廢業致間敷候事

八 入院休業等ノ爲メ非常ノ立換金ヲ受ケ又ハ逃亡其他稼業ニ不誠實ナルカ爲メ滿期ノ節借用殘金有之候トキハ廢業ノ即日壹時皆濟可致候事

九 滿期又ハ癈疾ニ罹リ廢業セシトキ及死亡シタルトキハ保證人ニ於テ引取リ貴殿ヘ御迷惑相掛申間敷候事

十 第九項ノ場合ニ於テ借用金返濟不相成トキハ保證人立合抵當品ヲ賣却シ該代金ヲ以テ償却可致候事

十一 第六項第七項第八項ニ違約シタルトキ又ハ逃亡後三十日ヲ經過スルモ立戻ラサルトキハ抵當品賣却代金ヲ以テ借用金償却ニ充テ尚ホ不足アルトキハ特約トシテ本證連署ノ人名一同連帶ヲ以テ辨償ノ責ニ任シ若シ連帶者中如何ナル事故有之候トモ殘リノ者ニ於テ引受ケ辨金可致候事

右之通リ結約候處如件

明治　年　月　日

本　人

保證人

貸座敷

殿

右之通リ結約仕候也

娼　妓

貸座敷

The following is the text (translated) of an actual agreement which was cancelled by mutual consent:—

Memorandum of Agreement.

(SEAL.)

2 Sen Revenue stamp.	2 Sen Revenue stamp.

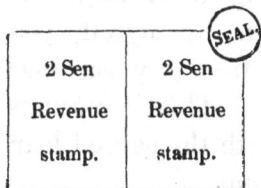

Yen 90. *Bearing interest at the rate of* 1% (*one per cent*) *per month.*

With respect to the above, owing to unavoidable circumstances, I agree, with the consent of my relatives, to practise the profession of a courtesan in your establishment. In this connection I have borrowed from you the sum of money herein-above-written, the due receipt of which I hereby acknowledge. In consideration of the premises, and with the intention of repaying the loan to you from my earnings, I hereby agree to the following clauses of this contract:—

1.—My fee for each guest is fixed at 25 *sen*. Out of each fee 12½ *sen* will appertain to myself, 3 *sen* being kept for my personal pocket-money while 9½ *sen* will be applied to the reduction of the principal and interest of my debt. You will please deduct the (latter) amount from the total of my daily earnings when the accounts are made up.

2.—Should I contract temporary loans during the period of my service, the monies shall be promptly returned out of my earnings for the current month, and such temporary loans shall be separate and apart from, and have nothing to do with, the capital loan contracted under this agreement.

3.—As my living expenses during detention in the hospital are a charge payable by myself, you will please deduct the same from my earnings during the current month. These expenses shall have no connection with the capital loan contracted under this agreement.

4.—Should I at any time be unable to repay out of my earnings temporary advances, or living expenses while in the hospital, during the current month in which such charges are contracted, you will please add the amount to the capital loan to be accounted for as per Article 1.

5.—My professional possessions are hereby pledged for the amount of my debt, therefore I will neither carry them out elsewhere, pledge them, nor sell them to other parties.

6.—The term of service contracted for is from the 20th December, 1895, to the 9th October, 1900, and during that period I will not fail to practise my calling in your house; but should I abandon the profession, or move to another establishment during the term, it is agreed that I am to repay forthwith the whole amount of loan and interest due thereon.

7.—Should I fall ill and become unable to attend to business, I shall leave the matter in the hands of the doctor and abide by his diagnosis, and I promise not to rest from work or abandon my profession on account of arbitrary personal caprice.

8.—When this agreement expires, should there be a balance of money owing to you by reason of extraordinary advances made by you in connection with my entering the hospital, resting from business, etc.; or in connection with my flight (abscondence) or other faithless (disloyal) conduct, I am to repay to you the whole amount of such balance on the same day that I give up the profession.

9.—When I give up business on the expiration of this agreement, or should I fall sick, be disabled, or die, my guarantor will receive me and will positively not cause you any trouble or annoyance.

10.—Under the circumstances mentioned in Art. 9, should the amount of debt not be duly repaid, the articles held in pledge by you shall be sold, in the presence of my guarantor, and the proceeds shall be applied to the clearing off of the debt.

11.—Should I commit a breach of agreement in violation of Articles 6, 7, or 8, or should I abscond and not return within 30 days, the articles pledged shall be sold, and the proceeds applied to the clearing off of the debt. Should a balance still be left, it is specially agreed that all the persons whose names appear as joint signatories to this contract shall be liable for the repayment of the amount involved. Should any of the persons liable be unable to discharge the debt, the remaining persons shall be responsible for repayment.

Agreement entered into is as above.

20th December, 1895.

Borrower........................(*signature*) (SEAL.)

Guarantor ....(*signature*) (SEAL.)

(Address)................................

To

MR. NISHIMURA ETSUSUKE

Brothel-keeper.

I have witnessed the above agreement.

(signed) SUNAGA YONEZŌ [SEAL.]

Vice-Superintendent of the brothels, tea-houses, and courtesans of Susaki.

No. 453.

The following is a specimen of an average contract from an actual document and will serve to illustrate the matter. This contract is one used by the Kanagawa brothel called "*Jimpurō*" (commonly known as "No. 9.")

Memorandum of Agreement.

Relative to a Loan of Money.

Yen—Four hundred.

Provided that interest on the above shall be in accordance with the Government Regulations.

With respect to the above I hereby acknowledge that as I have no means of livelihood, and practice the profession of a courtesan by official sanction, I have borrowed from you the above-written sum of money, and in consideration thereof I hereby agree to the following clauses of this contract:

1.—I will strictly comply with the regulations relative to courtesans.

2.—I will commence business on the.................. year............ month..............day of Meiji, and continue until the............. year........... month..... .... day of Meiji, and on the completion of this term of three years will forthwith return my license to the Government. It is understood that should I enter the Lock hospital during the term, the number of days shall be clearly noted in writing, and I shall apply for official sanction to continue longer in the business for a corresponding period of days. Should I not have repaid the loan when the time comes to return my license, I will enter into an agreement to repay the same entirely.

3.—I will gradually repay the loan from my earnings as a courtesan, and while the same is not all repaid, I will work faithfully and diligently. I will never rest from work without good reason, neither will I do anything calculated to interfere with or hurt your business.

4.—I will pay the prostitute tax provided by the regulations from my own earnings.

5.—I will divide the amount of my earnings into two portions, one of which I will give up to you as room-hire and other sundry expenses. From the remaining half I will repay the loan to you at the rate of 15 per cent of my receipts, and the balance (35 per cent) will be taken by me as my own. It is understood that having agreed to halve the money as above, even should the amount of my earnings be insufficient to pay the expenses of my board, I shall not pay out any other money.

6.—The account of repayments of the loan shall be balanced twice a month, for which purpose the landlord and the courtesan shall both keep books of the account wherein shall be set down entries to agree the one with the other, and at the end of each month such entries shall be stamped by both parties in each other's presence. With regard to the clothes which I use in the profession, and also my other effects as per separate list attached herewith, I hereby pledge and mortgage the same to you as security for the hereinbefore-mentioned debt.

7.—Should the owner of the prostitute house consider that the coming of any particular guest will be unprofitable, even although he (she) should send such guest away with a refusal I shall certainly not complain, but comply with his (her) wishes.

8.—Should I abscond during the term of engagement, fall sick, or desire to discontinue the business and change my residence owing to certain circumstances, but be unable to repay the above-written debt, I will not remove or cease practising the business until my guarantor has paid the entire amount.

9.—Any special debts which may be contracted by private arrangement between the parties shall have no connection with the present agreement. It is nevertheless understood that should I be unable to pay the fees and expenses while in the Lock hospital, any money I may borrow from you under that head will be added to the amount of the present loan.

10.—In respect to the monthly balancing of account as per above-written (Art. 6), in order that there may be no objection or dispute, the books of both parties shall be submitted to the Director of the "*Three Professions*," who shall be requested to seal the same officially after inspection.

In Witness whereof we the undersigned have hereunto set our seals together with those of the guarantors, in order that there may be no breach of the foregoing agreement hereafter.

Meiji.... ......year..............month........ day.

Borrower... .... L.S.

Guarantor (father) .... L.S.

Address ....

Guarantor (mother)............... .... L.S.

Address ....

To the Mistress of the Brothel.

I hereby seal the foregoing instrument in witness that its contents are in order.

Kanagawa Tachibana-gōri,

Kanagawa-Eki,

(*Signed*) SHIMAZAKI KYUJIRŌ. (SEAL)

Director of the "Three Professions."*

The Medical Aspect.†

According to a report of an investigation of venereal diseases, drawn up by Dr. Takai Hayao in 1892, and published

* Brothel-keeping; prostitution; introducing houses.

† See Appendix under the head of "Hospital Regulations."

in No. 4 of the "*Medical Monthly Report*" (醫務月報) for that year, the percentage of infection in the six prostitute quarters of Tōkyō was, during 1891, as follows:—

Shin-Yoshiwara	1.67	*Senji*	1.35
Susaki	1.88	*Shinjiku*................	1.99
Shinagawa	1.47	*Itabashi*	1.98

the stated average being 1.67509 per 100 women.

In Kanagawa Prefecture (including the prostitute quarters of Yokohama and Yokosuka) among 2634 women the average percentage of disease for 1898 was officially stated as 2.771. These very low figures must be regarded with great suspicion, as they are not only against the experience of medical practitioners in other countries *but are clearly proven to be misleading by the latest statistics of the Yoshiwara hospital.* In March 1899 the percentage of patients in the Yoshiwara rose to about 6½%, and this appears to be a more reliable figure. It is curious to note that in a work by Dr. O. Commenge (*Recherches sur les Maladies vénériennes a Paris, dans leur Rapports avec la Prostitution réglementaire de* 1878 *à* 1887) the percentage of prostitutes (registered by cards) suffering from *syphilis* alone was 7.3% while those registered in houses were diseased to the extent of 12.0%. In view of these figures, one cannot help regarding the Japanese statistics, which are supposed to include *all* venereal diseases, as somewhat untrustworthy and misleading, and to conclude that this trouble arises from the superficial nature of the inspection.

At the same time, it must not be forgotten that segregation of prostitutes in regularly appointed quarters *may* cause a difference in the percentage of disease, as this system gives a greater control over the licensed women.

According to the records of the Yokohama General Hospital (from 1868) the ratio of syphilitic cases treated diminished considerably after the present system of inspection and control was inaugurated in Yokohama. European medical practitioners states that it is a decided mistake to consider the form of syphilis in Japan as a peculiarly virulent or severe type. Among Japanese it is exceptionally mild, the more severe and deeper lesions being somewhat rare. It may be more severe in the comparatively pure-blooded European, but even with foreigners it is as amenable to treatment as in Europe or America.

Many Japanese doctors affirm that since the introduction of inspection and enforced hospitalization the more severe types of syphilis have become less common. Prior to the *Meiji* (present) era it was quite an ordinary thing to see noses eaten away by syphilis, whereas such a sight is comparatively rare nowadays.

Although there are a great many conflicting opinions on the subject, the concensus of opinion among Japanese medical men is that public prostitution is an unfortunate but necessary evil. They say that the present system is a safety-valve for society and that repressive measures would increase the number of cases of rape, seduction, adultery, unnatural vice, and illicit prostitution;* and that to abandon medical inspection would certainly tend to increase the ratio and virulence of venereal diseases.

One of the greatest evils of the system is that of permitting the custom called "*mawashi*" by which a woman accepts several

* Illicit prostitution *has* actually increased in Gumma and Wakayama since the abolition of licensed brothels.

guests and goes round from one to the other in turn all night. It is stated that the women wash themselves after each connection for the purpose of preventing the spread of disease, but unless the cleansing is done very thoroughly there can be no doubt but that infection is communicated to guests by this disgusting practice of accommodating several men at the same time. It appears that great trouble is experienced by the women when washing themselves in summer: the skin is apt to become inflamed and excoriated by excessive washing, and although iodoform would be an excellent antiseptic if applied, the smell of iodoform is offensive to guests, and this precludes its use.

The doctors, recognizing the one-sided feature of dealing with women alone, recommend that men entering houses of prostitution should be examined by a matron, so that all who are diseased can be eliminated, but they admit that this examination would not be infallible and that certain diseases would pass undetected: the brothel-keepers say that such a system would drive away guests and tend to encourage secret prostitution, and besides that the cost of medical attendance would be greatly increased.

There are a great many cases of heart disease, ***kakké*** (beri-beri), dyspepsia and hysteria among the inmates of the Yoshiwara, and also some cases of consumption.

Result of Medical Inspection in the Shin-Yoshiwara. 1898.

Month.	Number of inspections.	Number of infected cases.	Proportion per 100.	Number of guests entertained.
January........	10,590	574	5.42	135,100
February......	10,052	585	5.82	98,922
March	12,224	697	5.70	104,415
April	10,466	633	6.05	121,497
May	11,568	733	6.33	100,616
June...........	11,803	684	5.83	101,005
July	10,542	600	5.69	108,973
August	12,268	671	5.47	92,101
September	11,153	539	4.83	90,523
October	10,869	540	4.96	91,486
November	11,817	649	5.49	111,784
December	11,250	597	5.30	81,463
Total	134,602	7,506	5.58	1,237,885

Result of Medical Inspection in the Shin-Yoshiwara.

January to April 1899.

Month.	Number of inspections.	Number of infected cases.	Proportion per 100.	Number of guests entertained.
January........	11,545	732	6.34	133,410
February......	10,300	665	6.46	89,127
March	11,648	740	6.35	115,534
April	10,412	699	6.71	131,593
Total	43,905	2,836	6.47	469,664

Statistics *re* Social Evil in Japan in 1898.

The following figures are stated to be the result of official investigation, and they are given for reference. Readers will please understand that it is virtually impossible to verify the details, and therefore the correctness of the information cannot be guaranteed :—

Number of singing girls (adults)	24,261
Number of singing girls (children)	3,537
Number of women carrying on the profession of courtesans and singing-girls combined.	513
Waitresses in brothels and tea-houses*	34,015
Number of *geisha* houses	6,647
Number of restaurants	29,511
Various establishments frequented by *geisha*	5,650
Inspection offices	364
Number of courtesans	40,208
Introducers of courtesans	1,277
Number of prostitute quarters	546
Number of brothels	10,172

Pros and Cons.

As the writer has absolutely no axe to grind, and only desires to offer materials for further investigation of the subject, he has thought it well to annex some correspondence which appeared in the "*Japan Times*" in March 1899.

Correspondence.

A SOCIAL QUESTION.

To the Editor of the "Japan Times."

Dear Mr. Editor,—Will you kindly give the following "facts" a place in your paper. How long is the Government

* A great many of these women *are by no means virtuous*. These statistics are very incomplete, inasmuch as they fail to take into account the vast number of *secret prostitutes* in Japan. Even in the case of courtesans and *geisha*, it is almost certain that the numbers are understated.

of this land going to sanction a condition of things that permits of such cruel enslavement of her women ?—for, Mr. Editor, however the law may " read," morally, these girls have no liberty; and so long as legalized prostitutes are possible, so long will such sacrifices be forced upon the women of Japan.

If it be true that a nation is judged by the esteem in which her women are held,—is it not time for ambitious Japan to remove this blot upon her name?

In western Japan lives a widow and her three children —two daughters and a son. The eldest daughter when twelve years of age was adopted by another family. Three years later the adopted father died, when the adopted mother desired to be relieved of the child, but had no intention of giving her up without remuneration. She therefore wrote the true mother offering to return the girl on the payment of *yen* 150, and in the event of the mother not paying this price stating that she would sell the child for three years to a brothel. The price demanded was more than the poor mother could meet, for she was struggling to supply the needs of herself and other children; and this child of fifteen years was sold for " seven " instead of " three " years, the purchase money going into the hands of the foster mother.

Seven years rolled round, and the true mother expected to receive her child, but through the intrigue of the brothel manager and foster-mother—the latter was receiving a monthly percentage of the girl's earnings—it had been so managed that the helpless girl must earn still *yen* 300 before her slavery would end. The letters from this victim of man's passion and greed told only of repugnance of the life to which she was bound, and were full of entreaties to be freed. Finally a letter came saying death was preferable to the life she was leading. In despair the mother journeyed to the city where her child was in bondage, and succeeded in getting possession of her. *Ten years of enforced slavery* to which "death" is preferable has been this girl's portion. Happy in her freedom, she is now earning her living in an honest and respectable way, but on this innocent woman, who is but twenty-five years of age, will rest the blot of a *soiled life*. Where are the patriots? Surely the time has come for such to lift their voices and say these things shall not be.

Yours,

WHITE RIBBON.

Editorial Note, March 3rd, 1899.

The question of licensed prostitution, like every other problem under the sun, has two sides to it, and no judgment can be pronounced upon it until all the *pros* and *cons* have been duly considered and weighed. We do not profess to have studied the subject sufficiently thoroughly and dispassionately to record any authoritative opinion about it. But so far as we can see, the community at large certainly fares better from moral and sanitary points of view under a system which localizes social vices and exercises strict control over them, than under the alternative system—or rather absence of system—under which the evil is suffered to stalk about and stare at respectable men and women at every turn in the open streets, as is the case in many Christian cities in Europe and America. It is quite possible that the system of efficient control is not free from individual cases of hardship, cruelty, and injustice, such as that cited by "White Ribbon" in a letter published elsewhere. But the question is whether such cases of hardship upon innocent girls will be removed when the present system of licenced prostitution shall have been done away with. Supposing that there were no licenced houses of ill fame, would not the same greedy and cruel adopted mother in the present case have found some other means of making money at the sacrifice of the unfortunate girl's virtue? Would the girl's lot be any the better in such event? Until a times arrives when these questions can be answered in the decided affirmative, it seems to be mere waste of useful energy on the part of social reformers to cry out against the system of administrative control of vice. They had better devote their attention to the elevation of the general moral tone of society.

Dear Sir,—The case of the girl sold by her mother-in-law into a life of prostitution, reported by "White Ribbon" in to-day's issue of your paper, is certainly not an exceptional one in this country. That the majority of the girls filling the houses of prostitution in this country are there not of their own free will, but are practically held as slaves, is the current opinion among Japanese. That the government does not recognize such "sales" is of course understood. The first and most important step for social reformers undoubtedly is, as you suggest, the elevation of the general moral tone of society. This is the purpose of the "White Ribbon" movement and of much other moral and religious work. I am also ready to grant that, at least for the present, it may be an open question whether the legal control of the social evil is not perhaps the wiser course to pursue. But the question remains; what is the Government of Japan doing towards the elevation of the moral tone of society, making such cases as reported by your correspondent at least hideous in the eyes of the people, and rare in occurrence? Does not the *manner* in which the Government regulates this vice tend rather towards encouraging than towards discouraging such practice? Henry Norman in his "The Real Japan" has given us a pretty clear insight into the procedure by which girls receive the Government's permission to lead the profession of courtesan. As Henry Norman says, "the whole system is based upon the theory of a civil contract" and if the poor girl, hating the life into which she has been forced, tries to escape it by flight, is it not true that the keeper of the house of prostitution "recovers possession of her by a civil action for debt against her parents and surety"? Would not much be gained if the Government should cease authorizing the entrance of any girl upon a life of prostitution? If the police were to keep strict account of the number of prostitutes in the houses of ill fame, the medical examination could be continued compulsorily as now; and in this lies, as far as I understand, the great advantage claimed by the advocates of licensing the evil. But if a girl has been allured or has been sold into a life of shame, she could then escape from it without fear of being forced back by a civil suit against her parents or against those who had to do with leading her into it. If any keeper of a house of ill fame advances money in order to have additions to his stock of prostitutes, let him do it entirely at his risk, knowing that there is no legal redress if he loses his money through the flight of the girl.

Dear Sir, I write in no carping or fault-finding spirit. While I wish with all my heart that this whole awful evil could be wiped from the face of the earth and all men might treat every woman as their own mother or sister, I recognize that this cannot be gained at one jump. Social reformers as well as temperance reformers ought to avoid impracticable extremes. But while we are working for the elevation of the general moral tone of the people, is it not possible for the Government to do more towards the discouraging of the evil than it is doing? Can the Government do nothing towards making it easier for a girl, longing for freedom and purity, to secure it? Can the Government not do something to allow a girl to hide herself from the gaze of voluptuous men rather than be driven by a wretch of a brothel-keeper to sit for hours exposed to the gaze and the foul talk of vile men, for the mere purpose of swelling the brothel-keeper's income? Is the Government doing all it can do, all it ought to do, towards making it easier for any girl to keep out of a life of shame if she wishes to, and at the same time make it harder for the keepers of these houses of hell to capture and to retain these poor girls? With regard to these two points the authorization of a girl by the Bureau of Prostitution, and the permission for publicly exposing the inmates of a house of prostitution to public gaze, Japan certainly is far behind other civilized nations, and it is these two points that appear most hideous to foreigners. Can not the newspapers of the country, who so powerfully influence public opinion, do more than they are doing at present towards changing the existing state of things?

Thanking you for your kindness in granting me your valuable space, and inclosing my card, I remain,

Yours respectfully,

March 8th, 1899. ADJUTOR.

Dear Sir,—In commenting on a contributed article entitled " A Social Question " in a recent issue, the editor states that he has not studied the subject—licensed prostitution—sufficiently thoroughly and dispassionately to record any authoritative opinion about it, but that fact did not deter him from allowing his remarks to convey the idea that he considers the present system the best that can be had under the circumstances.

The writer *has made* a study of the social evil question and hence begs space for the following comments:

The statement that the community fares better under license than under the alternative system—prohibition,—cannot be supported by facts. On the contrary in Gumma and Wakayama provinces, which prohibit prostitution, venereal diseases are no more prevalent than in places under license—in fact the greatest percentage of venereal cases are to be found in provinces and cities which license the evil. This ought to settle the sanitary side of the question, and the fact that under prohibition hundreds and thousands of powerless girls are freed from the most damning form of moral slavery ought to settle the moral side of the same.

The editor speaks of "efficient control," conveying the idea that the evil is actually being controlled and localized by license, but such is far from being the case. Take the editor's own city, Tokyo, for instance. There were in 1897, 6,393 licensed prostitutes and over 2,000 *geisha* plying their trade according to law, but at the same time there were between 3,000 and 5,000 women who plied their trade secretly, that *were not controlled,* except the 304 who were arrested for fornication.

The fact, that licence or no licence, the evil will exist to some extent however, certainly does not justify the State in making its existence easy and secure, for surely the proper idea of license is to confine, lessen, and prohibit outside of certain specified places, but a careful investigation will prove that the evil is not confined and that instead of being lessened is actually augmented.

Because some women will sell their bodies and inhuman parents will sell their daughters for immoral purposes does not justify the State in becoming a partner to the transaction and making from 30 to 35 *yen* per year on each girl as at present. Neither can the writer understand how the general public is benefited by laws which compel helpless girls to abide by the terms of contracts made by others going so far as to fine and imprison those who attempt to escape from the brothels.

A case like the one cited, and there are thousands of such in Japan to-day, *could not occur in either Gumma or Wakayama Ken,* neither could anything very near it occur.

Trying to elevate the moral tone of society while leaving this question as it is means a great loss of effort, as every one who has much experience in reform work must know.

The State must withdraw its support and sanction and take the only logical and safe position a State can take, that of absolute prohibition of everything essentially evil, then we can have a much better chance at elevating the moral tone of society.

As to the evil stalking about the streets in many European and American cities, etc., the editor draws on his imagination or that of some one else's if he means to convey the idea that such is carried on to any great extent. Hoping that the time is near at hand when the welfare of helpless, innocent girls will receive consideration as well as the safety and convenience of lustful men,

I am, yours for

REFORM.

March 10th, 1899.

Japan Times Editorial, 14th March, 1899.

We feel considerable reluctance to take up the question of licensed prostitution, it is too delicate in its nature and complicated in its bearings to be a proper subject for journalistic discussions which are unavoidably brief and incomplete and which, in the case of questions like this, are particularly liable to become the source of misunderstandings and misleading inferences. However, having already ventured some remarks in connection with a recent communication on this subject, we cannot very well refuse to take cognizance of some of the points raised by the two other correspondents whose letters are published in another column.

" Adjutor " says :—" That the majority of the girls filling the houses of prostitution in this country are there not of their own free will, but are practically held as slaves, is the current opinion among Japanese." We may ask our correspondent if the majority of the unfortunate girls of the same class in other countries are not nearly in the same predicament as their sisters in this country with regard to the exercise of free will in the choice of their profession, the only difference being in the nature of motives that influence their decision. If misery, starvation and vicious habits constitute the principal influences that drive women to the immoral calling in other countries, the determing motive is here, in many cases, a mistaken idea of filial piety. In either case, the choice is equally free or otherwise, according to the way in which one likes to understand the meaning of the expression "freedom of will." This certainly has little to do with the question of licensed prostitution. So long as some girls are willing to enter upon a life of shame in obedience to mistaken ideas of filial duty, and so long as society remains as it is, the abolition of licensed prostitution will not prevent the occurrence of cases like that of the girl mentioned by "White Ribbon."

"Adjutor," however, is not positively opposed to the system of licensed prostitution, on the contrary, he is "ready to grant that, at least for the present, it may be an open question whether the legal control of the social evil is not perhaps the wiser course to pursue." But he is opposed to the manner in which the system is carried out and maintained, and complains that the Government is not doing enough to discourage the evil. He suggests that much improvement can be effected if all legal sanction be removed from contracts which at present bind the prostitutes to their employers, so that the latter, in the event of the escape of their employées, may not be able to enforce the contract. There is something in this suggestion, but we doubt very much whether its adoption will not practically tend to make the lot of the unfortunate girls harder than it now is. Supposing that the keeper of a house of ill-fame had no legal means of proceeding against any girl who may escape from his establishment, he will certainly take every precaution to prevent such desertion. And what does this mean? It inevitably means a complete curtailment of the liberty of his employees who will then be no better than galley slaves. Our correspondent may say: Why, the police can interfere in such cases. They can, to a certain extent, but it is not to be expected that, however assiduous and rigorous their exertions may be, their interference will effectually prevent the unscrupulous and ingenious brothel-keepers from exercising their oppressive control over the movements of the prostitutes under them. The result will simply be an immense increase in the hardships of the lot of those unfortunate creatures.

As to the charge that the Government is not doing enough to discourage the social evil, all that we need say is that the police authorities, before whom all girls about to enter upon a life of prostitution are required to appear before official authorization is issued, are under strict instructions to see that no unfair means have been employed to force the girls against their will. And there have been a number of cases where the discovery of the use of such unfair means has led to the withdrawal of official authorization. We may, however grant that the system as it is now carried out admits of reforms and improvement. One of these is, as "Adjutor" points out, the abolition of the exposure of the inmates of the houses of ill-fame to public gaze. We hope this desirable change will be speedily carried out by the police authorities.

The other correspondent, "Reform," who declares that he "has made a study of the social evil question," denies that "the community fares better under license than under the alternative system." He says that "in Gumma and Wakayama provinces (*sic*), which prohibit prostitution, venereal diseases are no more prevalent than in places under license," and that "in fact the greatest percentage of venereal cases are to be found in provinces and cities which license the evil."

This is a bold statement, a statement which certainly is not in accord with the opinion of those scientific experts who have made a special study of the matter. Unfortunately statistics are wanting, but it is a well known fact that the sanitary authorities at the Home Office are agreed in the verdict that venereal diseases are far more prevalent in places where no public prostitution exists than localities where it is licensed.

"Reform" takes exception to our expression "efficient control," and cites some figures about the existence of unlicensed prostitutes in Tokyo. We need hardly say that the expression was used in a relative sense, no right-minded person will expect that the evil can be controlled in an absolutely efficient manner. Neither will such person deny that the relative freedom of the streets of Tokyo from the presence of those objectionable beings who swarm in cities claiming to be more civilized and enlightened, is attributable to the system of localization followed here. We do not of course expect that "Reform" will recognize this fact unless he makes a short visit to his native land and sees how the evil stalks about in the open streets in some of the cities there. Such a trip will be of immense benefit to many another social reformer.

Note on "Jigoku" or Illicit Prostitutes.

The Jigoku: These women are the legitimate representatives of the ancient *Yo-taka* (night-walker). The origin of the word "*Yo-taka*" is given in an accepted Japanese encyclopœdia as follows: In the eighteenth century, there was, in Yoshida Street, Tokyo City, a house called the "*Yotaka-ya*" (the sign of the "Night-hawk") where women repaired to be painted and decked out when the ravages of disease had made them unpresentable. Thus women who were full of disease were painted and made up to look like young girls, and old hags had their eyebrows blackened with charcoal and their hair fashionably dressed in order to add to their attractions. Many of these prostitutes had their noses eaten away by syphilis, so they had the damage repaired by coloured candle drippings. Among them were deaf, dumb, lame, persons suffering from amaurosis and other maladies owing to syphilis which preventing them from practising in a regular brothel. These whitened their dirty complexions with powder, and the syphilitic sores and wounds in their faces were filled up and concealed by cosmetics, while the handkerchiefs which they bound round their heads did the rest, and guarded against too close an inspection.

These women in their dirty, greasy cotton garments, haunted the public streets, and might be seen by the sickly light of the waning moon, flitting about like the spirits of the damned, hunting for victims. They were in the habit of carrying with them a piece of matting or a rug, the use of which was only too self-evident and requires no explanation. They would accost passers-by with the utmost effrontery, and the price of their favours was a few cash per night! During the period 1711 to 1735, the nuisance grew so bad that a large number of these women were compelled to become regular prostitutes, being forcibly handed over to the Yoshiwara by the Government. From 1711 to 1746, the number of women who had been forced by the Government to enter the Yoshiwara as regular courtesans, served their time there, and been released was, according to a return made the 27th March, 1746, just 246 women.

APPENDIX.

THE GOVERNMENT OF THE NIGHTLESS CITY.

Since the first edition of the "Nightless City" was published in June 1899, many changes tending to ameliorate the condition of prostitutes have been made in the Japanese laws, and the writer believes it may be of more than a passing interest to foreign readers to be presented with a brief digest of the minute regulations at present governing the Yoshiwara in Tōkyō.

One word of warning is, however, essential as a preliminary to what follows. Taken as a whole, the rules are apparently well drafted and seemingly just, but let not the reader be deceived by their plausible provisions!

It must be remembered that, in a place inhabited by those whose business is the unholy trade in human flesh and human honour, there cannot be, broadly speaking, much room for benevolent sentiments and deeds of mercy! Be assured that in the so-called "Nightless City," populated as it is by heartless bestial men and abandoned shameless women, and frequented by bully, habitual criminal, and the scum of creation, no laws or regulations, however wise or humane, can be made completely effective! Notwithstanding all that has been, and is being done, the Yoshiwara is a very inferno of black despair, for it is the common resort of the most wicked and depraved of the male part of the community who hold high carnival within its precincts. Once entrapped in this grave of modesty and virtue—this home of concentrated debauchery and sexual perversion—a woman becomes a virtual slave to the brothel-keepers, many of whom set the law at defiance within the four walls of their unhallowed dens, and, aided by toadying satellites, terrorize and oppress the unfortunate females doomed to spend years of misery with none but shameless libertines and strumpets for their associates! Someone may ask—"If these women have legal rights, why don't they appeal to the police or to the Courts?" The question is easily answered. Some few do, and out of these a certain number obtain relief; but the majority suffer in silence owing to the very force of circumstances and environment. Most are—naturally—quite uneducated, do not know their rights, and are moreover possessed with a vague indefinable sense of terror which prevents them from making a struggle for independence. Others again, from a false sense of duty towards relatives and friends (who have made themselves liable for debts contracted with the brothel-keepers), refrain from making complaints or raising trouble; and above all, the ancient customs of the quarter die hard and hold the victims in their relentless clutches. The police, from their familiarity with this class of women, are more or less harsh and unsympathetic, and, to crown all, even the Supreme Court of the Empire—to the unspeakable disgrace of the judges—has decided that debts incurred by prostitutes, although based upon a clearly immoral consideration, are binding upon the women and their guarantors! With the above preface, we will proceed to describe the present system of control in force in the Yoshiwara, which is the largest and most important of the brothel-quarters in the Tōkyō Urban Prefecture, and therefore a typical institution.

The general status of persons engaged in the practice of prostitution is defined in detail by Notification No. 44

"Regulations for the Control of Prostitutes" issued by the Home Office on the 2nd October, 1900, under the signature of the late Marquis Saigo Tsugumichi, then Minister of State for Home Affairs. This Notification applies to the whole Empire, but various supplementary rules ancillary thereto provide for the control of prostitute quarters in the different prefectures. The regulations prescribe (*inter alia*) that no female under eighteen years of age can either become a licensed prostitute or pursue her calling until her name has been actually inscribed on a "Register of Prostitutes" (*Shōgi Meibō*) to be kept in the Police Station having jurisdiction within the locality, and that all women thus registered are subject to the control of the Police authorities.

In order to safeguard inexperienced applicants as far as possible, females desirous to prostitute themselves are required to appear personally at the Police Station, where they are closely interrogated and warned against taking the fatal step. They are then required to file a document giving full details as to the following matters, viz:—

(1) The reason and necessity for becoming a prostitute.

(2) The date of birth.

(3) As to whether the consent of her nearest ascendant relative, or the head of her family, has been obtained.

(4) As to whether (in the case of a minor) the consent of her real father, or failing him the consent of either her (*a*) real mother, (*b*) real grandfather, or (*c*) real grandmother (in the preferential order given) has been obtained.

(5) The place where she proposes to engage in prostitution.

(6) Residence subsequent to registration.

(7) Present means of livelihood; and if supported by some other person, the facts.

(8) As to whether she has previously practised prostitution or not, and, if so, the date of commencement and relinquishment; the place, her former residence, and the reason for her having discontinued the business.

(9) Special name to be adopted by the prostitute while in the brothel.

(10) The proposed term of service.

(11) Any supplementary details specially demanded by the Authorities in the various Prefectures.

To further guard against fraud and forgery, the above application must, in every case, be accompanied by:—

(1) A copy of personal registration (*koseki-tōhon*) certified to by the Registrar.

(2) Documents of consent (*shōdaku-sho*) signed and sealed by the proper parties.

(3) Certificates of the seals of the consenting parties (*shōdaku-sha no inkan shōmei-sho*) duly verified by the heads of cities (*shi*), districts (*ku*), towns (*chō*) or villages (*son*).

The Police may, in the exercise of their free discretion, refuse to enroll any applicant, but, when the application is granted, the woman is bound to submit to a preliminary medical examination at the hands of the physician on duty in accordance with the rules in force in the various administrative districts.

Women who have been prohibited from carrying on business as prostitutes, or giving up the life, have their name obliterated from the Police Registers. In the case of voluntary retirement, the applicant is, as a general rule, required to attend personally and prefer her request either in writing or orally, but the Police have discretion to dispense with personal attendance if they deem such attendance to be unnecessary under certain circumstances. No person can object to the cancellation of a registration, and any person proved guilty of causing entries to be made in the registers against the will of a woman is punishable with fine or imprisonment.

Once enrolled on the register of prostitutes, the woman's freedom of action is naturally much circumscribed, as she is neither allowed to exercise her calling except in a licensed brothel, nor to reside outside the district assigned to houses of ill-fame by the various Prefectural Governments. Moreover, she cannot leave the appointed precincts for any purpose other than that of attending at a Police Station, unless, indeed, she has received permission from the police, or is acting in accordance with some law or regulation, or in conformity with some official order. When, however, the local laws allow her freedom within certain fixed limits, the above restrictions are varied *mutatis mutandis.*

To prevent coercion and unwarranted interference with the private concerns of women inhabiting brothels, Article 12 of the Notification provides that it is unlawful for any person to prevent them from enjoying the rights of free communication and interviews with friends, freely receiving and perusing letters and papers, owning and possessing articles, making purchases, and other rights of personal liberty. Persons infringing these provisions are liable to major imprisonment for a term not exceeding 25 days, or a fine of not exceeding Yen 25 (say U. S. $ 12.50 or £2 10/- sterling).

All women whose names are inscribed on the Police Registers are obliged to submit to periodical physical inspection, and if found suffering from any contagious disease, or any sickness incapacitating them, they are suspended, under pain of fine or imprisonment, from continuing their business pending treatment and the obtaining of a certificate of complete recovery.

As previously stated, the Police Authorities have discretion in the matter of granting or withholding licenses. Prefectural Governors may either suspend or prohibit the trade of prostitution, and the various Prefectural Governments are empowered to issue further detailed regulations within the scope of the Notification.

Women who were actually engaged in public prostitution when the new regulations came into effect in 1900, were registered without being required to make any of the formal applications hereinbefore mentioned.

There are several penal clauses in the Notification, imposing fines or major imprisonment on persons infringing the various regulations.

Brothels (*kashi-zashiki*), introducing-tea-houses (*hikite-jaya*) and prostitutes (*shōgi*) are further governed in the Tōkyō Urban Prefecture by Notification No. 37 issued on the 6th September, 1900, by the Tōkyō Metropolitan Police Board, under the signature of Mr. Ōura Kanetake, Commissary of Police. This Notification, which superseded Notification No. 40 issued in July 1896, provides (*inter alia*) that brothel-keeping, the keeping of introducing-tea-houses, and public prostitution can only be carried on within the limits of certain quarters (*yūkwaku*) determined by the Metropolitan Police

Board; but an exception to this rule is made in favour of persons who up to the time of the promulgation of the Notification had carried on business outside such quarters, and of the successors (*sōzoku-nin*) of such persons.

Persons desirous of engaging in the businesses of brothel-keeping or "tea-house-keeping" are required to submit plans and all details of the buildings to the Police, and to obtain a license. The same applies when any change is made in the buildings. As a precaution against accidents, staircases of a certain width have to be provided, and for every 1080 (30 tsubos) feet increase in the superficial area an extra staircase is required. The legal maximum width of these staircases is four feet, and the minimum three feet.

No building can be used until officially inspected, approved, and licensed, and no buildings of three-stories and upwards, calculated to attract the public gaze, can be erected outside the brothel-quarters.

Buildings at present existing are to be made to conform to these requirements upon the occasion of extensive repairing or rebuilding.

Brothel-keepers are only allowed to attend to their own particular business, and are absolutely forbidden, under pain of having their licenses cancelled or suspended, to further engage in the businesses of restaurant-keepers or *geisha* (singing girl) keepers. The carrying on of such secondary businesses was stopped on the 1st October, 1900.

Licenses will be cancelled if business is not commenced within three months, or if suspended for twelve months, and all changes of personal status, change of domicile, etc, etc, are to be reported to the Police within three days.

Dancing, singing, music, etc, is forbidden after midnight in brothels and tea-houses outside the actual brothel districts; and such establishments are forbidden to display attractive sign-boards, bright lamps and lanterns, etc, which produce a showy appearance in the road.

Keepers of brothels and tea-houses are bound to provide guest registers (*yūkyaku-jin-meibō*) and to enter therein a minute description of all guests. These registers have to be stamped by the Police, and if lost or damaged the Police must be notified within three days.

In order to check the movements of employees, brothel-keepers and tea-house-keepers are prohibited from engaging employees who possess no "*Employee's Book*" ("*yatoinin-meibō*"), and when engaging or discharging persons, the Police have to be notified, within three days, of the status, domiciles, names, and ages, etc, of such parties.

To prevent secret prostitution in brothels, brothel-keepers are bound to report to the Police, within twenty-four hours, the presence of any woman lodging in their houses.

For the protection of the public, brothel-keepers and "introducing tea-houses" are strictly enjoined; (1) not to force guests to consume food and drink not voluntarily ordered; (2) not to send out touts (*kyaku-hiki*) or to induce people to dissipate either by means of advertisements or other means; (3) not to harbour persons under age or students and pupils wearing the insignia of schools or colleges; (4) not to conceal the presence of guests or deny persons interviews with guests; (5) not to accept clothes or other articles from guests in lieu of cash payment, or in pledge, except the guest has accompanied the keeper to the Police Station, and consented to such transaction in the presence of a Police Officer.

In order to prevent brothel or tea-house keepers from evading responsibility, they are required to obey all instructions given by the Police in connection with the control of their businesses; and they are moreover held personally responsible for the laches and torts of their servants, or members of their household, in regard to business matters.

For the purpose of maintaining public order in the streets of the brothel quarters, the planting of flowering trees and shrubs, organized decorations, and spectacular shows are forbidden unless the sanction of the Police has first been obtained. Outside the quarters the Police absolutely prohibit any public displays connected with the brothels or tea-houses; and in the case of outside brothels the regulations require the rooms to be so screened as to be practically invisible from the public road. Such houses are also forbidden to expose their bedding* to public view.

To protect women from harsh treatment, brothel-keepers are strictly prohibited from treating inmates in a cruel manner, and forbidden to compel them to incur needless expenditure. In case of sickness, the brothel-keepers are bound to provide medicine and medical attendance; and in order that the girls may be made aware of their rights under the law, it is provided that a copy of the regulations shall be posted up in each brothel in a conspicuous place where it can be easily seen and read by all whom it may concern. While the law is thus solicitous for the welfare of the women, they are by no

* It used to be the custom for lower class houses to air all their showy bedding on the balconies facing the road.

means allowed too much license, for the regulations provide that any infringement thereof by the prostitutes shall be notified to the Police by the brothel-keepers obtaining knowledge of such infringement.

For the purpose of localizing prostitution as far as possible, introducing tea-houses are forbidden to allow either guests, public women, or *geisha* (singing and dancing girls) to lodge or sleep therein.

To simplify the work of the Police and to ensure a more efficient control over these haunts of vice, the regulations provide for an elaborate system of what might be termed "local self-government," in which all classes concerned participate in a greater or lesser degree. Article 26 of Notification No. 37 of the Metropolitan Police Board says:—"Brothel-keepers, introducing tea-house keepers, and prostitutes, belonging to each and every brothel-district, shall form a Guild (*Kumi-ai*) and frame a constitution* therefor. Notice thereof shall be given to the Metropolitan Police Board through the Police Station having jurisdiction, and permission obtained in respect thereto. When the constitution is revised or altered, the same rule applies."

The Guilds are required to elect a director (*tori-shimari*) and a vice-director (*fuku-tori-shimari*), but the Police possess the power of vetoing such appointments, may cancel their approval of appointments, or may order fresh election. Directors of Guilds attend to the collective interests of the members, and are bound to notify the members of all changes

* The actual word used is "*Ki-yaku*" (規約) "an agreement" or "covenant," but, in the sense in which it is used here the term "*Constitution*" seems most appropriate.

in the laws and regulations, and of the purport of any special instructions issued by the authorities.

Articles 30 to 39 (inclusive) of Notification No. 37 deal in detail with the status of prostitutes, and provide (*inter alia*) that in case of an alteration of the term of service the same must be registered in the Police Station; that no woman may live or practice outside licenced houses; that if she changes her house such change must be notified to the Police under the joint signatures of herself and the keeper of the brothel in which she is presently staying; that changes of residence must be registered at the Police Station; that when a woman removes to a brothel situated in another jurisdiction, the change must be notified through the Police having jurisdiction over her former residence; that all changes of names, status, pseudonyms, fees charged (*age-dai*), suspensions and resumptions of business must be notified to the Police within three days. The regulations further provide that prostitutes may only hire as servants such persons as are possessed of "*Employee's Books*," and that when employees are engaged or discharged the facts are to be notified to the Police within three days; that they shall submit to certain physical inspections prescribed as necessary to prevent the communication of venereal disease; that they shall not leave the brothel-quarters without official permission, and that they shall respect all special orders of the Police. The women are also forbidden to oppear outside the quarters dressed in a loud or showy manner, or to loiter about in the public road or a place visible from a public road.

Articles 40 to 46 (inclusive of Notification No. 37 provide for a complete system of control over employees of brothels, tea-houses, and prostitutes. Such persons are required to carry with them pass-books wherein are set down particulars of their service record, and details of any punishments they may have undergone. All the movements of employees are thus known to the Police, who inspect and seal the books from time to time, and who have power to confiscate the books and thus prevent the subsequent employment of persons offending against the regulations. If a book be damaged or lost, application for a new book must be made within three days, and, should the bearer of a book entirely quit his employment, an application for cancellation of the same must also be made within three days.

In case the proprietor of a brothel or introducing tea-house is a minor of less than twelve years, or an incompetent person (*kinji-san-sha*) his legal representative (*hōtei dairi-nin*) may be held responsible for his acts. In the case of a quasi-incompetent person (*jun-kinji-san-sha*), his curator (*hosa-nin*) may be held responsible.

In case of an infringement of the regulations by a juridical person (corporation) the managing member (*gyōmu-tantō-nin*) may be punished by a police fine.

Details of "Employees' Books."

These are made of strong Japanese "*Mino*" paper, folded in four, and contain at least six such sheets. The cover is made of stout paper and the whole is bound together with an extra sheet at the back which is pasted securely to both covers (*fukuro-toji*). Remarks which should properly be entered by the Police cannot be entered by the holder.

Roughly speaking, the books are divided into two portions; (*a*) entries *re* employer, employment, discharge, and date; (*b*) *re* changes in personal registration, domicile, or name; also *re* actions of the authorities.

The form of the books is as follows:—

(FRONT)	(BACK)
Date................ **EMPLOYEE'S BOOK.** *Name*. .... Of No..........(name of village, town, district, county, prefecture), or urban prefecture.) *Lodging at* c/o................. No..........(name of village, town, district, county, prefecture, or urban prefecture).	Caution to employee carrying this book. 1.—Changes in registration of citizenship, domicile, or name, the date, and details of such changes must be personally entered. 2.—When employed or discharged, the date, house-name, and name of the employer, as well as all facts concerning such engagement and discharge, must be personally entered. 3.—This book must be constantly carried with you. Date................ (No...... ..... Seal of the Police Station having jurisdiction.

Specimen entries in an Employee's book.

Changes in registration of citizenship, personal status, domicile, and name.	Employer and date of being engaged and discharged.
Removed on the..........day of the......month of the.......year, to No......(name of village, town, district, county or prefecture.) *Removed* on the..........day of (same as above.)	*Employed* on the (.....date....) by (.........name........) of the (name of brothel or tea-house) of No....... (ward) Shin-Yoshiwara. *Discharged* on the (....date....) by the aforesaid (.....name.....) upon the expiration of the term of service.

Matter of Disposition.
Punished by the imposition of a police-fine of (amount) on account of (offence). Date................ ....*Police-Station.*

The Medical Inspection of Prostitutes.

NOTIFICATION No. 39 of the Metropolitan Police Board, issued on the 10th October, 1900, under the signature of Ōura Kanetake, Commissary of Police, which superseded Notification No. 22 of March, 1894, provides for the medical inspection of public women as follows:

All prostitutes are to undergo both regular and special inspections. Regular inspection is to take place once a week, and the days appointed in Tōkyō are :—

DISTRICT.	INSPECTION DAYS.
Shin-Yoshiwara................	Monday, Tuesday, Wednesday and Thursday.
Susaki..........................	Friday and Saturday.
Shinagawa.....................	Monday.
Natiō Shinjuku................	Wednesday.
Senju-machi and Minami Senju-machi	Thursday.
Itabashi-machi................	Saturday.
Hachiōji-machi................	Friday.
Fuchū-machi....................	Tuesday.
Chōfu-machi....................	Tuesday.

Special Inspection takes Place :—

(1) When a woman becomes a prostitute.

(2) When a woman has been resting outside the brothel to which she is attached, and is going to resume her calling after the lapse of seven days.

(3) When a patient is about to be discharged from a hospital.

(4) When a patient who has been sick has recovered her health and is about to resume her calling.

(5) When a woman discovers that she is infected.

(6) When a special inspection is considered necessary or expedient by the physicians.

The special inspection days in Tōkyō are :—

DISTRICT.	INSPECTION DAYS.
Shin-Yoshiwara.................	Every day except Sunday.
Susaki..................	Every day except Sunday.
Shinagawa-machi..............	Monday, Wednesday, Friday and Saturday.
Naitō Shinjuku-machi..........	Monday, Tuesday, Wednesday and Friday.
Senju-machi and Minami Senju-machi	Tuesday, Thursday, Friday and Saturday.
Itabashi-machi	Monday, Tuesday, Thursday and Saturday.
Hachiōji-machi................	Monday, Thursday, Friday and Saturday.
Fuchū-machi..	Monday, Tuesday, Thursday and Saturday.
Chōfu-machi...................	Monday, Tuesday, Thursday and Saturday.

Upon being inscribed upon the *Registers of Prostitutes*, new-comers are to be examined, on one of the special inspection days, by the surgeons of the Inspection Office (*Kensa-jo*). Special provisions are made to meet all cases needing inspection, aud the regulations require all infected women to enter the Lock Hospital for proper treatment under penalty of a fine of not exceeding Yen 1.95 (U. S. $0.97½, or a little under 4/-s sterling.) Patients intending to leave the hospital must procure a certificate (*shindan-sho*) from the President of the hospital. As a regular thing, examinations are to be conducted between the hours of 10 a.m. and 3 p.m., and at the close of each such examination the woman is to procure a sealed certificate of inspection (*juken-shōsho*) from the surgeon.

Hospital Regulations.

Various regulations exist, but those of the great Yoshiwara Lock Hospital are typical of the others. They were revised in March 1900, and provide substantially as follows:—

OBJECT OF THE HOSPITAL.—The hospital is established for the purpose of treating prostitutes who are suffering from venereal diseases, consumption, and other contagious maladies contracted or developed in the Yoshiwara brothel-quarters.

STAFF.—The permanent staff consists of about fifty people, including several surgeons, a secretary, four pharmacists, nurses, clerks, servants, etc., and is presided over by a chief doctor. The hospital arrangements are subject to Police supervision.

MEDICAL STAFF.—The patients must be visited at least twice a day, and on each occasion details of their condition and treatment entered in a report sheet (*byōshō nis-shi*) for the information of the President. In case of serious illness or slow recovery the matter must be reported to the President, and should the symptoms denote immediate danger, the brothel-keeper of the woman's house must be notified forthwith. Upon recovery, the report sheet has to be signed by the attendant physician, after which the President himself has to examine the patient. It is the duty of the doctors to prescribe the diet of patients, to instruct and supervise the nurse to see that all necessary instruments are provided and kept in proper condition; and each of the doctors are bound to take night-duty alternately. To prevent scandal and collusion, the doctors are prohibited from entering the wards unless accompanied by a nurse, and, as a precaution against incurring unnecessary risks in treatment, surgical operations can only be performed with the approval of the President. When not otherwise engaged, the hospital doctors may employ their leisure time in making medical investigations, and may, subject to the permission of the President, publish the results of their labours in this direction.

Records, Accounts, Statistics and Reports.—Proper records must be kept of the work and accounts of the hospital, the admissions and discharges, and a monthly and yearly report prepared containing detailed statistics. Monthly reports must be prepared by the 5th of the following month, and the annual report by the 10th of January of the following year. The chief pharmacist is also bound to prepare a daily report of all drugs dispensed and to submit same to the President.

Sundry.—Detailed rules are laid down for keeping the bedding and premises in a clean and sanitary condition, for disinfection, etc; and for the control of the nurses.

Salaries.—That the staff of the hospital is very much underpaid will be recognized upon perusal of the following scale of monthly salaries:

	YEN.	U. S. $	£ STERLING.
President..........	80 to 150	40 to 75	8 to 15
Vice-President......	50 " 80	25 " 40	5 " 8
Physicians..........	25 " 50	12½ " 25	2.10/– " 5
Secretary............	20 " 30	10 " 15	2 " 3
Chief Pharmacist....	25 " 50	12½ " 25	2.10/– " 5
Pharmacist.........	10 " 25	5 " 12½	1 " 2.10/–
Clerks..............	10 " 25	5 " 12½	1 " 2.10/–
Chief Nurse.........	10 " 20	5 " 10	1 " 2
Nurses.............	3 " 10	1½ " 5	0.6/– " 1
Servants............	4 " 10	2 " 5	0.8/– " 1

P.S.—If absent for upwards of two weeks, no salary is paid for the current month, and if absent for upwards of one month they may be discharged from the service. The rules do not, however, apply in cases of sickness.

FINANCIAL.—Funds for the support of the hospital are raised by way of forced contributions from the brothel-keepers of the Yoshiwara, and the basis of the annual expenditure is a written estimate prepared prior to the 20th March every year by the President of the institution and the Director of the Brothel-keepers Guild, and approved by the Police authorities. In case of a deficiency occurring, steps may be taken to make good the same by the President and Director acting in concert.

ALTERATION OF HOSPITAL REGULATIONS.—When necessary, the regulations may be altered by the President of the hospital and the Director and Vice-Director of the Guild acting in concert, provided that the consent of the Police authorities has been obtained to the proposed changes.

Sick-Rooms and Sanitary Precautions.—The regulations require that separate wards* be provided for various classes of patients, and that contagious cases be properly segregated; also that the premises be kept swept and clean, and all infected matter be destroyed by fire. Bedding and towels are not to be used promiscuously, sheets are to be disinfected by means of hot steam, spittoons containing a 5% solution of carbolic acid are to be provided, table utensils are to be washed in hot water containing corrosive sublimate (1 in a 1000), infected waste paper must be burnt, and even waste paper which is not infected must not be sold until properly disinfected. Patients who have obtained permission from the physicians are bound to take a bath every morning before the periodical examination.

Visitors.—Are not allowed in the wards or rooms unless the patient is unable to move and special permission has been obtained from the physician in attendance. Visitors may, however, under certain conditions, see patients between 9 a.m. and 3 p.m. in a room (*ōsetsu-jo*) set apart for that purpose.

Rules for Patients.—While under treatment, patients are required to be civil and respectful in their language and demeanour towards the members of the hospital staff, to wear the regular cotton dresses worn by all inmates, and to observe

* The wards are divided of follows:—

(1) For syphilis.
(2) " gonorrhœa.
(3) " chancres
(4) " skin diseases.
(5) " miscellaneous diseases.
(6) " cases of serious illness.
(7) " isolated rooms for infectious diseases.

the regulations governing the institution. No patient is allowed to leave the hospital while under treatment. Patients are required to do their hair up in a simple style, to refrain from entering other wards or rooms except for proper reasons, to refrain from wearing the thick-soled high sandals (*taka-zōri*) ordinarily worn in brothels, to carefully place all waste-paper in the receptacles provided, to refrain from creating noise or disorder, singing, quarreling, and scribbling nonsense on the walls or furniture. They are also prohibited from lending or borrowing money, gambling, etc; and (except with the permission of the physicians) from taking food and drugs brought in from outside. In case of wishing to make purchases outside the hospital, permission must be obtained from the physicians through the nurses.

EXERCISE.—Exercise may be taken daily in the hospital gardens within prescribed hours.

COMPLAINTS.—Complaints against the nurses or other persons must be made direct to the physicians in attendance.

As to the actual working of the Yoshiwara Hospital, some caustic remarks, contained in a book entitled *Yūkwaku no Rimen* (**遊廓の裏面**) "*Behind the scenes in the brothel-quarters*") published in Tōkyō in 1903, are appended. In the course of an exceedingly severe arraignment, the author says substantially as follows :—

"The filthy state of the Yoshiwara Hospital, and its "utter lack of proper appointments, is so notorious that "it is hardly necessary for us to dwell upon this par- "ticular phase of the subject; but we propose to enquire "into some of the details of the institution. When we "try to picture to ourselves what a hospital is, or should "be like, we naturally imagine a fine lofty building

" surrounded by beautiful green trees, grateful shrubs " and flowering plants, containing well-ventilated wards " kept scrupulously neat and clean and furnished with " beds covered with snowy-white counterpanes free from " even a suspicion of stain or dirt; but the Yoshiwara " Hospital is indeed far from being like that. We are " tempted to compare it to a prison, but, as a matter of " fact, a prison like the Sugamo Gaol is far more clean " and complete, so from the point of general dirtiness " and disorder the comparison would be quite inappro- " priate! The sick rooms have an area of from about " 144 to 180 square feet, and as many as twelve or " thirteen people are sometimes collected together in " such stuffy chambers. The inmates often sleep two " in a bed, and women belonging to different brothels, " who are indeed entire strangers to each other, share " the same couch. As to their treatment, they are medi- " cally examined twice a day, they have to pay for their " own food, and although attendance and medicine is " supposed to be supplied by the brothel-keepers, the " patients have to get the money from their masters in " the form of a loan and repay it in due course. Even " in these expensive times, when living is far dearer than " formerly, it appears that the cost of the regular hospital " food is only estimated at from 7 to 8 *sen* (3½ to 4 cents " U. S. money or say 2d in sterling), so that for the " women to be supplied with appetizing or nourishing " food is simply impossible. The food they actually get " three times a day is far worse than good prison fare, " and consists of:—

" (1) In the morning: boiled barley and rice mixed (*baku-han*).

" (2) At noon: boiled barley and rice mixed (*baku-han*), some vegetables or a small fish.

" (3) In the evening: boiled barley and rice mixed (*baku-han*) and some indigestible malodorous pickled vegetables (*kō-no-mono*).

" Periodical examination of all prostitutes takes place " once a week, the different streets each having special " days. For instance if Edo-chō It-chō-me has its inspec- " tion on Friday, the inspection of Ageya-machi will be " on a Wednesday. When the inspection time arrives, " the name of each prostitute is called by turn, and one " by one each undergoes a local examination. If a woman " is visibly infected, the doctor orders her into hospital, " but prior to her entering the establishment she is permit- " ted to temporarily return to her brothel, where she " makes up a bundle of such little things as she needs " and, accompanied by a servant of the house, proceeds to " the hospital and applies for admission. In the hospital " several nurses are in attendance, but while the name " 'nurse' sounds fine enough in itself, the women who " bear this title are terrible females, something like the " old brothel hags (*yarite*) themselves, and are ready to " do anything for a consideration. For this reason, " the prostitutes need some pocket-money when enter- " ing the hospital, and if they only are provided with " this they have very little trouble in getting their " whims gratified in every respect. After a prostitute " has been in the hospital three or four days, if she " happens to be a popular woman, the brothel-keeper, and " others who lose by her absence, do their best, by judicious " presents, to get her discharged as soon as possible, so " she is not put to any great inconvenience. On the other " hand, if the woman is an unknown new comer, or un- " popular, she is treated in a manner painful to witness, " only getting what may be given to her out of sheer pity " by one of the senior prostitutes of the brothel to which

" she belongs. The moment they hear the signal for " dinner, these wretched girls rush into the dining hall, " and scrambling for food devour it in the same greedy " wolfish manner as we can imagine the hungry spirits " doing in the Buddhist hell! As to the condition of the " inmates of the hospital, most of them spend their time " in reading obscene novels and stories, but this does not " last long, and they begin to discuss their guests and the " men they know, to talk about their lovers, to sing, and " to make abusive remarks about their masters and the " servants in their respective brothels. Or they dance " and skip about, play cards, write begging letters, and " generally raise a pandemonium as if the institution was " a low-class boarding-house. Such being the conditions " of this horrible place, with the exception perhaps of a " few disappointed women, or women who get on badly " with the brothel-keeper, the prostitutes regard with " dread the ordeal of entering the hospital. The majority " of the public place considerable faith in the efficacy of " the medical examination, but they are woefully mistaken " in thinking that immunity from disease is secured by such " inspection, because many of the doctors of the prostitute " quarters are miserable quacks, apparently regardless " of their conduct, and so venal that they receive bribes " from the brothel-keepers to deliberately pass unchal- " lenged women who are plainly affected with venereal " diseases—an act as dangerous as letting loose wild tigers " to prey upon the public! Not only that, but some of " the youngster assistant doctors who, though of course " licensed, are still in the course of perfecting their " medical knowledge by practical training, often inten- " tionally overlook serious cases which, unless treated in " the hospital, are incurable and likely to spread infec- " tion. This is done partly out of sympathy and partly

" for the sake of winning popularity with some of these " ill-famed wenches who know so well exactly how to bewitch the impressionable young men with their sidelong " looks and amorous glances. No doubt it is very wrong, " but then what a potent influence for good or bad there " is in the eye of a young and pretty woman! Moreover, " many of the girls are in collusion with their masters for " the purpose of hoodwinking the examiners. These " girls employ some of the low quacks who haunt the " quarters to make preliminary inspections, and if they " are found infected and likely to be ordered into " hospital on the examination day, they get 'fixed " up' for the official inspection by having the inflamed " parts treated with medicinal applications which temporarily, but effectually, conceal all visible symptoms of " disease. For these reasons, it is by no means safe to " put one's trust in the medical inspection. But these " are not the only tricks of the trade. It sometimes " happens that the quacks discover cases which it is impossible to conceal from the examiners by any known " method of 'fixing,' and when this happens, the brothelkeepers often request the mercenary charlatans to prepare false certificates stating that a change of air is " necessary. Armed with these certificates, keepers pretend that the patient has gone into the country, whereas she is carefully hidden in the house and secretly " treated by the quacks. The consequence of this is that " many women who are actually in attendance on guests, " and apparently healthy, are a frightful menace to " society and dangerous as the sharp points of poisoned " needles concealed in a bag, whose awful pricks spread " death and desolation in the paths of those with whom " they come into contact. As to the sanitary conditions " of the quarters, the laws of hygiene are utterly defied, for

" notwithstanding the exterior splendour of the palaces of " vice in the Yoshiwara, filthiness is the order of the day, " and in unseen corners, and dirty yards and alleys, lie " heaps of festering garbage containing the germs of every " imaginable form of virulent disease. While some " attempt is made to detect venereal maladies by means of " periodical inspections, internal diseases are practically " left uncared for, therefore the callous and selfish " brothel-keepers, taking advantage of this fact, are apt " to force girls (who are really ill and ought to be " inmates of a hospital ward) to wait on guests, and allow " women suffering from such sicknesses as consumption " and syphilitic eye diseases to continue their calling. " Partly owing to the heartlessness of the masters, and " partly owing to their carelessness in matters of sanita- " tion, many instances have occurred where women have " not only communicated to their guests the most loath- " some diseases, but actually died from illness while " sleeping beside their patrons. Decency forbids a too " close description of all the horrors of these brothels, but " one or two more instances of the terrible inattention to " sanitary precautions may be pardoned. In some of the " smaller houses the keepers are too mean to provide " daily baths, so it often happens that the women appear " before their guests innocent of the use of soap and " water. In these houses the girls are treated like " veritable dogs and cats, and remain year in and year out " in cramped unclean chambers, known as *kwambeya*, " furnished with dirty ragged bedding which is so filthy " that it gives off a strong sweaty effluvium! In these " dens, owing to the absence of hot water, the inmates are " supposed to wash in cold water, but in the winter-time " the low temperature causes them to dread their ablu- " tions, and so the risk of infection to themselves and

" guests is materially increased. On the other hand,
" when they do cleanse themselves as expected, the
" frequent application of cold water results in bringing
" on various forms of uterine affections and dooming the
" unfortunate wretches to life-long misery. In the alleys
" where the restaurants (*daiya*) stand, lie piles of mouldy
" fish-bones, rejected articles of food in a high state of
" putrefaction, and even heaps of excrement, all vieing
" with each other in the exhalation of offensive and
" poisonous odours, and advertising far and wide the
" 'sanitary' ideas of the charming residents of this sink
" of corruption. Thus are the laws of hygiene observed
" in the great Yoshiwara of Tōkyō!"

Whether the author's scathing denunciations of the medical staff of the Yoshiwara are justified or otherwise is not known, but, collating the results of enquiries instituted, the writer is of the opinion that the allegations are somewhat sensational, although of course scandals may occasionally arise, and it must be remembered that the miserable salaries paid are not likely to tempt high-class practitioners to remain in the service for any great length of time. That a host of shady quacks haunt the quarters and assist the brothel-keepers to enable the women to hoodwink the regular examiners is, the writer is informed on reliable authority, a sober fact, and it is probable that in some cases the official doctors have to bear the opprobium of sins committed by these unscrupulous outside charlatans.

As to the gross inattention to sanitary methods charged against the denizens of this immense social sewer, it is probably impossible to exaggerate the mephitic abominations of the disgusting place, or to overestimate the danger of infection run by its thoughtless frequenters in consequence of the virulent disease-germs which are incubated in and infest every hole and corner of the unclean stews, vitiating the atmosphere and spreading the seeds of sickness and death far and near.

The monthly report sheets of the hospital contain blanks analysing the various forms of disease as follows :—

INFECTIOUS DISEASES.

Syphilis :

1 Primary sclerosis and ulcers.
2 Painless buboes.
3 Disease of the lymphatic glands.
4 Skin diseases.
5 Diseases of the mucous membranes.
6 Opthalmia.
7 Diseases of the bones and periosts.
8 Diseases of the joints.
9 Diseases of the muscles.
10 Diseases of the viscera and brain.
11 Soft chancres.
12 Acute buboes.
13 Gonorrhœa.
14 Itch.
15 Tuberculosis.
16 Unenumerated.

NON-INFECTIOUS DISEASES.

17 Diseases of the digestive organs.
18 Diseases of the respiratory organs.
19 Diseases of the circulatory organs.
20 Diseases of the urinary organs.
21 Diseases of the generative organs,

22 Diseases of the nerves and sensitive organs.
23 Diseases affecting the general development and nutrition of the body.
24 Diseases of the skin and muscles.
25 Diseases of the bones and joints.
26 Surgical diseases.
27 Unenumerated.

Medical Statistics.

The medical statistics of the Yoshiwara for seven years (1898 to 1904 inclusive) are as follows :—

Year.	Number of inspections.	Number of infected cases.	Infected per 100.	Number of guest entertained.
1898..........	134,602	7,506	5.58	1,237,885
1899..........	108,268	5,333	4.95	1,367,639
1900.........	108,109	5,117	4.76	1,428,136
1901..........	108,572	4,864	4.48	1,157,492
1902..........	107,260	4,635	4.33	1,065,674
1903..........	106,121	5,006	4.74	1,167,969
1904..........	119,148	8,592	7.22	1,285,424

The figures show that during seven years the average ratio of infection was 5.18 per 100, but whether these show the true facts of the case is hard to determine. However, they have the merit of being "official" even if somewhat erroneous.

Taking into consideration the above results, it appears that the figures for the whole Empire given in the "*Annual Report of the Central Sanitary Bureau of the Home Department*" (published in 1905) must be misleading, as they show the ratio in 1901 to range from only 0.43 in Kōchi Prefecture to 6.20 in Kagoshima Prefecture. In Hyōgo Prefecture, Iwate Prefecture and Aomori Prefecture the ratio is stated to be 9.69, 13.75 and 14.52, respectively, and the average for the whole country works out as only 2.75 for all the forty-six prefectures enumerated. It is hard to reconcile these differences except on the assumption that the severity of the examination varies according to the localities.

The following table shows the alleged results of examination of prostitutes throughout Japan for *ten* years, the average ratio being 3.31 per 100.

EXAMINATION OF PROSTITUTES FOR SYPHILIS, IN EACH OF THE LAST TEN YEARS.

YEARS.	Places of examination at the end of each year.	Each day's average of the total number of prostitutes.	NUMBER OF EXAMINATIONS.					Number of affected per 100 examined
			AFFECTED.			UN-AFFECTED.	TOTAL.	
			TRUE.	FALSE.	True cases per 100 affected.			
1892	484	30,687	8,364	43,237	16.21	1,379,598	1,431,199	3.61
1893	487	31,253	9,339	40,858	18.60	1,408,813	1,459,010	3.44
1894	476	34,023	6,327	52,963	10.67	1,553,422	1,612,712	3.68
1895	471	37,518	5,937	50,056	10.60	1,644,110	1,700,103	3.29
1896	472	39,079	7,231	65,049	10.00	1,707,565	1,779,845	4.06
1897	498	43,570	8,856	61,004	12.68	1,960,407	2,030,267	3.44
1898	495	48,780	11,692	56,816	12.07	2,190,325	2,258,833	3.03
1899	518	49,553	8,650	52,508	14.14	2,171,964	2,233,122	2.74
1900	536	52,305	11,493	59,406	16.21	2,249,276	2,320,175	3.06
1901	530	40,855	9,117	50,493	13.29	2,427,909	2,496,518	2.75
TOTAL.	Average. 496.7	Average. 40762.3	Average. 8700.5	Average. 54139.0	Average. 13.45%	Average. 1869338.9	Average. 1932178.4	Average. 3.31%

Digest of the Regulations of the Yoshiwara Guild.

General.—In December 1901, in accordance with Article 26 of the Metropolitan Police Board Notification No 37, issued in 1900, the brothel-keepers, introducing-tea-house-keepers, and prostitutes of the Yoshiwara established a Guild, and in February 1904 the rules of this Guild were revised.

Object.—The object of the association is to secure and maintain intimate relations between its members, to protect the common interests of the "trade," and to preserve ancient picturesque customs of the quarter.

Director.—The Guild, which has its office at No. 462 Ni-chō-me, Senzoku-machi, Asakusa district, Tokyō City, is governed by a Director (*tori-shimari*) and a Vice-Director (*fuku-tori-shimari*) both of whom are elected, by means of an open ballot, by the members, all of whom enjoy the "franchise."

When the number of votes is equal the individual who is senior in birth is deemed to be elected, and when the dates of birth are identical the vote is decided by lot. The term of office is two years, and in case of a vacancy occurring a bye-election is held. The Director has a staff of clerks and other employees under his control.

Undertaking by Members.—Persons joining the Guild are required to subscribe to the articles of association and to give a written promise to observe the same. Moreover the new member has to provide a guarantor who will actually make performance of his duties should he himself fail to do so. Guarantors must be persons in the same line of "business," and the brothel-keepers have to guarantee the prostitutes belonging to their respective houses.

Contracts to be Submitted to Director.—All financial arrangements relative to contracts entered into between the brothel-keepers and prostitutes have to be reported to the Director under the joint signatures of the parties.

PASS-BOOKS.—The brothel-keepers and the women are required to prepare and keep pass-books in the following form, and to send in the same (duly entered up) for the approval of the Director before the 10th of every month :—

Entries in this book are to be made for one year from the .... 19.... to the .... 19....

Revenue Stamp

(L.S.)

Name of prostitute ....

Date ....

Total .... Yen........

Fee for one entertainment out of which.... Yen.........

(1) Portion of the Keeper................ " ....

(2) Portion of the woman................ " ....

Agreement relative to the income of the woman of.......... out of the fee for one entertainment as shown in the above division, has been duly notified to the Police Station.

As to the pocket-money .... for each entertainment fee, it will be paid at the time of accounting.

Number of entertainments ....

	Yen	Sen
Entertainment fees	......	......
Actual amount to be paid to the woman.......	......	......
To be applied to the interest on loan for (name of month)	......	......
Pocket money of the woman	......	......
Applied to repayment of debit balance in books	......	......
Balance is as follows:—		
Loan	......	......
Advance in current a/c on the books....	......	......
Total....		

Changes in Membership, Etc.—All changes in regard to membership and movements of employees are notified to the members generally through the Director, and the members are bound not to engage discharged employees except with the consent of the former employers.

Precautions Against Fire.—To guard against fire, periodical examinations are made by an expert (appointed by the Director) of the kerosene oil used in lighting, and the use of oil of under 70° (C) is forbidden.

Power to Expel.—Persons infringing the rules of the Guild may be expelled by a resolution of a general meeting.

Revision of Articles.—The articles of association of the Guild may be revised by a general meeting called by the Director at the request of thirty members.

Brothel-Keepers Consultation Committee.—To protect their mutual benefit the brothel-keepers appoint a consultation committee (*kyōgi-in*) the members of which are elected in the same manner as the Directors. This committee may request the Director to call a meeting at any time.

Reports of Income.—Every day each brothel keeper is obliged to report his gross income, and number of guests entertained, to the Director.

Charges.—An entertainments tariff, legibly written, must be conspicuously displayed in every guest-chamber. This table must also include the prices of various refreshments provided. Persons who accompany guests, but who do not engage a woman, are charged half the amount of the highest fee charged for a woman.

Exhibition of Women.—Women may not be publicly exhibited in the " cages " after 1 o'clock a.m. from November to April, or after 2 o'clock a.m. from May to October; and in case of pregnancy are forbidden to practice their calling for three months before and after parturition.

Medical Expenses.—Brothel-keepers are required to pay daily to the accountant of the Guild for transmission to the hospital the charges incurred in consequence of any of their women undergoing medical treatment.

Brothels who may use Tea-Houses.—Brothels employing women whose fee is Yen 1.50 (U. S. $ 75 or 3/- sterling) may do their business through tea-houses, but they are obliged to pay a commission to the latter.

Insurance of Accounts.—As an insurance against loss the brothel-keepers pay to a separately organized office, called the "*Uke-harai-jo*," one per cent of the amount of money received from tea-houses, and in return for this premium the "*Uke-harai-jo*" guarantees the tea-house accounts. All monies due to the brothels by tea-houses are paid to the "*Uke-harai-jo*" and not direct, and should any tea-house fail to meet its liabilities all business with such defaulting establishment is discontinued until settlement is made. In case of the tea-house people having committed any improper act, the brothel-keepers may boycott the tea-house and refuse to do business with its proprietors.

Expenses to be Defrayed by Brothel-Keepers.—Brothel-keepers have to bear the following expenses: (1) of the Yoshiwara Hospital; (2) of the office for the inspection of venereal diseases; (3) of the Director's office; (4) of emergencies; (5) of displays and shows; (6) of meetings; (7) of salaries of Director and employees; (8) reserve fund. These expenses are estimated and passed by the Consulting Committee in May and November each year, and notified to the brothel-keepers through the Director. In January and July of every year the Director prepares and submits accounts for the previous term. A supplementary budget may be passed by the Consulting Committee, but if the expenditure is for an object not contemplated in the eight items mentioned above, the sanction of a general meeting of brothel-keepers must be obtained.

ACCOUNTS FOR MEDICINES.—Accounts for medicine must be settled at the latest by the 25th of each following month, but these drugs are supplied to members at half-price as compared with the prices charged by ordinary physicians to the general public.

TEA-HOUSE-KEEPERS.—Introducing-tea-house-keepers appoint by ballot a Consulting Committee, two accountants and several *nemban* (" year guards.") General meetings of tea-house-keepers are convened by the Director in accordance with resolutions of the Consulting Committee. Members of the tea-house fraternity deposit Yen 50 as a guarantee that they will pay accounts due to the brothels with whom they deal. The members must join the *Uke-harai-jo* or " clearing house " of the Guild, and all monies are paid to the brothels through its medium, and not direct. A commission of 10 (ten) % is charged to brothel-keepers on the gross sums of money paid to the latter by the tea-houses, but this is subject to alteration by agreement between the Committee and the brothel-keepers. Monthly statements of accounts relative to the number of guests, money received for refreshments and *geisha* fees, etc., must be sent to the Director by the 3rd of each following month. When tea-houses fail to meet their liabilities in respect to brothel accounts, the " clearing-house" (*uke-harai-*

jo) makes good the amount, and the defaulter is either suspended or expelled.

Duties of Prostitutes.—Prostitutes belonging to the Guild are required to "take care of their health, be economical, and use their leisure time in study, sewing, etc, to the end that they may be prepared to resume their normal position in society." They are expected to dress like ordinary women when outside the brothel-quarter, to maintain good relations with their comrades, to treat their guests fairly and show proper respect towards them, and not to refuse acceptance of guests unless for "valid reasons."

The Validity of Debts.

At present, debts contracted by prostitutes are held to be valid and legally recoverable, although contracts binding women to serve in brothels in consideration of a loan would probably be held illegal. The leading case on the question is *Ōkuma Kin* (*and two others*) v. *Watanabe Mase* decided in the First Civil Division of the Supreme Court of Japan (Case "*O*" 398 of 1901) on the 6th February, 1902. The principles enunciated are thus stated in the digests:— "*Prostitution being* "*a publicly recognized business, it is not in the least contrary to* "*public order or good morals for a prostitute to enter into an* "*agreement with her creditors to devote the profits arising from* "*her own business to the satisfaction of her debt towards* "*them.*" It is the writer's strong opinion that the Judges have committed a very serious blunder in interpreting the law as stated above, as they appear to have overlooked the distinct intention of the legislature. Prostitution, even in Japan, is not intended to be authorized as a legitimate business, and, while it is *tolerated* by the law, this *toleration* is the outcome of a desire to control and regulate the evil for considerations of public policy. Public and personal safety require a constant inspection, and Japanese experience has shown that such inspection can be best enforced when the brothels are all gathered together in one central locality, but to dignify the infamous and ruinous calling by placing it upon a level with other permitted callings *is tantamount to protecting* the business itself by affording the security of the law to persons engaged in earning money by means of leading and encouraging a notoriously profligate course of life. There can be no doubt but that the Japanese system is excellent so far as it goes, but for the courts to virtually hold that the mere fact that brothel-keepers and prostitutes are *tolerated* and taxed entitles them to be ranked as ordinary worthy citizens, and their disgusting transactions protected by the Imperial laws, suggests a somewhat loose idea of morality in the Judges, and a wrong perception of the proper status of a class of persons whose professed business is to foster vice and pander to the libidinous desires of the multitude. Eradicate the evil we cannot, regulate it we can and ought, but surely the law goes far enough when it imposes certain obligations upon the unholy trade without going to the length of upholding claims based upon what is—no matter how plausibly you argue it—an immoral consideration!

Yarō.

"Peccatum illud horribile, inter Christianos non nominandum."

The subject is so horribly repulsive and distasteful that the writer would have preferred to close his eyes to the existence of this awful phase of human depravity and pass it by in silence, but friends, in whose judgment he places entire confidence, have pointed out that the very nature of this work demands at least a passing allusion to one terrible form of venery which prevailed in Japan in the later Middle Ages.

In the early part of the Yedo period (commenced 1587,) traces of the surviving customs of the preceding civil wars lingered on, and as unnatural practices (which had grown up in armed camps) had been introduced into the metropolis, and were rife in the city, there were, of course depraved persons who provided accommodation to gratify the infamous tastes of the times. Among the play-actors were a number of vicious and wholly abandoned characters who did not hesitate to pander to their patrons and submit to outrageous physical indignities for hire.

After the performance of theatrical representations in the province of Idzumo, female actors became all the rage, and, as society was corrupted and injured in consequence, the authorities forbade actresses to appear on the stage in future. This interdiction brought young men-actors into vogue, and the performances of these handsome looking young fellows also fascinated and charmed the minds of the public and captivated a large class of voluptuaries. The fearful evil which subsequently developed having become prevalent, male actors were also prohibited in the 1st year of Shō-ō (1652), but in the 2nd year of the same period (1653) in accordance with the petition of certain persons, permission was granted for dramatic performances to be held under the name of *mono-mané-kyōgen-zukushi* (various comic plays).

Warned by experience, and in order to prevent the recurrence of the vicious practice, the authorities caused all actors to

" *Yarō.*"

shave the hair above their foreheads, and the cognomen of "*wakashu*" ("lad") was officially changed into that of *yarō* ("a low fellow"). To circumvent the law and nullify its operation, actors who took the part of women wore towels arranged so as to conceal their shaven pates, and, hitting upon a further expedient, wore hats made of floss silk or purple crêpe. The prepossessing appearance of these men so greatly outrivalled the beauty of real women that, far from the regulations effecting any reform, the habit of enjoying unnatural pleasure spread through the city. Following the trend of prevailing tastes, games known as "*yarō-karuta*" (cards with figures of *yarō* upon them), and *yarō-sugoroku* (*yarō* backgammon) were invented and hawked around for sale, while some enterprising people manufactured pictures of *yarō* for sale and others published a *hyōban-ki* (Notes and criticism) about them. To such an extreme did the craze run that some insensate fanatics even went so far as to present votive tablets to shrines and temples bearing representations of these disgusting *yarō*!

The resorts of this vile fraternity were in Yedo (Tōkyō), Negimachi; in Kyōto, Miyagawa-machi; and in Ōsaka, Dōtonbori. The houses in which *yarō* were kept were colloquially known as "*Kodomo-ya*" (children's houses). These establishments hired and offered to their patrons the services of attractive boys much in the same manner as the regular brothels dealt in women. The youths were taught various accomplishments, and after they had become proficient as actors they were placed on the stage. Those who performed in plays were styled *butai-ko* (stage children), those who only waited at entertainments were called *kagema*, and those who travelled about the country were known as *tobi-ko* (jumping or "flying" children).

It was chiefly members of the military class and priests who came to houses of assignation (*age-ya*) and engaged these young men, but their services were also requisitioned by not a few women. At first the lads only appeared at banquets as pages in waiting on the guests, danced for the amusement of the company, and were engaged by enthusiastic patrons in the ordinary way, but eventually their exclusive business led them to become as familiar with their guests as ordinary female prostitutes. They aped the style of females, blackened their teeth with *ohaguro* (like the women of those times), and gave themselves languid effeminate airs in imitation of the fair sex. Originally they dressed in a distinctive costume, and their get-up was known as *wakashu-sugata* (young man style), but gradually their mode of dress underwent a change, and in the Meiwa and An-ei periods (1764 to 1780) they attired themselves in graceful garments dyed in rich designs, adopted long flowing sleeves such as were worn by females, wore wide girdles around their waists, and did their hair up woman-fashion.

In the Genroku period (1688 to 1703) the common practice of the vice had declined, but the custom of hiring *yarō* was as popular as that of hiring courtesans, and in the Meiwa and An-ei periods (1764 to 1780) it had reached its zenith. At that time there were as many as ten places in Yeyo where *yarō* could be hired—namely in Yoshi-chō, Kobiki-chō, Hatchō-bori in Kanda, in the grounds of the Shrine of Yushima Tenjin (!), in front of the Shimmei Shrine (!) in Shiba near the Hirakawa Tenjin Shrine (!) in Kōjimachi, near the Hachiman Shrine (!) at Ichi-ga-ya, etc. The number of *yarō* carrying on their infamous calling in the city was two hundred and thirty at this period.

Before long, nature either began to assert itself or the laws against the vice passed in Kwansei period (1789 to 1800) were severely applied, for in the Tempō period (1830 to 1843) only four places remained where *yarō* could be found.* Of these Yushima was patronized most extensively, but only twenty-two lads were kept there. In the 13th year of Tempō (1842), in the time of Ieyoshi, the 12th Tokugawa Shōgun, the vice was utterly rooted out in consequence of searching reforms instituted by Midzuno Tadakuni, Lord of Ichizen, and from that year unnatural sexuality ceased almost entirely in Yedo. In the Kwan-ei period (1624 to 1643) a number of so-called "incense-dealers" (*Kōyu-uri*) appeared in Yedo who offered unnatural services to their customers, and by the era of Genroku (1688 to 1703) the business was firmly established and the practice prevailed far and wide. Beautifully dressed, handsome, and effeminate looking young men wandered through the city carrying about with them various kinds of incense in *kiri*-wood boxes wrapped in light-blue silk cloths, and, under the guise of selling incense, wormed their way into the mansions of the nobility and gentry, but in course of time the custom was abolished. In those days it was quite general for lewd and abandoned women to hire actors and indulge in immoral pleasure. Such women, when they attended a play, would call actors to the tea-houses and there enjoy themselves with the players in the same way that male libertines were wont to call courtesans.

The above description of *yarō* is condensed from the *Nihon-Fuzoku-Shi* (日本風俗史), but the writer desires to add that the literature of the Genroku period, as typified in several

* Yoshi-chō, Hatchō-bori, Shimmei, and Yushima.

ancient volumes in his possession, clearly reveal the fact that the vice was practised quite openly, and apparently without any sense of shame, in the 17th century. Curious readers are referred to the *Danshoku Ō-kagami* (published in 1687) and the *Danshoku Ki-no-me-dzuke* (published in 1703) as specimens of this precious literature*.

* Copies of these works are rare and the Japanese Government will not allow them to be reprinted for sale. The language of these books is not in any way disgusting, and the style is florid and pleasing. It is the subject only which is "off colour."

The Grave of a Courtesan.

The following sad description of the last hours, death, and burial of an inmate of the Yoshiwara is gleaned from the "*Yūkwaku no Rimen*" (遊廓の裏面), published in 1903:—

"Even in the case of a courtesan who for a time has been famous as the star of her brothel, and who has become so skilful that she has robbed many men of their very souls, what will her ultimate fate probably be when suddenly attacked by a serious disease? I believe that there is no fate more piteous than that of a courtesan whose body has been sold to this prostitute quarter from a distant province, and who finds herself, sad and lonely, without a single acquaintance or relative, and with none to whom she can look for aid!

"Now that she is sick and has given up her business for one or two months, the myriads of guests, who formerly came crowding to see her in a never-ending stream while she was yet elegantly attired and beautiful to behold with her comely face and perfectly pencilled eyebrows, do not send her even a single letter. The servants who called her '*Oiran, Oiran*' * when she was in the zenith of her pride and popularity and who served her obsequiously in consideration of the many gifts she lavished upon them, gradually become unaccommodating and churlish. But that is by no means all, for they even speak ill of her and backbite her. Then she falls into low spirits, and alone by herself she writhes in solitary agony. Her debit account for medicine increases. There is no one to soothe or comfort her, and indeed it is impossible to imagine how great is her misery as she dozes uneasily upon her pillow, in this unhappy place, among things hard to bear and painful to hear.

"In this manner her sickness increases in severity, and finally, falling into a state which offers no hope of recovery, she can only await the awful approach of death. Our imaginations fails to picture the unhappy state of the wretched courtesan who is about to draw her last breath, lying on a cold hard thin mattress in a miserable and lonely little room beneath the back staircase of the brothel, without a soul in the world to help the absolutely forsaken creature. When death is about to enter through the torn paper-covered windows of her room, there is no light in the chamber, and all is dark as pitch. In the upper portion of the house singing girls are probably playing merrily upon their *samisen* (banjo), while dancing-girls are dancing and frisking to the music. The sounds of boisterous laughter, music, and cheerful voices pierce the ears of the sick woman and grate upon her nerves, and she, lying in misery at the very point of death, with none

* "The most beautiful of flowers." Complimentary name for a superior harlot in the Tōkyō Yoshiwara.

to attend or nurse her, totters on the brink of the grave writhing and struggling in pain and anguish, and when she breathes her last she is mocked in the hour of her mortal agony by the babel of voices telling of licentious joy and happiness and voluptuous pleasure. Her limbs grow cold and rigid, her eyes, which have lost the light of life, become dull and glazed, and, remaining wide open, stare horribly into the darkness. Just at this moment some courtesan who has come down the stairs for a sitz-bath, or a brothel hag (*yarite*) coming along the passage, noticing that the faint noise of breathing has ceased, and wondering if anything has happened, may open the door and look in and exclaim—'Ah! all is over.' That is about all the expression of astonishment which will be ejaculated, and although perchance two or three of her courtesan friends may shed a few tears of sympathy and pity, this ends the matter. The brothel keeper immediately states that there is no one to take delivery of the corpse, and, without even waiting for the dawn, the mortal remains are hurriedly born away to the crematorium and disappear forever in the smoke of the furnace. Ah! what a fearful and cruel thing this is to contemplate!

"And to where are the calcined bones carried, and where are they interred?

"If there be any person who desires to know where the white bones of the miserable courtesan are going, and who wishes to follow the unhappy woman to the end of her terrible fate, I beg that he will go out of the great gateway of the Yoshiwara—where the flower has withered and fallen—past the Go-jikken-dōri road, up the Emon-zaka hill, and grope his way along to the left of the dike at Dote-Hatchō.

"Before the eyes of the traveller spreads out on both sides of the dike a vista of beautiful fields and gardens. On the right, so far as the eye can see, separated by vast stretches of irrigated rice-fields, rise to varying heights the rows of the roofs of the brothels of Kotsugappara and Senju. Passing by this cluster of habitations, there are clumps of green trees and bamboo groves. Further on, if the weather be clear and fair, the white sails of craft on the upper part of the stream of the Sumida river can be faintly discerned, and, of course, the purple mountain of Tsukuba-yama can be seen among the clouds. Glancing around to the left of the dike, there will be noticed towns composed of tenant houses lately erected on ground reclaimed from the fields. Between the trees may be seen here and there the high roofs of various temples. The sight of the forest which crowns the high ridge of land reaching from Ueno to Higurashi and on to Dōkwan-yama creates a pleasing sensation in the mind. As one goes on among this beautiful scenery, he at length nears the gate of the slaughter-houses, and his nostrils are assailed by the scent of blood borne on the breeze. Going on a little further beyond the dike, a road commences which forms an old fashioned avenue with rows of trees on both sides. Having arrived at this point, if one turns round and glances back he will be able to see, between the trees, just the numerous roofs of the Yoshiwara prostitute-quarter stretching out all over. The lofty buildings of the quarter, such as the clock-tower of the "Ebi-ya," "Hikota," and the "Shinagawa" rise up in such conspicuous majesty that one imagines that he is looking at some great castle-town. Quickening one's steps, and going on one or two *cho* more, the dike disappears, and you see the railway embankment crossing

Tombs of Courtesan and Guest who Committed Suicide together on the 1st October, 1880.

diagonally in front. Beneath this railroad line stands a temple, and this temple is indeed the place where the unfortunate courtesan is doomed to have her bones decay and rot! By the left side of the bank oozes a little dirty ditch-like stream, spanned by a small old-fashioned stone bridge. This stream skirts the temple grounds, and, washing the luxuriant growth of wild bamboo grass which overgrows into boundaries, disappears at the back of the railway track. Pleased with the extreme quietness and privacy of the place, you cross the little bridge and come to a black gateway which you recognize as that of the *Jō-Kan-ji* temple. Ah! the *Jō-Kan-ji* at Minowa! Men of the world with their loves and hates, even if they have not already explored the actual place itself, have probably become acquainted with its name through the various books they have read.

"Having entered the gate, you will see a little hut where flowers are sold. Proceeding to the rear of the not very large *hondō* (main temple) by the left side of the building, you will come to a place thickly studded with numberless graves, tombstones and *sotoba* (stûpa). Near the thicket-like hedge, and here and there between the tombstones, stand clumps of gnarled and ancient *e-no-ki* trees whose branches quiver sadly and mournfully as the wind soughs through them with a plaintive sobbing sound like the burthen of a requiem. Glancing at the well-nigh undecipherable inscription carved on the first tombstone that meets the eye, we can trace a posthumous name such as 柳生院花容童女之墓 (*Ryū-sho-in Kwayō-dōjō no haka,*) or the words ロロ樓代々の墓 (the family grave of the ....brothel). Or we may even see stones on which two names are carved together, one name being that of a man and one that of a woman. None of these stones are more than two or three feet in height—they are all small and dirty—and for a very long period of time no incense has been burned or flowers offered before them.

"Going on into the heart of this lonesome place one at length arrives behind the main temple. Here the whole surface of the earth is damp and humid, and a dismal grave-like smell of mouldy earth pervades the locality. Probably the sunshine has never penetrated to this spot for centuries. The dead leaves of the *e-no-ki* trees have been allowed to lie as they have fallen year after year, so they have piled up, crumbled, mouldered, and rotted on the dark ground, and from the purulent mildewed soil have sprung into being myriads of weird uncanny poisonous toadstools and foul fungi fearful and horrid in shape and strangely ghastly in colour. Ah!, what a desolate uncanny appearance the place has; persons visiting it soon experience a deep sense of commiseration and sympathy, and feel as if they had entered a chilly underground vault. In this gloomy dismal place lie the bones ot the courtesan who only up to yesterday resembled a beautiful butterfly or lovely blossom when seen in all the glory of her gorgeous apparel, with her glossy black hair ornamented with gold and her snowy-white body clad in rich brocade robes now exchanged for the cerements of death.

"And look! at the rear of two great *e-no-ki* trees rises a high stone wall. Upon it stands a stone column bearing the six Chinese characters 新吉原無緣墓 (*Shin Yoshiwara Mu-en-dzuka*) "*The tomb of those of the Shin Yoshiwara who are without kith or kin.*" Around it is a rank growth of various weeds and grasses, and near by still stands undecayed a huge

The "*Mu-en-dzuka*" in the "*Jō-kan-ji*" temple at Minowa.

stûpa which was erected as an offering to the spirits of the dead at the time of the great earthquake of the 2nd year of the Ansei period (1855).

" As a matter of fact such things really do occur, but the courtesan who is thus buried in the *Mu-en-dzuka* must be counted as the most truly unfortunate, because most of the women are given burial in the family burying places of the brothel-keepers, while the bodies of those who cannot obtain even this latter consideration, who are from a far country and without a friend to take delivery of their remains, are carried stealthily out of the back entrance of the brothels in the grey light of the dawn, and here transformed into a heap of grisly bones. In any case the end of these brothel women is very sad and lamentable, and looked at from this point of view there is indeed nothing so miserable or so awful as the brothel quarter."

Five Curious Legal Documents actually used in the Yoshiwara in 1902.

(No. 1.) AGREEMENT.

Whereas I ...., being unable to maintain myself, have consented to.........................'s practising prostitution in your establishment for the purpose of aiding in my support, it is hereby agreed as follows:—

ART. 1.—I acknowledge and confirm the fact that I have consented to.........................'s practising prostitution in your house for a period of...................... .

ART. 2.—I hereby acknowledge the receipt of the sum of Yen.......................which you have advanced to me at the rate of......................per annum as regards interest

ART. 3.—The principal and interest mentioned in the proceeding Article shall be repaid out of.......................'s income derived by her in her practice of prostitution. Provided that her entertainment fee per head shall be fixed at........, whereof... ....is to be given to her as pocket-money, and the balance of...................is to be applied to the repayment of principal and interest.

With regard to the "entertainment fee" mentioned in the preceeding paragraph, it is agreed that you may, at your convenience, either increase or decrease the rate, and that even in such case the money is to be applied according to the same proportion as that mentioned in the said preceding paragraph.

The portion of her earnings hereinbefore mentioned as yours is to be applied for the expenses of maintaining the

Yoshiwara Hospital and other fixed expenses ; but the cost of board while in the hospital is to be paid by herself.

If at any future time further advances are made by you, or if you kindly disburse for us the cost of medicine and the expenses of board in the hospital, such monies shall be repaid in the following order and manner :—

(1) Cost of medicine. (2) Board in hospital.

(3) Interest on all loans. (4) Principal of further loans.

(5) Principal of original loan.

Art. 4.—It is further agreed that she will, of course, lodge in your house and practice the business faithfully during the term of the agreement, that she will strictly observe the regulations relating to the business, and any other Articles or customs which should be respected for the regulation of the brothel-quarters ; and further that, no matter what be the circumstances, she will neither relinquish or suspend the business nor change her lodging place until both the principal and interest of the liability towards yourself are finally cleared off. Provided, however, that in case you should, at your convenience, alienate your brothel-keeping business, or require us to change the lodging-place, your directions will be respected and no objection to the change will be raised against your wishes, except for proper and valid reasons.

Art. 5.—My portion of the profit being determined according to the rate specified in paragraph 1 of Article 3 hereof, I shall not be interested or concerned in respect to any other income derived in connection with your brothel-keeping business.

Art. 6. With regard to any personal property belonging to........................it is agreed that the same is pledged as security for the loan mentioned in Article 2 hereof, irrespective as to whether it is now actually in existence or may be acquired at any future time in the course of practising the business; and the said property shall be neither taken out, delivered to others, pledged, sold, nor otherwise alienated.

Art. 7.—In case....................falls ill before the loan from you is cleared off and consequently cannot practice the business, she shall undergo a medical examination by a physician at the Yoshiwara Hospital; and if his diagnosis shows that there is no prospect of her being able to resume her calling, it is agreed that the pledged articles belonging to the said ... .shall be sold by you in the presence of one of the guarantors, and that the proceeds of the sale shall be applied to the repayment of the principal and interest of the loan. In case any deficiency arises, the liability in respect thereto will be undertaken and fulfilled jointly and severally by the guarantors and the principal, the said guarantors assuming joint and several liability among themselves.

Art. 8.—Should the principal party abscond, conceal her whereabouts, etc., the guarantors will forthwith enquire after her and bring her back to resume her business; and as to the time which has elapsed during the period of her desertion, application will be made forthwith to the Police Station for the purpose of having the term of agreement mentioned in her license extended by the number of days during which she was absent, and of procuring renewal of the said license. If her whereabouts cannot be ascertained, or if she dies, the pledged articles belonging to her are to be sold by you in the presence of one of her guarantors and the proceeds to be applied to the repayment of the principal, and interest of the loan. Any deficiency will be made good by the guarantors and the principal all being jointly and severally responsible, and the guarantors undertaking the liability jointly and severally among themselves. In case of the death of the principal, the guarantors will take delivery of her corpse.

Art. 9.—Should there be any portion of the loan standing unpaid at the time of the maturity of the term of the agreement, you are at liberty to sell the pledged articles belonging to the said....................and to apply the proceeds towards the repayment of such unpaid portion of the loan. Any deficiency arising will be made good by the guarantors themselves, and you will be protected against any loss or annoyance.

Art. 10.—It is specially agreed that in case any of these Articles should be infringed, or should any other dispute arise between the parties, the case shall be considered as within the jurisdiction of either the Tōkyō Local or District Court.

The above Articles of Agreement being duly accepted by the parties, we hereby undertake not to infringe the provisions thereof; and in order to avoid future misunderstanding and trouble, we have drawn up this document and signed and sealed the same hereunder.

Dated..............................

(Signatures)........................ .....

(No. 2.) Deed of Loan.

The sum of Yen ....together with interest at the rate of.......... ....per annum.

We hereby acknowledge that the above sum of money has been borrowed from you to meet the requirements for.........'s carrying on of the business of a prostitute. Repayment of the money will be made according to the provisions of an agreement dated ...., and we have therefore no objection to your treating the matter accordingly.

In order to avoid future misunderstanding and trouble, we have drawn up this document and signed and sealed it hereunder.

Dated............................

(Signatures)............................

(No. 3.) POWER OF ATTORNEY.

I,......................., being about to commence business as a prostitute at........................in the Urban Prefecture of Tōkyō, hereby give and grant unto....... ....the following powers:—

1.—To manage all matters connected with the application for a license for practising as a prostitute, and to sign and seal as attorney for me all necessary papers and documents.

2.—To contract any further loan or loans from the brothel-keeper, while I am practising as a prostitute, to the actual amount of Yen.............., and to sign and seal as my attorney the documents relative to such loan or loans.

3.—In case of the alteration of the lodging-place at the convenience of the brothel-keeper, to borrow money from the new brothel-keeper, to determine the manner in which the money is to be repaid, to enter into any other agreement or contract in connection with the practice of the business of a prostitute, to sign and seal as my attorney various papers and documents, and to perform any other acts or deeds.

4.—To manage all my personal affairs while I am practicing prostitution.

5.—To appoint a substitute to manage or perform any of the matters entrusted to you.

I hereby certify that the above matters are duly entrusted to you, and beg that you will manage everything in accordance with the regulations; I pledge you my word that I will not raise any objection at any future time to anything which may have been done by you in the premises; and it is further specially agreed that this power of attorney will not be cancelled unless with your consent.

In witness whereof, I have drawn up this power of attorney and signed and sealed the same hereunder.

Dated ....

(Signature)..............................

(No. 4.) RESOLUTION OF THE FAMILY COUNCIL.

RESOLVED :—

ART 1.—That permission is given to........................to practice as a prostitute in the Urban Prefecture of Tōkyō.

ART. 2.—That ....may borrow the sum of .... from............... a brothel-keeper, contract any further loans not exceeding the actual amount of................., and enter into an agreement (as per draft) hereto attached.

ART. 3.—That in case the brothel-keeper .... alienates the brothel-keeping business at his convenience, or causes .... , change her lodging place, ... may borrow from the new brothel-keeper the sum of Yen ..... or contract any further loan not exceeding the amount of Yen................, he may determine in the exercise of his discretion the manner in which the repayment of the loans are to be paid, enter into further various agreements relating to the practice of the business of a prostitute, and do any and all other acts and deeds in connection therewith.

Art. 4.—That for the purpose of performing any acts or deeds in relation to Articles 2 and 3,......................may appoint any substitute under him and give to such substitute power to perform all such acts and deeds.

Date..........................

(Signatures)..........................

(No. 5.) Letter of Request.

..........................being now prepared to practice as a prostitute, I am very much obliged to you for your kind consent to my request to guarantee the agreement. Under these circumstances, I promise that I will respect and observe the said agreement and not cause you any trouble whatsoever. When it is necessary to sign and seal papers filed with the proper authorities in connection with the practice of prostitution, I beg that you will kindly sign and seal the same, and that you will, when necessary, sign and seal the documents *re* additional loans as attorney for.............., and kindly guarantee the repayment of the said loans. I further request that you will look after her in all matters affecting her interests while engaged in the business of prostitution. If you act as above, the principal party will never act contrary to your directions, and..............too will raise no objections.

In witness whereof, I have hereby drawn up this letter of request and signed and sealed the same hereunder.

Dated..........................

(Signature).... ....